Economic Nationalism and Development

Published by arrangement with
Polish Scientific Publishers PWN.

This book was translated with
a subsidy from the Batory Foundation.

Economic Nationalism
and Development

Central and Eastern Europe
Between the Two World Wars

Jan Kofman

WestviewPress
A Division of HarperCollins*Publishers*

For Masia

Copyright © 1992, 1997 by Wydawnictwo Naukowe PWN

Published in 1997 in the United States of America by Westview Press, 5500 Central Avenue, Boulder, Colorado 80301-2877, and in the United Kingdom by Westview Press, 12 Hid's Copse Road, Cumnor Hill, Oxford OX2 9JJ

Library of Congress Cataloging-in-Publication Data
Kofman, Jan.
    [Nacjonalizm Gospodarczy-Szansa Czy Bariera Rozwoju, English]
Economic nationalism and development : Central and Eastern Europe
between the two world wars / Jan Kofman;
translated by Maria Chmiclewska-Szlajfer.
       p.   cm.
    Includes bibliographical references and index.
    ISBN 0-8133-8725-6
    1. Europe, Central—Economic policy.   2. Europe, Eastern—Economic
policy.   3. Protectionism—Europe, Central.   4. Protectionism—
Europe, Eastern.   I. Title.
HC244.K595   1997
382.7'0943—dc21   97-8090
                                                                        CIP

The paper used in this publication meets the requirements of the American National Standard for Permanence of Paper for Printed Library Materials Z39.48-1984.

10   9   8   7   6   5   4   3   2   1

Contents

Part Two
Protectionism as a Response to Underdevelopment

Acknowledgments

I am pleased to thank the people who went to the trouble of acquainting themselves with a part or the whole of this work. First and foremost, I want to thank very much Professor Jerzy Tomaszewski, who at various stages of my writing this book, was always ready to offer his own interesting remarks and suggestions. I could always rely on his help and considerate interest. I also want to thank very much the book reviewers. I am particularly grateful to Professor Zbigniew Landau for his detailed and penetrating comments. Professors Piotr Łossowski and Juliusz Łukasiewicz voiced many precious opinions, and for these I am much obliged to them. I also want to warmly thank Doctor Henryk Szlajfer. In its interpretative parts, the book owes a lot to the discussions, and sometimes the polemics, that we carried on. My sincere thanks go to Mrs. Maria Chmielewska-Szlajfer who translated the book into English—I greatly appreciate her effort and useful suggestions. I would also like to thank Mr. John Guardiano for his perfection in copyediting the manuscript. Needless to say, I myself bear responsibility for all of the book's imperfections.

Jan Kofman

Introduction

In this book I set out to present the phenomenon of economic nationalism in interwar East-Central Europe[1] and to define its role in the region's development. Did it constitute a barrier to growth, or a stimulus? I argue that economic nationalism did advance entry of the region's usually backward countries onto the road of modernity.

Historical treatments mention economic nationalism only occasionally and indirectly, both in reference to particular countries as well as to the entire East-Central European region. As a result, the interwar economic, political, and social history of this area is significantly oversimplified.

Historians, economists, and political scientists often use the term "economic nationalism" to indicate a variety of phenomena, predominantly in the economic policy sphere, and without going into details. By "economic nationalism" they usually mean protectionism or, even more narrowly, a policy of foreign trade. Only very few scholars (nearly all of them economists) in the interwar and immediate postwar periods showed intent interest in the phenomenon, and they all used the tools of neoclassical and liberal economics and hence were critical of economic nationalism. Students of underdeveloped Third World economies have shown greater interest in the issue, but only some works from the 1960s and later years contributed any interesting results.[2]

Previous studies have commonly pointed to the roots of this kind of nationalism, emphasized the importance of ethnocentrism as its binding factor, and distinguished it from other ideologies; sometimes they have traced its evolution. Yet, neither in their theoretical nor in their descriptive aspects have they tackled a number of issues and threads of crucial importance to the subject of this book. For this reason, I often found myself moving into areas essentially unexplored.

The book consists of two parts: Part One (Chapters 1–4) is of a general nature and deals with the occurrence of economic nationalism in the region, and Part Two (Chapters 5–8) is in effect a case study of protectionism. I approach these phenomena historically and theoretically.

In the Part One I propound, among other things, a few theoretical concepts of economic nationalism and put forward a concept of my own, which emphasizes both theoretical and historical points of view. I present the sources and causes of the phenomenon's spread in East-Central Europe and the scale to which it influenced ideology and economic policy. I ask: To what extent did this phenomenon result from unique circumstances, and to what extent did it represent a considered, consistently pursued line of action? In this context, I discuss the main areas of expansion and the manifestations of economic nationalism. I also consider why in certain countries industrialism and in others agrarianism were its major element, and what the causes and effects of this inward-oriented nationalism were. I conclude this part with an attempt to sum up the ideology and practice of economic nationalism in the countries of the region.

For methodological and heuristic reasons I separate and analyze more thoroughly the question of protectionism in particular countries of the region. I believe that protectionism is the binding agent of economic nationalism and, at the same time, its distinctive feature—one without which it cannot take root. In presenting all the various interwar concepts of protectionism, understood as either ideologies or specific policies, I give special attention to the ideas of Mihail Manoilescu, which won recognition also outside East-Central Europe. I identify three kinds of protectionism according to the extent of state economic interventionism. I try to verify my categorization against historical and economic data, which serves also the purpose of verifying the correctness of more general conclusions concerning the protectionist policy. To this end, I conduct a more detailed analysis of the cases of Poland, Czechoslovakia, and Bulgaria. Next, I discuss, among other things, the question of what might be the outcome if protectionism were attenuated or abandoned by those countries that only recently ceased being a part of larger economic units. Last but not least, in the context of interdependence between particular elements of economic nationalism, I discuss the relationship between economic growth and protectionism as well as the prospects it offers for achieving strategic development goals.

My conclusions are broader than usual. They include questions pertaining to certain issues crucial to the understanding of the main subject of the book, even though they reach beyond the strict limits of the book— for example, the choice of the paths of industrial development, the relationship between economic growth and the political system, and an assessment of the degree to which economic nationalism (and protectionism) brought about and influenced changes in the international division of labor.

*   *   *

This work is based on a voluminous and diverse literature (synthetic, monographic, and analytical publications, including statistical ones) because of the largely interdisciplinary nature of my subject. It proved to be necessary to reach for papers pertaining not only to economic or political history but also to economic thought, the theory of economics, and political science. Wherever useful, I referred to archival materials (from the Archiwum Akt Nowych in Warsaw and the Public Record Office in London), both published and unpublished. The exemplification method I employ does not embrace all the countries of the region to the same extent. It is thus only occasionally that I cite the examples of Austria or Albania, and I refer more often to Romania, Yugoslavia, or the Baltic countries, and most often to the countries situated centrally and of the greatest importance to the region—Poland, Czechoslovakia, and Hungary, but also Bulgaria.

Notes

1. By East-Central Europe I mean Austria, Czechoslovakia, Hungary, Poland, Lithuania, Latvia, Estonia, Romania, Yugoslavia, Albania, Bulgaria, and Greece. In the broadest sense the borders of East-Central Europe or Eastern Europe run from the Baltic Sea in the north to the Black Sea and the Adriatic Sea in the south, from Germany and Italy in the west and southwest to the Soviet Union in the east; so defined, the region embraces twelve to fourteen states. Narrower definitions usually exclude from the region Finland, Turkey, Albania, and Greece and sometimes also Austria. Quite often the region is understood to embrace the succession or Danubian countries (the meaning of these two terms is not identical, although in some publications they are treated synonymously). Sometimes it is understood simply as several randomly chosen neighboring countries, for example, Poland, Czechoslovakia, Hungary, Romania, and Yugoslavia, and the perceptions of the region's borders have no doubt been affected by postwar history, when some of these countries became Soviet satellites. In this book I use the broader definition of the region. For different books referring in their titles to the region and its territorial range, see, for instance, C. A. Macartney and A. W. Palmer, *Independent Eastern Europe: A History* (London, 1962); J. Żarnowski, ed., *Dyktatury w Europie Środkowo-Wschodniej 1918–1939* (Wrocław, 1983); I. T. Berend and G. Ránki, *Economic Development in East-Central Europe in the Nineteenth and Twentieth Centuries* (New York and London, 1974); J. Rothschild, *East Central Europe Between Two World Wars* (Seattle, 1974); B. Puchert, *Ekspansja gospodarcza niemieckiego imperializmu w Europie Środkowej i Wschodniej 1900–1933* (Warsaw, 1975); M. C. Kaser, ed., *The Economic History of Eastern Europe, 1919–1975*, vols. I–II (Oxford, 1985–1986). The methodological problems related to the definition of the region are discussed in R. Havranková, Z. Sládek, J. Valenta, "O močnosti integračniho pojetí: Studia dějin 'vychodni Evropy' ve 20 stoleti," in *Slovenské historické studie*, vol. VII, 1968 (Prague).

2. Among the outstanding authors who wrote on this subject before and immediately after World War II are O. Lange, L. Pasvolsky, T. E. Gregory, J. M. Keynes, W. Rappard, W. Röpke, F. Hertz, and M. A. Heilperin. From the angle of the un-

derdeveloped countries, the issue of economic nationalism has been tackled by R. Prebisch, G. Myrdal, J. D. Wirth, E. B. Burns, D. Seers, and others. A. Breton and H. G. Johnson tried a model-building approach, and J. F. Karcz and J. M. Montias analyzed economic nationalism within the communist bloc. I write about the theoretical problems of this form of nationalism and about protectionism in Chapters 2 and 5 in particular.

PART 1

Economic Nationalism:
Description

1

Theoretical and Research Approaches

Nationalism and Economic Nationalism

Nationalism has turned out to be one of the most attractive twentieth-century ideologies and one of the main springboards of political, social, and economic changes taking place in the world, especially in less developed areas such as East-Central Europe (with the exception of Czechoslovakia). Economic nationalism, both a manifestation and a component part of nationalism, played a significant, if rarely noticed by historians, role in the process of national and social integration in the countries of the region.

There is no need to enter here into the complicated interpretations of the definition of nationalism.[1] Let us only draw attention to the various ambiguities and often fundamentally different interpretations. It is also important to point out at the outset that Western historians fairly often fail to differentiate between nationalism of a defensive kind displayed by an oppressed nation and the nationalism of a nation that has its own statehood. This is the case, for example, with applying the nationalist label to national-liberation aspirations lacking a strong ethnic idiosyncrasy or to a policy aimed at consolidating an already won freedom (there are cases, however, in which this label is axiologically indifferent).[2]

Established English-language dictionaries and encyclopedias often equate nationalism with patriotism. For example, the most popular English dictionaries from Oxford define nationalism as patriotic feelings, principles, and efforts and as a policy of national sovereignty (independence). A patriot is defined as one who defends the well-being, freedom, and rights of his country and has an ardent attitude toward it. A dictionary of social sciences published in the 1960s only lists a similarly defined nationalism and has no entry for "patriotism." The same is true of an authoritative international encyclopedia of social sciences.[3]

Western scholars do not usually differentiate between the contents of nationalism and patriotism. Some social scientists even use the two terms synonymously,[4] ignoring the distinction between the two phenomena, which, right or wrong, appears obvious to Polish, Hungarian, or Czech researchers (and probably to the inhabitants of the region as well). If the former acknowledge this distinction, they usually reduce it to the degree of intensity of national feelings and to the size of the areas in which these phenomena are observed.[5] This approach, especially in the case of anglophone authors, is explained not only by the adherence to theoretical assumptions but also by the different histories of the Western and the East-Central European countries. At the same time, however, such an approach has its rationale (which does not outweigh its disadvantages) because it is difficult for those who make this distinction to define the historical and psychological moment at which patriotism becomes nationalism. Though Czech and Polish national democrats, for example, were—by definition, so to speak—nationalists, could one say the same about Czech social-democrats, or about Polish socialists when they advocated Poland's independence? To many Anglo-Saxon researchers, there is no doubt that the answer is yes. They classify, for instance, both Giuseppe Mazzini and Adam Mickiewicz as representatives of the nationalist attitude, along with not only Gandhi but Mussolini and Hitler too.[6]

Obviously, such a broad interpretation of nationalism blurs the distinctions and homogenizes ideological positions that often oppose each other completely. Unlike their French counterparts, Anglo-Saxon historians rarely refer to the patriotism-nationalism-chauvinism triad that characterizes the contents and intensity of national emotions.[7] It might be interesting to note that George Orwell laid still different emphases when describing the relationship between the two phenomena. He sharply contrasted the contemporary patriotism, regarded as a defensive attitude, with nationalism conceived as an aggressive one.[8] Anglo-Saxon historians, who as a rule inertly follow the historians of ideas, rarely distinguish between nationalism and patriotism in the countries of the region.[9] Let us note, however, that in the context of Europe's traumatic twentieth-century experience, the notion of patriotism is sometimes used to camouflage emotions and views that are clearly nationalistic.

I subscribe to the view that there are fundamental differences between nationalism and patriotism.[10] I leave aside the relationship between them as having little relevance to my argument in this book (although, of course, the problem will be further discussed later on).

Nationalism is a complex structure, composed of elements and relations that can be identified according to various criteria. It is thus possible to approach nationalism from the genetic, functional, or political-system points of view. Using the latter approach, one can identify, after Hans Kohn, liberal, democratic, integral, and totalitarian nationalisms, or, after Carlton J. Hayes, nationalisms that are humanitarian, Jacobin, traditional, liberal, and integral.[11] It is possible to make more such divisions on the basis of various other criteria.[12] For example, nationalism examined both in historical perspective and from the point of view of its objectives, can also be divided into cultural, political, and, especially interesting to us, economic nationalism.

Researchers rarely refer to economic nationalism,[13] and when they do, they usually do it in an indirect way. In major theoretical studies the problem of the relationship between political and economic nationalisms has hardly been touched upon.[14] Such classics as those by Kohn or Hayes as well as by the outstanding student of the subject, Karl W. Deutsch, usually identify only two kinds of nationalism: the cultural and the political.[15] On the rare occasions that economic nationalism is identified,[16] the authors want to see it as a tool to achieve the goals of political nationalism or as an extension thereof, without defining its place in the whole structure clearly.[17] They tacitly accept political nationalism as the supreme and definite form of nationalism.

Characteristically, the notion of economic nationalism rarely appears in studies dealing with economic or political problems of the region in the interwar period, and when it does, it is hardly ever accompanied by even a superficial analysis of its content, despite the fact that the term was in fairly widespread use in economic and political writing of the period.

The term "economic nationalism" seldom occurs in encyclopedias or dictionaries. It does not appear as a separate entry in any of the various editions of the best-known Polish, German (Meyers and Brockhaus), anglophone, Soviet, or Czech general encyclopedias or in the most renowned specialist encyclopedias. In *Encyclopaedia Britannica* it appears only once, in the "Protection" entry, and is not defined in detail. One American encyclopedia mentions it once, but in an indistinct context and under a different entry. Only an Italian encyclopedia lists economic nationalism in the "Nationalism" entry, emphasizing the specific character of the former, namely its origins, which go back to the period of mercantilism.[18]

However, it appears that although political and economic nationalisms by definition have ethnocentrism as the ideological and emotional binding agent, because of the different range of their meanings and their peculiar features they constitute complementary—but not identical—phenomena. What is more, a deeper analysis of the history of nationalist ideologies and movements justifies the hypothesis that, at least on a regional scale, the phenomenon referred to as economic nationalism is a very peculiar kind of nationalism, and at the same time, its crowning. No theoretical or historical work dealing with the region that I know of clearly formulates this kind of mutual relationship between the two kinds of nationalism. Józef Chlebowczyk, who does refer to this relationship, albeit without using the term "economic nationalism," relates it only to the process of an ethnic minority's forming a national movement in a multination state—that is, to only one aspect of the phenomenon.[19] Even if this process is brought to its conclusion (according to the triad of cultural, political, and economic nationalism), it does not at all mean that the minority in question demands self-determination.

Historiography of the Subject

Before 1945 economists and politicians showed greater interest in economic nationalism than they do now. However, the publications appearing at that time were to a large extent contemporary case studies (for the most part economic) rather than studies of a historical nature. There was the valuable study by Leo Pasvolsky, widely used to this day, which dealt with economic problems of the Danubian region from a certain perspective, although it did so only briefly. The works by Antonin Basch, written during World War II, were of a similar value.[20] There were also more-or-less penetrating studies and articles (some of them displaying rather theoretical ambitions), for example, by Thomas Balogh, Theodore E. Gregory, Arthur Salter and Lewis Lorwin,[21] in which this problem received only marginal attention, yet some of the statements contained observations that are interesting even today.[22]

The historiography (or social sciences for that matter) of post-1945 Poland, Czechoslovakia, Bulgaria, Yugoslavia, and Hungary or of the Baltic countries pays hardly any attention to the problem of economic nationalism, and when the subject is raised at all, it is usually in terms of a general statement about the existence of an interdependence between nationalism and the economic processes in the countries of the region. The text by Ivan T. Berend and György Ránki, which deals with the economic reasons for the development of nationalism, is one of the very few exceptions. However, it concerns Hungary at the turn of the century, a time frame outside of the scope of this study, and it does not analyze the structure of the phenomenon as such.[23] There have also been a number of works on the attitudes of economic nationalists toward minorities. Other noteworthy works include the study by Frederick Hertz, which appeared just after World War II.[24] Contrary to its subtitle, it is not actually a description of the policy of economic nationalism but a lecture on the economic history of the Danubian region.

Considering the methodological problems that social scientists and historians face, the paucity of separate monographs dealing with economic nationalism in East-Central Europe[25] is not really surprising. But it is also true that some of the researchers, including those representing the region, simply do not notice this phenomenon, whereas others examine it only from the ideological point of view; still others, who even use the term "economic nationalism," treat it in a traditional, formal, and narrow way—as yet another, if exceptionally glaring and widespread, form of protectionism, neoprotectionism, and autarky, of which they, as a rule, disapprove.

In this context, the pioneering nature of Pasvolsky's book should be strongly emphasized. He noticed and tried to describe the phenomenon not on the basis of an isolated case but on the basis of the countries that were formed out of the ruins of the Austro-Hungarian Empire in the first postwar decade (until 1928). Nevertheless, it is now easy to notice that while listing the conditions conducive to the rise of economic nationalism (to which I shall refer later), Pasvolsky mixed causes with effects and also emphasized the significance of symptoms that, in my opinion, had little or nothing to do with his topic. His interpretation of this ideological current and the resulting economic policy defined as economic nationalism everything that did not fit in with the liberal vision of economy and development, usually conjured up in a doctrinaire manner.[26] All the same, Pasvolsky's interpretation strongly influenced researchers' approach to the problems of the region's economic development.

Hertz, for example, followed Pasvolsky's approach to the extreme. His study, written from the neoclassical position, presents the history of the Danubian region from the angle of a defender of the Austro-Hungarian Empire, and his political, historical, and ideological message, to which the selection of arguments was wholly subordinated, is obvious. Hertz painted a compelling picture of the successor countries, which were economically weak and isolated from one another and which, for irrational nationalistic reasons, squandered their Austro-Hungarian heritage. The author used the term economic nationalism liberally, yet without giving its precise definition. He also blamed all the misfortunes that befell the region on the nationalistic ideology of its people.[27]

Hertz's appraisal was characterized by a peculiar cognitive monocausalism. He regarded economic nationalism as an almost exclusive cause of all evil, and, professing integral economic neoclassicism, he viewed all the limitations imposed on the economy—be it foreign exchange, import and, less often, export restrictions, protectionist measures regarded as defensive ones (high import tariffs, bonuses, subsidies, customs and tax concessions, import quotas), restrictions affecting foreigners, the expansion of the defense industry, the development of state enterprises and other forms of state control, and so on—as its manifestations. Such interpretation prevented him from identifying the actual objective causes and symptoms of economic nationalism, which were born of the uneven development of capitalism and the petrifaction of the existing pattern of international specialization.

Hertz's impact nonetheless remains strong to this day (a new edition of his book appeared in 1970). The fact that traces of a similar approach may be found in the thinking of the historians of the countries concerned, such as Austria or Hungary (e.g., Berend and Ránki), can be given a rational explanation. During a 1964 conference on the heritage of Austria-Hungary, there was a characteristic clash of views between Hungarian and Romanian scholars. Whereas some Hungarian historians suggested that the disintegration of the empire was essentially a step backward, their Romanian counterparts insisted that the emergence of the national states was a logical consequence of the historical process and marked a progressive tendency.[28]

Theoretical Approaches: Liberalism
Versus Economic Nationalism

The fact that the subject of economic nationalism has not received sufficient attention may be due to problems in defining of the exact area of the relevant studies. Economic nationalism has posed analytical and interpretative difficulties also because of its blurred contour, the ambiguity and amorphousness of the subject matter, and the multiplicity of its features; moreover, in definite political-economic incarnations it has both common and specific characteristics. For this reason it is difficult to draw the demarcation lines separating economic nationalism from other ideologies and to describe it accurately. It is also difficult to delimit the variants of economic nationalism and enumerate the tools resorted to in its name. For instance, there is the fundamental question of whether every manifestation of protectionism can be termed economic nationalism. Is then industrial protectionism of the early stage of industrialization a symptom of economic nationalism, be it in Germany in the times of Friedrich List, in Napoleon's France, in the Balkan states at the turn of the century, or in the present underdeveloped countries?[29] And if it is not, at what point does this legitimate—to put it this way—protection becomes a *nationalist* tool? Or another question: Does economic nationalism embrace any striving for self-sufficiency, including limitations on the flow of capital and labor? After all, these and similar instruments are at the same time part of economic policies and as such require a proper procedure. It is possible to ask more questions of a similar nature to demonstrate the relative, at least dual, nature of economic nationalism.

Usually the students of these problems, consciously or not, refer to neoclassical conceptions of economic processes and liberal political doctrines. This is especially true of researchers from developed countries with a big-power status and/or of those from those countries in which for various reasons economic nationalism hardly manifested itself in the period discussed or did so on a relatively small scale. Things looked different to researchers from those countries of the region that, due to external and internal conditions, were receptive to this ideology and its practical application, and they were at the same time its major propagators.

Before 1945 there were a few more-or-less theoretical discussions about economic nationalism, and they were characterized by an excessive immediacy of their judgments and a tendency to generalize from isolated phenomena or from phenomena that are today regarded as being of secondary importance. Along with the aforementioned Lange, Gregory, and Balogh, it is worth mentioning the works of Mihail Manoilescu, William Rappard, and Wilhelm Röpke as well as Edward H. Carr and even Antonin Basch.[30]

Michael Heilperin is the noteworthy economist to have dealt with the problem of economic nationalism after 1945.[31] However, it was only more or less toward the end of the 1950s, in the period of increased interest in the Third World, that political science, and the burgeoning political economy of the underdeveloped regions in particular, showed greater interest in this problem. It is possible to identify two main approaches.

The first approach is one in which economic nationalism is not regarded as a separate subject of study but rather either as a minor component of the economic policy of an underdeveloped country or as an element of external conditions that this policy must take into consideration.[32] The second approach formally emphasizes the role of nationalism, including its economic variety, as a fundamental characteristic of modern times, which seriously affects the economic policy of the underdeveloped countries. A separate and characteristic stream is the theory of dependency (center-periphery).[33] The scholars who programmatically refer to it (e.g. the Wallerstein school), that is, those whose analysis proceeds first of all from ideological premises, view nationalism and its economic variety as an active (and progressive) factor of the process of reconstruction of the world economic order.[34] Nevertheless, the representatives of this approach, too, have not delved more deeply into these problems, being content with some general statements. The relevant issues are usually examined only on the side, especially in the context of the evaluation of the role of the national state as a stimulator (or inhibitor) of growth.

On the whole, it is hard to find a deeper theoretical analysis of the problem, one that would present the inner structure of economic nationalism.[35] When such attempts are made (e.g., Carr), they are usually done as part of a general analysis of nationalism, which, along with obvious advantages, has one fundamental drawback, namely, that the unquestionably specific nature of the economic aspect of the problem gets blurred.

Of the more theoretical works, I should mention the articles by Eliezer B. Ayal, Harry G. Johnson, Peter J. Burnell, and—the most interesting of all and the one that offers the most food for thought—the text by Albert Breton,[36] which are useful as comparative materials even if they exceed the geographical and chronological scope of the subject of this book and are more applicable to the problems of the present underdeveloped countries. John Montias, E. Bradford Burns, and John D. Wirth are some of the authors who made some limited effort to define the phenomenon of economic nationalism.[37]

Among the authors from the interwar period, Manoilescu was the most outspoken advocate of economic nationalism.[38] His writings were a manifestation of that ideology, supplying it at the same time with theoretical economic foundations. He explained his doctrine in his best-known book, which was published in 1929 and translated into English, French, Italian, Portuguese, and, in a revised edition, German.

The backbone of Manoilescu's argument was the thesis, acceptable from the point of view of economic theory (although strongly criticized precisely in this area),[39] that the maintenance of the present economic pattern of the agricultural countries meant the perpetuation of their status as clients of highly developed countries.[40] To use the terminology borrowed from the dependence theory, this would be a case of petrifaction of a relationship existing between the center and the periphery. Manoilescu's conception was based on the following assumption: Only industrialization, which is a natural right of every country, will allow agricultural countries to break out of the vicious circle of backwardness and dependency and lay the foundations for economic independence. (In this case protection of industry is justified because in new industries productivity is higher than the national average.) This striving for industrialization does not really clash with the interests of the developed countries. On the contrary, in their own well-conceived long-term interest, the developed countries should support the industrialization of the backward nations, which would then be able to participate in international trade as buyers of industrial products. In this way all countries would benefit from the growth of the world market. In other words, only by moving to a higher level of economic development can the less developed countries join in the bloodstream of the world economy, which is also to their advantage. Only when a certain level of economic development is reached is it possible to achieve, slowly and gradually, the independence of domestic production and to confront it with international competition, which can further stimulate development and progress.

This main idea extracted from the book in no way contradicts the tenets of political economy of less developed countries. However, one must also accept the view of Michał Kalecki, who, while generally supporting the advocates of protectionism in underdeveloped countries—in defiance of the views of orthodox economists—wrote that "Manoilescu's recognition of protectionism as a universal solution to the problem of industrialization of agricultural countries is certainly misleading." According to Kalecki, there are other, more important, obstacles to the economic growth of underdeveloped countries (e.g., their social structures).[41]

The popularity of Manoilescu's conception in the countries of the region and in underdeveloped countries in general should not be surprising. After all, it offered theoretical arguments for a policy of economic "egoism" that, even though they were not fully coherent, constituted a novelty in comparison to earlier works (e.g., by representatives of the German Younger Historical School[42] to say nothing of the works by List and especially by Henry C. Carey[43]). Manoilescu's conception was favorably received both by certain state bureaucracy circles and influential milieux, and by the local bourgeoisie in particular, who urged the state authorities to employ the policy of industrial protectionism. In Romania his book served as an important argument—though not the only one—to justify such a policy[44] and was pursued in an almost integral manner. In Poland Manoilescu's arguments were referred to by the *Lewiatan Group*.[45] In distant Brazil in the 1930s business circles quoted Manoilescu's book to fend off the repeated calls from various quarters for a lowering of import duties, claiming that this protectionism made it possible to build economic independence.[46]

Along with economic arguments, Manoilescu's work, which laid the foundations of the theory of economic nationalism,[47] contained an equally important ideological component. Manoilescu, a Romanian economist and politician, fiercely opposed the tenet of liberal economy that recognized individual profit as the sole criterion for the evaluation of a given economy. In his opinion, capitalist profit is a superficial issue, whereas the benefit of the state and the nation is of decisive importance.[48] Manoilescu accepted the possibility of developing production that was not profit-oriented—or that even caused losses—and was undertaken primarily by the state because it was advantageous to the country as a whole. These considerations applied to areas in which the interests of capitalists could differ from the interests of a higher order, articulated by the state or the nation, or, more precisely, by groups socially and politically authorized (or pretending to be authorized) to represent the people.

Liberal economists, in turn, rejected the formula of production that was advantageous despite the fact that it meant losses to the enterprises directly involved in it; for them this was a contradiction in itself. As the famous Polish theoretician Adam Heydel had, they argued that though the state might engage in production on its own behalf, "it must be realized that the whole society paid a certain price—in the form of a loss of social income—for the political goals attained in this way."[49] This conviction was shared by all private capitalists, who were nonetheless only too eager to win protection and concessions.[50]

Manoilescu's reasoning with regard to concrete decisions and his appeal for greater role of the state was not unusual in the countries of that region.

However, in regard to economic nationalism, liberals, who were in a majority in the academic community, confined themselves to a negative evaluation of the phenomenon, although there were some exceptions. Certainly the critical analysis of economic nationalism presented by Gregory deserves attention. The appearance of his article in 1931 was not incidental, for the Great Depression had triggered a widespread tendency on the part of governments to resort to protective measures that were at odds with the economic policy based on the rules of neoclassical economics that had pursued up until then.

By economic nationalism Gregory meant "the point of view that it ought to be the object of statesmanship in economic matters to increase the power [of the state]." The proponents of this view in the event of a conflict between the prosperity of individuals and the power of the state deliberately chose the power of the state rather than the prosperity of individuals as a matter of rational calculation and as their ultimate goal. The ideology of nationalism, Gregory went on, subordinated economic interests to the prestige of national strength, putting one's own nation above the others.[51] Therefore nationalism based on race, characteristic especially of Eastern Europe and Asia, was a prerequisite of the emergence of economic nationalism.[52]

Leaving aside the problem of the relationship between racial and economic nationalisms,[53] to which there is more than Gregory saw, let us note that he marked clear boundaries between the social and the state goals, and even set them against one another. In reality, however, the avowed advocates of economic nationalism (with the exception of the extreme radicals who, in a totalitarian spirit, equated the state with the nation) pointed to the complementary nature of these goals, arguing that the improvement of the economic conditions of society depended directly on the growth of the strength, including the economic strength, of the state or the nation. In other words, a policy that strengthens the state also strengthens its citizens. Nor is there much truth in Gregory's claim that "you have to keep the minority economically weak in order that you may dominate it politically." On the contrary, political domination is usually enough for an ethnic minority, regardless of its economic standing, not to play any major political role. This is evidenced by the situation of the Jews in Hungary at the time of the Compromise, in Romania at the end of the nineteenth century, or in Poland between the two world wars, and the position of the Chinese in Southeast Asia or of Asians in South Africa.[54]

Only if one interprets economic nationalism in an integralist way—and also limited to domestic context alone—one can argue that economic nationalism makes a part of the policy of racial ascendancy, for by increasing the economic power of your own people and weakening that of alien elements, it consolidates the political power of a distinct social group, with this power following from premises and rules other than economic.[55] It should be added here that the ethnic criterion is the only one by which the group is to be favored. Such a categorical junction between both kinds of nationalism was by no means a rule. It was not a rule in the nineteenth-century economic history of Germany, Russia, or the United States.[56] Nor was it a rule in the interwar foreign trade policies of the East-Central European countries. For example, export and/or import concessions were awarded regardless of the applicant's ethnic origin; in Czechoslovakia they were granted to both Czechs and Germans, and in Poland to Poles, Germans, and Jews. The important thing was that the goods produced in the country should be sold abroad. In other words, as long as there were no formal or actual differences in the treatment of various citizens on the basis of ethnic or religious principles, one can hardly speak about any junction between the two kinds of nationalism. However, it is a fact that toward the end of the 1930s the situation began to change, reflecting the ascendant inward-oriented economic nationalism.

Interpretation problems stem precisely from the fact that Gregory was not precise in his argument, treating economic nationalism as a homogeneous phenomenon not clearly differentiated in terms of the direction of its expansion; indeed, at times it is difficult to be sure whether he means outward or inward expansion. He was right, however, to observe that economic nationalism flourished in an atmosphere of an impending war[57] (although I will add to this that one could pursue the policy of economic nationalism even without developing the defense industry). Gregory's observation is most applicable, as it has turned out, to Hungary, and possibly to Bulgaria—that is, the countries interested in a revision of the Treaty of Versailles. These countries exploited the atmosphere of war preparations, which pervaded Europe in the late 1930s, and the actual relaxation of the restrictions the treaty had imposed on them, and they openly reached for classic economic nationalism policy tools to expand their defense industries. According to Gregory, this nationalism was also spurred by the growing competition in international trade, especially during a business slump. This popular view was of course correct, although the increasingly fierce competition seems to me to have been merely an external symptom of deeper economic processes.

On the whole, Gregory's observations were strikingly penetrating for that period. His analysis of the racial—or, to be more precise, ethnic—undercurrent of the ideology and practice of economic nationalism brings

him close to the conception formulated thirty years later by Albert Breton, who in fact drew much of his inspiration from Gregory). However,
Gregory scarcely explained the historical reasons for the development of
this ideology and failed to appreciate the role of its socioeconomic background. Therefore his outlook on the world economy, seen in the Anglo-
Saxon perspective, ignored those aspects of economic nationalism that
were obvious and rational in less developed countries.[58] Then, when examining economic nationalism essentially from the angle of international
economic relations, he overlooked that ideology's positive role as an element of development ideology.[59] Gregory's bias was the reason why he
emphasized mainly the negative sides of economic nationalism, that is,
the unequal treatment of ethnic minorities who were looked upon as
competitors for a limited number of jobs, and for business opportunities
in general.[60] But it should also be said that Gregory formulated his opinions, as it were, on an ad hoc basis, at a time when the world was plung-
ing into probably its worst crisis ever, and when economic interventionism was, for that matter, still in its infancy.

Oskar Lange attempted to present the essence of the phenomenon in
the Marxist perspective, but also in one marked by the liberal vision of
the economy. In a short article published in 1927 Lange defined economic
nationalism as a protectionist (or even a prohibitive) tariff policy. Lange
went on to present an argument in which he disqualified the ideology
and practice of economic nationalism, describing them as anachronistic
and reactionary, as they were slowing down the process of the formation
of a uniform system of world economy and seeking to put up barriers between national economic systems. According to Lange, the main driving
force of economic nationalism, especially in underdeveloped countries,
was the part of the bourgeoisie that lost its economic independence as a
result of advancing monopolistic concentration. On the other hand, the
bourgeoisie that was tied to big international capitalist monopolies opposed that ideology.[61]

Lange's reasoning did not stand the test of time, however.[62] Firstly,
Lange limited the scope of the phenomenon to customs policies. Secondly, he wrongly equated economic nationalism with self-sufficiency.
Thirdly, he did not distinguish between economic nationalism of small
and large countries. Finally, he did not identify very accurately the subjects that were stimulating the development of the phenomenon. Even if,
for example, the Czechoslovak business circles did at a certain time oppose high import tariffs (primarily on farm produce), large industrialists
in Poland opted for strong protection through tariffs.[63]

It can therefore be said that young Lange defended, paradoxically, the
enclave (and, to some extent, compradore) character of industrial development in underdeveloped countries, at least over some, by no means

short, period of time. Lange's views from that period reflected his confidence in the efficient operation of Ricardo's mechanism of reducing development inequalities, at least on the European scale.

In 1934 George D.H. Cole, an outstanding Labor Party leader and a renowned economist, presented a short and fragmentary argument meant to demonstrate the discord between the policy of economic nationalism and the principles of efficient management. Cole pointed out that the protectionism and dumping inherent in this policy and regarded as an almost fundamental economic objective, by eliminating competition, led to a growth of wages and thus to a growth of costs as well. Besides, the dumping of goods on foreign markets—by precluding the use of the benefits of international specialization and by offsetting the losses by high prices on the domestic market—upset the functioning of the economy as these higher prices naturally affected the population's living standard.[64] This reasoning, derived from neoclassical economics (although Cole himself frequently referred to Keynes), is not convincing, at least in relation to the countries of the region discussed here (and, to a large extent, to Italy and Germany as well). Though the exports of those countries were predominantly of a dumping nature,[65] the needs of the labor market (huge labor surpluses) made the prospect of high wages in industry and in the economy as a whole very remote.

The view of Bertil Ohlin deserves to be mentioned here as an example of an interesting and rare opinion that did not reject a priori the ideology of economic nationalism. Understanding its rational roots, he pointed out that on the whole its practical application produced economic losses and led to a drop in national income. He believed, nevertheless, that the effects of the policy of economic nationalism of the 1920s and 1930s were not as dangerous to the world economy as several decades earlier (if only because of the easier access to technological developments).[66]

A broader analysis of economic nationalism could be found in the famous report of the Royal Institute of International Affairs (RIIA). Proceeding from the tenets of neoclassical economics, its authors said that this ideology had its sources in mercantile practices and the explosion of vested interests around the turn of the century (various forms of monopolies and restrictions on production, curbs on distribution and the labor market), to which the state was giving its assent with increasing vigor. This process, speeded up by the effects of World War I and the emergence of new states, was facilitated by the eclipse of the economic expansion of the developed European countries, the technological progress that brought about a huge increase in food and raw materials production, and the change of political systems in some of the countries, which threatened social stability. The scope of economic nationalism and its diverse effects, especially in the 1930s, cannot be compared to earlier manifestations of the phenomenon (let us note that on this point the authors of the report took a view different from Ohlin's). This incomparability was supposed to result from mutual interference between political and economic nationalisms. However, this progression of events could not have been taken for granted, as it was not at all certain that Central Europe (mainly Austria, Hungary, and Germany) would have embarked on this path had it not been for the postwar inflation and the credit and finance crisis of 1931. On the whole, the report emphasized the significance of political reasons for the development of economic nationalism after World War I.[67]

This analysis contains several noteworthy points. First of all, it clearly identifies the phenomenon of economic nationalism as such, and it rightly emphasizes the role of the state in stimulating its evolution. However, it is a mistake to point to the allegedly inevitable bond between economic nationalism and the totalitarian character of the state and at the same time to underrate the internal impulses that were pushing the young nations (although not them alone) toward economic nationalism.

One researcher who took a deeper interest in economic nationalism was William E. Rappard. He correctly distinguished between the economics of nationalism and economic nationalism of the countries not "animated by the spirit of nationalism" (because after World War I economic nationalism was applied by practically all states). He also pointed to the close mutual relationship between economic and political nationalisms[68] and the resulting need for a precise definition of the two. According to Rappard, the aim of economic nationalism was not so much to contribute to the well-being and wealth of a nation as to the growth of its independence from foreign influence. Therefore "economic nationalism is the policy of national self-sufficiency."

As the most important features, which are also goals, of that nationalism, Rappard identified: the tendency to buy locally produced goods; support for production deemed indispensable to the state; the striving for a favorable balance of payments; and the demand for more living space. Appeals to the patriotism of fellow citizens and the use of various protectionist instruments and methods made the achievement of these goals possible.[69]

Both the definition and the list of characteristic features of economic nationalism arouse misgivings. First of all, the advocates of this ideology emphasized its beneficial material results. Secondly, the first two features did not go beyond the standard (rather narrow) interpretation of the phenomenon (limited to protectionism). As for the third feature, the striving for a trade surplus was indeed the essential task of the economic policy in the region. It resulted, however, from the meagerness of foreign currency reserves, not from any doctrine. In the 1920s the accumulation of foreign trade surplus was not that important and was hardly ever used as an argument for protectionism. The fourth distinguishing factor, the demand for more living space, was characteristic mainly of imperialism or totalitarianism but was not a prerequisite of economic nationalism. However, if one went strictly by this list of features, then, contrary to Rappard's intention, the list of countries pursuing economic nationalism would be drastically cut down to just a handful.[70] The same would happen if all those features or goals were to appear in every single case. Therefore it seems that Rappard's endeavor to define and classify the phenomenon was not consistent enough.

Wilhelm Röpke, an outstanding liberal economist, made some interesting remarks on economic nationalism. He recognized this nationalism—a phenomenon whose "total" dimension in the interwar period distinguished it basically from the protectionism of the earlier period[71]—as a symptom and a cause of a profound and dramatic crisis (which he calls a historic one[72]) that gripped Western society and its economy. According to Röpke, the crisis dated back, symbolically, to July 1914. Inasmuch as for the no-less-famous Karl Polanyi the events of the 1930s were revolutionary in terms of the building and strengthening of the framework of a new international economic, political, and social order that he treated as an answer to the failure of nineteenth-century liberal capitalism,[73] to Röpke that period was characterized by confusion, malady, and disintegration of the world economy. The salvation—practically the only one—was a return to the status quo ante. Otherwise economic nationalism might lead to "economic collectivism," to "political and even cultural Totalitarianism," and in the field of international relations, to the "growing advantage of the greater political units [i.e., states] over the smaller ones" (e.g., of Germany over the Balkan states) due to the surge in economic bilateralism.[74]

But in contrast to the more or less parallel extreme liberal criticism of economic nationalism (Hertz, Heilperin), Röpke emphasized the great influence of noneconomic objective and subjective factors on the development and durability of the phenomenon that, though irrational (from the liberal point of view), could hardly be ignored altogether. Although on the whole economic nationalism was harmful (be it the agrarian nationalism of the developed countries, the monetary variety, or that articulated in the conception of "full employment"[75] or the wasteful autarky), this assertion does not apply to the industrialism of backward countries, whose negative effects are of a merely transitional nature.

In these circumstances, industrial nations should give up excessive protection of their agriculture in favor of the so-called third road, which was an alternative to both self-sufficiency in food production and to dropping such ambitions altogether. Meanwhile, the "industrial nationalism" of the agricultural countries was not only supposed to help them get out of their backwardness but was also to be advantageous for international economic relations. Hence, whereas "the effect of the policy of agricultural protectionism on international economic disintegration is indisputable," it is by no means clear whether the parallel development of the industrialization of "new countries," as furthered by protective measures, is to be considered also as a disintegrating factor. In fact, it is just the opposite: In the long run, this industrialization served precisely the integration of the world economy.[76] This is usually the path toward Western civilization and capitalism, he wrote. So it can be said that on the issues of the re-agrarianization of the industrially developed countries and the industrialization of the backward nations Röpke went a long way toward meeting the arguments of the advocates of industrialism as the proper development strategy for the region.

However, one thing I find rather surprising about this book, which remains a source of inspiration today, is the lack of a clear distinction between protectionism and economic nationalism (which, incidentally, are approached in a traditional manner), two phenomena that are, after all, the core of his book. Also, Röpke's pessimism regarding the sociopolitical effects of economic nationalism, though somewhat justified in the case of Germany and Italy, proved to be unfounded in relation to the Western democracies.

E. H. Carr, who was the editor and coauthor of the aforementioned RIIA report, was interested in economic nationalism in the context of the broader problem of nationalism. In 1945 he published a small but important and still valuable book on nationalism (*Nationalism and After*), in which he presented the origins of the phenomenon. He correctly perceived the modification of the role of the state in the economy in the last quarter of the nineteenth century—that is, the striking growth of its significance as the subject of economic activity and the stimulator of economic nationalism in Western Europe (and in the United States, for that matter)—as the turning point in the history of nationalism. Carr identified three periods in the development of nationalism, with the third period occurring in the years 1914–1939. In his opinion, that period was characterized by socialization of the state, which, while defending the level of earnings and employment of its citizens, had to turn, out of necessity, against the national policies of other countries.

Though passing a negative judgment on the nationalism and the economic nationalism that prevailed in the whole world, including the Soviet Union, Carr, unlike other authors (e.g., Gregory and Lionel Robbins), seemed to some extent to understand the rationale of the underdeveloped countries, eager to partake of the privileges thus far reserved for the industrialized countries,[77] even if he may have put too much emphasis on the selfish nature of these aspirations.

In presenting the post–World War II major contributions to the subject, we should begin with Michael Heilperin, a Polish-born economist, who is probably the most often quoted liberal expert on economic nationalism. Already in *Trade of Nations*, whose title refers to the famous book by Adam Smith, he signaled ideas that he subsequently developed in the interesting *Studies in Economic Nationalism*, published in English and French.

The ideological pivot of Heilperin's views is the contrast between the so-called collectivism and the free enterprise system.[78] Economic nationalism, in its radical variant engendered by the Great Depression, was to be characterized by such features—new and old—as the influence of the state, guided by its *raison d'état*, on the balance of payments, chiefly by means of currency controls; the pursuit of a policy of full employment by means of limiting imports and stimulating exports; the use of protectionist methods and tools to create a foreign trade surplus and a desired pattern of trade; and the emphasis on bilateralism in international commerce. These features, which reduce economic nationalism to a set of national policies that regulate the relations between a country and the rest of the world,[79] suggest a rather traditional understanding of economic nationalism.[80] Economic nationalism interpreted in this way not only restricts the free-enterprise system but also is actually its opposite.

From among the broader and the narrower definitions of the phenomenon, Heilperin chooses the latter as more convenient for the description of the reality. The narrower definition equates "economic nationalism with policies aimed at national self-sufficiency" but "excludes from its scope policies which *interfere* with international economic relations but *without effectively insulating* a country from the outside world." According to Heilperin, the use of the broader definition (which, in my opinion, would be more correct from the methodological point of view) would blur the distinction between the nineteenth-century protectionism and the "new economic nationalism." Whereas the former is essentially compatible with liberalism (and in fact is a symbiotic component thereof), the latter—especially under autarky—has little or nothing in common with liberalism,[81] being closely related to collectivism and totalitarianism of various hues.

Heilperin finds the roots of economic nationalism back in mercantilism and the Fichtean conception of a closed commercial state (*Der geschlossene Handelsstaat*). He perceives contemporary impulses in the rise of economic interventionism, especially in planning, which is inseparably linked with the idea of autarky, implemented in Germany in the 1930s by Hjalmar Schacht and propagated with some success by John Maynard Keynes in the democratic countries. The conception of full employment in particular was blamed for the extraordinary surge in new economic nationalism.[82]

This view leads Heilperin to the repeatedly voiced opinion that the only remedy for the fatal syndrome of economic nationalism is a return to the healthy liberal principles, especially in trade. As a result, what was the beginning of something new for Polanyi was for Heilperin (and probably even more so than for Röpke) a step backward in comparison to the golden age of the nineteenth century, almost a retrogression to premodern times.

In his presentation and criticism of the ideology of economic nationalism (incomplete as it was), Heilperin did not avoid inconsistencies, methodological ones included. His fundamentalist liberal world outlook was inconsistent with, for example, the rational proposal for differentiating between economic nationalism in both the broader and the narrower senses. This restrictive approach must have been responsible for the unabashed presentism of his argumentation.[83]

A different approach to the problem of economic nationalism was presented by a representative of political sciences, E. B. Ayal. Analyzing the relationship between ideology and economic development, he proceeded from the assertion that the potential of the nationalist ideology was stronger and more durable than that of other contemporary ideologies, such as fascism or communism,[84] that is, the ideological trends that were explicitly political and more or less universalistic, in which, incidentally, the national element quickly became manifest and even predominant. To follow Ayal's reasoning, when a country's leadership maintains that national interest entails development, it means that the leadership plans to focus the nationalistic feelings of the population on economic objectives. The leadership resorts then to direct sociotechnical influence or to indirect but more effective methods of exploiting people's emotions to tie up concrete social forces with the goals set by the state authorities. In his view Ayal referred (not quite justifiably) to the experiments of Zionists, of Kemal Atatürk's Turkey, and of Japan (cf. Chapter 9). As regards the countries of the East-Central European region, the prevalence of authoritarian regimes there neither precluded nor facilitated the use of this method of manipulating nationalist feelings for the sake of economic development.

The analysis produced by Albert Breton, who used economic and sociological research methods to approach the problem of economic nationalism, is ambitious, modern, mature, and comprehensive. In the theoretical part of his work, Breton's findings indicate what I think to be the right direction of the further study of the phenomenon. Breton follows the classics in differentiating between cultural and political nationalisms. These two variants were not clearly delimited,[85] and thus by overlapping they only strengthened each other. The crucial point of Breton's analysis is the assertion that the economists overlooked the kind of investment that he terms "investment in nationality or ethnicity." Indeed, it can be safely assumed that societies that are guided in their behavior primarily by nationalism do embark on this kind of investment project—or rather, as I would term them, quasi-investment projects, as they hardly ever take a physical shape (and if so, only in an indirect way, as investments are usually made in such specific areas of public life as education or the mass media). The specific nature of this kind of "investment" in nationality lies in the fact that it does not so much generate new income or promote its maximization as redistribute the income already produced. Hence these investments are not profitable for everyone in a society but only for specific and identifiable groups[86]—for a part of or for all of the middle class, to be precise.[87]

Breton's definitions of nationality and nationalism are original, and the hypotheses derived from them seem to be important because they try to describe nationalism in economic terms. It can therefore be quite safely assumed that the sphere related to "investment" in nationality or ethnicity is, to a large extent, what used to be described as economic nationalism. However, in contrast to, for example, Johnson,[88] for Breton economic nationalism is only a substratum and at the same time a form of political nationalism. This is what can be concluded from his own definition, according to which at the roots of nationalism there always are definite political interests.

The aim of a nationalistic policy is to increase the national possessions, which can be achieved either through nationalization or through tariffs, taxes, bonuses, subsidies, or a special pricing policy (meaning "setting prices at nought"), and the like, which take more time and are more complicated.[89] The benefits of such moves, especially in the access they generate to high-paying jobs and positions of authority, fall primarily to the national (or ethnic) middle class (this specifically applies to the strata that has joined that class relatively recently). If the number of high-paying jobs is limited, there can develop a conflict within the middle class itself.[90] It remains unclear to me, however, why this conflict could not be neutralized, at least partly, by advantages other than financial ones. A stream of nonpecuniary benefits, which would be hard to measure, is of a psychological nature (pride, sense of identity, etc.). When offered to workers— and, I would add, other social groups, for example, peasants—such benefits make it easier for them to reconcile themselves to a policy from which they draw no economic advantage.[91] Therefore, Breton suggested, this stream is a hoax, a false advantage, in fact a way of manipulating the working class.

The main aspects of this conception prompt me to offer several comments, both of a detailed and of a general nature:

First, one can detect some Marxist inspiration in it, for example, in the terminology used, in the references to class stratification, and in the novel attempt to express definite spiritual values in economic terms.

Second, this conception draws on the achievements of the psychological school of political economy, which is especially manifest in the placing of the nonpecuniary stream of benefits in a separate research category. In a way, Breton touches upon a problem I would define as the noneconomic rationale of economic nationalism (more about which later).

Third, in Breton's theory one can paradoxically discern the neoclassical influence as well, which can be seen both in certain arguments and in the possibly unintentional choice of the preliminary assumptions to the effect that the limitations of the flow of manpower, capital, and goods are symptoms of nationalism and hence that the internationalization of economic relations is a more advanced stage in the development of management. Without denying the argument about the internationalization of economic relations, one can nevertheless note that his position in this regard could in part result from the nonhistorical approach common among economists, and in part from some confusion of the merits, which obliterated the two phenomena's distinctive features.

Fourth, it is worth noting the original, if unproved, assertion that nationalism is essentially little more than a mechanism of redistribution of the existing national income (or, more accurately, that it sets such a mechanism in motion). This is the foundation of the conception, its starting point, and its target. It is at this point that Breton's model reveals its methodological flaw, that of a partial tautology of this assertion. Besides, even if we assume that "investing" in nationality influences the allocation of the tangible assets engaged in material production, the choice of the evaluation criteria still remains to be explained. We can assume that these criteria are formulated *ex post facto*, when the effects of this "investing" can already be seen. But even then it is not possible to avoid the arbitrariness and subjectivity of the evaluation. Though the model incorporates the category of national interest, which, by generally defining the groups interested in definite economic moves, is supposed to facilitate the formulation of more-or-less correct answers, I do not think it is possible to identify these groups with a large degree of accuracy. Furthermore, a rigorous application of Breton's scheme virtually precludes the existence of the category of nationwide advantages (even if perceived only subjectively), whereas in reality such a category does exist beyond all doubt. The manifestation of the common interests of the whole of society, or at least of its prevalent part, at the time of the Great Depression can serve here as an example.[92]

Fifth, I do not think it is in any way possible to rule out the possibility that nationalistic ideals, like almost any other ideals, by releasing the intellectual and/or physical reserves of some circles of society or the whole of it, may be conducive to the growth of the national income. The significance of this trend is certainly much smaller when the edge of nationalism is directed inward.

Sixth, the radical critics of economic nationalism tend to interpret any intervention they believe to be of the protectionist nature as, almost by definition, an articulation of nationalist intentions. This is how those who express such an extremist point of view classify, for example, protective measures taken in times of crisis. Breton hardly fits into this category of critics even though his conception does not contain clear reservations that would rule out such a broad interpretation of economic nationalism.

Harry G. Johnson has paid a relatively great deal of attention to economic nationalism in the Third World countries, and he even held a special seminar devoted to these problems. On the basis of works by Gary S. Becker, Anthony Downs (both from 1957), and Breton, in 1965 he proposed an outline of a comprehensive interpretation of the phenomenon. According to his theory, the policy of economic nationalism places emphasis on industrialization and the development of those industries that now are the symbols of "national identity" in the developing countries and at the same time are conducive to the preservation of the cohesion of the state, that is, to the development of heavy industry. The supreme aim of this policy is to create and then to increase the numbers of the middle classes and/or the group of educated people and to provide them with prestigious and well-paying jobs. The attainment of these goals is made possible by the development of public ownership (which is precisely what facilitates the offering of good jobs to fellow citizens) and the redistribution of the material product first of all to the educated middle class, at the expense first and foremost of the poorer classes. Outside the economic sphere, the attainment of these goals is facilitated by the so-called psychological income, which takes the shape of nationalistic satisfaction.[93]

This interpretation lacks the Breton conception's theoretical foundations, and it can hardly be called a model one, as the author would wish it to be; but even so it contains interesting observations. I refer in particular to its basic assumption, that is, to the category of mental income, borrowed from Breton and subsequently transformed, and to the ensuing conclusion that investing in the domestic middle classes is a prerequisite of the establishment of a national state capable of surviving. This assumption corresponds to some extent with the tenor of the deliberations presented in Johnson's essay. Nonetheless, Johnson's argument, too, gives rise to reservations of a more general nature. The point is that (similar to Breton) he described the policy of economic nationalism in terms of neoclassical economics, whereas his conclusions hardly fit with its vocabulary. On the one hand, Johnson's interpretation emphasized that mental income is attained at the expense of material income, and so from the point of view of the principles of economics it is a waste (assuming,

of course, that an income exists there in the first place, which in itself represented a certain breakthrough in neoclassical thinking), while on the
other hand, it pointed—rightly, in my opinion—to the positive aspects of
the phenomenon. It may even be, writes Johnson, and at this point he
goes further than Breton, that nationalist policies are the cheapest and
most effective way to raise real income in less developed countries. This
internal contradiction can be removed by assuming that a nonhyper-
trophic economic nationalism is indispensable in certain circumstances
and that it may be conducive to the modernization of the economies of
the developing countries, and in this way it may contribute to their incorporation into the national economy on better terms.

The applicability of Johnson's interpretation to the subject of my analysis is another problem; matters become complicated insofar as the aforementioned goals of economic nationalism and the means of attaining
them were not as pronounced in the interwar East-Central European
countries as they were in the postcolonial countries. First of all, the
process of establishing a national identity was already complete and,
with very few exceptions, did not involve the overcoming of ethnic "trib-
alism," which has been the case in many young countries. Hence the nationalistic and state tendencies were of a somewhat different nature from
those of present-day postcolonial countries. Due to a different historical
context, especially in the 1930s, the East-Central European countries, as a
rule, adopted moderate political and economic systems, oriented rather
toward preventing changes in their respective social structures, especially in Poland, Romania, Yugoslavia, Bulgaria, and Hungary—or at
least toward this structure's slow transformation. This was partly because the nationalist elites, who sought a fast growth in the numbers and
in the role of the middle classes identified according to ethnic criteria, did
not gain a decisive influence on economic policies in any of these countries. As for the Baltic states, Johnson's observations usually apply to
them, even if the role the state played in their economy was smaller than
the role the state plays in, for example, many African countries at present. But the same Baltic states did much in the interwar period to speed
up greatly the process of building modern national consciousness.

The undeniable universalistic aspirations of both conceptions (which is
more true of Breton's than of Johnson's) turn out to be a bit unfounded in
the light of the questions and reservations I have expressed. Nonetheless,
these pioneering theories, which contain, especially in the case of Breton,
a number of important arguments, can help historians to understand the
complex fabric of nationalism, especially its economic variant, irrespective of its variability in time and space and the large dose of subjectivity
in its appraisals. Interestingly, the attempts in the 1960s to incorporate
the phenomenon of economic nationalism in the theory of nationalism on

the one hand and the theory of economics on the other have usually met with no reaction or criticism.[94]

Among the few, mostly descriptive, definition-like presentations of economic nationalism, it is worth mentioning John M. Montias's proposal, even though it was to serve different research purposes. By economic nationalism he meant any commercial policy detrimental to the economic interests of a group or "bloc" of countries, pursued in the name of some domestic objectives.[95] This formula is not precise enough. On the one hand, it is too broad, as there can be no commercial policy that would produce only benefits.[96] Of any commercial policy it can be said that it is guided by "some domestic objectives." On the other hand, this definition is too narrow, because in practice it confines the existence of the phenomenon to foreign trade. Finally, Montias ignored the domestic aspect of relations between states and/or blocs.

The notion of economic nationalism can be found also in works dealing with Latin America. The notion is widely used in the historical studies concerning the modern history of Brazil and Mexico.[97] For example, J. D. Wirth, in describing the development of the Brazilian economy in the years 1930–1954, emphasized the role played by economic nationalism, a notion by which he understood a policy aimed at the attainment by the state of an economic strength sufficient for ensuring its political independence. Economic nationalism construed in this way is based on two principal assumptions: (1) that the country's natural resources should remain under the control of the citizens or the state, and (2) that while defining the priorities and assessing the effects of an economic policy, one should refer to a system of values expressed in terms of the nation's needs. This makes it possible, for example, to weigh the proportions of growth between heavy industry and agriculture, between defense and purely economic needs, or to define with greater precision the time needed for the state to attain big-power status.[98]

In contrast to Montias's definition, Wirth emphasized the positive element of economic nationalism (rather than the negative, i.e., activities detrimental to other countries). However, the tendency to narrow down the scope of the notion to politics—to the sphere of practical action—puts the two authors in the same league. Wirth was aware, however, of the ideological aspect of the problem when he took up the question of the circumstances and the time of the transformation of economic nationalism into a future-oriented "ideology of development."[99] The phenomenon was interpreted in yet another way by Robert F. Dernberger, who saw it as a policy that stresses the creation of an independent economy.[100] This is too general and imprecise a formula, even though it clearly delimits the scope of the phenomenon to relatively few countries.

George Macesich and Burnell are two other authors who have recently dealt with economic nationalism in the Third World.[101] Burnell argued that in the face of the dramatic tangle of North-South contradictions, it is in the interest of the underdeveloped countries to remain in the orbit of the capitalist world economy; at the same time, their clear economic self-determination will have a positive impact on the shape of the international division of labor.[102] Meanwhile Macesich, another representative of the liberal critique of economic nationalism, saw the rise of nationalism in the underdeveloped countries solely as a source of threat to their internal stability, arguing that the ideological nature of the goals of a nationalistic economic policy, understood in a very broad sense, predetermines its failure. While this policy may be viewed as an investment for the benefit of building a common good—a viable national state[103]—the alternative liberal solutions, especially in the monetary and financial field, are undoubtedly more advantageous for the developing countries.[104]

On the whole, however, the authors I have mentioned define and identify the features of economic nationalism in too general a manner, without formulating the necessary reservations, which makes many of their judgments questionable. For example, it is necessary, if only for methodological reasons, to differentiate between the nationalism of a strong state, which may evolve into expansive and/or militarist tendencies, often camouflaged by slogans of free trade and the internationalization of the economy, and the economic nationalism of an underdeveloped country, which is mainly of a defensive nature and which is viewed—whether correctly nor not I shall discuss later—as a chance to increase the freedom of maneuver, including political maneuver, a chance to extricate the country from its backwardness by developing domestic production.

Economic Nationalism: The Component Parts

Economic nationalism is a broad, complex, and variable phenomenon and, as the foregoing implies, has been characterized by the amorphousness of its contents and practice. For this reason the observations contained in this section, far from trying to exhaust all of the phenomenon's characteristics, have a more modest goal, that of capturing the most important components of the ideology of economic nationalism. Unfortunately, it is not possible to avoid a measure of arbitrariness in the selection of assumptions and consequently of arguments.

In no country of the region did the ideology of economic nationalism receive a clearly defined and logical shape, one that would form a coherent whole, with the possible exception of Manoilescu's conception. As a rule it was an ideology relying on several plain slogans or demands (industrialization, support for domestic producers, state control, cautious attitude toward other countries, dislike of or aversion to ethnic minorities), bonded together by the idea of state or national interests. With this general amorphousness, it offered a choice of various interpretations. It is important to note that none of the variants was officially recognized as the only correct one (even in Romania, where the ideology and practice of economic nationalism were probably most strongly propagated[105] and where the prestige of its leading advocate was the greatest, although he did not hold a monopoly on being right). Later on I shall consider the state as the subject implementing the guidelines of economic nationalism, for it was the state that took up the challenges of the ideology of economic nationalism on behalf of definite groups and strata by focusing on itself and by transforming their clearly articulated interests. (This does not mean that the state was not guided at the same time by considerations recognized as general, national ones.)

Some influential milieux in the countries of the region recognized nationalism also as a key to the desired economic development. This conviction became particularly strong in the 1930s, which can be attributed to the weakening of the influence of other ideologies, especially those of a universalist nature, such as liberalism and internationalism.[106] Only rarely, however, did economic nationalism offer a sensible program for modernization of the country, which would at the same time be correlated with a suitable commercial and tariff policy.

Economic nationalism was and is engendered, not only in theory, by excessive protectionism[107] and autarky. With the exception of fascist and communist countries,[108]) autarky was a characteristic strategy of economic policy that external circumstances forced the developing countries to pursue. However, the popular view (repeated after Hertz) that autarky, conceived as a prerequisite and a means of obtaining economic autonomy, was an essential feature of economic nationalism in the region contains a methodological error, because it identifies the verbal statements with the practice, which was actually remote from them. What is more, these two phenomena cannot be equated: protectionism allows the policy of autarky to be carried out, but protectionism is not autarky. In reality, the intensification of autarkic tendencies in the 1930s was more a result of spontaneous processes than a deliberate choice and implementation of a definite conception, and it was obviously a consequence of the Great Depression and external conditions in general. Protectionist tendencies in those countries were, however, growing stronger, and these tendencies were conducive to the use of economic policy instruments that either limited or altogether eliminated foreign competition on the domestic market.

The program of industrialization was often recognized as the most important segment of the ideology of economic nationalism. In the countries ruled by peasant parties, though, the ideology had a different hue: Agrarianism was propagated instead of (or parallel to) industrialization. This was the case in Bulgaria in the years 1920–1923 and, with much less intensity, in Romania during the short period of the rule of the Iuliu Maniu party. The agrarianist movement had the strongest political and economic backing in the Baltic countries. In Czechoslovakia, which is often cited as an example of the domination of farming circles, the situation was in reality more complex than that. The Agrarian Party, despite the hegemonic position it had been enjoying for a long time (owing to a peculiar distribution of political forces), was not quite able to push through its conception of the development of the country. Besides, in contrast to, for example, Aleksandŭr Stamboliyski's party in Bulgaria, the agrarianists appreciated the role and importance of industry for the development of the country. Unable to impose their policy on the others in the end, they nevertheless managed in practice to secure the protection of agriculture and the food industry.[109]

As for the distribution of group interests, the industrialization program was a characteristic distinguishing feature of the strata interested in it, either for material or for superior patriotic reasons. The aim of an economic policy guided by these principles (especially the industrialization imperative) was the attainment of economic independence, which was construed as a prerequisite of political sovereignty and understood, verbally for the most part, in a maximalist manner. The prevailing opinion was that the creation of appropriate conditions for domestic production, especially industrial production, would sooner or later make it possible to set in motion an engine of internal accumulation of capital, which, in view of the insufficient availability of foreign capital, should facilitate the development of the available resources and provide jobs, ultimately making it possible to solve the problem of agrarian overpopulation within the foreseeable future.

Therefore it is not surprising that another constituent part of this ideology, one of only slightly lesser status to the aforementioned ones, was the striving for the so-called nationalization of capital, that is, the reduction of foreign influence on the economy, especially in the sectors regarded as vital for a country's security. Such nationalization was achieved by administrative and legislative means. In the 1930s attacks were directed at capital termed as disloyal, at usurious interest on loans, and the like. The scope of state interference was a function of political intentions and possibilities, but since the bargaining position of the two parties was uneven the moves were often as spectacular as they were ineffective. Foreign capital, backed by political pressure from the country of its origin, was strong enough to neutralize any hostile action. Besides, the countries of the region were essentially very much interested in attracting foreign capital. This resulted in a significant lack of coherence between the chronic shortage of capital (Czechoslovakia and Austria being the two notable exceptions) and the articulation of dislike of foreign capital. This obviously affected the cohesion of the ideology of economic nationalism.

The other side of the attitude toward foreign capital, antiforeigner feelings, much stronger in the 1930s than previously, was expressed in curbs on the economic activities of foreigners[110] and in immigration restrictions. The U.S. immigration acts of 1921, 1924, and 1928, by hampering permanent immigration, produced negative economic and social consequences in a number of countries of the region. This was offset only to a small extent by the readiness of France and some Latin American countries to accept foreigners. However, in the 1930s economic emigration almost disappeared (with the exception of migration to Latin America), though there was some seasonal migration (e.g., of Hungarians, Poles, and Lithuanians to Germany and Latvia and of Poles and Czechs to France).[111] From the angle of interstate relations this antiforeign sentiment was one of the important features distinguishing the economic nationalism of the late 1930s from its traditional variant.[112]

Etatism was another of its constituent parts. As a form of nationalization, and as a manifestation of state interventionism, etatism automatically became a peculiar part and form of economic nationalism, in keeping with the logic of its doctrine (but also with the formally reigning liberal values). Of course the ideologues of economic nationalism by no means questioned the superior status of private ownership. Nevertheless the practice of the 1930s demonstrated that a flexible interpretation of the dogma of private property was received with greater understanding when restrictions imposed by the state such as nationalization and ethnicization were spearheaded against ethnically different fellow citizens. On the whole, etatism construed as a form of economic nationalism on the internal plane had genuine advocates only among the state bureaucrats and naturally, for tactical (and, in a sense, ideological) reasons, among socialist movements.

Protectionism, autarky, and industrialism[113] (or, less frequently, agrarianism), the three basic ingredients of economic nationalism, along with the dislike of foreign capital, each one on its own and all of them together formed only one side of the projection of the future contained in this ideology. Its full scope can only be seen when it becomes imbued with the ideological element, a certain intensity of national emotions, and when national (state) interests, regarded as the supreme ones, impart an ideological tint to economic policies. The state bureaucracy—which also aspired to the title of the main articulator of the idea and which generally interpreted it more in the spirit of state than national ideology—was the coordinator of these moves, its executor to some extent, and, finally, the arbitrator in disputes between groups representing different economic (and sometimes class) interests. It can be assumed that this was really the case in the countries of the region (with the exception of the late 1930s).

It is not easy to identify any precise moment from which the ideology and eventually also the practice of economic nationalism began to focus primarily on the domestic scene, assuming a totalitarian hue and undergoing a qualitative transformation. It seems that this development was especially due to the inability of these countries to attain sufficiently rapid economic progress and to cope with the economic, commercial, and political pressures exerted by the highly developed countries. In that situation the ruling elites saw no choice but to resort to solutions of an internal nature. At this stage, economic nationalism transformed public discontent into hostility toward outsiders, whether the neighboring nations and states or ethnic minorities at home, who were blamed for rampant exploitation, injustice, and poverty. Proceeding in most cases from the slogans of national solidarity, the advocates of economic nationalism recommended (and tried to implement) the policy in which development was based on the redistribution of wealth, incomes, and rights at the expense of the minorities, especially the Jews, but also foreign capitalists and people living on unearned income. In international economic relations, they proposed the so-called beggar-my-neighbor policy. Apart from the alleged economic benefits of this set of policies, the ruling circles set great store by its political and psychological advantages, that is, the neutralization (with varying effects) of the influence of the extreme right and the winning over of some of its clients. But this policy also had unforeseen side effects, as it was conducive to a general shift of the public mood to the right and to a dominance of nationalistic attitudes. This was so because in practice the ruling elites yielded to the populist and anticapitalist demands of the extreme right as well as to the purely nationalistic ones. By the end of the 1930s this race to the right between the ruling authoritarian circles fighting to retain power and the extreme right trying to take it over became so fierce in some countries (Hungary, Romania, and to some extent Greece) that the former almost found themselves implementing the ethnic goals of the latter.[114]

Notes

1. Numerous studies have already been devoted to nationalism. See, for example, bibliographies by Koppel S. Pinson, *Bibliographical Introduction to Nationalism* (New York, 1935), Karl W. Deutsch, *Interdisciplinary Bibliography of Nationalism, 1935–1953* (Cambridge, Mass., 1954), and also extensive bibliographical annexes in Anthony D. Smith, "Nationalism: A Trend Report and Bibliography," in *Cur-*

rent Sociology, vol. XXI, no. 3, 1973, and Heinrich A. Winkler, ed., *Nationalismus* (Athenäum-Main-Scriptor-Hanstein, 1978).

2. See the classical work by Carlile A. Macartney and Alan W. Palmer, *Independent Eastern Europe: A History* (London, 1962), written with great sympathy for the nations of the region.

3. J. B. Sykes, ed., *The Concise Oxford Dictionary of Current English* (Oxford, 1978), pp. 725, 809; Albert S. Hornby, ed., *Oxford Advanced Learner's Dictionary of Current English* (Oxford, 1980), pp. 561, 614; Charles P. Schleicher, "Nationalism," in Julius Gould and William L. Kolb, eds., *A Dictionary of the Social Sciences* (Chicago, 1969), pp. 456–457; Hans Kohn, "Nationalism," in David L. Sills, ed., *International Encyclopedia of the Social Sciences* (Chicago, 1968), vol. 11, pp. 63–70.

4. For instance, Barbara Ward, *Five Ideas That Change the World* (New York, 1959), p. 27, writing on Soviet Russia after 1927.

5. See Carlton J.H. Hayes, *Essays on Nationalism* (New York, 1926), and *Nationalism: A Religion* (New York, 1960); Hans Kohn, *The Idea of Nationalism: A Study in Its Origins and Background* (New York, 1967). This tendency has been strengthened by Boyd C. Shafer, *Nationalism: Myth and Reality* (New York, 1955); Louis L. Snyder, *The Meanings of Nationalism* (New Brunswick, N.J., 1954); Aira Kemiläinen, *Nationalism: Problem Concerning the World: The Concept and Classification* (Jyväskylä, Finland, 1964). See also Miroslav Hroch, *Evropská národni hnuti v 19 stoleti: Společenskě přepohlady vzniku novodobných národů* (Prague, 1986), pp. 7–30, 369–372.

6. Compare Edward H. Carr, ed., *Nationalism: A Report by a Study Group of Members of the Royal Institute of International Affairs* (Oxford, 1939), p. xx.

7. Precise definitions of patriotism and nationalism were offered by Karl W. Deutsch, *Nationalism and Social Communication: An Inquiry into the Foundations of Nationality* (Cambridge, Mass., 1967), p. 288. See also Frank Tachau, "Nationalism," in *The World Book Encyclopedia*, Field Enterprises Educational Corporation, vol. 15, p. 175.

8. George Orwell, "Uwagi o nacjonalizmie," in G. Orwell, *Eseje* (London, 1985), p. 127.

9. One should remember, however, that they understand patriotism in its narrow sense, in a different way that is usually understood in the scientific literature of the countries of the region. Compare Hroch, *Evropská národni hnuti*, p. 372. One of the few exceptions is in an essay by Peter F. Sugar, "External and Domestic Roots of Eastern European Nationalism," in Peter F. Sugar and Ivo L. Lederer, eds., *Nationalism in Eastern Europe* (Seattle, 1973), although even he, like Hayes, is inclined to see patriotism as a stage preceding nationalism proper. In the collection edited by Sugar and Lederer, Sugar's approach does not find any following. For example, Tajar Zavalani, "Albanian Nationalism," p. 91, recognizes the events of spring 1939 as the first manifestation of true nationalism (at that time Albanians put up armed resistance to the Italian invasion). What he understands as nationalism, I would call patriotism.

10. Polish literature usually sharply opposes nationalism to patriotism. See interesting analyses in Stanisław Ossowski, *O ojczyźnie i narodzie* (Warsaw, 1984), pp. 26–30, and his "O osobliwościach nauk społecznych," in *Dzieła* (Warsaw, 1967), vol. IV, p. 157, where he makes a distinction between patriotism and its de-

generated form—democratized nationalism. See also entries "Nacjonalizm" and "Patriotyzm" in *Wielka Encyklopedia Powszechna* (Warsaw, 1966), vol. 7, p. 575, and vol. 8, p. 524, and Jerzy J. Wiatr, *Naród i państwo—Socjologiczne problemy kwestii narodowej* (Warsaw, 1969), p. 416.

11. See Kemiläinen, *Nationalism*, in which he makes a very scrupulous comparison between Hayes's and Kohn's concepts.

12. For example, the subject index to the book by Anthony D. Smith, *Nationalism in the Twentieth Century* (Oxford, 1979), lists over twenty kinds of nationalism.

13. Carr's *Nationalism: A Report* belongs to the few studies that clearly distinguish political and economic nationalism.

14. This term has not been used in many outstanding theoretical works in sociology, political science, or philosophy dealing with nationalism (for example, by Hayes, Kohn, Kemiläinen, Shafer, Berlin, Hroch, and Gellner). Ward, *Five Ideas*, p. 24, used it once without, however, analyzing its meaning and specific character.

15. Kohn believed that nationalism was directly related to political questions. See his *Nationalism*.

16. This is more frequently done by political and economic historians, economists, and political scientists than by historians of ideas. As regards the former it is more frequently done by students of Latin America than by students of Europe.

17. See Lewis L. Lorwin, "Economic Nationalism and World Co-operation," in L. L. Lorwin, *Time for Planning: Social-economic Theory and Program for Twentieth Century* (New York, 1945), pp. 218ff. He made this point in 1933, probably the only economist to do so.

18. See W.A.S.H., "Protection," in *Encyclopaedia Britannica* (1960 edition), vol. 18, p. 604 (the term is used in reference to the German economic policy in the nineteenth and early twentieth centuries). Compare John B. Whitton, "Nationalism-Internationalism," in *Encyclopedia Americana* (New York, 1958), vol. XIX, p. 751. The term is used several times, although without explanation, in the popular encyclopedia of Latin America. See Samuel L. Baily, "Nationalism," in Helen Delpar, ed., *Encyclopedia of Latin America* (New York, 1974), p. 407. See also entry "L'nazionalismo economico," in *Dizionario Enciclopedico Italiano* (Rome, 1958), vol. VIII, p. 267.

19. Józef Chlebowczyk, *Procesy narodowotwórcze we wschodniej Europie Środkowej w dobie kapitalizmu (od schyłku XVIII do początków XX w.)* (Warsaw-Kraków, 1975), p. 266.

20. Leo Pasvolsky, *Economic Nationalism of the Danubian States* (London, 1928); Antonin Basch, *The Danube Basin and the German Economic Sphere* (London, 1944); *A Price for Peace: The New Europe and World Markets* (New York, 1945).

21. Theodore E. Gregory, "Economic Nationalism," *International Affairs*, vol. X, no. 3, 1931; Thomas Balogh, "Some Theoretical Aspects of the Central European Credit and Transfer Crisis," *International Affairs*, vol. XI, no. 3, 1932; Arthur Salter, "The Future of Economic Nationalism," *Foreign Affairs*, vol. 11, no. 1, October 1932; Lorwin, *Economic Nationalism*.

22. See Oskar Lange, "Nacjonalizm gospodarczy (1927)," in O. Lange, *Dzieła*, vol. 1, *Kapitalizm* (Warsaw, 1973), pp. 33–39; G.D.H. Cole, *Studies in World Economies* (London, 1934); Charles Schrecker, "The Growth of Economic Nationalism and Its International Consequences," *International Affairs*, vol. XIII, no. 2, 1934 (he incorrectly identified economic nationalism with autarky); Maurice

Coulborne, *Economic Nationalism* (London, 1933) (he tried to interpret the phenomenon in ideological categories of Fabianism); G. G. Hodgson, *Economic Nationalism* (New York, 1933); Oscar Jászi, "Kossuth and the Treaty of Trianon," *Foreign Affairs*, vol. 12, no. 1, October 1933; John Maynard Keynes, "National Self-Sufficiency," *New Statesman and Nation*, July 8, 1933; John Maynard Keynes, *The General Theory of Employment, Interest, and Money* (London, 1936); Lionel Robbins, "Economic Nationalism and Monetary Policy," *Banker*, no. 125, June 1936; Carr, *Nationalism: A Report*.

23. Ivan T. Berend and György Ránki, "Economic Factors in Nationalism: A Case Study of Hungary at the Turn of the Twentieth Century," in I. T. Berend and G. Ránki, *Underdevelopment and Economic Growth: Studies in Hungarian Economic and Social History* (Budapest, 1979).

24. Frederick Hertz, *The Economic Problem of Danubian States: A Study in Economic Nationalism* (London, 1947).

25. See Nicolas Spulber, *The State and Economic Development in Eastern Europe* (New York, 1966), and John M. Montias, "Economic Nationalism in Eastern Europe: Forty Years of Continuity and Change," *Journal of International Affairs*, vol. XX, no. 1, 1966. Spulber discusses the phenomenon in reference to Romania in the nineteenth century and the Jewish question; Montias concentrates on trade among European Communist countries. See also Jerzy F. Karcz, "Reflections on the Economics of Nationalism and Communism in Eastern Europe," *East European Quarterly*, vol. V, no. 2, June 1971. However, he employs a slightly different approach and concentrates on the period that extends beyond our interest here.

26. Pasvolsky, *Economic Nationalism*, passim.

27. Hertz, *The Economic Problem*, passim.

28. See Robert R. King, *Minority Under Communism: Nationalities as a Source of Tension Among Balkan Communist States* (Cambridge, Mass., 1973), p. 175.

29. This is how Ivan T. Berend and György Ránki seem to interpret this stage in their book *The European Periphery and Industrialization, 1780–1914* (Budapest, 1982), p. 71.

30. Mihail Manoilescu, *The Theory of Protection and International Trade* (London, 1931); Edward H. Carr, "States and Nationalism: The Nation in European History," in D. Held et al., eds., *States and Societies* (Oxford, 1985), pp. 181–194; William E. Rappard, *Le nationalisme économique et la Société des nations*, Recueil des Cours de l'Académie du Droit International de la Haye, 1937, III (Paris, 1937), and "Economic Nationalism," in *Authority and Individual* (Cambridge, Mass., 1937); Wilhelm Röpke, *International Economic Disintegration* (London, 1942). See also works quoted in notes 20–22.

31. Michael A. Heilperin, *The Trade of Nations* (London, 1946), and *Studies in Economic Nationalism* (Geneva, 1960).

32. See the studies by Harry Leibenstein, W. Arthur Lewis, Amar N. Agharwala, Sampat P. Singh, Paul N. Rosenstein-Rodan, Alexander Gerschenkron, and Tamas Szentes, and by such Polish economists as Oskar Lange, Michał Kalecki, Jerzy Kleer, and Zofia Dobrska.

33. This famous formula was coined by Raul Prebisch. For further contributions, see, for example, the works by Celso Furtado, Fernando H. Cardoso, Theotonio Dos Santos, Andre Gunder Frank, Samir Amin, Arighi Emmanuel, and

Immanuel Wallerstein. In Polish literature see Henryk Szlajfer, *Modernizacja zależ
ności: Kapitalizm i rozwój w Ameryce Łacińskiej* (Wrocław, 1985), and Tadeusz Łepkowski, ed., *Dzieje Ameryki Łacińskiej od schyłku epoki kolonialnej do czasów
współczesnych*, vols. I–III (Warsaw, 1977–1983). See also contributions by Jan Kie-
niewicz, Marcin Kula, Tadeusz Łepkowski, and Ryszard Stemplowski.

34. Immanuel Wallerstein, *The Capitalist World-Economy* (Cambridge, 1979);
Barbara H. Kaplan, ed., *Social Change in the Capitalist World Economy* (Beverly
Hills, 1978); Samir Amin, Giovanni Arrighi, Andre Gunder Frank, and Immanuel
Wallerstein, *Dynamics of Global Crisis* (New York, 1982).

35. The only exceptions are the essays by Heilperin cited earlier and a collection of studies edited by Harry G. Johnson, *Economic Nationalism in Old and New
States* (London, 1968).

36. Eliezer B. Ayal, "Ideology and Economic Development," *Human Organization*, vol. 25, no. 3, 1966; Johnson, "A Theoretical Model of Economic Nationalism
in New Developing States," *Political Science Quarterly*, vol. LXXX, no. 2, 1965
(reprinted in Johnson, ed., *Economic Nationalism*); Albert Breton, "The Economics
of Nationalism," *Journal of Political Economy*, vol. LXXII, no. 2, August 1964; Peter
J. Burnell, *Economic Nationalism in the Third World* (Brighton, 1986); Frank H. Golay, Ralph Anspach, M. Ruth Pfanner, and Eliezer B. Ayal, *Underdevelopment and
Economic Nationalism in Southeast Asia* (Ithaca, 1969).

37. Montias, "Economic Nationalism;" E. Bradford Burns, *Nationalism in Brazil:
A Historical Survey* (New York, 1968); John D. Wirth, *The Politics of Brazilian Devel-
opment, 1930–1954* (Stanford, 1970); James Petras and Robert LaPorte, Jr., "U.S.
Response to Economic Nationalism in Chile," in James Petras, ed., *Latin America:
From Dependence to Revolution* (New York, 1973); fragments of works by Barry
Supple, Edward H. Carr, and Tom Nairn, in Held, *States and Societies*.

38. Mihail Manoilescu (1891–1950), was a professor at the Technical University in
Bucharest. He held several government positions: undersecretary of state in
Averescu's government in the years 1926–1927; minister of public works in 1930;
and later minister of state at the Ministry of Industry and Commerce and president
of the National Bank of Romania. In 1936 he founded a national corporate league.
He was a close associate of King Carol II, maintaining at the same time contacts
with the Iron Guard. In 1940 he was minister of foreign affairs in Ion Gigurtu's cabinet and then in Ion Antonescu's cabinet (until September 1940). Manoilescu elabo-
rated the concept of integral corporationism and a quantitative model of internal
colonialism based on the case of Romania, and he also published some important
sociological studies. See *Le sìecle du corporatisme* (Paris, 1936); *Der Einzige Partei*
(Berlin, 1941); "Le triangle économique et social des pays agricoles: La ville, le village, l'étranger," in *Internationale Agrarrundschau*, June 1940; *Rostul și destinul
burgheziei romanesti* (Bucharest, 1942). For more information on Manoilescu, see *Enciclopedia Italiana*, Rome, vol. XXII, 1934; *Enciclopedia Italiana 1938–1948*, Rome, Sec-
onda apendice I–Z, 1949, p. 260; *Dictionar Enciclopedic Roman*, vol. III (Bucharest,
1965), p. 229; Philippe C. Schmitter, "Reflections on Mihail Manoilescu and the Political Consequences of Delayed-Dependent Development on the Periphery of
Western Europe," and Andrew C. Janos, "Modernization and Decay in Historical
Perspective: The Case of Romania," in Kenneth Jowitt, ed., *Social Change in Romania, 1860–1940: A Debate on Development in a European Nation* (Berkeley, 1978);

Joseph L. Love, *Modelling Internal Colonialism: History and Prospect* (paper presented at the conference "Models of Development and Theories of Modernization in Eastern Europe Between the World Wars," Rackeve, September 10–15, 1988).

39. See Bertil Ohlin, "Protection and Non-competing Groups," *Weltwirtschaftliches Archiv*, vol. 33, no. 1, 1931, and Jacob Viner's review in *Journal of Political Economy*, vol. XL, no. 1, February 1932. Manoilescu answered charges in "Die theoretische Problematik des Aussenhandels. Synthese-Beweisfuehrung-Polemik," *Weltwirtschaftliches Archiv*, vol. 51, 1940, pp. 1–78.

40. Manoilescu, *The Theory of Protection and International Trade*, p. 208.

41. A review of the German edition of the book *Die Nationalen Produktivkräfte und der Aussenhandel* (Berlin, 1937), *Economic Journal*, vol. XLVIII, no. 4, 1938, pp. 708–711.

42. For example, Gustav von Schmoller, Adolph Wagner, Ludwig (Lujo) Brentano, and Werner Sombart. Compare Y. S. Brenner, *Theories of Economic Development and Growth* (London, 1966).

43. See Heilperin, *Studies in Economic Nationalism*; Fritz Machlup, *A History of Thought on Economic Integration* (London, 1977).

44. There were more economists thinking likewise in Romania. See M. F. Iovanelli, *Industria Româneasca 1934–1938* (Bucharest, 1975), p. 45. Stefan Zeletin, an outstanding economist whose ideas helped to justify the protectionist policy of the Liberal Party, was among Manoilescu's predecessors. Compare Daniel Chirot, "Neoliberal and Social Democratic Theories of Development: The Zeletin-Voinea Debate Concerning Romania's Prospects in the 1920s and Its Contemporary Importance," in Jowitt, *Social Change*, pp. 31–52.

45. Jan Kofman, *Lewiatan a podstawowe zagadnienia ekonomiczno-polityczne Drugiej Rzeczypospolitej: Z dziejów ideologii kół wielkokapitalistycznych w Polsce* (Warsaw, 1986), chapter 7.

46. Wirth, *The Politics of Brazilian Development*, p. 47. In all underdeveloped countries the argument ran along similar lines. Compare Love, *Modelling*, p. 27.

47. Manoilescu's further evolution at the end of the 1930s goes beyond the subject of our study. Let us only point out that, nolens volens, Manoilescu became a supporter of the concept of *Grossraumwirtschaft*. Compare also Schmitter, "Reflections."

48. Manoilescu, *The Theory of Protection and International Trade*, pp. 19ff.

49. Adam Heydel, "Etatyzm," in *Encyklopedia nauk politycznych*, vol. 2 (Warsaw, 1937), p. 118. See also *Etatyzm w Polsce* (Kraków, 1932), and Ferdynand Zweig, *Zmierzch czy odrodzenie liberalizmu?* (Warsaw, 1938).

50. For Poland, see Kofman, *Lewiatan*. For Czechoslovakia, see publications by industrial circles, particularly in the 1930s, in *Sbirka přednašek pořadaných Českou společnosti ná rodohospodá řskou v obdobi* (1928–39), and reports *Ústředni svaz československých průmyslniku v roce . . .* (1921–38).

51. Gregory, "Economic Nationalism," pp. 289ff. Hertz, *The Economic Problem*, p. 88, expressed similar opinions several years later, after the experience of World War II.

52. With this approach, Gregory seems to be ahead of the conclusions drawn by Kohn from his famous dichotomy, presented in *The Idea of Nationalism*. For more on the latter, see Snyder, *The Meanings of Nationalism*, and Kemiläinen, *Nationalism*.

53. Gregory's thesis that in Eastern Europe and Asia the consciousness of race and racism inevitably leads to the policy of ruining one's political opponents and of justifying it by means of economic arguments is by no means obvious. It is difficult to decide whether the ethnic (racial) characteristic of certain fellow citizens and foreigners is the primary reason for fighting their economic position, or vice versa—the sense of racial distance grows stronger in the face of genuine or imagined threats to one's own economic interests.

54. See William O. McCagg, Jr., "Hungary's 'Feudalized' Bourgeoisie," _Journal of Modern History_, vol. 44, no. 1, 1972; Janusz Żarnowski, _Społeczeństwo Drugiej Rzeczypospolitej 1918–1939_ (Warsaw, 1973); Zbigniew Landau, "Oligarchia finansowa," in Zbigniew Landau and Jerzy Tomaszewski, _Druga Rzeczpospolita. Gospodarka—społeczeństwo—miejsce w świecie_ (Warsaw, 1977), pp. 191–216; Stephen Fischer-Galati, _Twentieth-Century Rumania_ (New York, 1970), pp. 24–26; Spulber, _The State and Economic Development_, pp. 89–115.

55. Gregory, "Economic Nationalism," p. 291.

56. Compare A. G. Kenwood and A. L. Lougheed, _The Growth of the International Economy, 1820–1960_ (London, 1971), pp. 82ff.; Jerzy Ciepielewski, Irena Kostrowicka, Zbigniew Landau, and Jerzy Tomaszewski, _Dzieje gospodarcze świata do roku 1980_ (Warsaw, 1985), chapter 10; Elżbieta Kaczyńska and Kazimierz Piesowicz, _Wykłady z powszechnej historii gospodarczej (od schyłku średniowiecza do I wojny światowej)_ (Warsaw, 1977), chapter 18.

57. Hertz, _The Economic Problem_, pp. 222ff., and Lionel Robbins, _The Economic Problem in Peace and War_ (London, 1947), p. 64, were exaggerating when they treated economic nationalism as one of the primary causes of the last war. Carr, "States and Nationalism," p. 193, also saw the process of socialization of the state (combined with the growing nationalist feelings in the world and nationalization of economic policy) as a cause of the two world wars.

58. This problem was quite well understood by Lorwin, "Economic Nationalism," pp. 217–219. This, however, was probably an exception.

59. On Brazil, see Burns, _Nationalism in Brazil_, p. 11.

60. Gregory, "Economic Nationalism."

61. Lange, "Nacjonalizm gospodarczy," pp. 36–38.

62. Several dozen years later, Lange abandoned his earlier approach, and declared himself (both in theory and practice) to be in favor of the development of the industrial base in communist countries at the initial stage of their development.

63. See "Hospodářská politika čs. průmyslu v letech 1918–1938," _USČP_, v roce 1937, Prague, pp. 2, 24; Kofman, _Lewiatan_; Zbigniew Landau and Jerzy Tomaszewski, _Gospodarka Polski międzywojennej 1918–1939_, vol. III, _Wielki kryzys 1930–1935_

64. Cole, _Studies in World Economies_, p. 15.

65. With the exception of German industrial exports to southeastern Europe, based on clearing transactions favorable to Germany (for other than economic reasons), and of agricultural imports from the countries of the region (e.g., from the Baltic countries). Until the present day, benefits from that trade have not been obvious to everyone.

66. Bertil Ohlin, "Introductory Report on the Problem of International Economic Reconstruction," in _International Economic Reconstruction_ (Paris, 1936), p. 63. A divergent opinion was more common. See _Unemployment as International Problem_, Royal Institute of International Affairs (Oxford, 1935), p. 187.

67. Carr, ed., *Nationalism: A Report*, pp. 225–239.

68. The two being possibly two aspects of one and the same reality. Rappard, "Economic Nationalism," pp. 77ff. Quoted after Heilperin, *Studies in Economic Nationalism*, pp. 18–21.

69. Ibid.

70. Italy, Germany, the Soviet Union—the totalitarian states. Rappard's approach juxtaposed too strongly the motivations behind economic nationalism to other motivations.

71. Röpke, *The International Economic Disintegration*, pp. 201ff.

72. Historic in the understanding of Jacob Burckhardt, ibid., pp. 1, 20–22.

73. Karl Polanyi, *The Great Transformation* (Boston, 1957).

74. Röpke, *International Economic Disintegration*, pp. 40ff., 208.

75. This point was aimed against the ideas of John Maynard Keynes.

76. Röpke, *International Economic Disintegration*, pp. 165ff.

77. Carr, "States and Nationalism," pp. 180, 189–192.

78. The ideologies that emphasized the prevalence of the collectivist element over the individualistic one, such as communism, socialism, and fascism, were termed by Heilperin as collectivist one, and such terms as "free enterprise," "market economy," and "liberalism" were used in various contexts as synonyms of "capitalism." Heilperin, *Studies in Economic Nationalism*, p. 16.

79. Ibid. But Heilperin understood at the same time that this nationalism was also expressed in domestic economic policies.

80. Heilperin, *The Trade of Nations*, pp. 73–77.

81. Heilperin, *Studies in Economic Nationalism*, pp. 24ff., 81.

82. *Ibid.*, pp. 19, 24, 63, and chapters 5 and 6; Heilperin, *The Trade of Nations*, pp. 92, 95–100.

83. Unless the *Studies in Economic Nationalism* are regarded also as a sign of an ideological crusade, as is suggested by some threads of selected essays (e.g., on Fichte and Keynes).

84. Ayal, "Nationalist Ideology."

85. Breton, "The Economics of Nationalism," p. 367.

86. Ibid.

87. Ibid., p. 386.

88. Harry G. Johnson, "The Ideology of Economic Policy in the New States," in Johnson, ed., *Economic Nationalism*, p. 126. He pinpoints the political nationalism, which has its counterpart in economic nationalism.

89. Breton, "The Economics of Nationalism," pp. 377ff.

90. Ibid., p. 378.

91. Ibid., p. 379.

92. Carr, "States and Nationalism," p. 191, raised this problem indirectly, emphasizing the common interest of both workers and employers in the protection of and subsidies to industry.

93. Johnson, "A Theoretical Model," pp. 183ff.

94. But see Peter J.D. Wiles, "Foreign Trade of Eastern Europe: A Summary Appraisal," in A. A. Brown and E. Neuberger, eds., *International Trade and Central Planning: An Analysis of Economic Interactions* (Berkeley, 1968), pp. 167–169. Wiles reproaches Johnson (and, indirectly, Breton) for presenting a concept of *public goods* that is a case of "intellectual imperialism." In the same collection Johnson

rejects this criticism ("Notes on Some Theoretical Problems Posed by the Foreign Trade in Centrally Planned Economy," pp. 369–370).

95. Montias, *Economic Nationalism*, p. 61.

96. Naturally, if one adheres to one of the numerous versions of the neoclassical doctrine, one can think so. It should be remembered, however, that the practical implementation of their provisions was, even under the most favorable circumstances, quite distant from the Ricardian principles they were adducing. Compare Joan Robinson, "Introduction" in *Economic Heresies: Some Old-fashioned Questions in Economic Theory* (New York, 1971).

97. Along with the works by Burns and Wirth, see, for example, Alfred Stepan, ed., *Authoritarian Brazil: Origins, Policies, and Future* (New Haven, 1973); and, especially, Manning Nash, "Economic Nationalism in Mexico," in Johnson, ed., *Economic Nationalism*, pp. 71–84, for the use of Breton and Johnson's categories.

98. Wirth, *The Politics of Brazilian Development*, p. 7.

99. Ibid. Compare H. Martins, "Ideology and Development: 'Development Nationalism' in Brazil," in *Sociological Review Monograph*, no. 11, 1967.

100. Robert F. Dernberger, "The Role of Nationalism in the Rise and Development of Communist China," in Johnson, ed., *Economic Nationalism*, p. 49.

101. George Macesich, *Economic Nationalism and Stability* (New York, 1985); Burnell, *Economic Nationalism*.

102. Burnell, *Economic Nationalism*.

103. Macesich accepts some conclusions and elements of older conceptions, especially those by Breton.

104. Macesich, *Economic Nationalism*, pp. viiff., 2.

105. For information on economic nationalism in nineteenth- and twentieth-century Romania, see Spulber, *The State and Economic Development*, pp. 89–106; Fischer-Galati, *Twentieth-Century Rumania*, pp. 25–27, 30ff.; Jowitt, *The Sociocultural Basis*; Henry L. Roberts, *Rumania: Political Problems of an Agrarian State* (New Haven, 1951).

106. Macartney and Palmer point indirectly to this phenomenon, in *Independent Eastern Europe*, p. 285.

107. Recognition of a certain economic phenomenon as too extensive can always give rise to a discussion. One can agree, however, that the situation in which foreign goods have practically no access to a particular domestic market is the extreme case of protectionism. In the 1920s Romania, ruled by the National Liberal Party led by Ion Brătianu, and, to a lesser extent, Bulgaria under Andrei Liapchev, were those countries in the region that adhered to the extreme version of economic nationalism understood in this fashion.

108. Socialist countries chose the path of autarky at the first stages of their development. In the Soviet Union, it was primarily internal political and ideological reasons that determined the choice of autarky. However, in the people's democracies the policy of autarky was rather a result of external influence, in particular the pressure to follow the example of the Soviet path.

109. Among the works on agrarianism in Poland, see Stanisław Miłkowski, *Agraryzm jako forma przebudowy ustroju społecznego* (Warsaw, 1934); Aleksander Łuczak, *Społeczeństwo i państwo w myśli politycznej ruchu ludowego II Rzeczypospolitej* (Warsaw, 1982); Bohdan Cywiński, *Potęga jest i basta: Z minionych doświadczeń*

ruchów społecznych na wsi (Paris, 1983). For Bulgaria, see Aleksandŭr Stamboliyski, *Izbrani proizwedeniya* (Sofia, 1979); Joseph Rothschild, *The Communist Party of Bulgaria: Origins and Development, 1883–1936* (New York, 1959); Nisson Oren, *Revolution Administrated: Agrarianism and Communism in Bulgaria* (Baltimore, 1973); John D. Bell, *Peasants in Power: Alexander Stambolijski and the Bulgarian Agrarian National Union, 1899–1923* (Princeton, 1977). For Yugoslavia, see Jozo Tomasevich, *Peasants, Politics, and Economic Change in Yugoslavia* (Stanford, 1955). For Czechoslovakia, see Jaroslav César and Bohumil Černy, "O ideologii československého agrarizmu," in *Československý Časopis Historický*, no. 2, 1959. For the Baltic countries, see Piotr Łossowski, *Kraje bałtyckie na drodze od demokracji parlamentarnej do dyktatury (1918–1934)* (Wrocław, 1972). For works on agrarianism in the entire region (with extensive remarks on Romania, Yugoslavia, and the Baltic countries), see David Mitrany, *Marx Against Peasant: A Study in Social Dogmatism* (London, 1951); Ghita Ionescu, "Eastern Europe," in Ghita Ionescu and Ernest Gellner, eds., *Populism: Its Meanings and National Characteristics* (London, 1969); Mariusz N. Goranowicz, *Krakh Zelenogo Internacyonala* (Moscow, 1967); and unpublished papers by Drago Roksandić "Agrarne ideologije i teorije modernizacije u Jugoslaviji od 1918 do 1941 godine," Luben Berov, "Appearance of Ideas for a Co-operative ('Intermediate') Road of Socio-economic Development in Bulgaria During the Period Between the Two World Wars," and Keith Hitchins, "Rumanian Peasantism: The Third Way," presented during the conference "Models of Development and Theories of Modernization in Eastern Europe Between the World Wars," Rackeve, September 10–15, 1988.

110. Endeavors by Brazil and Argentina provide a good example here. See Burns, *Nationalism in Brazil*; Wirth, *The Politics of Brazilian Development*; Ryszard Stemplowski, *Zależność i wyzwanie: Argentyna wobec rywalizacji mocarstw anglosaskich i III Rzeszy* (Warsaw, 1975); Łepkowski, ed., *Dzieje*, vol. III, *1930–1975/80*, I: *Kryzys rozwoju zależnego*.

111. Dudley Kirk, *Europe's Population in the Interwar Years* (Princeton, 1946); Edward Kołodziej, *Wychodźstwo zarobkowe z Polski 1918–1939: Studia nad polityką emigracyjną II Rzeczypospolitej* (Warsaw, 1982); Andrzej Brożek, "Polityka imigracyjna w państwach docelowych emigracji polskiej (1850–1939)," and Halina Janowska, "Emigracja z Polski w latach 1918–1939," in Andrzej Pilch, ed., *Emigracja z ziem polskich w czasach nowożytnych i najnowszych (XVIII–XX w.)* (Warsaw, 1984), pp. 132–140, 326–450.

112. For more on autarky and industrialization, see Chapter 9.

113. Economic nationalism is correctly related to industrialism. See, for example, Ward, *Five Ideas*; Johnson, ed., *Economic Nationalism*; Carr, "States and Nationalism," p. 192; Barry Supple, "States and Industrialization: Britain and Germany in the Nineteenth Century," in Held, ed., *States and Societies*, pp. 174–176. This relationship, however, does not have to exist as a universal rule as illustrated by the ideology and practice of the peasant parties in the Baltic countries, Bulgaria, Romania, and even Czechoslovakia. In the latter, because of the high level of economic development of the country, agrarians gave strong emphasis to the requirements of industrialism.

114. See, for example, Bélla Vago, *The Shadow of the Swastika: The Rise of Fascism and Anti-Semitism in the Danube Basin, 1936–1939* (London, 1975), pp. 137ff.

2

Economic Nationalism:
Overview, Sources, and Causes

Overview

Depending on the period, area, and society, economic nationalism in the countries of East-Central Europe assumed different shapes and intensities. The proportions of the constituent parts differed as well. These were determined by external and internal conditions such as the form of statehood, national and state sovereignty or their absence, and the social and ethnic structure of the population. The 1930s brought a qualitative change in the development and expansion of nationalism, which was increasingly often put into legal and institutional frameworks and given the highest sanction. Propitious to this change were the growing authoritarian trends in the societies and states of the region[1] and the consolidation of totalitarian rule in the countries bordering the region, notably Germany, Italy, and the Soviet Union.[2] This was of course a case of reciprocal coincidence: Nationalism, which was the impulse and the binding agent of totalitarianism, in Italy and Germany became one of the main ideas, if not the central idea, organizing social, political, and economic life,[3] thereby influencing the evolution of authoritarian political systems toward totalitarianism in other countries of the region as well.[4] The stronger the influence of Nazism and Italian fascism became in the region in the late 1930s, the more strongly the idea of the nation competed with the respective state ideology.

I wish to emphasize that in keeping with my definition of economic nationalism, the state is its main subject. Therefore I do not analyze, although I sometimes mention, the grassroots economic nationalism of national minorities. Although this is itself an important subject, and one hardly approached in the literature, it exceeds the scope of the present book.[5]

Each of the two basic ways of hierarchizing the component parts of nationalism into a sequence—that is, the cultural, economic, and political order, as some scholars would have it, or the cultural, political, and economic order that a minority of researchers (including myself) prefer—can be indirectly supported by historical materials, although the degree of this support is open to discussion. The suggestions presented in this chapter are formulated as working hypotheses since as yet no relevant studies have been conducted to verify the three-stage conception of nationalism.

In the case of Hungarians and Poles, cultural and political nationalism (not to be confused with patriotism) drew its strength from the existence of a modern national awareness and the memory of state tradition, and it appeared relatively early, with only a short delay vis-à-vis Western Europe.[6] In Bohemia, in contrast, cultural and economic nationalism came first, and clear manifestations of political nationalism occurred only later (at the beginning of the twentieth century). The Albanian, Greek, Serbian, or Croatian nationalisms were first articulated in the cultural arena and only later in the political. Cultural nationalism pervaded the Estonians, Latvians, and Lithuanians until the early years of the twentieth century.[7]

Let us take a closer look at this problem. For example, it appears that the Czech economic nationalism, which emerged toward the end of the nineteenth century and was aimed primarily at German property, surpassed the manifestations of political nationalism in terms of intensity and aspirations. It is possible and in fact probable that this was a substitute means of professing Czech nationalistic tendencies as well. Such an explanation would allow the advocates of the former hierarchization to eliminate a disturbing inconsistency between their assumptions and the actual situation. After all, in the political system and conditions prevailing in Austria-Hungary, people did have the opportunity to express even radical political aims of nationalism. It is also worth remembering that the Czechs advanced the demand for separate statehood only during World War I, and even then they did not do it straight away.

In Polish society economic nationalism manifested itself differently in each of the partition sectors. In the Prussian sector it was of a defensive nature, and it sought to preserve the Polish possessions as well as to recover the possessions lost previously as a result of an intensive Germanization campaign. In the Kingdom of Poland it was directed not so much against the Russian ruler as against the minorities, especially the Jews (from the 1890s onward). In the largely autonomous Galicia it was relatively the weakest, which may have been due to the sector's general backwardness (and at the same time may have been the result of Galicia's autonomy, which made it possible for Poles to achieve limited national goals). It can also be said that in Polish lands economic nationalism accompanied rather than followed political nationalism.

In the Hungary of the age of Compromise (after 1867) economic nationalism, which in terms of intensity was rather secondary to political nationalism, came to the surface only after the ruling classes attained their main political goals. Hungarian economic nationalism expressed itself in the emphasis given to the development of domestic industry.

It is therefore possible to formulate the general hypothesis that in the Danubian and Balkan countries of the turn of the century and the interwar period, political nationalism occurred prior to economic nationalism (as in, for example, the slogans of "Great Bulgaria," "Great Greece," and "Great Romania" as well as in the Hungarian revisionism) and was the driving force of the latter.

Economic nationalism manifested itself in protectionist practices (sometimes with a prohibitive hue, especially in Bulgaria and Romania) and was aimed at initiating or consolidating industrialization processes. In addition, it had the aforementioned clear domestic dimension. In the Baltic states economic nationalism as a perceptible phenomenon and objective was a derivative of the inferiority complex and resulting political nationalism (one of a quite recent vintage, especially in the case of the Lithuanians) of nationalities that, to their own surprise, had recently gained independence.

I think that the historical development of the countries of the region at the turn of the century and in the interwar period seems to prove that the nationalist idea receives its full shape and develops most dynamically only when it is based on economic foundations. As long as such economic support is insufficient, nationalism does not develop in full, including in its political dimension. Therefore, the phenomenon referred to (correctly or not) as economic nationalism acquires its prime importance in the region when it turns out that independence by itself does not yet guarantee full autonomy from foreign decisionmaking centers.

The history of Latin American countries also carries weight as a powerful argument for the notion of an interplay between the two kinds of nationalism (irrespective of their sequence), and probably a more powerful one than the history of the East-Central European countries. Consider, for example, Brazilian nationalism in its contemporary, twentieth-century phase, which most scholars divide into two periods; the first one was characterized by the predominance of cultural and political nationalism, whereas economic nationalism prevailed in the second period, which began with the takeover of power by Getúlio Vargas in 1930.[8] The time shift is characteristic: Economic nationalism appeared in Brazil in a fully developed form and acquired its prime importance after the country had already been independent for more than a century. Let me add, too, that this could be one of the reasons for such a violent outburst of economic nationalism following the 1930 coup, when power changed hands from the representatives of coffee interests to the enterprising representatives of the industrial bourgeoisie and the middle classes.[9]

In contrast, in the countries of East-Central Europe, an outward-oriented economic nationalism appeared almost immediately after the regaining (or gaining) of independence, even if there had been no advantageous conditions for its development previously, as in the case of the Baltic countries.[10] That shortcut was, I believe, a result of the attainment by a given country of the necessary level of economic development, of the relevant social transformations, and also, to a considerable degree, of external circumstances. As for the choice of a growth model, in the nineteenth and twentieth centuries the so-called demonstration effect was probably felt more strongly, for example, in Bulgaria, Serbia, Romania, and the backward outskirts of the three great monarchies than, say, in the young nations of Latin America.

Therefore, it seems legitimate to assume that economic nationalism was gaining ground (usually stepwise) and leaving an imprint on economic and social policies when capitalist relations of production had already been built up or when groups interested in a redistribution of income had already stood apart. It should be noted, however, that there are also researchers who subscribe to the view that the onset and spread of nationalism (also in East-Central Europe) was closely related to the development of the capitalist system and to the industrial revolution. This line of opinion is questionable, however.[11] As a brief reply to the advocates of this view, I would note that at present, as in the underdeveloped Third World countries, it is the external factors—for example, a transplant of ideas or a side effect of a political and ideological struggle between the big powers—that offer the strongest stimulus to the development of economic nationalism.[12]

The advocates and opponents of economic nationalism are locked in a perennial dispute—seen by both sides to be of fundamental importance to economic nationalism's correct valuation—on whether this nationalism produces any economic advantages, and if so, how big they are. The opponents, who appear to be in the majority, emphasize that the negative effects of this ideological and political trend predominate. In my opinion, the dispute cannot be resolved definitively. If only for methodological reasons, it is not possible to draw a fully objective balance sheet of the gains and losses of pursuing a policy of economic nationalism. Besides, it should be remembered that along with economic effects there are also psychological and emotional effects, or effects that have to do with consciousness. Any given appraisal is also influenced by factors of a rather subjective nature, such as the scholar's nationality or citizenship, the position he or she occupies in the life of the country (in its ethnic, social, or economic structure), and his or her personal views. Despite all these reservations, though, it is possible to make some important, if only very general, observations.

Let us begin with the statement that if historians or economists single out economic nationalism, they treat it as a homogeneous phenomenon. It is hard to accept such an attitude, if only because the very direction of the dynamics of economic nationalism influences its valuation. But then, the basic categorization of the phenomenon is made by means of defining the subjects it influences. Like elsewhere, in the countries of East-Central Europe this nationalism was directed outward—against the economic interests of other countries or in defense of domestic interests—as well as inward (against the interests, often vital ones, of fellow citizens belonging to ethnic minorities). What matters are the proportions between the two directions of nationalist influence in political practice. It must be said straight off that in the 1930s inward influence was very much in evidence in the countries of the region (see chapter 3).

However, the qualification of the moves aimed against foreign capital remains an unresolved question. Foreign investors, although they put up their money in a country, tend to transfer their profits abroad. Due to this dual nature of foreign investments, the moves directed against it may be regarded as an outward or inward expression of economic nationalism (depending upon whether or not they are viewed as merely an agency of foreign interests). This, needless to say, influences the appraisal of the role of foreign capital and of the phenomenon of economic nationalism as well.

Nonetheless, the view—and one can hear this even today—that the xenophobic feelings toward foreign capital, which are said to characterize the region's societies and economic policies, are an integral and durable part of these policies must be regarded as carrying things too far.[13] It is nearer the truth to say that when industrialization recedes into the background in a country's economic policy, xenophobic reactions *might* take place. This is what happened in Bulgaria under Aleksandŭr Stamboliyski, which was a consequence of his distinct antiurban, antiindustrial and antifinance bias,[14] and in Romania under Ion Brătianu's Liberals. The openly demonstrated dislike of foreign capital in the 1930s was due first of all to its withdrawal on a scale threatening to the economic existence of the states of the region. The limitations of the freedom of movement of foreign capital and the requirements put to it in the face of these threats had, of course, an additional aspect: By reflecting public feelings, they demonstrated the desire for independence and for the severance of unequal relations (goals that they achieved in a small part only).

In general, however, apart from the rhetoric (e.g., the Geneva declarations of the Kimon Georgiev regime[15]), foreign investors were usually offered advantageous conditions in the East-Central European countries,[16] but they were in no hurry to invest there, as they did not find the prospects for a return on their capital to be alluring enough. The situation still looked relatively well in the 1920s, especially in the years 1924–1928, when a fairly large amount of capital flowed into the region. But this soon changed dramatically. Czechoslovakia was the only exception, recording even a surplus of capital flow.[17]

The main question that has given rise to much controversy concerns the economic rationale of the economic nationalism. The representatives of various schools of economics and politics have always found it difficult to agree on the criteria according to which this rationality would be decided. It is therefore not surprising that we may come across a whole range of opinions, from extreme to moderate views. On one pole there were those who questioned this rationality altogether, especially the advocates of integral liberalism, who viewed economic nationalism as a collection of inner contradictions and absurdities because it clashed with the binding precepts of economic theory and political conceptions of those times. The students of the phenomenon, both historians and economists, who referred to these conceptions rejected economic nationalism a priori, negating the choice of noneconomic criteria for the evaluation of the rationality of economic moves. A middle-of-the-road attitude discerned some rationality in the economic nationalism on theoretical and even on practical grounds (the justification was to be supplied by the results of protectionist economic policy moves).[18] Finally, at the other extreme, one could come across passionate approbation of the rationality of economic nationalism, both from the theoretical and the practical points of view. This rationality was proved, argued the advocates of economic nationalism, by the achievements of the fascist, totalitarian, and also some authoritarian regimes, for example, in the Balkan countries, Latvia and Estonia, and, on the American continent, Mexico, Brazil in Vargas's time, Argentina under Juan Perón. The figure among the theoreticians of the time—and not just in the East-Central European region—was Mihail Manoilescu. Apart from Marxist economists (in the broad sense of the term), economists associated with the corporative state, fascism, and Nazism (even though the latter proceeded from different assumptions) also proclaimed the irrationality and the failure of economic liberalism. However, it must also be pointed out here that especially the Nazi conceptions proceeded from the concept of *Grossraumwirtschaft*, an intellectual trend that, in my opinion, was essentially in conflict with the common understanding of economic nationalism.[19]

The next question that should be asked is the following: To what extent did economic nationalism implement the state goals en masse, and to what degree did it concentrate on the pursuit of group interests? The way the question is put immediately suggests a positive answer, at least to its second part. No matter what economic views one professes, it is clear that some groups or strata were interested (also from the material point of view) in the pursuit of a policy based on economic nationalism, or else they would not have referred to it. Also, from the point of view of the national economy as a whole, economic nationalism could be and indeed was profitable, at least in the short run. It should be added, however, that the appraisal of the implementation of national economic objectives is even more difficult in light of the multinational character of the populations of Poland, Romania, Czechoslovakia, and Yugoslavia, and that no matter whether one applies nationalist criteria in making this appraisal or not.

The advantages of economic nationalism to particular countries, classes, strata, and groups were not obvious because of:

- the complex and varying interactions of social strata and groups;
- the relative weakness of the standard-bearer of economic nationalism, that is, the national bourgeoisie as a whole;
- the fact that economic nationalism tended to be advanced rather by the middle classes—by the state bureaucracy and the intelligentsia in some countries (e.g., Romania, Hungary and Poland), and in others also by the peasantry (e.g., the Baltic states, Czechoslovakia, Bulgaria);
- the internal divisions within the domestic bourgeoisie, illustrated by the fact that some of its groups, which had ties to foreign capital or foreign economic decisionmaking centers (directly or indirectly, e.g., through international cartels), opposed some economic and especially commercial policies.[20]

However, there can be no doubt that the interest groups directly involved in economic life obtained the greatest advantages (reaping profits in periods of boom and losing relatively the least during recessions)—first of all, those associated with banking and industrial capital, and also, in certain cases (e.g., in Bulgaria and Czechoslovakia), agrarian capital as well. The policy of economic nationalism, by protecting selected branches of industry from foreign competition, sometimes was advantageous also for some groups of the working class or peasants (for example, in supporting the regulation of agricultural prices, as was the case especially in Czechoslovakia, Latvia, and Estonia, and to some extent in Bulgaria).

The above mentioned problem of advantages relates to other than the state subjects of the ideology of economic nationalism, and hence to a more precise definition of its social base. Certainly, the list of economic nationalism's subjects includes businessmen's associations, which, through their writings and demands addressed to the government, significantly influenced both the content of economic nationalism and, even more so, its practical economic policies. The leading political subjects of this ideology were right-wing and radical movements and parties, representing for the most part the middle classes, including the petit bourgeoisie, but sometimes certain bourgeois sections as well. In Romania these were the National Liberal Party and its offshoot, the New Liberal Party; in Hungary, the (ruling) Party of Unity in various phases of its evolution and, at the opposite end, Ferenc Szálasi's Arrow Cross Party fascists; in Poland, the broad national camp, and in the 1930s its most radical, totalitarian-minded National Radical Camp (ONR), some factions of the ruling camp and the Camp of National Unity (OZN) in particular; in Czechoslovakia, first of all the Agrarians (who, contrary to their unofficial name, did not reject industrialization out of hand but rather placed a different emphasis on its priorities), but also Edvard Beneš's National Socialists, or, in the 1930s, Andrej Hlinka's and Josef Tiso's Slovak People's Party, and finally Karel Kramář's National Democrats; in Bulgaria, the Progressive-Liberal Party representing on the one hand the bourgeoisie, and on the other Stamboliyski's Bulgarian Agrarian Union, which interpreted economic nationalism in a peculiar way, rejecting one of its cornerstones, namely, industrialization and the resulting urban growth, and replacing it with ubiquitous and essentially totalitarian agrarianism; finally, in the Baltic states, attention was especially attracted by peasant parties who relied on the authoritarian variety of the agrarian doctrine.

In practice, economic nationalism meant something different to the representatives of conservative views and of more-or-less liberal views, and something else still to extreme-right movements. Needless to say, this division only very roughly corresponds to the stratification of society. Generally, it could be said that, for example, the conservative opinion had the support of landowners in Poland, Hungary, and Romania; the liberal opinion was dearer to the circles of the big bourgeoisie and part of the intelligentsia (to a different extent in each of the countries); the totalitarian option was peculiar to part of the petit bourgeoisie, the intelligentsia, and the proletariat, of its poorer rather than better-off groups (although even here there were exceptions, such as the relatively strong support of workers from large enterprises for the phraseology of the Iron Guard or for the Hungarian Arrow Cross fascists[21]).

Also, it should be emphasized that inward-oriented economic nationalism sometimes, especially in the case of the extreme right (the ONR, the Arrow Cross fascists, and the Iron Guard being only the most significant examples), had anticapitalist overtones. These movements were characterized by the syndrome of anti-Semitism and hostility toward capitalism; the capitalist system was symbolized by international capital, which in all extreme-right ideologies was synonymous with evil and Jewishness. Thus conceived, economic nationalism was self- contradictory. By being both antisocialist and anticapitalist, and by referring to the slogan of independence, it essentially amounted to a return to conservative thought rather than to the revolutionary thought that one might have been expected. Economic nationalism of the extreme right proposed an anachronistic vision of development, static rather than dynamic. Given the realities of the region, radical right-wing ideologies were in most cases a herald of small industry, crafts, and farming, tied to the idea of some form of the corporate state for the organization of society.[22]

In enumerating the classes or groups interested in economic nationalism, one must not ignore a very special formal group, namely, the army. The army was an autonomous factor that usually stimulated economic nationalism quite automatically. In the countries of the region, the armies were always in favor of building from scratch or expanding and modernizing the armaments industry, which is not to say that in each of the countries of the region their demands were equally forceful or stood an identical chance of being satisfied.

In Czechoslovakia defense considerations received priority treatment, and the army's equipment was of the highest world standard, and yet until 1938, that is, until the period immediately following the Munich agreement, the army did not play any autonomous political role. In the relatively economically weaker Poland the armed forces in the 1930s, though they exerted a considerable political leverage, were not able to impose an accelerated inflation-based development of the defense industry. In Hungary the army was an autonomous force and an important cradle of revisionist ideology and policy, and it also played a decisive role in advancing the development plan for strategically important branches of industry, called the Győr Program; it also demanded the shedding of the constraints imposed on Hungary by the Treaty of Trianon. In that country there was actually a consensus of the politicians and the army as to the goals of military significance. In Romania the armed forces were subordinated to the supreme political power, which was King Carol II, but in the decisive years of 1939–1940 they entered the political scene through General Ion Antonescu's dictatorship. In Yugoslavia the officers' corps, permeated with the spirit of great Serbian nationalism and the centralist idea, played a stabilizing role as a mainstay of King Alexander's authoritarian rule; in 1941 the army determined an important change of the country's foreign policy line. In Bulgaria the military played a decisive role in shaping the political system of the country twice, first in 1923, when the Military League organized the coup against Stamboliyski's government, and then in 1934, when the same revived League along with the Zveno Group was a key force in the May coup d'état. In Bulgaria, as in Hungary, the officers' corps sought to free the country from the constraints imposed by the relevant clauses of the Treaty of Neuilly. In Greece, the army played the key role in the overthrowing of the oligarchic parliament. Its intervention in 1922 led to the proclamation of a republic in 1924 and to the restoration of the monarchy eleven years later. After Ioannis Metaxas became premier in 1936, strengthening the country's defenses was the prime goal of the state's economic policy. In the Baltic countries, the support of the officers' corps facilitated the imposition and stabilization of an authoritarian rule, under which the army was quite successful in securing increased military spending.

In sum, the armed forces of all the countries of the region except Czechoslovakia tried to influence their governments to give preference to a broad understanding of military expenditures. However, the financial, economic, and technological conditions prevailing in those countries definitively diminished the chances of satisfying the military needs. It should be added here that the armies also lent crucial support to authoritarian regimes. Although from the ideological point of view the officers' corps's main characteristic usually was their strong nationalism, it was nevertheless of a conservative or populist rather than a fascist nature (although among the military, especially in Hungary but also in Romania, there were also such men, who took the example of Italy and Germany).

The foregoing helps to illustrate the scale of support that economic nationalism enjoyed in all the countries of the region, without exception. It influenced peasants, big industrialists, state bureaucrats, and members of extreme-right movements of the middle class. Economic nationalism can therefore be said to have been a universal ideology, in the sense that it appealed to various social strata and political groups whose programs and fundamental ideologies might be incompatible with one another. Also, economic nationalism expressed, not always fully realized, the longing for progress.

To complete this overview of economic nationalism in East-Central Europe, let me note that each country, apart from general similarities, evinced also its individual characteristics due to certain differences in the country's internal and external situation. This fact must not be forgotten when assessing economic nationalism in particular countries. For example, until 1936 Poland's financial and monetary policies had clung to classical rules. As a result, its economic policy was based on industrial protectionism, dumping, import bans, a limited use of subsidies, but not on currency restrictions or continuous huge state purchases of grain (the latter being the case in some other countries of the region).[23]

On a hypothetical ranking list of states of the region, compiled according to the intensity of the measures employed to fend off foreign competition, Poland should be placed behind the Balkan countries and Hungary, and probably also behind Czechoslovakia. This is my subjective opinion, however, and the criteria used for arriving at it are open to question. But it is virtually impossible to weigh in a fully objective manner the effect of the protective measures employed by each of the countries concerned or to define each country's place on such a list, unless we adopt the effective protection rate proposed by theoreticians of foreign trade, which historians seem not to have done as yet.[24]

Other issues that should be included in our theoretical balance sheet of the benefits and losses of the policy of economic nationalism in the 1930s are the strong ambitions of the ruling elites who have a real say about the fate of their countries, which until recently amounted to the goal of unchecked foreign expansion. These aspirations in themselves should not be regarded as manifestation of excessive economic nationalism. If that was indeed the case in some instances, it depended more on the economic policy as implemented in practice than on the tenor of ideologically tinged extremist statements. At any rate, the attitude toward foreign capital and foreigners residing in a given country and engaging in economic activity there was a criterion of the actual degree of integrity of the ideology and practice of economic nationalism.

The Sources and Causes of Economic Nationalism

Contemporary students of economic nationalism have compiled a more-or-less full list of the direct and indirect causes of and circumstances conducive to the expansion of economic nationalism. Let us look, for example, at the causes the keen observer Theodore E. Gregory regarded as important. He believed that the growth of economic nationalism was structurally linked with the world agricultural crisis. This crisis followed from the overproduction (which in turn was a consequence of enormous strides in farming technology) that led to a disastrous fall in agricultural prices over a very short period of time (a year and a half). The spread of the ideology and especially the practice of economic nationalism were made easier by phenomena from the area of modern social psychology: certain moods, frustrations, fears, and strivings stemming from a definite economic and political background. Gregory's list of such phenomena included, among other items:

- the fear that excessive export-oriented production could lead to an excessive dependence of domestic producers on foreign demand and customs tariffs;
- the fear of foreign capitalists interfering with the domestic market (this was an especially popular excuse in East European countries, Gregory alleged);

- the reluctance to place strategic raw materials at foreign disposal (such reluctance could be detected even in England, a mainstay of liberalism);
- the striving for self-sufficiency in food production for strategic and defense reasons, including the need to attain independence from foreign supplies in the event of war, and the objective of maintaining a definite level of employment in agriculture, dictated by noneconomic considerations, such as the need to preserve the species of tough man, prepared to bear the hardships of war (it is worth noting, however, that the latter motive was characteristic of prefascist and fascist ideologies);
- the ambition to ensure to the national intelligentsia a due place in economic life, until then more often than not occupied by foreigners.[25]

It may be said that Gregory pinpointed important causes of the expansion of economic nationalism, although he scrambled them, which was not at all unusual at the time. A more orderly and generalized approach, however, can be found in the Royal Institute of International Affairs (RIIA) study, prepared after the Great Depression and shortly before the outbreak of World War II. This report lists three sets of factors that, though not exactly new, had the strongest impact on the development of economic nationalism because of their scale and interaction: the imminent end of the economic expansion of industrialized Europe; the use of new inventions and innovations that revolutionized the production of both raw materials and food; and the social and economic changes transpiring partly from the first two causes, which in certain countries effected radical transformations in political organization.[26]

It is difficult to systematize both the set of reasons proposed by Gregory and those enumerated in a more synthetic fashion in the RIIA report, according to their role and importance. Leo Pasvolsky, in his by now classic work that was written before the Great Depression, mentions moreover the conviction, particularly strong among the ruling elites and state bureaucracies, that without economic independence political sovereignty is questionable.[27] Thus Pasvolsky refers simultaneously to the ideological and to the psychological factors.

1. The conviction mentioned by Pasvolsky—that economic independence is a prerequisite of political sovereignty—can serve as a convenient starting point for further deliberations on economic nationalism. That conviction was indeed very important. It was shaped first of all under the influence of experience (especially in the case of Hungary, Poland, Czechoslovakia, and Romania) from the period during which the boundaries of those countries were being decided. In exchange for more favorable territorial solutions, those countries often had to award economic

preferences (e.g., appropriate trade concessions) to the big powers, huge monopolies, major industrial firms, and commercial or insurance companies. Hungary had an especially unpleasant experience from that period as its political and economic interests were wholly subordinated by the big powers to their policy of support for the countries of the future Little Entente. Czechoslovakia and Romania, in contrast, benefited a great deal from the bargaining between the Allies—even if only in the short run, as it was to turn out in the end—when they offered economic advantages to France. Incidentally, France displayed an unusual diplomatic activity in this region, particularly in the 1920s, forcing the countries concerned to grant customs privileges (as in agreements with Poland in 1922 and next, with Czechoslovakia) and other economic concessions to itself.[28]

2. The countries of the region were aware of the nature of the concessions they had granted. They also realized that—aside from some unique political configurations that could positively or adversely affect their room for maneuver—their bargaining position vis-à-vis the highly developed countries was, in some measure, an outcome of their own economic strength. The effects were real in the case of Czechoslovakia, and potential in the case of Romania, which had relatively large oil deposits, or that of Yugoslavia, which had rich deposits of rare metals. It is therefore not surprising that Czechoslovakia could obtain better conditions of exchange than Poland.

3. The new vistas that opened up before the classes, strata, and groups within nations that until recently had little or no rights became a powerful psychological engine of change in patterns of ownership as well as in a radical remodeling of the traditional status hierarchies.

4. In the backward countries of the region advocates of effective state control in particular were exhorting intensive industrialization, regarded as a prerequisite of the country's independence. They used any arguments they could seize upon (even to the point of invoking some of the Soviet experience, as in the case of Polish etatists).[29] They had enlisted firm support of the advocates of private industrial capital. The view that without economic independence political independence was not possible acted as a powerful incentive to industrialization, just as Pasvolsky had pointed out.[30]

In particular, the trends mentioned in points (3) and (4) manifested themselves in the opinion (quite widespread in the succession countries) to the effect that genuine independence was not possible without the nation's ridding itself of the financial dominance of Vienna, Berlin, or—on a smaller scale—Budapest, and without the creation of strong domestic financial centers. It should be remembered that the massive repatriation of foreign capital during the crisis of the years 1930–1935 was an especially powerful impulse for the development of economic nationalism; it also served as a sort of justification of a certain distrust of these centers, which at that time extended to London, New York, Zurich, Paris, Brussels, and Amsterdam as well.

5. In the 1930s significant shifts developed in the ranks of the advocates of economic nationalism. The proponents of a greater role of the state in the economy, including state ownership of enterprises, had an increasingly great say. This, in view of the dismally low level of capital formation, inevitably led to a clash with the interests of the private sector. Some other reasons for this evolution included the inability of the private sector to meet the investment targets set by the national plans that were passed in some countries (Poland, Hungary, and to some extent Czechoslovakia). In this situation, there occurred, particularly in Poland but to a lesser extent in other countries as well, discord among the earlier allies and animators of industrialization.

6. Purely political considerations also played a part in stimulating economic nationalism. These political considerations included, for example, the East-Central European countries' persistent fear that their national status might be questioned. The binding agent of the Little Entente was the desire to prevent the restoration of the Habsburg monarchy (in any territorial shape whatsoever[31]), and even more so the fear of Hungarian revisionism; in the case of Yugoslavia, it was the fear of Italian and (to a much smaller degree) Bulgarian claims; in Lithuania, the search for protection from Polish and German moves; in Greece, an apprehensiveness of Bulgarian and especially Italian policies.[32]

7. Those fears, going back to the 1920s, were fueled by the behavior of the defeated states (Germany, Hungary and, on a smaller scale, Bulgaria) that accepted the end-of-war treaties reluctantly and with much resistance. As time went by and various shifts took place in the international arena, they began to question those treaties more or less openly. The buildup of armed forces in the Little Entente countries—in Poland, Greece, and even the Baltic states—also stimulated economic nationalism to some degree by requiring a certain degree of self-sufficiency.[33] That buildup was not only a logical consequence of the emergence of new states but also of their fear for their independence. (These circumstances were particularly important in the latter half of the 1930s, offering a psychological justification for the development of the ideology of economic nationalism). In Poland this tendency to arm was additionally heightened by the perception of its duties resulting from its leadership in the region, at least in the area stretching from the Baltic to the Black Sea, quite widespread in the ruling circles and among the influential political groupings.

8. Among the internal conditions conducive to the development of economic nationalism, the need to build uniform economic organs out of the

new national territories appears to have been the most important (only in Bulgaria was this no longer such a burning issue). This called for an enormous effort to eliminate administrative, transport, legal, tariff, educational, and other differences.

9. Inevitably the countries concerned (and Poland in particular) saw the policy of economic egoism as a chance to overcome the postwar disruption (shortages of provisions, raw materials, and foreign exchange) and to repair the war damage.

10. Historical experiences, ethnic tensions in the early 1920s resulting from, among other things, the peace treaties, and the social and economic shock caused by the Great Depression, all fueled the growth of nationalist feelings in countries with sizable ethnic minorities (usually exceeding 10 percent of the population). As a result internal policies (educational policy included) inevitably aimed at the consolidation of "state nations" (*Staatsvolk*). The policies toward the nationalities in the first place, and sometimes also the attitude of the minorities (especially of the Germans in Czechoslovakia and Poland but also in other countries of the region,[34] and toward the end of the 1930s, of the Hungarians in Romania and Slovakia) also provoked manifestations of inward-oriented economic nationalism (see Chapter 3).

11. The Great Depression produced new and powerful stimuli to the spread of this ideology, leading to the development of various forms of protectionism, autarky, and etatism in particular. In the face of an impending financial disaster (especially in Austria, Hungary, and Bulgaria), the lack of response to appeals addressed to Western governments and foreign capital and the failure of attempts to establish international economic guarantees, the countries of the region had no other choice but to resort to extreme restrictions and protectionist measures. Hence, whatever the reasons for taking these steps—whether they were forced by circumstances, or born of nationalist ideological premises, or both—the result was the same: the spread of economic nationalism.

12. In addition, in the 1930s the ideology and practice of economic nationalism were influenced in the region by the dangerous evolution of the international situation. It was characterized by particular tension and the imminence of war resulting from the rise in the extreme revisionism of Nazi Germany, which also encouraged similar trends in Hungary and to some extent in Bulgaria, while also becoming an incentive to armaments throughout Europe.

13. The domestic economic difficulties and social problems of that decade and the impoverishment of a large part of the population (sometimes extending to whole social strata) had a radicalizing effect on the public mood. The social and occupational structure of the population and antagonisms arising out of an ethnic background, intensified further

by the influence of movements of the extreme right, sought an outlet in nationalism that was directed, first of all, inward—that is, against the ethnic minorities inhabiting those countries, and against Jews primarily.

14. As a result of the development of authoritarian forms of government, there came a process of intermingling of state and national ideologies, with economic nationalism becoming, to a greater or lesser degree, the state ideology. The fascist and Nazi ideologies definitely influenced its hue. More and more often, the so-called national interest was invoked as the most important element of economic nationalism, the basic criterion of the usefulness and advisability of various moves, including economic ones. But it was not the only element. Only the extreme nationalist movements (e.g., the ONR, the Arrow Cross, the Iron Guard, Croat extreme nationalists, the fascists of the Baltic states, Rudolph Gajda's fascist followers, the radical factions of Hlinka supporters) made the national interest—interpreted in a maximalist way, full of phobias and aggression—the cornerstone of their political, social, and economic programs.

15. Paradoxically, in the latter part of the 1930s the aforementioned influence of German foreign policy and the conception and practice of *Grossraumwirtschaft*, extending to some countries of the region, opened up new development vistas for economic nationalism. It is interesting to note that the more those countries (Hungary, Bulgaria, Romania, Yugoslavia, and even Greece) depended, both politically and economically, on the Third Reich, the more forcefully they invoked the attributes of economic sovereignty. In a condensed form these attributes reflected precisely the slogans of economic nationalism, which, as a matter of fact, were little more than ideological ornamentation. Economists and politicians in charge of the economy, to say nothing of ideologues in those authoritarian countries, were aware of this state of affairs. Some of those people, like Manoilescu, tried to find a way out of this inner contradiction.

While examining the factors conducive to the expansion of economic nationalism, it is also worthwhile to point out the circumstances that might impede this development. The psychosocial conditionings, though external to that ideology, were nevertheless an important factor. It must be realized that the societies of the countries in question and also a large proportion of the population of Czechoslovakia (Slovaks and Transcarpathian Ruthenians) were going through a transitional period before they would become industrial societies. This was attested to by their occupational structure (the share of the agricultural population could be as high as 80 percent in the Balkan countries), the structure of the national income (with the share of agriculture ranging from about 30 percent to nearly 50 percent) and of foreign trade (predominance of agricultural raw material exports—with the exception of Czechoslovakia, of course—

which, in the cases of Lithuania, Yugoslavia, Romania, Bulgaria, and Albania, ranged from 83 to 100 percent of their overall exports), and the general level of development (i.e., the condition of material infrastructure as well as of education, health care services, etc.).[35]

With the exception of highly industrialized areas such as Bohemia, Upper Silesia, Budapest, and some parts of the former Kingdom of Poland, the ethos of an industrialist, a wholesaler, a manager or, in general, a businessperson in the modern sense of the word, or of an economist, bookkeeper, technician, and the like, rather slowly gained the appreciation of the middle classes and of influential circles, especially of those who, as in Poland, Hungary, and to some extent in Romania, descended from the nobility. The traditional values cherished by the peasantry, however, such as the cult of work in the field and attachment to native tradition, family, and faith, remained strong in those societies. Agrarianism assimilated these values in part; however, their adoption by extremist right-wing ideologies made them degenerate.

At the same time, however, the rural population, and especially its proletarianized strata, viewed the moving to town, the obtaining of education and of a definite job, to say nothing of joining the ranks of the working-class aristocracy, as a promotion, a rise in social status. This appeal to rustic values was in apparent as well as real contradiction with the ambition to improve the peasant lot *also* through industrialization (no matter how it was understood), proclaimed by their agrarian, radically conservative or radically right-wing propagators. It was apparent because those rustic values were usually propagated by people who had little to do with the countryside (mainly the intelligentsia) or by those whose financial situation was relatively good (rich and fairly rich peasants). These "country-lovers" appealed to the feelings of the people whose only hope for rising in life was to find any job at all. Yet at the time of economic recovery it was easier to find work in the town than in the overpopulated village. But the contradiction was also real because the only solution to the internal problems at the time was a genuine forced industrialization, which was bound to undermine and destroy these values. Regardless of the nature of industrialization, its process as such led to a total break with the previous environment and lifestyle—despite the attempts to build safety valves into the social sphere, such as the corporatist system and a peculiar kind of industrialization based on private crafts.

Therefore, for a certain definite period of time the proindustrial ideology in the region did not have an outwardly aggressive hue. That hue only came to light at higher levels of social consciousness, especially the consciousness of the national bourgeoisie. Once it consolidated its position, it began to aspire, with varying degree of justification and success, to the leading role in the economic life of the nation or state. It is hard to define accurately at which historical moment this took place. At any rate, the capitalist ideology had already begun to make ever greater inroads into East-Central Europe at the turn of the century. Nonetheless, in the interwar period the bourgeoisie was only one of the forces aspiring to exercise power. The aristocracy, landowners, and to some extent other social groups and strata, such as peasants, the intelligentsia, and the military, were their rivals.

Considering the country's level of productive forces, the Czech National Democrats were objectively the strongest political party to directly represent the development ideology of the future big capital. But even so they never exercised power in Czechoslovakia on their own, not even in the brief period of their flourishing (1919–1920). They were eventually (in the 1930s, which are of special interest here) pushed to the sidelines.[36] The rule of the bourgeois parties in the Balkans and in Romania reflected less the actual role and strength of the bourgeoisie in the economy than the specific political situation in those countries.[37] In medium-developed countries, such as Poland and Hungary, things looked still different. In Hungary, the ruling team led by the outstanding conservative-liberal politician István Bethlen (who served as premier from 1921 to 1931) effectively represented the interests of big industrialists and landowners. The successor governments of Gyula Gömbös, Kálmán Darányi and Béla Imrédy appeared to be closer to the interests of the petit and middle nationalist bourgeoisie and the middle classes,[38] despite the fact that it was precisely the Darányi administration that undertook the Győr Program. In Poland, in the period of parliamentary rule, National Democrats (*Narodowa Demokracja*) were closer to capitalist circles, yet it was the so-called Castle Group rallied around President Ignacy Mościcki and Vice Premier Eugeniusz Kwiatkowski who in the late 1930s initiated a worthwhile industrialization program.[39] In the Baltic countries, the proindustrialization ideology was definitely of secondary importance, playing only a subservient role to the blend of agrarianism and corporatism in the ideological and political field. The peasant parties that played a dominant part in those states prioritized their economic policy according to the interests of the countryside.[40] What industrialization was there was for the most part connected with the expansion of the industrial infrastructure of agriculture rather than bearing the marks of a "development ideology."

For these reasons the idea of industrialization took a long time to garner broader public support. Consequently it fell to the state bureaucracy to spread the industrialization variant of economic nationalism. In Bulgaria, Poland, Romania, Hungary, and in some measure Greece, the state bureaucracy proved to be quite effective in this respect; it was relatively less effective in Czechoslovakia and Austria and quite ineffective in the Baltic states and in Albania.

This overview of determinants of economic nationalism does not exhaust the whole of their spectrum. However, it is important to realize that together, they form a complicated web of interdependent causes and effects that are difficult to identify with any greater measure of accuracy and that can only be arranged into a hierarchical order with a great deal of trouble. Any hierarchy, including the one proposed here, is therefore arbitrary.

Notes

1. See J. Żarnowski, ed., *Dyktatury w Europie Środkowo-Wschodniej 1918–1939* (Wrocław, 1973).

2. See Hannah Arendt's classic, *The Origins of Totalitarianism* (New York, 1973); Carl J. Friedrich, ed., *Totalitarianism* (New York, 1964); and Leonard Schapiro, *Totalitarianism* (London, 1972).

3. From among Western publications, see, for example, Renzo de Felice, *Interpretacje faszyzmu* (Warsaw, 1976); Walter Laqueur, ed., *Fascism: A Reader's Guide* (Berkeley and Los Angeles, 1978); S. G. Payne, *Fascism: Comparison and Definition* (Madison, Wisc., 1983); Richard Grunberger, *A Social History of the Third Reich* (London 1977). Among Polish ones, F. Ryszka, *Państwo stanu wyjątkowego*, 3d rev. ed. (Wrocław, 1985); J. W. Borejsza, *Mussolini był pierwszy . . .* (Warsaw, 1979); J. W. Borejsza, ed., *Faszyzmy europejskie (1922–1945) w oczach współczesnych i historyków* (Warsaw, 1979); *Studia nad faszyzmem i zbrodniami hitlerowskimi*, vol. III, *Faszyzm — teoria i praktyka w Europie* (Wrocław, 1977).

4. See Hans Rogger and Eugen Weber, eds., *The European Right: A Historical Profile* (London, 1967); Samuel P. Huntington and Clement H. Moore, eds., *Authoritarian Politics in Modern Society: The Dynamics of Established One-Party Systems* (New York, 1970); Peter F. Sugar and Eugen Weber, eds., *Native Fascism in the Successor States, 1918–1945* (Santa Barbara, 1971); Joseph Rothschild, *East Central Europe Between Two World Wars* (Seattle, 1974); Żarnowski, *Dyktatury w Europie Środkowo-Wschodniej.* Compare Nicos P. Mouzelis, *Politics in Semi-Periphery: Early Parliamentarism and Late Industrialization in the Balkans and Latin America* (London, 1986).

5. Some information on this subject is dispersed in different works. We know relatively more on the manifestations of the economic nationalism of the Germans in Czechoslovakia and Poland, and to a lesser extent, in Hungary, Yugoslavia, and Romania. See Elisabeth Wiskemann, *Czechs and Germans*, 2d ed. (London, 1967); J. W. Bruegel, *Czechoslovakia Before Munich: The German Minority Problem and British Appeasement Policy* (Cambridge, 1973); Stanisław Potocki, *Położenie mniejszości niemieckiej w Polsce 1918–1938* (Gdańsk, 1969); Karol Grünberg, *Niemcy i ich organizacje polityczne w Polsce międzywojennej* (Warsaw, 1970); Thomas Spira, *German-Hungarian Relations and the Swabian Problem: From Károlyi to Gömbös, 1919–1936* (Boulder, 1977); G. C. Paikert, *The Danube Swabians* (The Hague, 1967).

6. Contrary to Aira Kemiläinen, *Nationalism: Problem Concerning the World: The Concept and Classification* (Jyväskylä, Finland, 1964).

7. See Józef Chlebowczyk in his books *Procesy narodowotwórcze we wschodniej Europie Środkowej w dobie kapitalizmu (od schyłku XVIII do początków XX w.)* (Warsaw and Kraków, 1975), chapters 3–5, and *Między dyktatem, realiami a prawem do*

samostanowienia: Prawo do samookreślenia i problem granic we wschodniej Europie Środkowej w pierwszej wojnie światowej oraz po jej zakończeniu (Warsaw, 1988); M. Hroch, *Evropská národní hnutí v 19 století: Společenské předpoklady vzniku novodobých národů* (Prague 1986), chapter 3. Compare Edward H. Carr, ed., *Nationalism: A Report by a Study Group of Members of the Royal Institute of International Affairs* (Oxford, 1939); Karl W. Deutsch, *Nationalism and Social Communication: An Inquiry into the Foundations of Nationality* (Cambridge, Mass., 1967); Peter F. Sugar and Ivo L. Lederer, eds., *Nationalism in Eastern Europe* (Seattle, 1973); Kemiläinen, *Nationalism;* George von Rauch, *The Baltic States: Estonia, Latvia, and Lithuania: The Years of Independence, 1917–1940* (Berkeley and Los Angeles, 1974).

8. E. Bradford Burns, *Nationalism in Brazil: A Historical Survey* (New York, 1968), pp. 8ff., 72–89.

9. For more on this subject, see Henryk Szlajfer, *Modernizacja zależności: Kapitalizm i rozwój w Ameryce Łacińskiej* (Wrocław, 1985), chapter 4; Marcin Kula, *Historia Brazylii* (Wrocław, 1987), pp. 174–186, 226–231; Mouzelis, *Politics in Semi-Periphery,* p. 27.

10. Compare Royal Institute of International Affairs, *The Baltic States: A Survey of the Political and Economic Structure and the Foreign Relations of Estonia, Latvia, and Lithuania* (London, 1938), pp. 116–118; Carr, *Nationalism: A Report,* pp. 230ff.; P. Łossowski, "Problem mniejszości narodowych w Europie Środkowo-Wschodniej na przykładzie państw bałtyckich 1919–1940, in J. Żarnowski, ed., *"Ład wersalski" w Europie Środkowej* (Wrocław, 1971).

11. See e.g., Carr, *Nationalism: A Report,* p. 9. More cautious is the opinion that "nationalism has assumed many forms since its birth in the eighteenth century, especially since its fusion with *etatism,* the doctrine of the supremacy in all spheres of the state, in particular the nation state, and after its alliance with forces making for industrialization and modernization, once its sworn enemies." I. Berlin, "Nationalism: Past Neglected and Present Power," in his *Against the Current: Essays in the History of Ideas* (Oxford, 1981), p. 345.

12. Compare Johnson, "The Ideology of Economic Policy in the New States," in Johnson, ed., *Economic Nationalism in Old and New States* (London, 1968).

13. See e.g., Frederick Hertz, *The Economic Problem of Danubian States: A Study in Economic Nationalism* (London, 1947), pp. 86–90, and Nicolas Spulber, *The State and Economic Development in Eastern Europe* (New York, 1966), p. 42.

14. See Joseph Rothschild, *The Communist Party of Bulgaria: Origins and Development, 1883–1936* (New York, 1959), and R. J. Crampton, *A Short History of Modern Bulgaria* (Cambridge, 1987), pp. 87–99. More favorable in their opinion of Stamboliyski are John D. Bell, *Peasants in Power: Alexander Stambolijski and the Bulgarian Agrarian National Union, 1899–1923* (Princeton, 1977), p. 155, and Jerzy Tomaszewski, "Bulgaria 1923: profesor Cankow ratuje monarchię," in Andrzej Garlicki, ed., *Przewroty i zamachy stanu: Europa 1918–1939* (Warsaw, 1981), pp. 82–85. Stamboliyski's xenophobia did not hinder his passionate striving for the unity of southern Slavs.

15. On January 19, 1935, Bulgarian Foreign Minister K. T. Batolov told the League of Nations Finance Committee that its recommendations were favoring foreign creditors as concerned transfer of capital from Bulgaria. He said that this was unacceptable to his country. See *Public Record Office FO 371/19487, R 575/1/7.* Romania, however, signed the so-called Geneva Plan, on slightly better terms, for

the amelioration of the country's finance. See Juliusz Demel, *Historia Rumunii* (Wrocław, 1970), p. 302.

16. Unless a given country's security was at stake. For example, Poland refused an electrification license to Harriman's group, which acted as a cover for German capital. Compare Zbigniew Landau and Jerzy Tomaszewski, *Anonimowi władcy: Z dziejów kapitału obcego w Polsce (1918–1939)* (Warsaw, 1967), pp. 167–175.

17. See Rudolf Nötel, "International Capital Movements and Finance in Eastern Europe," *Vierteljahrschrift für Sozial- und Wirtschaftsgeschichte*, vol. 61, no. 1, 1975, pp. 76–99; Rothschild, *East Central Europe*, p. 20.

18. So did Bertil Ohlin, although with many reservations, in "Protection and Non-competing Groups," *Weltwirtschaftliches Archiv*, vol. 33, no. 1, 1931. At the time John Maynard Keynes had no reservations; see his *The General Theory of Employment, Interest, and Money* (London 1936), chapter 23. Michał Kalecki recognized this rationality in his review of M. Manoilescu's book, *Economic Journal*, vol. XLVIII, no. 4, 1938, pp. 708–711. After World War II, the theory of underdevelopment followed the same line.

19. For the economic ideas of the Nazis, see Franz L. Neumann, *Behemoth: The Structure and Practice of National Socialism*, 2d ed. (New York, 1944); Stuart J. Woolf, "Did a Fascist Economic System Exist?" in Woolf, ed., *Nature of Fascism* (New York, 1969); Alan S. Milward, "Fascism and the Economy," in Laqueur, ed., *Fascism: The New Order and the French Economy* (Oxford, 1970), and *War, Economy, and Society, 1939–1945* (Harmondsworth, 1977); Jerzy Chodorowski, *Niemiecka doktryna gospodarki wielkiego obszaru (Grossraumwirtschaft) 1800–1945* (Wrocław, 1972); and Eckart Teichert, *Autarkie und Grossraumwirtschaft in Deutschland 1930–1939* (Munich, 1984).

20. For example, the union of Upper Silesian industrialists active in Poland, which in the 1920s was dominated by German capital, stubbornly opposed, among other things, the introduction of new tariffs and changes in the existing economic ties. See Franciszek Biały, *Górnośląski Związek Przemysłowców Górniczo-Hutniczych, 1914–1932* (Wrocław, 1967).

21. Bélla Vago, *The Shadow of the Swastika: The Rise of Fascism and Anti-Semitism in the Danube Basin, 1936–1939* (London, 1975), p. 42.

22. For more general and comparative works, see, for example, Juan J. Linz, "From Falange to Movimiento-Organización: The Spanish Single Party and the Franco Regime, 1936–1969," and Andrew C. Janos, "The One-Party State and Social Mobilization: East Europe Between the Wars," in Huntington and Moore, *Authoritarian Politics*. See also Philippe C. Schmitter, "Reflections on Mihail Manoilescu and the Political Consequences of Delayed-Dependent Development on the Periphery of Western Europe," in Kenneth Jowitt, ed., *Social Change in Romania, 1860–1940: A Debate on Development in a European Nation* (Berkeley, 1978), pp. 123–148, and Mouzelis, *Politics in Semi-Periphery*.

23. Zenobia Knakiewicz, *Deflacja polska 1930–1933* (Warsaw, 1967); Zbigniew Landau and Jerzy Tomaszewski, *Gospodarka Polski międzywojennej 1918–1939*, vol. III, *Wielki kryzys 1930–1935* (Warsaw, 1982); Marian M. Drozdowski, *Polityka gospodarcza rządu polskiego 1936–1939* (Warsaw, 1963).

24. Warner M. Corden, *The Theory of Protection* (Oxford, 1971). For the calculation of the effective protection rate for different British industries, see Ferrest

Capie, "The British Tariff and Industrial Protection in the 1930's," *Economic History Review*, 2d series, vol. XXXI, no. 3, August 1978.

25. Theodore E. Gregory, "Economic Nationalism," *International Affairs*, vol. X, no. 3, 1931, pp. 295–298. Compare Josef Hanč, *Tornado Across Eastern Europe: The Path of Nazi Destruction from Poland to Greece* (New York, 1942), pp. 97ff.

26. Carr, *Nationalism: A Report*, pp. 231–233.

27. Leo Pasvolsky, *Economic Nationalism in the Danubian States* (London, 1928), p. 66.

28. See, for instance, Piotr S. Wandycz, *France and Her Allies, 1919–1925* (Minneapolis, 1962); Landau and Tomaszewski, *Gospodarka Polski międzywojennej 1918–1939*, vol. I, *W dobie inflacji 1918–1932*, chapter 13; Zbigniew Landau and Jerzy Tomaszewski, *Sprawa żyrardowska* (Warsaw, 1983), pp. 157–168; Wiesław Balcerak, *Powstanie państw narodowych w Europie Środkowo-Wschodniej* (Warsaw, 1974); Alice Teichova, *An Economic Background to Munich: International Business and Czechoslovakia, 1918–1938* (Cambridge, 1974); P. L. Cottrell, "Aspects of Western Equity Investment in the Banking Systems of East Central Europe," Claude Beaud, "The Interests of the Union Européenne in Central Europe," G. Ránki, "The Hungarian General Credit Bank in the 1920's," comments by B. Michel and François Crouzet, all in Alice Teichova and P. L. Cottrell, eds., *International Business and Central Europe, 1918–1939* (New York, 1983).

29. See Jerzy Gołębiowski, *Sektor państwowy w gospodarce Polski międzywojennej* (Warsaw, 1985), pp. 79ff.

30. Pasvolsky, *Economic Nationalism*, p. 73.

31. The countries of the Little Entente remembered the 1918–1921 activities of the legitimists trying to recover the thrones of Austria and Hungary. See Balcerak, *Powstanie państw narodowych*, pp. 259, 265–267.

32. Compare Henryk Batowski, *Między dwiema wojnami: Zarys historii dyplomatycznej* (Kraków, 1988).

33. Pasvolsky, *Economic Nationalism*, p. 67.

34. Henryk Batowski, ed., *Irredenta niemiecka w Europie Środkowej i Południowo-Wschodniej przed II wojną światową* (Katowice and Kraków, 1971); Antoni Czubiński, ed., *Rola mniejszości niemieckiej w rozwoju stosunków politycznych w Europie 1918–1945* (Poznań, 1984); Czubiński, ed., *Państwa bałkańskie w polityce imperializmu niemieckiego w latach 1871–1945* (Poznań, 1982); Paikert, *The Danube Swabians*.

35. See E. A. Radice, "General Characteristics of the Region Between the Wars," p. 31; Eric Lethbridge, "National Income and Product," p. 533; Zdeněk Drabek, "Foreign Trade Performance and Policy," pp. 470–474; E. Ehrlich, "Infrastructure," p. 326, all published in Michael C. Kaser (gen. ed.), *The Economic History of Eastern Europe, 1919–1975*, vol. 1, M. C. Kaser, E. A. Radice (eds.), *Economic Structure and Performance Between the Two Wars* (Oxford, 1985); and *Mały Rocznik Statystyczny* (Warsaw, 1939), p. 174.

36. In 1934, in protest against the devaluation of the Czechoslovak koruna, National Democrats resigned from the government coalition. See Alena Gajanová, "Přispevek k objasněni přičin roztržasy v táboře česke buržoazie v roce 1934," *Československý Časopis Historycký*, no. 4, 1956; V. Fic, "Národní sjednocení v politické struktuře buržoazniho Československá v letech 1934–1935," *Československý Časopis Historycký*, no. 1, 1978.

37. See Josef S. Roucek, *The Politics of the Balkans* (New York and London, 1939), pp. 11–22; Robert L. Wolf, *The Balkans in Our Time* (Cambridge, Mass., 1954). Among Polish historical publications, see the interesting contribution by Andrzej Ajnenkiel, "Ewolucja systemów ustrojowych w Europie Środkowej 1918–1939," in Żarnowski, *Dyktatury w Europie Środkowo-Wschodniej,* pp. 27–55.

38. Ivan T. Berend and György Ránki, *Underdevelopment and Economic Growth: Studies in Hungarian Economic and Social History* (Budapest, 1979), pp. 196–199, 201–205.

39. Drozdowski, *Polityka,* chapter 6; Żarnowski, *Społeczeństwo,* chapters 7 and 8; Jan Kofman, *Lewiatan a podstawowe zagadnienia ekonomiczno-polityczne Drugiej Rzeczypospolitej: Z dziejów ideologii kół wielkokapitalistycznych w Polsce* (Warsaw, 1986), chapter 3.

40. Rauch, *The Baltic States;* Piotr Łossowski, *Kraje bałtyckie na drodze od demokracji parlamentarnej do dyktatury (1918–1934)* (Wrocław, 1972, pp. 210–213, 270–277, and "Ideologie reżimów autorytarnych (kraje bałtyckie 1926–1934–1940)," in J. Żarnowski (ed.), *Dyktatury w Europie Środkowo-Wschodniej,* pp. 127–128.

3

Directions and Instruments
of Economic Nationalism

General Remarks

Reports and notes by, for example, Polish and British foreign services abound with charges of excessive protectionism, restrictions, and autarkic inclinations—in short, economic nationalism—against East-Central European countries. There is no reason to think that reports by Bulgarian, Czechoslovak, or Hungarian diplomats were any different. It is of major importance to establish precisely the extent to which a specific economic policy resulted from particular circumstances (temporarily to defend the national economy) and the extent to which it was a consistent, deliberate course taken to stimulate the economy, its sectors, and its industries to develop in a definite direction.

Expansive economic nationalism is characterized by maximalist goals defined in categories of national and/or state interest. The multitude of instruments used by economic nationalism was indeed impressive. From nationalization aimed primarily against foreign capital (relatively infrequently employed under capitalism), to instruments typical of a command economy (including even long-term development plans), to traditional measures such as tariff and taxation policies. It is their specific usage that decided whether they ultimately became instruments of economic nationalism.

Economic nationalism found its practical expression, for example:

- in the legislation of such countries as Romania, Albania, and Yugoslavia, which instituted the state as the owner of natural resources;[1] in laws concerning important areas of a given country's life (as the Czechoslovak national defense act of 1936);[2] in the legislation amending the existing ownership system so as to curtail the property rights of ethnic minorities or foreigners (e.g., the laws on land reform, on licenses,[3] or the so-called nostrification, which I discuss below); and in special discriminatory laws and ordinances against the Jewish minorities in Hungary, Slovakia, and Romania, issued in the late 1930s;[4]

- in such tariff and foreign trade policies as to improve economic conditions in general and to curtail foreign competition on the domestic market (through export subsidies and bounties, high tariffs, reimbursement of duties, import bans and quotas, and so on);
- in tangible support for domestic production, usually industrial but in the case of Czechoslovakia agricultural production in particular (through tax and investment reliefs, produce procurement, and the like);
- in a definite policy toward foreign capital (through, for example, foreign exchange legislation, laws pertaining to joint stock companies, "ethnicization" of enterprise managements and boards of directors);
- in legislation discriminating against foreigners in taxation, capital transfer and management, ownership, and so on;
- in control over the labor market (e.g., the tendency to "ethnicize" this market even at the skilled-workers' level)[5] and in curbing immigration (e.g., in the United States and South America);
- in propaganda activities such as, in Poland, the spreading of a naval and colonial ideology, and in all countries of the region, an official propaganda of hostility toward minorities;
- in advertising domestic products and boycotting foreign products[6] (e.g., in Germany, in the period of the postwar crisis and in the 1930s, there succeeded an appeal to buy German products only; in other countries the trend was similar).

It should be borne in mind that these instruments of economic nationalism only seldom were a genuine regional invention. Indeed, particularly those of a protectionist and autarkic nature had been known already earlier or were resorted to following the example of neighboring Italy, Germany, and the Soviet Union.

It is striking that certain instruments recognized as typical of economic nationalism can in fact be treated as instruments of state interventionism. The relatively large-scale intervention employed in East-Central European countries did indeed start from psychological and ideological assumptions that were, in some measure, an expression of economic nationalism. Besides objective reasons such as pressing internal requirements, this was an effect of the conviction, stronger than elsewhere, of the local power elites and segments of the public that national (or state) interest demands that the command economy be expanded. Yet to perceive in nationalism the main reason and expression of state interventionism[7] makes its interpretation too far-fetched. In extreme cases, this can mean treating the whole of the economic policy, and not just some of its fragments, as both a form and an expression of nationalism. The proponents of such a view ignore the internal causes of the development dynamics of modern societies, the rising complexity of the organizations of economic and social life, and the effects of successive revolutions in science and in production.

Admittedly, the development of labor legislation, social insurance, or education could be welcomed by the working class, the petit bourgeoisie, or certain groups of white-collar workers, particularly if the government policy limited the rights of foreigners. Yet it is difficult to agree with those scholars who recognize this kind of progress in social relations as a manifestation of nationalism (or economic nationalism).[8] As regards foreigners' rights, the policy adopted reflected first and foremost the labor market situation. Unlike, for instance, North and South America,[9] East-Central European countries, with their labor surplus and rural overpopulation, did not have to introduce special legislation discriminating against foreign workers because there were hardly any foreign workers there. At the end of the 1930s Estonia and Latvia, which had seasonal labor shortages, handled the problem by signing relevant international agreements.[10]

Once again we must concede that the economic policies of the East-Central European countries in the 1930s more often than not were merely a momentary defensive reaction to the social and economic dangers of the Great Depression. This notwithstanding, such policies were to a certain degree a manifestation of economic nationalism, and they differed from the nationalism used as an ideological sword in the struggle for economic transformation. Most often, however, the countries of the region subscribed to both economic and ideological nationalism.

Nostrification

In East-Central Europe nostrification was the most common manifestation of economic nationalism. However, the term itself is ambiguous, providing for a multitude of interpretations.

Nostrification in such countries as the Baltic states, Czechoslovakia, Poland, and Romania concerned agriculture, industry, transport, banking, and insurance. The aim of nostrification was to strengthen those countries' independence. Yet its domestic political and social context was no less important. Nostrification was often seen not only as a way to settle historical accounts and to claim the due national rights but also as a

necessary mechanism to rectify particular people's property status, political position, or prestige—in keeping with the interests of the new political elite. By now, a number of scholarly works have been written on the
real as well as the more—or-less imaginary harm suffered by the German
minorities in Poland and Czechoslovakia, by Hungarians in Romania, by
Poles in Lithuania, and by Ukrainians and Byelorussians in Poland.[11]

It is difficult to get to the core of these very complicated matters. From
the point of view of the liberal economic, political, and social concepts,
nostrification—irrespective of its initial assumptions—must be seen as a
manifestation of nationalism. However, such an appraisal happens to be
cognitively sterile, ahistorical, anachronistic, and in fact conservative because it tacitly assumes a relative unchangeableness in time and space of
the already existing political and state structures—on the global, conti-
nental, or regional scale, regardless of the national liberation aspirations.[12]

My criticism does not, however, indicate an approval of the abuses that
occurred and that were raised by the Hungarian, German, Polish, and
Lithuanian press and on the international forum (the international court
of the League of Nations in The Hague).[13] The Versailles Treaty provisions allowed the allied countries (Poland, Czechoslovakia, Romania,
and the Kingdom of Serbs, Croats, and Slovenes among them) to manda-
torily purchase public and private properties owned by the defeated
countries (and their nationals) but situated on the territory of the victori-
ous countries. These provisions were favorable to the policy of ousting
the German, Austrian, and Hungarian elements from the successor and
Baltic states. As a rule, nostrifications were mandatory but also compen-
sational.

Sometimes the ideological factor played a very important role in the
nostrification process. In Czechoslovakia, for example, it was apparent in
the policy of the outstanding national-democratic leader, until 1923 the
economic policy czar, Finance Minister Alois Rašin.[14] In Czechoslovak
land reform there immediately was a clear tinge of a national clash. As
large private estates subject to parceling were usually owned by either
Germans or Hungarians, land reform meant significant changes in the
land property's national structure. At this point, it must be forcefully emphasized that contrary to German opinion, German peasants and land-
less Germans benefited from the reform too, although the Czechoslovaks
did not avoid unequal treatment of nationalities.[15]

Needless to say, nostrification caused certain economic perturbations.
It was often carried out in conditions one could hardly describe as favorable to the nostrified property (whether private or public). The expropri-
ated owners were particularly critical of the amount of compensation
they were awarded. Critics of the nostrification acts argue that immedi-

ately after the war, they could help to overcome chaos and economic difficulties but did not produce any regular profit. This argument seems to hold water. First, economic reasons were secondary to political ones when the extent of nostrification was being considered. Both expressed the national interest. Economic context, despite appearances, was also favorable to nostrification. Second, the economic rationality of nostrification statutes can as a rule be estimated in retrospect only. It should be remembered, moreover, that nostrification's basic aim was to build up economic, financial, and social relations corresponding with the needs of the newly established territorial units.

The literature of the subject quite often imprecisely defines nostrification as something that, from the formal point of view, was not actually nostrification. I mean here the taking over by Czechs, Slovaks, Poles, Romanians, Serbs, Croats, and Balts the property of their fellow citizens who were part of the German, Hungarian, Russian, or Polish minority. This was another aspect of the process of "ethnicization" of property and capital and, legally, had nothing to do with nostrification.

For example, in Czechoslovakia changes in the national ownership structure were made easier by the fact that Sudeten and Austrian Germans and Hungarians in Slovakia had bought Austro-Hungarian war bonds and had been very strongly involved in their former government's military endeavors. In the postwar crisis, that involvement made the relevant German and Hungarian businesses face bankruptcy. In that situation, Czech capitalists, supported by their government, took over the bankrupts' shares. Conducive to the "ethnicization" campaign were also upper- and middle-class Germans' ties with, primarily, Vienna and Berlin, and Hungarians' with Budapest—that is, with the centers that had become foreign. Those ties proved to be real fetters to the minorities in the situation of the currency crisis (inflation) that affected Austria, Hungary, and Germany in the first postwar years.[16] These circumstances did not, of course, rule out changes in the ownership structure within the minorities themselves, but in their case, for the reasons given earlier, the process of change was slower. Similar processes took place, for example, in Poland, Romania, Yugoslavia (in the two Danubian countries the object of "ethnicization" was first and foremost Hungarian firms), and the Baltic states (where they concerned primarily German, Polish, and Russian estates).[17]

Thus the nostrification procedures of the 1920s were as if indirect. In the following decade, the progressive "ethnicization" of capital and property, for instance, in Czechoslovakia, was again to a considerable extent a result of the German minority's economic ties with German capital and industry. The failure of the banks in Vienna, and particularly those in Germany in the years 1931–1932, inevitably caused financial troubles for German-owned businesses in Czechoslovakia. The charges that the authorities in Prague took unfair advantage of the difficulties the German-minority-owned industrial, commercial, cooperative, banking, and insurance businesses faced at the time of crisis seem unconvincing.[18] The Czech authorities, by not providing them with effective aid, are alleged to have conduced to their takeover by the Czech element. The fact remains, however, that gross infringements of German property were committed. Thus in the years of the Great Depression the government imprudently transferred money to investment projects in particular *kraje* (regions), or insufficiently counteracted the effect of the grain monopoly on the condition of German flour-milling, or allowed only a certain quota of margarine, which was produced largely by the Sudeten food industry.[19]

The changes in property relations in the heavy industry of the Polish Upper Silesia of the second half of the 1930s, too, came about as a result of purely economic considerations. It was only on that occasion that the Upper Silesian industry became "ethnicized." To be precise, the Wspólnota Interesów Górniczo-Hutniczych (Community of Mining and Metallurgical Interests) was actually nationalized when the Polish state took over from the Germans the concern connected with financial centers in the Reich.[20]

To recapitulate, it may said that the nostrification and "ethnicization" campaigns carried out in the region in the two interwar decades, but most intensively in the early 1920s, were inevitable—if one considers the existing antagonisms between nationalities, and their political context. Thus, for example, wide circles of German bourgeoisie and gentry were noisily demonstrating their open hostility to the new Czechoslovak state, even demanding statehood for the Sudeten-German area.[21]

Also, by their carrying into effect what we call the Versailles order, nostrifications acquired international political dimensions. Specially, France was in favor of nostrifications, seeing in them an element of strengthening the position of its allies and of weakening that of the potentially revisionist countries, Germany in particular. Besides, it is worth remembering that the process of Czechization, Romanization, Polonization, Latvianization, or Lithuanization of business did not mean the exclusion of Western European or American capital. On the contrary, the governments and businesses of the region were interested in seeing Western European or U.S. capital replace the capital they had ousted.[22]

Inward-Oriented Economic Nationalism

Depending on the emphasis given to fundamental goals, whether to the power of the state or to the strength of the nation, we can speak of the primacy of either the state or the national element in the ideology of economic nationalism. In the 1920s and 1930s, save the close of that period, East-Central European governments were giving priority to the goals and reasons of the state when enforcing the policies of protectionism and industrialism. It should nonetheless be remembered that such notions as the interest of the state or the interest of the nation are extremely vague, flexible, and subject to different interpretations. The recourse to the state ideology was a result, among other things, of a large percentage of national minorities living in several countries of the region (Poland, Czechoslovakia, Romania).

To clarify the intentions of the proponents of economic nationalism, it is necessary to consider whether a particular country's policy aimed to take over economic control from the former metropolises (Vienna, Berlin, Moscow) or to limit the business opportunities of the new and old national minorities, including those who had managed to place themselves in important segments of the economy. I mean here, for instance, Jews, who in nearly every country of the region comprised a significant part of the capitalist and middle classes, the Sudeten Germans, who formed a strong enclave in the Czechoslovak economy, Polish landowners in the Baltic countries, Swabians in the Hungarian countryside, Hungarian peasants in Romania, German capitalists (and, to a lesser extent, landowners and rich peasants) in Poland, and so on.[23]

Economic nationalism adopted as a state policy sometimes (if rarely) was a means to mobilize the positive energy of the public for the authorities-assigned tasks of greater economic importance. Such was the aim of the propaganda campaign, for example, that the Camp of National Unity (OZN) launched to establish the Central Industrial Basin (COP), or that of the Hungarian governmental party to implement the Győr Program.[24] At the same time, however, the trend of peremptory argumentation began in an increasingly obvious way to follow another bent: to emphasize the primacy of the nation or to identify the national with the state interest. Nationalistic moods, which at the close of the 1930s reached their apogee, only aggravated the separation between the ruling nation and the national minorities. But in this regard, too, there were many interpretations and varieties of implementation. Unlike the governments in Italy and Germany, the governments in East-Central Europe for a long time could not and did not want to identify the national with the state interest.[25]

Conflicts were usually about the Jewish share in the economy. In Poland, Romania, Slovakia, Hungary, Austria, and to some degree the Baltic states, the new middle classes (but not just they alone) saw Jews as competitors for limited opportunities in trade and the professions. The public believed business to be primarily in the hands of Jews, and it directed its discontent against them. A Hungarian peasant in debt, for example, knew well that in nine out of ten cases, his promissory note would fall "in the hands of a Jewish creditor."[26] The right-wing propaganda increasingly often identified Jews with interests and forces alien or even hostile to the nation or the state. There is much to indicate that the historian was right who observed that it was neither the Marxism of the left, nor the monarchist loyalism, but anti-Semitism that was the true, powerful, international ideology of the region.[27]

It is interesting that the opinion that Jews exercised vital control over the economy has filtered even into historiography. Such opinion, however, excessively general, represents a confounded and thus adulterated consciousness. Inasmuch as such opinion about Jews applied in a large measure to relations in Hungary, and much less to those in Czechoslovakia, it hardly corresponded with the facts at all in Bulgaria. In Poland, one can demonstrate that a mere fourteen of the country's industrial, financial, and landed oligarchs could be recognized as Jews (and this quite apart from how they themselves felt about it). Even if we assume that this number has been underestimated, it will still turn out that in Poland's big business Jews were in a decisive minority.[28]

To some extent, people also felt rancor against, for example, Germans in Poland and in Czechoslovakia or Hungarians in Romania. Needless to say, such feelings affected a particular line of economic nationalism, which was by various means tending toward "ethnicization" of capital, entrepreneurship, land, and other realty. The intensity with which these instruments were employed was conditioned by many factors, usually political (as noted earlier in the section on nostrification).

Hence economic nationalism as carried out in practice for some time deviated from the point the radical right was trying to carry. The accumulation of national (in the chauvinist meaning) assets was taking place at the expense of the minorities (of Jews in Poland, Romania, Hungary, Slovakia, the Czech regions following the Munich agreement; of Germans in the Baltic countries, Poland, and Czechoslovakia; of Byelorussians and Ukrainians in Poland; of Hungarians in Romania and Slovakia, and so on). It was only toward the end of the 1930s, however, that the governments' policies distinctly evolved toward totalitarianism. The authorities' attitude toward minorities was becoming increasingly hostile, perhaps the least so in Bulgaria. It became relatively easy to level out the differences between the respective governments' practice and the nationalists' demands concerning the Jewish minority. Particular countries differed, though, in the extent to which they identified national interest with the discrimination of Jews. For instance, Bulgaria, Czechoslovakia, and the Baltic countries did not officially express anti-Semitism in their respective legislation or economic policy.[29] Still, there was a difference between the qualified approval of representatives of a country's top authorities (e.g., the famous quotation from Premier Sławoj Składkowski: "Economic struggle—fine, but no violence [against Jews],")[30] and the legalized discrimination in Hungary and, to some extent, in Romania (and at the end of 1940 in Bulgaria).[31]

The degree of oppressiveness toward particular minorities differed. It was higher, for example, especially in the second half of the 1930s, toward Jews than Hungarians in Romania (out of fear of the spread of revisionist feelings among the latter). Sometimes minorities were almost not oppressed at all, as in the case of the Sudeten Germans in Czechoslovakia after February 1937. Sometimes minorities were even given special privileges—as Swabians in Hungary, around 1938, as a result of Hungary's having got into the Third Reich's sphere of influence.[32]

Wherever the German minority made up a substantial percentage of population, the host countries reckoned with them, although reluctantly. They did so because of this minority's ties, first, with the Weimar Republic and then with the Third Reich. The German minority in other countries became an instrument of German foreign policy, particularly useful after 1933.[33]

German organizations in Czechoslovakia, for example, frequently complained about being discriminated against economically. The conditions of working-class and petit-bourgeois families in the Sudetenland were indeed very difficult, as the Great Depression hit that area more severely than the Czech regions. The resulting frustration of the Sudeten Germans, combined with grievance and at the same time a sense of superiority, which fed on spite against Czechs and on pride in the growing importance of the Third Reich, produced the aggressive nationalist movement of Konrad Henlein. From 1935 or so, having backing from Berlin, the movement began increasingly boldly to dispute Czechoslovakia's integrity. The SdP Sudeten German Party used its electorate's complaints to struggle against the non-Nazi groups that had until the end of 1938, on the strength of the relevant 1925 agreement, been either members or supporters of coalition governments. In 1935 and 1936, the Third Reich, too, began to charge Czechoslovakia with ethnic discrimination. Despite Prague's efforts, the movement of non-Nazis was gradually losing influence. In the years 1937–1938 they found themselves in a pathetic minority among their fellow countrymen and facing complete disintegration.[34]

Sober historians indicate that what embittered Czechoslovak Germans could take for discrimination (e.g., job discrimination) often turned out on closer examination to be an effect of misinterpretation of facts, of inadequate information, or of the general economic situation of the Sudetenland.[35] Unfortunately, cases of ethnic discrimination practiced by Czech officials in the region were by no means unusual. Thus, for instance, the everyday interpretation of the law on the defense of the state, made in accordance with the instructions of Minister František Machnik, or the placement of government orders with and subsidies to enterprises according to the nationality of the owner, or the financing of public works routinely to the advantage of the Czechs justified complaints against the conduct of the Prague authorities.[36] The opinion seems irrefutable that the agreements signed with the non-Nazi groups among the Sudeten Germans in February and at the end of 1937 could have removed some of the reasons for the German complaints.[37]

The status of the German population in Poland was better than that of other minorities,[38] although in certain situations the government acted against the Germans. Polish Germans repeatedly appealed to Berlin, to the League of Nations, or to the international court in The Hague. The German minority regularly stressed the fact that Poland was not abiding by the minority treaty, which to all intents and purposes it renounced in 1934 anyway.[39] The Polish government acted against the German minority, for example, by the virtual nationalization of large heavy-industry and mining enterprises or by the steps taken as of mid-1938 to neutralize German economic influence. The Polish government restricted German firms' access to certain investment projects, speeded up the parceling of German estates, limited loans to German businesses, was very strict about taxes, and planned to sequester German citizens' shares in enterprises when official Polish-German relations began to deteriorate rapidly.[40] The relevant decisions should be seen, however, in the wider perspective of Poland's foreign policy. Polish decisionmakers could have doubts about the line that representatives of Germany's big capital would take in case of a conflict between the two countries. And yet in the 1930s Poland did not seriously back any anti-Nazi groups this way to offset the German minority's ill will. That was a result of the 1930–1938 foreign policy line, which ruled out any meaningful ventures toward this end.

In the 1930s the governments of Hungary, Romania, and to some extent Yugoslavia and the Baltic countries were quite effectively supporting the moderate cultural and political movements of the German population, particularly those acceptable to the Third Reich. However, in view of the patronage the Reich was giving to the minority, and of these countries' increasing economic dependence on trade with Germany, from around 1938 and 1939 the German minority in those countries began to enjoy a privileged status.

I believe, therefore, that despite the sometimes strong wording (particularly in the 1920s), East-Central Europe's policy of economic nationalism toward Germans was defensive in nature. Even if we accept the distinction between defensive, neutral, and aggressive types of economic nationalism, it is still difficult to answer the question of whether the extent to which the decisions of the late 1930s, related to the country's defense (development of the defense industry, raw materials reserves, etc.), reflected the country's economic nationalism at all. If our answer were in the affirmative, then we should say the same about the similar moves of, for example, Great Britain or France—which is not usually done.

The economic situation of the Hungarian minorities in Slovakia and Transylvania also constituted a problem, though of a lesser international importance. The Hungarian minorities in those two countries fared worse than before 1918. That was a result of the express policy of revindication launched by the governments of Czechoslovakia and Romania. Also Poles in Tesin were treated badly.

As a rule, the inward-oriented economic nationalism infringed upon the economic rights of minorities. Security reasons, that is, reasons of state or nation, were usually given as an explanation. Kazimierz Dziewanowski is one of those to have observed that such reasons often acted as a blunt screen for someone's appreciable practical interests.[41] In its extreme form, the inward-oriented nationalism served, first and foremost, a political game or mobilization. It directed national feelings toward issues often distant from the real economic, social, or political problems of the country. In a sense that was the reason behind the previously mentioned Hungarian anti-Jewish laws. They were used, for example, as instruments in the struggle for influence between the increasingly rightist governmental party and Ferenc Szálasi's extreme right. At the same time, those laws made an instrument of redistribution of national income and wealth.

Zbigniew Landau and Jerzy Tomaszewski give a sensible answer to the question about the true effects of inward-oriented economic nationalism with regard to the Jewish problem. They are of the opinion that to bar Jews from Poland's economic life at the time (considering the rigid immigration restrictions, land hunger, unemployment, etc.) would have not met the expectations. Instead it would have caused, for an unspecified period of time, a further decline in the already small domestic market.[42]

Extrapolating this opinion for the situation of other minorities, we observe that, whether lawfully or unlawfully discriminatory, in the short run inward-oriented economic nationalism constituted yet one more attempt at redistribution of national income and social wealth. (It is difficult to foresee the long-term effects of such discrimination.) Although this allowed the neutralization of the effect of certain internal social and economic difficulties, for a time at least, it did not solve the region's most important problems: to accelerate industrialization and to eliminate the endemic agrarian overpopulation.

Industry or Agriculture?

Until the 1930s industrialization was the strongest tenet of economic nationalism of the less developed countries of the region. The strategic reasons of the 1930s made them add self-sufficiency in food and/or in raw materials to their program. In order to achieve a certain level of self-sufficiency in food, those countries, particularly the backward ones among them, had to resort to protectionism. Nevertheless, it is not easy to sum up its effects.

In Czechoslovakia, for example, the general line of the policy of economic nationalism was a subject of perpetual controversies and bargaining. The disputing parties were primarily the proponents of self-sufficiency in food and of the development of the food industry (the Agrarians) and of further industrialization, based on the development of the processing and heavy industries, or at least on the full utilization of their capacities.[43] Among the advocates of the latter policy were political organizations representing otherwise conflicting interests, such as national democrats, social democrats, and communists. It is only at first sight that it seems odd to mention the Social Democratic Party and the Communist Party of Czechoslovakia (KSC) (or the Polish Socialist Party [PPS], the Communist Party of Poland [KPP], etc.) as advocates of nationalism. The socialist and communist movements' support for further industrialization meant that they were opting not merely for the development of local industry and the working classes but also for the protection of the urban labor market against foreign competition and, more generally, for a change in the international division of labor—that is, they were rejecting the classic Marxist view on that matter.[44]

Proponents of Czechoslovakia's further industrialization saw in it the only way to retain Czechoslovak industry's position on foreign markets and, indirectly, to resolve the country's economic and social problems. The economic policy's heading toward self-sufficiency in food reflected the strength of the Agrarians. It had a negative impact on Czechoslovakia's international standing, however. Still, it must be admitted that the country's stubborn and successful (e.g., in grain production) aspiring to semiautarky (as indicated by the import tariffs from 1924 and 1929 and by the change of the import taxes at the time of the Great Depression) had the positive effect of enforcing the modernization of industry and a change in its export directions.[45]

Poland sanctioned no option, neither that promoting industrialization nor that championing agriculture and the food-processing industry. Despite the protection given to industry by import restrictions and the increased import tariffs of the years 1924 and 1933,[46] businessmen com-

plained that the level of protection was too low.[47] The problem of self-sufficiency in food did not exist in Poland in the 1930s. It was the unex-
portable agricultural surplus that was the problem. In any event, the
proindustry policy was strengthened only under the four-year plan.[48]

In the case of Hungary, which lost a major part of its territory as a result of World War I, the argument that what was left of it had no real possibility of independent economic development is unconvincing. It could
be true only if by independent economic development one understood a
self-sufficient but utterly backward economy, capable of supplying the
domestic market only with absolutely basic goods and services. Hungary
was principally inclined to support the development of local industry.[49]
That development took place partly at the expense of rural economy. But
still, politicians tried to find a bigger and, at the end of the 1930s, a more
differentiated market for agricultural products. First, talks with Mussolini in Rome in 1934 brought an increase in Hungarian wheat exports
to Italy; then, from around 1935–1936, the country could increase its food
deliveries also to Germany, which gave local agriculture one more incentive to diversify.[50] Hungarians were spreading the slogan of self-reliance
in the entire interwar period,[51] and particularly from 1938. But the slogan
was put out to propagate internal policy aims rather than a conscious
economic concept.[52]

In the entire interwar period, save the short rule of Maniu's peasant
party (which tried to enact a proagrarian policy and encouraged foreign
competition in industry),[53] the popularity of economic nationalism allowed Romania to carry out its proindustrial policy at the expense of
peasants, that is, of nearly 80 percent of the country's population. Romania imposed, particularly in the second half of the 1930s, high industrial
import tariffs and bans[54] and provided numerous reliefs to local industry.[55] Both the tariffs and reliefs are believed to have been the most protectionist in the entire region.

Compared to Romania, Yugoslavia did not show such a strong inclination to industrialize. The Yugoslavs gave attention especially to the textile and leather industries. In the 1930s, specifically in response to the
economic expansion of Germany, Yugoslavia gave emphasis to the development of the raw-materials industry as well.[56] It did not, however, adopt
a more definite policy line in this respect.[57]

Except for the short rule of the Bulgarian Agrarian National Union,
Bulgaria, too, opted for further industrialization, even if primarily with
regard to the food, textile, and clothing industries.[58] Like other countries,
Bulgaria, too, introduced high import tariffs.[59] At the same time, in the
1930s, the country was carrying out, with some success, a policy not so
much of a protection of farming as of the farmer,[60] and also of a certain di-

versification of agricultural production.[61] It may be said about the Bulgarian policy of economic nationalism that it was better coordinated than in neighboring Romania and Hungary.

Generally auspicious economic and political circumstances in Lithuania, Latvia, and Estonia in the 1920s facilitated the finding of a balance between laying foundations of industry and the heeding of agricultural interests. In the 1930s they made a characteristic volte-face to give a decided preference to agriculture. The change was most remarkable in Latvia, followed by Estonia and Lithuania.[62] This is how the previously mentioned Baltic (and Bulgarian under Stamboliiysky) peculiarity of economic nationalism came into prominence. However, those countries adopted their peculiar line reckoning their economic ties with the Third Reich and with Great Britain.

Notes

1. See the Yugoslav constitutions of 1921, 1929, and 1931; that of Albania of 1928; and those of Romania of 1923 and 1938. The Portuguese constitution, prepared by Antonio Salazar himself, contained a similar entry; so did the relevant articles (directly referring to the Portuguese constitution) of the Brazilian constitutions of 1934 and 1937, which also provided for the nationalization of certain industries. In Estonia, a special law secured the nationalization of natural resources. See "Konstytucja Królestwa Serbów, Kroatów i Słoweńców," and "Konstytucja Rumunii," both in *Nowe konstytucje* (Warsaw, 1925), pp. 257, 334; Leszek Gembarzewski, "Nowe konstytucje (Jugosławia)," in *Biuletyn Urzędniczy*, no. 11-12, 1931, p. 10; "Konstytucja Portugalii," in *Biuletyn Urzędniczy*, no. 5-6, 1935, p. 8; "Konstytucja Albanii," in *Biuletyn Urzędniczy*, no. 3-4, 1939, p. 9; *Konstytucja Królestwa Rumunii z dnia 27 lutego 1938* (Warsaw, 1938), p. 13; E. B. Burns, *Nationalism in Brazil: A Historical Survey* (New York, 1968), p. 82; *Soviet Estonia* (Tallin, 1980), p. 138. See also G. Ránki and J. Tomaszewski, "The Role of the State in Industry, Banking and Trade," in M. C. Kaser, ed., *The Economic History of Eastern Europe, 1919–1975*, vol. 1, *Economic Structure and Performance Between the Two Wars* (Oxford, 1985); H. L. Roberts, *Rumania: Political Problems of an Agrarian State* (New Haven, 1951), p. 123.

2. See *Dejiny štatu a práva na území Československa v období kapitalizmu*, vol. 2, *1918–1945* (Bratislava, 1972), pp. 377–381. The law also included regulations that were aimed against German-owned property and against German ethnics.

3. In Romania, for example, the process of issuing licenses started from the four laws from 1924 concerning mining, the use of electric power, transport, and government monopolies. Their aim was to minimize foreign influence; they provided for a maximum 40 percent share of foreign capital in the industries mentioned. See Roberts, *Rumania*, p. 123; E. A. Radice, "General Characteristics of the Region Between the Wars," in Kaser, *Economic History*, p. 43.

4. See C. A. Macartney, *October Fifteenth: History of Modern Hungary, 1928–1945*, vol. 1 (Edinburgh, 1961), pp. 214–220, 324ff; Bélla Vago, *The Shadow of Swastika: The Rise of Fascism and Anti-Semitism in the Danube Basin, 1936–1939* (London,

1975); J. Rothschild, *East Central Europe Between Two World Wars* (Seattle and London, 1974), pp. 180, 197ff.; Halina Donath, *Przemiany ustrojowo-prawne na Węgrzech, 1939–1949* (Wrocław, 1978), pp. 45, 50–54; Václav Průcha, ed., *Historia gospodarcza Czechosłowacji* (Warsaw, 1979), pp. 137–139; Ezra Mendelsohn, *The Jews of East Central Europe Between the World Wars* (Bloomington, Ind., 1983), pp. 116, 120–122, 207–209.

5. That is why, for example, in Bulgaria, preference was given to enterprises employing, above all, Bulgarians. The new industrial law of 1928 was more restrictive, determining the percentage of Bulgarian experts to be employed in enterprises at 75 percent in the first five years and 100 percent from then on; the percentage of the operating personnel was to be 50 percent and 75 percent respectively, and the administrative staff was to be Bulgarian exclusively. The law of 1936 went even further. In Romania, the relevant laws from 1924 regarding enterprises using energy sources and also transport enterprises provided that 75 percent of their staff and two-thirds of their directors had to be Romanian citizens. However, the practical implementation of those laws depended on circumstances. It seems to have been more consistent in Romania, and less so in Bulgaria, where it seems improbable that the laws could have been observed strictly, mainly because of the shortage of skilled labor. See Dinko Toshev, *Industrialnata politika na Bŭlgariya sled Pvrvata svetovna voyna* (Varna, 1943), pp. 153ff.; Roberts, *Rumania*, p. 123. Mieczysław Grzyb, *Narodowościowo-polityczne aspekty przemian stosunków własnościowych i kadrowych w górnośląskim przemyśle w latach 1922–1939* (Katowice, 1978).

6. See Theodore E. Gregory, "Economic Nationalism," *International Affairs*, vol. X, no. 3, 1931, p. 289.

7. See, for example, L. Robbins, *The Great Depression* (London, 1934), chapters 2 and 3; B. C. Shafer, *Nationalism* (New Brunswick, 1954), p. 238.

8. In reference to Brazil, see Burns, *Nationalism*, p. 85.

9. The regulations adopted in Cuba and Brazil were extremely discriminatory in this respect. See Burns, *Nationalism*, p. 85; T. Łepkowski, ed., *Dzieje Ameryki Łacińskiej od schyłku epoki kolonialnej do czasów współczesnych*, vol. 3, *1930–1975/80* (Warsaw, 1983), p. 50; M. Kula, *Polonia brazylijska* (Warsaw, 1981), p. 186.

10. Especially agreements with Hungary, Finland, Poland, and Lithuania. See E. Kołodziej, *Wychodźstwo zarobkowe z Polski 1918–1939*, pp. 230–235; Alfred Svikis, "Stosunki agrarne na Łotwie w okresie międzywojennym (1918–1940)," *Roczniki Dziejów Społecznych i Gospodarczych*, vol. XL, 1979, p. 39.

11. See, for example, some Polish publications: P. Łossowski, "Problem mniejszości narodowych w Europie Środkowo-Wschodniej," in J. Żarnowski, ed., *"Ład wersalski" w Europie Środkowej* (Wrocław, Warsaw, Kraków, and Gdańsk, 1971); Maciej Koźmiński, "Mniejszości narodowe w basenie Dunaju a węgierski rewizjonizm terytorialny," in Żarnowski, *"Ład wersalski"*; Waldemar Michowicz, "Problem mniejszości narodowych," in Jan Tomicki, ed., *Polska Odrodzona 1918–1939* (Warsaw, 1982); J. Tomaszewski, "Kwestia narodowa w Rumunii w 1931 r. w raportach polskich konsulatów i poselstwa," *Studia z Dziejów ZSRR i Europy Środkowej*, vol. XX, 1984, pp. 187–208; J. Tomaszewski, "Kwestia narodowa w Jugosławii i Grecji w raportach polskich poselstw," *Studia z Dziejów ZSRR i Europy Środkowej*, vol. XXI, 1985, pp. 181–189.

12. Jan Kofman, *Lewiatan a podstawowe zagadnienia ekonomiczno-polityczne Drugiej Rzeczypospolitej. Z dziejów ideologii kół wielkokapitalistycznych w Polsce* (Warsaw, 1986), p. 126; Z. Landau and J. Tomaszewski, *Polska w Europie i świecie 1918–1939* (Warsaw, 1984), p. 218.

13. See E. Wiskemann, *Czechs and Germans* (London, 1967), pp. 129ff.; Stanisław Sierpowski, "Polityka mniejszościowa Niemiec w Lidze Narodów," in A. Czubiński, ed., *Rola mniejszości niemieckiej*, p. 49; P. Łossowski, *Po tej i tamtej stronie Niemna: Stosunki polsko-litewskie 1883–1939* (Warsaw, 1985), p. 210; Koźmiński, "Mniejszości narodowe."

14. Opinions on Alois Rašin and the effects of his economic policy are discordant. Wiskemann, *Czechs and Germans*, pp. 141–143, seems to provide a balanced judgment in this regard.

15. See the penetrating remarks by Wiskemann, *Czechs and Germans*, pp. 147–160. See also Lucy E. Textor, "Agriculture and Agrarian Reform," in Robert J. Kerner, ed., *Czechoslovakia* (Berkeley, 1945), pp. 226ff.; J. Ciepielewski et al., *Dzieje gospodarcze świata do roku 1980* (Warsaw, 1985), pp. 316–319.

16. Wiskemann, *Czechs and Germans*, pp. 140–146; J. César and B. Černý, "The Policy of German Activist Parties in Czechoslovakia, 1918–1938," in *Historica*, vol. VI, 1962, p. 249; Rudolf Olšovský et al., *Přehled hospodářského vývoje Československá v letech 1918–1945* (Prague, 1961), pp. 34, 81.

17. G. von Rauch, *The Baltic States: Estonia, Latvia, and Lithuania: The Years of Independence, 1917–1940* (Berkeley and Los Angeles, 1974), pp. 87–91; P. Łossowski, "Związek Niemców bałtyckich z państwem niemieckim, 1919–1940," in Czubiński, ed., *Rola mniejszości*, p. 138; Ránki and Tomaszewski, "The Role of the State," pp. 7–11.

18. Wiskemann, *Czechs and Germans*, pp. 166, 282; *Czechoslovak Cabinet Ministers on the Complaints of the Sudeten German Party in the Czechoslovak Parliament* (Prague, 1937), pp. 50ff. See also J. W. Bruegel, *Czechoslovakia Before Munich: The German Minority Problem and British Appeasement Policy* (Cambridge, 1973); Rothschild, *East Central Europe*, pp. 123ff.; F. Gregory Campbell, *Confrontation in Central Europe: Weimar Republic and Czechoslovakia* (Chicago, 1975), p. 259.

19. See "Notatka na temat aktualnej sytuacji mniejszości niemieckiej, 7 grudnia 1934," in *Archiwum Akt Nowych, Poselstwo RP w Pradze*, vol. 54, pp. 11–15. For a German position, see "The Economic Fate of the Sudeten Germans in the Czechoslovak Republic," in *Weekly Report of the German Institute for Business Research*, October 7, 1938, pp. 77–79.

20. Some researchers were suspicious of the transaction, as it was too profitable to the German owner (F. Flick). See Józef Popkiewicz and F. Ryszka, *Przemysł ciężki Górnego Śląska w gospodarce Polski międzywojennej (1922–1939)* (Opole, 1959), pp. 425–428. See also J. Gołębiowski, *Sektor państwowy w gospodarce Polski międzywojennej* (Warsaw and Kraków 1985), pp. 181–186.

21. Wiskemann, *Czechs and Germans*, pp. 64, 93–97; Campbell, *Confrontation in Central Europe*, pp. 48–52; Rothschild, *East Central Europe*, pp. 78–81.

22. On this aspect of nostrification, see the contributions by P. L. Cottrell, Eric Bussière, B. Michel, and F. Crouzet, in A. Teichova and P. L. Cottrell, eds., *International Business and Central Europe, 1918–1939* (New York, 1983), pp. 316–334, 399–407, 350–353, 411ff.

23. See, for example, H. A., Winkler, *Statistisches Handbuch der Europöischen Nationalitäten* (Vienna, 1931); H. Batowski, *Z polityki międzynarodowej XX wieku* (Kraków, 1979), pp. 167–171.

24. For the theoretical aspects of this problem, see E. B. Ayal, "Nationalist Ideology and Economic Development," *Human Organization*, vol. 25, no. 3 (1966). Regarding Poland, see, for example, Jacek Majchrowski, *Silni-zwarci-gotowi: Myśl polityczna Obozu Zjednoczenia Narodowego* (Warsaw, 1985). See also Macartney, *October Fifteenth*, pp. 211–216.

25. See J. Żarnowski, "Reżimy autorytarne w Europie Środkowej i Południowo-Wschodniej w okresie międzywojennym—analogie i różnice," in J. Żarnowski (ed.), *Dyktatury w Europie Środkowo-Wschodniej*, pp. 24–39; F. Ryszka, "Autorytaryzm i faszyzm: Wprowadzenie semantyczne," *Kwartalnik Historyczny*, vol. LXXIX, no. 2, 1972, pp. 322–344; Ryszka, *Państwo stanu wyjątkowego* (Wrocław, Warsaw, Kraków, Gdańsk, and Łódź, 1985), pp. 46–79.

26. C. A. Macartney and A. W. Palmer, *Independent Eastern Europe: A History* (London, 1962), p. 285. A different and more idealistic view emphasizing the peasants' indifference toward anti-Semitic slogans and an alleged uniqueness of Hungary was presented by Bernard Klein, "Hungarian Politics and the Jewish Question in the Interwar Period," in *Jewish Social Studies*, vol. XXVIII, no. 2, April 1966, p. 94. According to Klein, the poor Hungarian peasant was grateful to his Jewish neighbor for his loans. For more precise data concerning the employment structure and the situation of the Jews who were concentrated primarily in commerce and the professions, see Milan Hauner, "Human Resources," in Kaser, *Economic History*, pp. 75ff.; Mendelsohn, *The Jews of East Central Europe*; J. Żarnowski, *Społeczeństwo Drugiej Rzeczypospolitej 1918–1939* (Warsaw, 1973); J. Tomaszewski, *Rzeczpospolita wielu narodów* (Warsaw, 1985), pp. 151–166; *The Jews of Czechoslovakia: Historical Studies and Surveys*, vol. 1 (Philadelphia, 1968); I. T. Berend and G. Ránki, *Underdevelopment and Economic Growth: Studies in Hungarian Economic and Social History* (Budapest 1979), pp. 196–205; David Koen, "Demografsko i sotsialno-ikonomickesko polozheniye na bulgarskite evrei (1926–1946)," in *Prouchvaniya za istoriyata na evreyskoto naseleniye v bŭlgarskite zemi XV–XX vek* (Sofia, 1980), pp. 157–186.

27. Rothschild, *East Central Europe*, p. 10.

28. Klein, "Hungarian Politics," p. 82; W. O. McCagg, Jr., "Hungary's 'Feudalized' Bourgeoisie," *Journal of Modern History*, vol. 44, no. 1, 1972, pp. 75–78; Berend and Ránki, *Underdevelopment*, p. 195; Landau and Tomaszewski, *Druga Rzeczpospolita*, p. 158.

29. Mendelsohn, *The Jews of East Central Europe*.

30. *Sejm RP. IV kadencja. Sprawozdanie stenograficzne z 26 posiedzenia, z dnia 4 VI 1936*, col. 7; Andrzej Chojnowski, *Koncepcje polityki narodowościowej rządów polskich w latach 1926–1939* (Wrocław, 1979).

31. Vago, *The Shadow of the Swastika*; Mendelsohn, *The Jews of East Central Europe*, pp. 89–122, 174–208; N. M. Gelber, "Jewish Life in Bulgaria," *Jewish Social Studies*, vol. VIII, no. 2, April 1946, pp. 124–126; Stojan Rachev, "Borbata na bŭlgarskiya narod za spasyavane naevreite ot unishtozhovane prez Vtorata svetovna voyna (1939–1944)," in *Prouchvaniya*, pp. 188–192.

32. See Vago, *The Shadow of the Swastika*, pp. 22–52; Ottakar Kána, "Mniejszość niemiecka pod wodzą Konrada Henleina na ziemiach czeskich" and Leonard

Tilkovszky, "Irredenta niemiecka a Węgry," both in H. Batowski, ed., *Irredenta niemiecka*, pp. 89, 186–188.

33. Wiskemann, *Czechs and Germans*, chapter 15; Kána, "Mniejszość niemiecka," pp. 91–95; Andrzej Szefer, *Mniejszość niemiecka w Polsce i Czechosłowacji w latach 1933–1938* (Kraków-Katowice, 1967), pp. 185–192; A. Szefer, "Niemcy sudeccy jako narzędzie agresji przeciw Czechosłowacji," in Czubiński, ed., *Rola mniejszości*, p. 171; Rothschild, *East Central Europe*, pp. 129–132. See also Bruegel, *Czechoslovakia Before Munich*; J. César and B. Černý, *Politika nemeckých buržoaznich stran v Československu v letech 1918–1938*, vol. 2, *1930–1938* (Prague, 1962); H. Batowski, *Austria i Sudety 1919–1938* (Poznań, 1968).

34. See, for example, Szefer, "Niemcy sudeccy."

35. Wiskemann, *Czechs and Germans*; Bruegel, *Czechoslovakia Before Munich*.

36. The Foreign Office was receiving numerous reports from its legation in Prague concerning the economic situation of the Sudeten Germans. The reports were based primarily on information provided by German circles. In light of Czech counterarguments and later studies, the analysis of German charges showed their biased character, convenient for the policy of appeasement. See, for example, "Hadow to Eden, 23 March 1936," *Foreign Office 371/20373 R 69, c. 248;* "The German Minority in Czechoslovakia, 20 February 1936," *Foreign Office 371/20376 c. 90*, pp. 4–7. For the German position, see "The Economic Fate," p. 78. However, some of the German charges were justified, as demonstrated by the 1937–1938 agreement between activists and the Czechoslovak authorities. César and Černý, *Politika*, pp. 14–28, admit this indirectly in a very crabbed style. So does Campbell, *Confrontation in Central Europe*, p. 248. On the other hand, Chlebowczyk seems to subscribe to a more critical opinion. Quoted in Żarnowski, ed., *Dyktatury w Europie Środkowo-Wschodniej*, pp. 218ff.

37. Bruegel, *Czechoslovakia Before Munich*, pp. 148–150; Kána, "Mniejszość niemiecka," pp. 89ff.

38. S. Potocki, *Położenie mniejszości niemieckiej w Polsce 1918–1939*; Żarnowski, *Społeczeństwo*; Tomaszewski, "Konsekwencje wielonarodowościowej struktury Polski 1918–1939," in H. Zieliński, ed., *Drogi integracji społeczeństwa w Polsce XIX-XX w.* (Wrocław, 1976), pp. 115–117, 121–124, 133. Compare Hans Roos, *A History of Modern Poland* (London, 1966), pp. 134, 160.

39. Chojnowski, *Koncepcje polityki*, pp. 144, 165; Michowicz, "Problem mniejszości," pp. 342ff.

40. See Drozdowski, *Polityka gospodarcza rządu polskiego 1936–1939*, pp. 244, 284; Kofman, *Lewiatan*, p. 225.

41. Kazimierz Dziewanowski, "Kto płaci za rację stanu?" in *Przegląd Powszechny*, no. 12, 1985, pp. 426–430.

42. Landau and Tomaszewski, *Polska w Europie*, p. 70. Earlier similar arguments, supported by data analysis, were given by Wiktor Alter, *Antysemityzm gospodarczy w świetle cyfr* (Warsaw, 1937). The representatives of the Jewish minority pointed to the discriminatory character of the tax system. According to some estimates, in 1928 only 16 percent of the national income was generated in trade (in which Jews dominated), but more than 34 percent of all direct taxes were paid by merchants. See also Desider Kiss, "The Jews of Eastern Europe," *Foreign Affairs*, vol. 15, no. 2, January 1937, p. 332. Much higher estimates were

provided by Paweł Korzec, "Antisemitism in Poland as an Intellectual, Social, and Political Movement," in Joshua Fishman, ed., *Studies on Polish Jewry, 1919–1939* (New York, 1974), p. 70.

43. A. Gajanová, "Přispevek k objasněni přičin roztržasky v táboře česke buržoazie v roce 1934," ČČH, 1956, no. 4; Vojtek Mencl and Jarmila Menclová, "Náčrt podstaty a vývoje vrcholné sféry předmnichovske československe mocensko-politické struktury," *Československý Časopis Historický*, no. 3, 1968, pp. 357–362; Průcha, *Historia*, pp. 56–68; Vlastislav Lacina, *Velká hospodářská krize v Československu 1929–1934* (Prague, 1984).

44. Looking at this problem from a different angle, one should take into account the extreme dispersion of opinions qualifying a certain policy as economic nationalism. For instance, hardly anyone in Czechoslovakia would recognize the tendency to promote export expansion as a manifestation of unequal relationships, but that is how this tendency was perceived in Hungary and Yugoslavia. On the other hand, Czechs found harmful the policy of blocking their industrial goods access to their traditional markets along the Danube. These two examples show clearly the ambiguities built into the notion of economic nationalism. Also, they show the need to take the odium off of this notion wherever it is justified.

45. See Ludwig (Ladislav) K. Feierabend, "Agriculture in the First Republic of Czechoslovakia," in Miloslav Rechcigl, ed., *Czechoslovakia Past and Present*, vol. 1, *Political, International, Social, and Economic Aspects* (The Hague, 1968), pp. 177–180; Průcha, ed., *Historia*, p. 79.

46. Landau and Tomaszewski, *Gospodarka Polski międzywojennej 1918–1939*, vol. 2, *Od Grabskiego do Piłsudskiego 1924–1929*, pp. 272–274, 285; Landau and Tomaszewski, *Gospodarka Polski międzywojennej 1918–1939*, vol. 3, *Wielki kryzys 1930–1935*, pp. 360–363.

47. Kofman, *Lewiatan*.

48. Kofman, *Lewiatan*, pp. 122ff. See also Drozdowski, *Polityka*, chapter 3; Landau and Tomaszewski, *Zarys historii gospodarczej Polski 1918–1939* (Warsaw, 1981), pp. 255–266.

49. Leo Pasvolsky, *Economic Nationalism of the Danubian States* (London, 1928), pp. 361–371; A. Basch, *The New Economic Warfare* (New York, 1941), p. 27; Julius Rézler, "The Hungarian Manufacturing Industry," *Hungarian Quarterly*, vol. 1, no. 1, Summer 1941, pp. 322–334; Berend and Ránki, *Underdevelopment*, pp. 173–176, 181–186.

50. See Basch, *The Danube*, pp. 158–165; Z. Sládek and J. Tomaszewski, "Próby integracji ekonomicznej Europy Środkowej i Południowo-Wschodniej w latach trzydziestych XX w.," in *Śląski Kwartalnik Historyczny* "Sobótka," no. 3, 1979, p. 391.

51. At that time Pasvolsky, *Economic Nationalism*, p. 372, was sceptical about those plans. Compare Berend and Ránki, *Underdevelopment*, p. 173.

52. See Rézler, "The Hungarian Manufacturing Industry," pp. 322, 327.

53. Virgil Madgearu, "The New Economic Policy in Rumania," *International Affairs*, vol. IX, no. 1, 1930, pp. 90–92; Roberts, *Rumania*, pp. 164–166.

54. Roberts, *Rumania*, p. 121; H. Liepmann, *Tariff Levels and the Economic Unity of Europe* (London, 1938), p. 383; Iovanelli, *Industria Româneasca 1934–1938*, pp. 51–57.

55. Ránki and Tomaszewski, "The Role of the State," pp. 15ff., 18.

56. Ránki and Tomaszewski, "The Role of the State," pp. 14ff., 17, 37ff.; Liepmann, *Tariff Levels*, p. 383; Berend and Ránki, *Underdevelopment*, p. 274; Teichova, "Industry," in Kaser, *Economic History*, pp. 233, 236.

57. Mijo Mirković, *Ekonomska historija Jugoslavije* (Zagreb, 1968), p. 350.

58. Pasvolsky, *Bulgaria's Economic Position* (Washington, D.C., 1930), pp. 223. 234; L. Berov, *The Economic Development of Bulgaria Between the Two World Wars, 1918–1944* (Oxford, 1972), pp. 6–10; Żak Natan, Veseli Khadzhinikolov, and L. Berov, eds., *Ikonomikata na Bŭlgariya*, vol. 1 (Sofia, 1969), p. 581.

59. Natan et al., *Ikonomikata*, pp. 518, 538; Berov, *The Economic Development of Bulgaria*, pp. 7–10; Liepmann, *Tariff Levels*, p. 383.

60. Despite certain reservations, this is what results from Berov, "Direktsiya 'Khranoiznos' 1930–1949 g.," *Trudove na Visshiya ikonomicheski institut Karl Marks*, no. 1, 1960, pp. 275–371.

61. See Ludmila Zhivkova, "Kym vyprosa za ikonomicheskata ekspanziya na Germaniya v Bylgariya (1933–1939 g.)," in *Bŭlgarsko-germanski otnosheniya i vrŭzki: Izsledvaniya i materiali*, vol. 1 (Sofia, 1972), pp. 381–389.

62. Łossowski, *Kraje bałtyckie*, pp. 65–72, 201, 269–277.

4

Tentative Conclusions

The advocates of the traditional economic order—politicians, financial experts, and the economists educated according to the canon of neoclassical economy—were eager to discern in the spreading nationalism (and in economic interventionism as its manifestation) the cardinal cause of the adjustment difficulties of the mid-1920s, of the Great Depression and its long duration, and certainly of the financial crisis of the years 1931–1932.[1] Even, for example, T. Balogh, shortly to become a severe critic of the neoclassical concepts of international trade, was among the traditionalists at the time. In 1932 he pointed to interventionism as a crisis-generating factor. He saw in it a consequence of "political and economic nationalism [which] has led us to where we are now." He saw the solution in the restoration of the classical mechanisms of capitalist economy.[2] L. Robbins, a leading representative of the neoclassical school, used similar arguments.[3] In Italy in 1932, at one of the several conferences on the role of the state in the economy, Professor Virgil Madgearu, the outstanding Romanian economist and agrarian politician, referred to economic nationalism as "this new mercantilism" that causes production growth in all countries and in every industry with no regard to natural or social conditions.[4]

In some measure economic nationalism was also blamed for the suspension of international debt payment and for the withdrawal from the gold standard.[5] Such was the opinion voiced already in 1932, for example, by A. Salter, the Foreign Office's outstanding international finance expert, who referred primarily to the policy of Germany but of other East-Central European countries as well.[6]

It is difficult to accept such unequivocally negative opinion of the effects of economic nationalism[7] with reference to the policies of the countries of East-Central Europe. Despite the liberal and theoretical Marxist arguments, and also the opinion of some later researchers,[8] this nationalism did not in fact cause any serious harm to the European economy. The healthy demand for the growing industrial and agricultural production of the region (a large part of which was exported) facilitated the reconstruction of domestic markets. We can even suppose that had the new elements of economic activity not been there, the severe crisis that these countries allegedly aggravated would have hit them more violently than it in fact did. It was precisely industrialization and the development of the infrastructure in the 1920s that created the conditions in some of these countries that led to another takeoff at the end of the 1930s. In the 1930s it turned out that in the face of the flight of foreign investors, the endangerment of industrial production, and the sharp fall of prices for raw materials (for farm produce in particular, the export of which was these countries' main source of foreign exchange—indispensable to the repayment of loans and supply imports), and last but not least the dire balance-of-payments predicament, resorting to protectionism and restrictions was the only option. East-Central Europe was by no means an exception in this respect, as the richer countries followed suit (especially the United States, but also Great Britain, France, and, of course, Germany). It is the latter that had a decisive impact on the running down of the East-Central European economy and on the worldwide protraction of the crisis. (In this respect the charges that liberals leveled against protectionism and restrictions, stating that they had brought such effects, were perhaps more plausible.)

It must be noted here that thanks to the boom of the 1920s, the negative effect of high import barriers on growth in foreign trade was not particularly acute as far as trade within the region itself was concerned. For example, bilateral trade between the succession countries, although showing a dwindling trend, remained nevertheless at a relatively high level. Prior to World War I, bilateral trade between the Danube countries (within Austria-Hungary and beyond) amounted to two-thirds to three-quarters of their turnover, and in 1928 Austria's imports from the other succession countries reached 43 percent of its total imports, against exports of 40 percent of the total; in Czechoslovakia the figures were 24 percent and 35 percent respectively; in Yugoslavia 48 percent and 38 percent; in Poland 15 percent and 28 percent; in Romania 38 percent and 40 percent; and in Hungary 55 percent and 73 percent. The structure of that trade remained as yet basically unchanged. For instance, the industrialized Czechoslovakia and Austria consumed more than one-third of the Hungarian, Yugoslav, and Romanian grain exports.

Needless to say, in the following decade the situation changed. In 1937 the breakdown of those countries' trade was as follows: Austria imported 30 percent of foreign merchandise from the succession countries, directing 32 percent of its exports to them; in Czechoslovakia the figures were 18 percent and 21 percent respectively; in Yugoslavia 27 percent for both; in Poland 11 percent and 12 percent; in Romania 32 percent and 21 percent; and in Hungary 40 percent and 28 percent.[9] Exports of grain and food products from agrarian countries to Austria and Czechoslovakia dwindled markedly because of the latter countries' policy of protecting their own agriculture.

The Baltic countries had been plying new trade routes since the 1920s. From closer ties with the Russian market before World War I, they redirected their trade primarily toward the German and British markets, which in 1923 took over 46 percent of Estonian, 54 percent of Latvian, and 70 percent of Lithuanian exports (the Soviet market still absorbed about 7 percent of Estonian and 4 percent of Latvian exports). The trend gained momentum in the 1930s, with the significance of the Soviet market sinking even deeper. Sixty-five percent of total Estonian, 74 percent of Latvian, and 63 percent of Lithuanian exports went to the German and British markets (the figures for exports to the Soviet Union were 4 percent, 2.5 percent and 5.3 percent, respectively).[10] At the same time, bilateral trade between the Baltic countries and the other countries of the region was at a very low level in the years 1919–1939.

J. M. Montias attributes this general tendency in the region, and in the succession countries in the 1930s in particular, among other things, to the "beggar-my-neighbor policies adopted by the East European states toward each other," including tariff increases, discriminatory exchange controls, restrictive quota arrangements and export subsidies that "aggravated the crisis in the region as a whole."[11] If these methods—applied by each of these countries separately to retrieve its own situation—further aggravated the regional crisis, then they did so in proportion to their respective roles in the European economy and trade and to—and this must be emphasized—their respective share in that trade. Their share, as we have seen, kept dropping more or less distinctly, being thus conducive to a further weakening of mutual ties, already weakened as a result of structural economic and political changes.

To sum up, we may say that the East and Central European countries' share in causing and then aggravating the world crisis was in exact proportion to their respective economic power and significance on the financial market. However, East-Central Europe's small economic role, and effects of crisis (particularly the unfavorable terms of trade everywhere except Czechoslovakia) usually more painful than in the developed world,[12] made the countries of the region face difficulties greater than signified by various indices of their share in the world economy or in the European economy. But even the relevant indices, the size of individual domestic markets (usually very small, with the exception of Czechoslovakia and, to a lesser extent, Austria), financial weakness, and other characteristics (including total separation of urban and rural economies)[13] revealed the actual significance of the regional countries' economic policy as an element that aggravated the crisis.

Salter's forecasts that economic nationalism would have sprouted until carefully planned countermeasures were undertaken[14] proved accurate only in part. The time of economic nationalism was just approaching, Salter's optimistic prediction did not come true. The years 1935–1939 demonstrated that economic egoism (whether of the national or the state variety) was not overcome as a result of a concerted action and, moreover, that, despite some attempts, such action was never taken. The fact that the recommendations of the 1933 World Economic Conference were ignored made a spectacular but by no means a rare case of corroborating the current state of affairs.[15] Paradoxically, the return to the more-or-less normal international trade relationships took place as a result of resorting, particularly in the most industrialized countries, to unconventional methods of state intervention in the economy. Liberals would say that the sick organism was cured with medicines that had caused the sickness in the first place. The paradox inherent in this statement is only an apparent one, as it cannot be solved by neoclassical theories, to which Keynesian economics had given a severe albeit momentary blow.[16]

Crisis in the East-Central European region in the first half of the 1930s was merely a part of the world crisis, and therefore its overcoming depended only to a very small degree (and perhaps none at all) on the relaxation of the restrictions mentioned earlier. It must be noted that in each of the region's countries, Czechoslovakia included, resignation from restrictions would have only exacerbated their internal difficulties. Bertil Ohlin was thus right when he argued that the international impact of the region's policies of economic nationalism could not stand comparison with the negative effects of, for example, the neoprotectionism of the United States at the turn of the century.

Considering these arguments, it is obvious that protectionist policy, or that of economic nationalism in general, cannot be blamed for all the economic and social disasters that befell the region in the interwar period or recognized as one of the basic reasons for other economic perturbations. The policy of industrialized countries was of a much greater consequence in this respect.[17] Therefore I believe that the otherwise convenient opinions uttered in this vein can be interpreted as the industrialized countries' ambition to preserve the existing relations in the European economy, that is, to maintain the advanced countries' domination. At the same time, I cannot negate the goodwill of at least some of the economists and politicians representing the industrialized world who professed that a global free trade should urgently be restored. It is only free trade, they argued, referring to the famous principle of Ricardo, that could reduce or even eliminate disproportions and dysfunctions of growth. This principle, in their opinion, should enable the less developed countries in time to find within the international division of labor an advantageous place for themselves.

Notes

1. See, for example, League of Nations, *The World Economic Conference: Final Report* (Geneva, 1927), pp. 8ff.; L. Robbins, *The Great Depression* (London, 1934); F. Hertz, *The Economic Problem of Danubian States: A Study in Economic Nationalism* (London, 1947), pp. 53ff.

2. T. Balogh, "Some Theoretical Aspects of the Central European Credit and Transfer Crisis," *International Affairs*, vol. XI (1932), no. 3, pp. 345ff.

3. Robbins, *The Great Depression*, p. 62.

4. Virgil Madgearu, in *The State and Economic Life: First Study Conference (Milan, May 1932)* (Paris, 1932), p. 81.

5. See, for example, the study by the Royal Institute of International Affairs (RIIA), *Money Policy and Depression* (Oxford, 1933), p. 2; Ranger Nurske et al., *International Currency Experience: Lessons of the Inter-war Period* (Princeton, 1944), p. 192.

6. A. Salter, "The Future of Economic Nationalism," *Foreign Affairs*, vol. 11, no. 1, October 1932, p. 13. See also F. Zweig, *Zmierzch czy odrodzenie liberalizmu?* (Warsaw, 1980), p. 151.

7. Although prevalent, that was not the only opinion. For a dissenting view, see A. Basch, *A Price for Peace: The New Europe and World Markets* (New York, 1945), p. 20. Basch saw—correctly I believe—the world crisis and built-up armaments as the main causes of consolidation of economic nationalism, and not vice versa.

8. See, for example, Sidney Pollard, *European Economic Integration, 1815–1970* (London, 1974).

9. See J. Tomaszewski, "Związki gospodarcze państw sukcesyjnych a Polska," in Z. Landau and J. Tomaszewski, *Druga Rzeczpospolita Gospodarka—społeczeństwo—miejsce w świecie* (Warsaw, 1977), pp. 367–370; I. T. Berend and G. Ránki, *Economic Development in East-Central Europe in the 19th and 20th Centuries* (New York, 1974), p. 209; and A. Basch, *The Danube Basin and the German Economic Sphere* (London, 1944), p. 39.

10. *The Baltic States: A Survey of the Political and Economic Structure and the Foreign Relations of Estonia, Latvia, and Lithuania*, RIIA (London, 1938), pp. 125, 165.

11. J. M. Montias, "Economic Nationalism in Eastern Europe: Forty Years of Continuity and Change," *Journal of International Affairs*, vol. XX, no. 1, 1966, p. 61.

12. J. Ciepielewski et al., *Dzieje gospodarcze świata do roku 1980* (Warsaw, 1985), pp. 385ff. Czechoslovakia's terms of trade in the 1930s were very favorable (in the worst year, 1930, the ratio reached 1.07); Hungary's, Yugoslavia's, and Romania's terms of trade were unfavorable (0.78, 0.71, and 0.59, respectively, in the worst year, 1933). See Z. Drabek, "Foreign Trade Performance and Policy," in M. C. Kaser, ed., *The Economic History of Eastern Europe, 1919–1975*, vol. 1, *Economic*

Structure and Performance Between the Two Wars (Oxford, 1985), p. 469. The terms of trade for the Baltic countries were probably similar—although not as unfavorable as in the three Balkan countries—considering the similarity of the foreign trade structure there.

13. For Poland, see Z. Landau, "Hamulce rozwoju gospodarczego związane z dwusektorową strukturą gospodarki," in Z. Landau and J. Tomaszewski, *Druga Rzeczpospolita*, pp. 70–92; Jan Kofman, *Lewiatan a podstawowe zagadnienia ekonomiczno-polityczne Drugiej Rzeczypospolitej. Z dziejów ideologii kół wielkokapitalistycznych w Polsce* (Warsaw, 1986), pp. 159, 249. It is likely that a similar phenomenon occurred in other countries of southeastern Europe as well. See, for example, I. Vinski, *Klasna podjela stanovnistva i nacionalnog dohotka Jugoslavije v 1938* (Zagreb, 1970), p. 170.

14. Salter, "The Future of Economic Nationalism," p. 19.

15. Henry V. Hodson, *Slump and Recovery, 1929–1937* (London, 1938); Charles P. Kindleberger, *The World in Depression, 1929–1939* (London, 1973), pp. 205–220. See also Z. Landau and J. Tomaszewski, *Gospodarka Polski międzywojennej 1918–1939*, vol. 3, *Wielki kryzys 1930–1935* (Warsaw, 1982), pp. 354–360.

16. D. McCord Wright, *The Keynesian System* (New York, 1961); Lawrence R. Klein, *The Keynesian Revolution* (London, 1968); Robert Lekachman, *The Age of Keynes* (London 1967); Gottfried Bombach et al., eds., *Der Keynesianismus*, vol. 1 (Berlin and New York, 1976); Robert Skidelsky, ed., *The End of the Keynesian Era* (London, 1977).

17. This was clearly stated in the League of Nations *Report on Exchange Control* (Geneva, 1938), p. 6. The report blamed industrial countries for the policy of self-sufficiency in food production and for closing their markets to agricultural imports from countries of the region. That was the main reason that the latter maintained currency controls that undermined, as was then believed, the foundations of international trade.

PART 2

Protectionism as a Response to Underdevelopment

Part Two tackles the protectionist measures to which particular countries of the region resorted. It is my intention to show the protectionist tendency distinct in the economic and political thought, and in the region's economic policies, in the interwar period. I wish, moreover, to point out this tendency's most characteristic features. Reference will be made to the examples of several countries, and in particular to Bulgaria, Czechoslovakia, and Poland. The choice of the countries is not quite arbitrary. It is of course determined by the availability of source materials but also by the fact that the selected countries represented certain typical characteristics.

Thus Czechoslovakia was the region's only industrial-and-agricultural country (with Austria the second most developed state of this part of Europe). Poland was an agricultural country but of relatively many industrial potentialities. Particularly at the end of the 1930s its economy showed development capacities to build at some time in the future an economic structure like that of Czechoslovakia. To some degree Poland's economic level corresponded to those of Hungary, Latvia, and Estonia. However, the economic position of those small Baltic countries was better and economic restructuring clearer, even if—unlike Poland—they were emphasizing the development of agriculture and of the food industry, and the general standard of their population was higher, consequently making them closer to Austria and Bohemia.

Bulgaria, Lithuania, Yugoslavia, and Romania were underdeveloped agricultural countries. Greece was slightly better developed, whereas Albania was extremely backward economically, socially, and politically.

In terms of territorial size, Poland represented a large country in the region, Czechoslovakia was middle-sized (smaller than Romania or Yugoslavia), and Bulgaria, Austria, Greece, and Hungary were small. Geographically, Poland represented northeastern, Czechoslovakia central, and Bulgaria southeastern Europe.

5

On Protectionism's
Theory and Practice

All the different opinions on protectionism were based on the common thesis that in a world divided into and among states, the national economy was the fundamental economic structure.[1] This thesis allowed protectionism to be interpreted in three ways.

According to the first interpretation, the state was obliged not only to protect but also to develop the national economy according to protectionist criteria. Those criteria, for their part, were based on the use of all means possible to achieve these ends, and therefore they admitted justifications that went beyond the strictly economic sphere. The protectionism thus described was in point of fact an integral development ideology. Translated into practice, it made such a policy where economic calculation sometimes yielded to other reasons. I define this kind of protectionism as *strategic*.

According to the second interpretation, protectionism meant the objective of developing local production, in order to shield domestic manufacturers from foreign competition, and of supporting one's own foreign trade expansion.[2] Compared with the first interpretation, this would comprise a narrower, *tactical* kind of protectionism.

The third interpretation identified protectionism with the shielding of one's own industries with foreign trade restrictions (according to Królikowski, protectionism is intervention in foreign trade[3]). This kind of interventionism is thus traditional and merely *operational*.[4]

The first ("holistic") interpretation was prevalent among die-hard advocates of protectionism. The second option showed a pragmatic attitude characteristic of economic policy makers, regardless of their respective doctrine of choice. Willingly or unwillingly they had to acknowledge foreign competitors' influence on local manufactures and balance of payments. As for the third interpretation, the most popular at least until the Great Depression, a vast number of overt proponents of free trade adopted it. However, with the experience of the 1930s and 1940s, even liberals seldom referred to this narrowest, operational interpretation, preferring a somewhat wider one.[5] Those three model positions nevertheless assumed—even the third option implied it—that economic liberalism, particularly in relations between countries at different levels of development, was not always (or was not at all) advantageous to the less developed nations.

Strategic protectionism in no way restrained the resort to economic and other instruments (including planning) in order to affect the sought-after development of the national economy. If need be, it permitted the seeking of foreign aid, economic, financial, or technological. Moreover, it did not rule out measures reaching beyond even the most broadly understood sphere of economic policy (e.g., policies toward foreigners and minorities). Apart from classical methods, protectionism of this kind also used detailed import quotas and involved the state in activities of both current and structural nature (where etatism played a prominent part[6]). To be more precise, this kind of protectionism reached in the first place for economic policy instruments—that is, for the policy of foreign trade (including, next to traditional measures such as state monopoly and protective duties, also the newer ones, such as import and export bans and the related quantity restrictions), foreign exchange policy (particularly with regard to exchange rates and control over foreign exchange), and financial, tax, investment, and transport policies.

Pragmatic, tactical protectionism, for its part, approved of any of these methods. It chose them, however, on more rational grounds, even if under the protectionist option. Operational protectionism, in practice, did not go beyond the area of foreign trade. It reduced the protection of domestic manufacturing to the relatively limited indirect (e.g., through protective duties) and direct control (through quotas and subsidies).[7]

It is worth remembering here that the first to advocate tariff protection was Friedrich List, who argued that "infant industry" needed to be shielded from foreign competition. In keeping with numerous variants of List's concept, the state protects by means of tariffs the development of domestic manufactures against foreign competition until a given industry achieves maturity. This way the period of tariff protection in economic policy was meant to represent a transitional stage in the process of a developing country's joining the world economy on the basis of free trade. So much for the theory.[8] In practice, every country interested presented this sort of policy to the outside world as a defensive one for as long as it could,[9] meanwhile elongating the use of tariffs to protect its infant industries. Such a policy reflected the reluctance of industrial and sectoral interest groups to give up their current comfortable position.

What is more, it soon turned out that this form of protectionism did not confine itself to tariffs alone, although they were definitely its backbone.

Many countries went through the stage of protectionism. First were European nations less developed than Great Britain, such as France and Germany. Then, in the last two decades of the nineteenth century, Russia and Austria, and on other continents, the United States and Japan, followed suit.[10] Some countries of East-Central Europe did the same at the turn of the century.[11] Stirred by World War I, in the interwar decades, with the exception of the short period of prosperity in the years 1923/24–1929/30, capitalist countries returned to protectionism.[12] Such was also the pre-1928 policy of the Soviet Union, which then ushered in the stage of autarky. In the 1930s protectionism reached its highest point in the century. It was widely resorted to by countries of quite different productive potentialities. In industrialized countries at the time, protectionism was undergoing an interesting transformation: from a particularistic ideology and policy to more "universalized" forms. Great Britain, for example, by defending the pound sterling and the country's imperial links and by lifting restrictions in 1931, brought about the birth in the following year of the British Commonwealth of Nations and of the system of imperial preferences (which, in part, had already been given before). France, within its own colonial empire, behaved in a similar way, although on a smaller scale.[13] Additionally, industrialized countries heightened the protection of their respective agricultural production and professed their aspiration to become self-sufficient in food.[14] However, more important than economic reasons[15] to the development of this form of protectionism, related to the industrialized countries' entering the stage of intensified agricultural production, were reasons of ideological and political (pleading the need to protect peasants) as well as of military nature.[16] At the same time, there prevailed a tendency to enlarge the range of the protectionist instruments used. The governments concerned adduced either general economic and social necessities or reasons of state or the nation.

For a long time practitioners and theoreticians set the greatest store by protective duties. Yet the impact of such duties was and is in fact slight. Protective duties played a greater role only when (in the second half of the nineteenth century) international relations did not drive governments to introduce other forms of protection as well. In the 1930s the situation was of course different. Protective duties were even temporarily reduced to a sideshow because foreign competitors were always inclined to employ every means (dumping, production subsidies, tax reliefs, reimbursement of duties, etc.) only to be able to go beyond their own domestic market. On the other hand, to sustain domestic manufacturing required measures to stop competitive imports, that is, among other things,

to impose import quotas and bans, veterinary restrictions, foreign exchange controls, and to prohibit imports of substitutes.

At that time, especially the developed states used to speak reprovingly
about East-Central European countries' reaching for protective measures
in too demonstrative a way. Nevertheless, nearly every country ushering
in the capitalist stage of economic development resorted, at least for a
time, to protectionism, treating it as a means to mobilize internal resources. The thesis applies to underdeveloped countries in particular.
The studies by Arthur Lewis seem to prove the assertion that as a rule, at
a certain stage of their respective development, when entering the level
of modernization and desiring to catch up with the more developed nations, willingly or unwillingly these countries resort to protectionism—
for better or for worse. Before Lewis, W. Röpke spoke in the same tone.[17]
   The protectionism of the less developed countries invariably met with
the opposition of the industrialized nations, which feared that industrial
development of the nations supplying food and raw materials would
check the process of the extension of the world market and endanger the
current division of labor.
   The origins of this opposition can be traced back to the second half of
the nineteenth century, when Great Britain thus reacted to the protectionism of Germany and France. It reappeared at the turn of the century, this
time in Germany, which was apprehensive of the industrial development
of the United States, Italy, and Eastern Europe, and in Great Britain,
which was once again alarmed by the protectionism-based economic expansion of Germany.[18] Then again, in the interwar period economists and
politicians of the more developed countries showed bias against those
nations of the region that, aspiring to industrialization, reached for protectionist methods.[19]
   The 1930s proved, however, that the resort to protectionism was based
on partly wrong assumptions and calculations. The reality of the world
economy was so complicated that the prescriptions of numerous neoclassical economists (which in fact were leading to the petrifaction of the existing economic structure) were of little value. What is more, it was impossible to observe them strictly even in one country, let alone on the
international scale. J. M. Keynes, J. Robinson, and W. Röpke understood
that very well. Arrivals and emigrants from Eastern Europe before and
during World War II, T. Balogh, Oszkár Jászi, David Mitrany, Paul N.
Rosenstein-Rodan, K. Polanyi, Kurt Mandelbaum, Michał Kalecki, and
Henryk Tennenbaum among them,[20] must have also exerted a great influence on the change of their colleagues' position. All of them argued that
economic development (resorting to protectionism), and especially the
growth of industry in backward countries, not only did not check the

global-scale integration processes but also led in the long run to a greater complexity (and thus progress) of the international division of labor and to a greater volume of world trade. Their view was corroborated by economic transformations following World War II, by statistical and economic research, and by economic theory.[21]

Therefore it is no surprise to anyone that more often than not it was representatives of the countries only entering upon the path of economic growth who pressed theoretical arguments for protectionism. This way both the protectionist ideology and economic thought (whose origins could be traced back to mercantilism[22]) chronologically were a reaction, first, to classical conceptions, and, next, to neoclassical ones. As a result of the expansion of the ideology of economic nationalism in the twentieth century, the rising protectionism got a new impetus and a theoretical basis. Such countries as Bulgaria, Yugoslavia, and Hungary adduced economic and political ideas implemented in Italy and the Third Reich. In the interwar period, particularly in its second decade, supporters of pure liberalism were on the defensive among economic policy makers. The reverse was true of the academic economic profession. However, in the 1930s a new school became popular, associated with the name of Keynes, which argued for the rationality of resorting under certain circumstances to protectionism as a special economic policy.[23] M. Manoilescu came up with a separate and original theoretical proposal that went down well in the region.[24] Although ignored by the academics of the time, his concept (which I discuss in greater detail later) can today be recognized as the precursor of the dependency theories, so popular in the 1960s to the 1980s.[25]

The argumentation for protectionism—going back, it is worth remembering here, to the Fichtean concept of *der geschlossene Handelsstaat*, to Hamilton's considerations, to the concept of List, who was recognized as the author of the first developed theory of protection, to Carey, and then to the theses of the younger German historical school, and last but not least to the theories of Josef Grunzel and of Manoilescu[26]—encountered criticism primarily from representatives of academic economics as eminent as Jacob Viner and Gottfried von Haberler.[27]

Besides adducing the need to protect national sovereignty and to lay the foundations for one's own independence, including economic independence, all sorts of economic and social justifications for protectionism were and are put forward, for example: the argument of the terms of trade, entailing countervailing (i.e. "just")[28] and optimum duties;[29] the already mentioned Listian argument of infant industry or educational protectionism, which is modernized as the times goes by;[30] the argument of protection aimed at attracting foreign capital or creating a domestic market; the argument for the diversification of production or for the second-best policies; and the argument for the redistribution of income on behalf of specific groups of interests and social strata.[31]

Keynes promulgated one of the most forceful arguments for protective duties. He maintained that, if properly employed, they could help to fight unemployment in a given country. It seems nevertheless that even this aspect of protective duties lost much of its weight in the years of Great Depression. The selfish beggar-my-neighbor policy (based on, e.g., dumping or protective duties) could be of advantage (at least for a short time) but at the expense of the country against which it was aimed.[32] Of course, retaliation in the form of, for example, offensive duties was a virtually routine reaction of the target country. This way the fine effect of protective duties on the economy was offset by the moves of the opponent party. For various reasons, including the fight against unemployment, encouraging investments was a better solution.[33] Unfortunately, the investment argument could hardly apply to the countries of the region (with the notable exception of Czechoslovakia and, to some extent, Austria) because of the scarcity of capital they could lay out, particularly in the 1930s.[34] Thus there remained nothing for them to do but to create an inflationary demand, on the condition, however, that in their economic policy they abandon the dogmas of classical economy. In some countries this did indeed take place but only at the end of the 1930s, and this on too small a scale.

In short, the crux of the changes lay in the increasingly strong inclination to hinder market-based price formation and in the desire to cut off domestic from world prices. In consequence, it allowed domestic demand to be boosted largely independently of the situation in the world market. In the 1930s the measures that led to this were first and foremost foreign exchange controls (suspension of payments included) and goods rationing, supplemented by compensatory and clearing transactions. The majority of the East-Central European countries were sooner or later compelled to resort to such methods.

Since World War II the arguments for protectionism have gained in sophistication. Theoretically, they have been substantially enriched by the political economy of the underdeveloped countries. The list of academic contributors in economics includes Harry Gordon Johnson, Warner M. Corden, and Béla Balassa, who lay greater emphasis on replacing the protection of development traditionally based on import substitution by supporting development based on export expansion.[35] Protectionists usually underestimate traditional exports or treat them as a preservative of the old economic structure. The former group of economists recognize exports (and new industries built with the idea of exports in mind) as an equally important element of the development strategy[36] (more on this subject in Chapter 8). In any case, today even the numerous advocates of economic liberalism incline toward the opinion that protectionism has its advantages, and therefore it can be appealing to underdeveloped countries.[37]

To understand the position of the economic and political elites of the region with regard to protectionism, it is worthwhile to become at least cursorily acquainted with the work of Manoilescu, first and foremost with his most famous work, *The Theory of Protection*. His work did not appear out of the blue. It constituted a link in the chain of arguments whose origins could be traced back to the epoch of mercantilism; indeed, protectionist trade had already had a long tradition in Romania.[38] It was the ambition of this Romanian politician and economist to devise a rational system that would justify the necessity of protectionism. Manoilescu's book is a treatise on the fringes of economics, politics, and social thought. His study imparts also an important ideological message, which can be summed up as follows:

For various reasons, none of the earlier attempts to develop a consistent theory of protectionism met expectations. Even the List's work was far from perfect, either in its purely economic or—although Manoilescu himself did not mention this attribute—its ideological part. As Manoilescu saw it, List's mistake lay in his recognition of protectionism as a necessary evil; List did not oppose the free-trade idea and in fact did not even question its rightness. What is more, List limited the use of protectionism to certain countries only, and this to certain epochs of their respective development. In protectionism he saw merely a period of transition. Manoilescu attributed this view to List's excessive attachment to the idea of infant-industry protection. Indeed, Lists's expectation that protective duties (to which he reduced protectionism), initially amounting to 40–60 percent, then to 20–30 percent, would be lifted once a given industry reached maturity was groundless, for at least two reasons: First, it never happened that protected industrialists decided of their own accord that it was time to give up the protection they enjoyed; and second, there were never any logical premises for recognizing the level of any specific duty as satisfactory (which boils down to the question, Why should the duties amount to 20–30 percent and not, for instance, to 60 percent of the good's worth?). We can therefore assume that in the opinion of the Romanian economist, the arguments of the founding father of the theory of protectionism were simply unconvincing and not without obvious errors. Moreover, in the eyes of Manoilescu, List committed not only an error but a downright sin by admitting that protectionism was necessary only in a limited time and territory under a specific political regime. He was thus an advocate of protectionism one might describe as defensive.

However, Manoilescu's historical and economic analysis of economic development led him to believe that, particularly when capitalism was developing, protectionism was the only instrument that would allow a backward country to catch up with the countries economically more advanced. The gist of Manoilescu's concept was the thesis that agricultural productivity was much lower than industrial productivity. Manoilescu tried to question Ricardo's analysis in its main point, that of comparative costs,[39] in the belief that it would take several centuries before agricultural productivity could approximate industrial productivity (p. 148). The resulting conclusion was as follows: The preservation by free trade of the present status of the agricultural countries is tantamount to keeping them for ever in the position of poor clients of the large industrialized countries (p. 208). Thus industrialization is the only chance such countries have to extricate themselves from underdevelopment. Industrialization is a prerequisite for the raising of productivity, which is possible only if the policy of protectionism is adopted. The undeveloped country must resort to protectionism if it does not want to remain forever a supplier of cheap raw materials and agricultural produce for the industrialized world. Only when the presently underdeveloped countries finally achieve an adequately high level of industrial development will they give up the use of protectionist measures.

The guiding principle of Manoilescu's theory was the belief that protectionism was favorable to the aspiration toward a new international division of labor, one based on the harmony of the developed local industries (p. 213).[40] Yet such harmony was unattainable within the system of generalized protection. Therefore protection would be extended only to those industries whose productivity exceeded the national average. A new global-scale international division of labor would result only from a "longer evolution" as a consequence of all countries of the world having taken effective measures on behalf of industrialization. Then global economic cooperation would no longer be an empty term masking mutual exploitation (p. 214). So much for the projecting part of Manoilescu's conception.

To support his theory, Manoilescu referred to statistics. He argued, correctly, that the largest importers of industrial goods were always the industrialized countries (p. xvi). Although slowly, this opinion gained economists' recognition. Earlier, for example, in 1927, the Polish delegate Hipolit Gliwic had made similar observations before the International Economic Conference.[41]

Manoilescu believed that the full satisfaction of the needs of the internal market in the developed countries inclined them to increase industrial imports (p. 204). Thus he emphasized, for example, that Europe's most important customer in 1913 was, as always, Europe. That meant that the industrialization of agricultural countries made international trade flourish. He concluded that those countries' adoption of the way of protectionism would, as a result, make them dependent on one another and would not lead them to autarky (p. 211).

However, Manoilescu underestimated the potential role of foreign trade as a factor of economic growth. He assumed that the share of international trade in world output would tend to fall. In the light of the prewar statistical data, his view seemed to be justified. Earlier, Werner Sombart had already put forward theoretical arguments in support of such a view.[42] For Manoilescu it was convenient to accept them inasmuch as this allowed him to refer (tautologically) to those data as the confirmation of an even wider tendency. As regards Sombart's idea, it took the dynamic development of international trade after World War II to reject it firmly.

Manoilescu, for his part, attempted to fully rehabilitate protectionism. One cannot help observing that his arguments were permeated with a peculiar economic metaphysics. He wrote that the role of protectionism should never disappear; in a world divided into rivaling countries, it should always be there. Although according to the advocates of free trade protectionism had no legitimacy apart from the license to represent the point of view of the public, from the economic point of view protectionism was legitimate while it was reduced by the public, Manoilescu argued (p. 143).

It must be emphasized here that economic development as Manoilescu saw it inevitably took for granted a very active role for the state—and he was very well aware of that. But then, he saw that role (he changed his mind several years later) not so much as the state's acting as direct producer (etatism) but as an "agent" indirectly creating conditions favorable to industrialization, and to *local* industrial capital in particular. It would be agriculture that would bear the cost of economic development thus conceived. Manoilescu hoped at the same time that in the country entering upon the path of development it would be feasible to neutralize the influence of the interests of European powers (furthered by definite political or economic circles). He foresaw vital importance for the state bureaucracy, experts, and managers in the further encouraging of transformations. Let me add here that in its central point, the concept Manoilescu meant to apply also to Romania was shortly questioned. It soon turned out that it was impossible to squeeze enough money from peasants, and from the agricultural sector in general, to allocate to industrialization,[43] to unsettle the superiority of German interests (which decided Romania's foreign trade structure, particularly at the end of the 1930s), or to smash the current party rule system. In those circumstances, Manoilescu's conception did not stand any chance of implementation.[44]

As mentioned in Chapter 1, Manoilescu's theory called forth a response especially among industrial circles and economic ideologues in East-Central Europe (e.g., in Poland, Bulgaria, and Hungary) and in

Latin America. To economic circles it appeared to provide a scientific confirmation of their common opinion and, above all, a proof of the validity of their demand that the economic policy of the government protect domestic manufacturers.

It was, however, a peculiar and very selective understanding of Manoilescu's philosophy. On a speculative note, one may still say that in certain East-Central European countries, proponents of industrialization would underwrite, if not the whole, then at least significant parts of Manoilescu's theory. In Poland, for example, advocates of etatism would welcome his arguments about the role the state should play in development; and to the supporters of Lewiatan, especially reassuring would be the part that stressed the importance of industrialization carried out by the local private sector. Likewise, it would be in Bulgaria where the well-known economist Konstantin Bobchev exalted the advantages of protectionism to the country's economy.[45] The absence of any wider interest in similar concepts in the Baltic countries is not surprising, as these countries chose a different path of development. In Latin America Manoilescu's theory was well received because spokesmen for local industrial groups (to be precise, for some of their factions) saw in it a convenient tool to be used in both their internal struggles (with agricultural circles and with those interested in traditional exports) and their external struggles (with foreign capital).[46]

The distinguished economists of the time either did not know Manoilescu's conception or passed it over in a cutting silence. Only Jacob Viner bothered to openly express his disapproval, from the neoclassical position denying any worth to Manoilescu's works. The notice by Bertil Ohlin and, a decade later, a review by the rising international scientific star Michał Kalecki were among the exceptions. Ohlin, although critical, proposed a discussion on Manoilescu's theory. Kalecki, unlike his predecessors, brought into relief its merits as well its errors, which were obvious in his opinion.[47] Then Röpke, even though he did not analyze Manoilescu's theory (knowing his views, one can imagine that he would explode it), stressed and understood the significance of the social conditions and the climate that made the theory acceptable to agricultural countries.[48] Needless to say, Third Reich economists accepted Manoilescu's proposals for quite different reasons.

Even after World War II, the acclaimed French theoretician Maurice Byé oversimplified Manoilescu's position (alleging that he recommended industrialization as an aim in itself, believing that since industry employed large numbers of people, it was particularly productive) to reject it as incompatible with the rule of "factors proportions."[49] At this point, it is worth remembering that (1) Manoilescu considered the question of industrialization from the perspective of the backward agricultural country, and (2) he emphasized that it was necessary for the underdeveloped country to achieve a certain economic level so that the principle of comparative costs could sensibly operate there. All in all, however, the assessment of the work of the Romanian theoretician changed, no doubt influenced by the experience of the Great Depression and the war economy. One can even speak about a certain rehabilitation of his views, at least in the eyes of some of the members of academic community.[50]

Notes

1. See Josef Grunzel, *Economic Protectionism* (Oxford, 1916), pp. 17ff. Grunzel, a supporter of protectionist measures, referred to the ideas of the younger German historical school. For Poland, see Stanisław Głąbiński, *Ekonomika narodowa: Teoria ekonomiki narodowej* (Lwów, 1927), pp. 10ff.

2. See the descriptive definitions given by Andrzej J. Klawe and Antoni Makać, *Zarys międzynarodowych stosunków ekonomicznych* (Warsaw, 1977), p. 259, and W. M. Corden, "International Trade Controls: Tariffs and Protectionism," in *International Encyclopedia of the Social Sciences*, vol. 8 (Chicago, 1968), p. 113.

3. Stefan F. Królikowski, *Zarys polskiej polityki handlowej* (Warsaw, 1938), p. 88. For the distinction between tactical and operational ("narrow") protectionism, see Corden, "Tariffs," p. 113.

4. See Grunzel, *Economic Protectionism*, p. 125; Głąbiński, *Ekonomika narodowa*, p. 11.

5. See Górski, "Protekcjonizm," in *Mała encyklopedia ekonomiczna* (Warsaw, 1958), p. 579.

6. For Poland, see Królikowski, *Zarys*, and A. Heydel et al., *Etatyzm w Polsce* (Kraków, 1932). For other countries, see F. Machlup, *A History of Thought on Economic Integration* (London, 1977).

7. See Maurice Byé, "Międzynarodowa polityka handlowa, jej skutki i założenia," in Zbigniew Kamecki and Józef Sołdaczuk, eds., *Teoria i polityka handlu międzynarodowego w kapitalizmie* (Warsaw, 1960), p. 431.

8. See M. A. Heilperin, *Studies in Economic Nationalism* (Geneva and Paris, 1960). In the Polish literature, see Edward Lipiński, *Historia powszechnej myśli ekonomicznej do roku 1870* (Warsaw, 1968).

9. Interpreting it as *Erziehungszölle* or *Erhaltungszölle* protectionism. See Królikowski, *Zarys*, pp. 11, 118.

10. See J. Ciepielewski et al., *Dzieje gospodarcze świata do roku 1980* (Warsaw, 1985); E. Kaczyńska and K. Piesowicz, *Wykłady z powszechnej historii gospodarczej* (Warsaw, 1977).

11. L. Pasvolsky, *Economic Nationalism of the Danubian States* (London 1928); N. Spulber, *The State and Economic Development in Eastern Europe* (New York, 1966); A. Gerschenkron, *Economic Backwardness in Historical Perspective* (London, 1976); John R. Lampe and Marwin R. Jackson, *Balkan Economic History, 1550–1950: From Imperial Borderlands to Developing Nations* (Bloomington, Ind., 1982); M. Mirković, *Ekonomska historija Jugoslavije* (Zagreb, 1968); Z. Natan, V. Khadzhinikolov, and L. Berov, eds., *Ikonomikata na Bŭlgariya*, vol. 1.

12. See the expanded edition of Albert O. Hirschman, *National Power and the Structure of Foreign Trade* (Berkeley, 1980). See especially "Appendix II: Resolutions of the Paris Economic Conference of the Allies, June 1916."

13. See A. G. Kenwood and A. L. Lougheed, *The Growth of the International Economy, 1820–1960*, pp. 216, 218ff.

14. For example, Great Britain and Germany. See J. P. Maxton, "Planning Measures for the Protection of British Agriculture," in *Proceedings of the Third International Conference of Agricultural Economics* (London, 1935), pp. 40–46; H. Zörner, "Agriculture in Germany," in *Third International Conference*; Z. Drabek, "Foreign Trade Performance and Policy," in M. C. Kaser, ed., *The Economic History of Eastern Europe, 1919–1975*, vol. 1, *Economic Structure and Performance Between the Two Wars* (Oxford, 1985), pp. 438–440. In the years 1929–1934, the duties levied on grain increased nine times in Germany and five times in France and Czechoslovakia. See Klara Romanow-Bobińska, "Związki gospodarcze Europy Południowo-Wschodniej okresu międzywojennego," in A. Czubiński, ed., *Państwa bałkańskie w polityce imperializmu niemieckiego w latach 1871–1945* (Poznań, 1982), p. 169.

15. Arguments employed in Germany and Great Britain were presented in *Commercial Policy in the Interwar Period: International Proposals and National Policies*, League of Nations (Geneva, 1942), pp. 125, 162, and Królikowski, *Zarys*, p. 118. The Méline Law from 1892 was referred to in justifying the French agricultural protectionism. See *The State and Economic Life: First Study Conference (Milan, May 1932)* (Paris, 1932), pp. 40–47.

16. W. Röpke, *International Economic Disintegration* (London, 1942), parts III and IV.

17. Röpke, *International Economic Disintegration*; W. A. Lewis, *The Theory of Economic Growth* (London, 1956) and *Growth and Fluctuations, 1870–1913* (London, 1978). See also S. Pollard, *Peaceful Conquest: The Industrialization of Europe, 1760–1970* (Oxford, 1981), pp. 258–261; Pollard, however, emphasized a negative influence of protectionism on industrialization.

18. See Alfred Maizels, *Growth and Trade* (Cambridge, 1970), pp. 2–4; Hirschman, *National Power*, pp. 55–80, 146–148.

19. See *The World Economic Conference: Final Report*, League of Nations (Geneva, 1927); *International Economic Conference (Geneva, May 1927): Principal Features and Problems of the World Economic Position from the Point of View of the Different Countries*, League of Nations (Geneva, 1927); *Commercial Policy*, League of Nations, chapter 4; Hirschman, *National Power*, p. 86. The connection between the postwar crisis and the industrialization of backward countries in Europe and other continents was emphasized in *Commercial Policy*, League of Nations, and in M. Manoilescu, *The Theory of Protection and International Trade* (London, 1931), p. 216.

20. Helmut W. Arndt, "Development Economics Before 1945," in Jagdish Bhagwati and Richard S. Eckaus, eds., *Development and Planning: Essays in Honour of Paul Rosenstein-Rodan* (Cambridge, Mass., 1973), pp. 27–29, and H. G. Johnson, "The Ideology of Economic Policy in the New States," in H. G. Johnson, ed., *Economic Nationalism in Old and New States* (London 1968), p. 131ff.

21. Röpke, *International Economic Disintegration*, pp. 153–186; Lewis, *Growth and Fluctuations*; Folke Hilgerdt, *Industrialization and Foreign Trade* (Geneva, 1945), chapter 7; Maizels, *Growth and Trade*; Ingvar Svennilson, *Growth and Stagnation in the European Economy* (Geneva, 1954), pp. 24–26. For the interesting discussion

among neo-Marxists (Emmanuel, Amin, Frank, Wallerstein, and others) and the first generation of dependency economists (Furtado, Prebisch, Hirschman), see also T. Szentes, *Theories of World Capitalist Economy* (Budapest, 1985).

22. See Eli F. Heckscher, *Mercantilism* (London, 1955); Machlup, *A History*.

23. Keynes, *The General Theory of Employment, Interest, and Money* (London, 1936); A. G. B. Fisher, *Self-Sufficiency* (London, 1939).

24. On his political ideas concerning corporatism, see A. C. Janos, "Modernization and Decay in Historical Perspective: The Case of Romania," and P. C. Schmitter, "Reflections on Mihail Manoilescu and the Political Consequences of Delayed-Dependent Development on the Periphery of Western Europe," both in K. Jowitt, ed., *Social Change in Romania 1860–1940: A Debate on Development in European Nations* (Berkeley 1978).

25. See Janos, "Modernization and Decay," p. 103ff.

26. For a review of these concepts, see Tommy Munk, *Le débat sur le libre échange et le protectionnisme à la lumière des structures nationales* (Geneva, 1953); Heilperin, *Economic Nationalism*; Y. S. Brenner, *Theories on Economic Development and Growth* (London, 1966); Machlup, *A History*; H. Szlajfer, "Economic Nationalism of the Peripheries as a Research Problem," in H. Szlajfer, ed., *Essays on Economic Nationalism in East-Central Europe and South America, 1918–1939* (Geneva, 1990), pp. 57–59.

27. See Jacob Viner, *Studies in the Theory of International Trade* (New York, 1937); Gottfried Haberler, *The International Trade* (Edinburgh, 1936), and also works by Robbins, Paul A. Samuelson, and Ludwig von Mises.

28. *The Tariff and Its History* (Washington, D.C., 1934).

29. See Béla Balassa et al., *Development Strategies in Semi-industrial Economies* (Baltimore, 1984).

30. See W. M. Corden, *The Theory of Protection* (Oxford, 1961); Johnson, "International Trade: Theory," in *International Encyclopedia*, p. 84.

31. See *The Tariff and Its History*, pp. 4, 94, and arguments by Wolfgang F. Stolper and Samuelson from 1941, and Barbara Kisiel-Łowczyc, *Protekcjonizm w handlu zagranicznym w teorii i historii myśli ekonomicznej: Przyczynek do analizy polityki handlowej rozwiniętych krajów kapitalistycznych* (Gdańsk, 1974), p. 119.

32. Keynes, *General Theory*, chapter 23. See also Joan Robinson, *Introduction to the Theory of Employment* (Cambridge 1937), chapter 11, and "Beggar-my-Neighbour Remedies for Unemployment," in *Essays in the Theory of Employment* (London 1937).

33. Keynes, *General Theory*.

34. V. N. Bandera, *Foreign Capital as an Instrument of National Economic Policy: A Study Based on the Experience of East European Countries Between the World Wars* (The Hague, 1964), chapter 6. For statistical data, see R. Nötel, "International Capital Movements and Finance in Eastern Europe, 1919–1949," *Vierteljahrschrift für Sozial- und Wirtschaftsgeschichte*, vol. 61, no. 1, 1975.

35. Corden, *Theory of Protection*; Balassa, *Development Strategies*; H. G. Johnson, "An Economic Theory of Protectionism, Tariff Bargaining, and the Formation of Custom Unions," *Journal of Political Economy*, vol. 73, June 1965.

36. See Gerard M. Meier, *Leading Issues in Economic Development* (New York, 1977), pp. 629ff.; B. Balassa, "The Structure of Incentives in Semi-industrial Economies," in B. Balassa, *Development Strategies*, pp. 16–59.

37. See Machlup, *A History*.

38. For example, works by Petru Aurelian and Alexander Xenopol. See Montias, "Notes on the Romanian Debate on Sheltered Industrialization: 1860–1906," in Jowitt, ed., *Social Change in Romania*.

39. Manoilescu, *The Theory of Protection*, p. 142. He remarked ironically that following the earlier patterns of development of the United States, Russia, and England, the first should stick to the production of cotton, tobacco, and corn, the second to industry, and the third to agriculture.

40. Janos, "Modernization," p. 104, seems wrong to claim that Manoilescu assumed no changes in the international division of labor.

41. Quoted in Manoilescu, *The Theory of Protection*, p. 208. See also Röpke, *International Economic Disintegration*, p. 12.

42. Werner Sombart, *Die deutsche Volkswirtschaft im neunzehten Jahrhundert* (Berlin, 1903), chapter 14. Quoted in Hirschman, *National Power*, p. 146.

43. Janos, "Modernization," p. 103.

44. Compare Schmitter, "Reflections," pp. 122ff.

45. See Jan Kofman, *Lewiatan a podstawowe zagadnienia ekonomiczno-polityczne Drugiej Rzeczypospolitej. Z dziejów ideologii kół wielkokapitalistycznych w Polsce* (Warsaw, 1986); D. Toshev, *Industrialnata politika na Bŭlgariya sled Pŭrvata svetovna voyna* (Varna, 1943), pp. 166–168; Konstantin Bobchev, "Protektsionisticheskata teoriya na profesor M. Manoilescu," *Spisaniye na Bŭlgarskoto Ikonomichesko Druzhestvo*, 1933, vol. 8; K. Bobchev, "Protektsionism i stopanska nauka," *Spisaniye na Bŭlgarskoto Ikonomichesko Druzhestvo*, 1935, vol. 8-9. For the contemporary criticism of his views, for Poland see A. Wakar, "Pojęcie produkcyjności i dochodu społecznego," *Ekonomista*, vol. 1, 1932, pp. 81–92; for Bulgaria, Toshev, *Industrialnata politika*; and in Romania, George Taşcă (quoted in Röpke, *International Economic Disintegration*, p. 181).

46. See E. B. Burns, *Nationalism in Brazil: A Historical Survey* (New York, 1968); J. L. Love, "Theorizing Underdevelopment: Latin America and Romania, 1860–1950," *Review*, vol. XL, no. 4, 1988, pp. 477, 484, 487; J. L. Love, "Modelling Internal Colonialism: History and Prospect," pp. 27ff.

47. See chapter 1, notes 39 and 41; and Ernst Wagemann, *Der neue Balkans: Altes Land—junge Wirtschaft* (Hamburg, 1939), pp. 65–69.

48. Röpke, *International Economic Disintegration*, p. 179.

49. Byé, "Międzynarodowa polityka handlowa," p. 447.

50. See Munk, *Le débat sur le libre échange*, chapter 3; G. M. Meier and Robert E. Baldwin, *Economic Development: Theory, History, Policy* (New York, 1957), pp. 335, 339; Johnson, "Theory;" Lewis, *Theory of Economic Growth*.

6

Policy of Protectionism in East and Central Europe: Overview

From the point of view of the countries of East and Central Europe, the protectionist tendency brought about at least two effects. First, it threatened that the industrialized world would close its markets to agricultural products and raw materials, which were the lion's share of the region's exports. That would be a result of preferences the more advanced countries had given, especially in the 1930s, to their own agricultural producers.[1] A League of Nations report stated that the Great Depression affected the countries of eastern and southeastern Europe particularly acutely.[2] Second, the protectionist tendency confirmed the region's governments' belief that in the given circumstances embracing protectionism was the only rational choice.

In the interwar period, however, Western observers tended to believe that the conspicuous process of increased protectionism resulted from a conscious political decision.[3] After World War II (although similar suggestions had been made even earlier[4]), East and Central Europe watchers were inclined to see in protectionism a by-product of the rise in nationalism of the states that emerged from the defeat of Austria-Hungary and Russia.[5] The historiography of the region, though, gave more emphasis to the objective character of the economic processes conducive to the expansion of protectionism.[6]

Needless to say, the approaches to protectionism described in Chapter 5 do not exhaust all possible interpretations. Protectionism in East and Central Europe was a product of the rising nationalism (and as such had its unmistakable ideological roots; see chapters 1 and 5), a spontaneous phenomenon resulting from objective economic processes, and also a consciously stimulated process. Yet the effect of these factors on each particular protectionist-autarkic tendency in the region varied. As it is impossible to determine this effect precisely, we must confine ourselves to some very general statements.

I believe that it is possible to conceptualize the evolution of protectionism at least according to formal and substantive criteria. The formal conceptualization refers primarily to the analysis of the regulations governing customs, treaties, and control. When conceptualizing protectionism according to substantive criteria, we must weigh the actual qualitative changes. Conclusions from the latter approach seem more important to our further considerations.

Historically, protectionism as a conscious policy emerged in the region together with the birth or rebirth of a given nation's statehood. There occurred at the same time a characteristic time lag. Greece, Serbia, Romania, Bulgaria, and Hungary were the first to have resorted to large-scale protectionist measures several or several dozen years after they had become independent states. However, the economic policies of Estonia, Latvia, Lithuania, Czechoslovakia, Austria, the post-Trianon Hungary, Yugoslavia, the enlarged Romania, and Poland showed the protectionist tendency practically immediately or soon after they had gained independence.[7] At this point one may conclude that the later a given country appeared on the map of Europe, the sooner it was likely to adopt a more or less protectionist line. That shortening of the time before protectionist measures were adopted resulted, first and foremost, from the economic dissimilarity of the development stage at which those countries were when they gained independence, and also from their own experience and their understanding of the development paths that the more advanced countries had trodden. Additionally, protectionism in the twenty interwar years was either, as in the case of Yugoslavia, Romania, Greece, and Bulgaria—albeit qualitatively different—an apparent extension of the earlier trend or, as in the case of Poland, Czechoslovakia, Hungary, Austria, Lithuania, Latvia, and Estonia, a specific continuation of the economic policy of the now-vanished empires they had all been part of. The policy of protecting their own manufactures, as pursued by Austria-Hungary, the German Reich, and the Russian Empire, was to some extent followed by the new states' emerging bureaucracies and business circles. Initially, they took over on a large scale the customs regulations and tariffs binding in the old metropolises (Austria, Czechoslovakia, and Hungary merely confined themselves to a conversion of the old rates).[8]

It must be remembered that in the first postwar years, all the countries of the region made their numerous protectionist moves spontaneously.[9] To a considerably smaller degree, such moves were an outcome of the economic leaders' doctrinaire professing of the rules of protectionism. Yet the role of the latter factor (which in the 1930s might even be a key influence in some of the countries) in the shaping of economic policy must not be disregarded. Soon after the end of the war, the countries of East and Central Europe resorted spontaneously to protectionism as a response to the direct adversities brought about by World War I (devastation, supply shortages, communication chaos), and to the relevant political decisions—with all the ensuing adjustment difficulties of the new states in administration, transport, currency, army, and so on. Another important factor, although secondary to those already mentioned, was the need to protect the local market from either the flood of manufactures and—less often—agricultural products that neighboring countries were selling at a loss or, vice versa, from exports that were harmful to the public.[10]

After the countries of the region mastered the postwar difficulties—including the beating of inflation in Poland, Austria, and Hungary and the stabilization of currency in all of them in the years 1922–1927[11]—they abandoned the extreme forms of autarky. Of course, protectionism did not dry up, though it became less conspicuous—maybe because the prosperous years of 1923/24–1929/30 alleviated its symptoms. Nonetheless, Western governments and business circles, not without reason, accused the succession states of carrying out a flagrantly protectionist policy. I have already quoted both the Western charges—for example, those laid during the International Economic Conference in 1927—as well as the answers of the governments charged. Needless to say, in the light of liberal concepts those charges were not unfounded. The booming end of the 1920s encouraged, particularly in the West, a flush of an illusory, as it turned out, optimism as regards the possibility of restoring the gold standard and the economic circumstances from before the war.[12] (It was only several years later that economists began to understand the anachronism of that belief.[13]) In the years 1927–1929, the antiprotectionist moods reached their apogee. They manifested themselves in the widely propagated demand that any further progress of protectionism be checked, and even that it be abandoned gradually by replacing it with, for example, a customs truce.[14] It is characteristic that the truce proposal was received most cautiously by the Central European governments of Czechoslovakia, Poland, and in effect, Germany. Ultimately, the customs truce never took effect, as it was not ratified by the required number of states.[15] (The Great Depression immediately exposed its illusiveness, anyway.) Such a position regarding the customs truce was not accidental. The countries of the region had already shown a similar cautiousness or open repugnance to the earlier suggestions on how to untie the knot of conflicting interests. For example, Austria, Hungary, and Czechoslovakia simply ignored the peace treaty–proposed mutual preferential duties that made—theoretically—the only sensible recommendation for their respective economies.[16]

But it must be remembered that the initially spontaneous protectionism generated certain habits in—and consolidated—interest groups with a stake in maintaining and even widening this tendency. Thus, even though after the period of the postwar reconstruction all countries of the region moderated the state intervention in the economy, protectionist measures were least affected by that moderation. Actually, something opposite took place: It was then that the ruling elites became confirmed in their opinion that a conscious plan for the development of the country's production and distribution was absolutely necessary. It should be no surprise that nearly all customs laws and tariffs enacted in the region (after economic stability had already been achieved) were more or less protectionist, even if we assume that they were often treated as a mere tool for improving a given country's bargaining position, particularly in dealings with its neighbors.[17] Yet that tool proved ineffective when used in negotiations with a partner who was strong either economically or politically. Still, a strong partner's concessions were of crucial importance to the East and Central European countries.

The Great Depression was a turning point in the evolution of protectionism, including on the regional scale. Quantity turned into quality, as Röpke put it. Thereafter we have a "new protectionism."[18] Hence the causes of the explosion of protectionism in the 1930s were only in part identical with the causes of protectionism in the previous decade. The impact of the Great Depression brought protectionism in the region to an unprecedented intensity, embracing the entire economic life and certain areas of social life as well. First, protective measures were introduced ad hoc, but then they were applied methodically, in response to economic events, particularly those in the spheres of finance and commerce, taking place on the global, the regional, and/or the national scale. Of note among the characteristic incidents that occurred in the central and southeastern parts of the region are the outbreak in 1930 of a trade war between Hungary and Czechoslovakia, the collapse of the great Central European banks in Austria, Hungary, and Germany in the years 1931 and 1932, the reciprocal termination of commercial treaties, the imposition of foreign exchange restrictions and, first and foremost, the disastrous and rapid decline in industrial production in Poland, Czechoslovakia, and Hungary and the socially and economically devastating agricultural overproduction. Similar occurrences, fortunately on a smaller scale, happened in the Baltic countries too.[19] These occurrences should be seen in the context of the global depression, as its effect and, at the same time, a constituent part. Falling prices for agricultural products and raw materials were the most powerful determinant of the economic situation in the region, leading to an extremely fierce competition among the region's exporters on their own and third countries' markets.

It is no wonder that the task of arresting the fall in agricultural prices was given a top priority in the majority of the region's countries (Austria and Czechoslovakia included). To check that falling trend, governments supported agricultural production by various means, initially with only moderate success. For example, in the Danube countries, where grain production had for the greater part of the interwar period been the main line of farming, in the years 1930–1933 produce prices plummeted.[20] Intervention purchases of grain and other produce at prices higher than both domestic and international prices in order to stockpile reserves or, possibly, to export them was a major remedy.[21] In Greece the government aided wheat cultivation to make the country independent of imports.[22] Such measures can be recognized as tools of economic intervention but also as instruments to protect one's own agriculture. Such countries as Hungary (where in the years 1930–1934 the government subsidized grain purchases and provided tax relief), Yugoslavia, Romania, and especially Bulgaria and Czechoslovakia (which established first a grain syndicate, and then a monopoly) enjoyed great success in this area.[23] Sometimes such measures produced gratifying results, as in Bulgaria and Czechoslovakia, where they had a widespread impact on the entire economy. In other countries, however, for example, in Poland, such efforts were not particularly successful.[24] The Baltic countries did not actually face the problem of overproduction of grain. The governments of Latvia and Estonia concentrated on the reduction of grain imports and on the stimulation of their own agriculture in order, first, to become self-sufficient in food, and, then, to export processed food products. Their effort was largely successful.[25]

The protectionism of the 1930s no doubt profited by the experience of neighboring countries, particularly of the Soviet Union and of Germany toward the close of the Weimar Republic and during the Third Reich in particular. As for the Balkan countries, their closer political ties with Germany were followed by their assuming German economic patterns. The patterns protectionist countries copied concerned predominantly agriculture, foreign trade, and autarky in general.

The situation at the time was characterized by a drastic decline in the value of the region's trade (with trade among the region's countries shrinking even more rapidly). The subsequent growth in the countries' foreign trade was usually very slow. Trade was declining more rapidly than production. Growth in domestic production, on the other hand, usually preceded an improvement in foreign trade indices.[26]

The relations observed permit the following interpretation: Inasmuch as in the first instance the government intervention (e.g., orders from state institutions) checked the decline in production, in the second instance, the growth in production resulted, after 1931/32, from an increasingly frequent government intervention on behalf of the domestic market and producers (e.g., by forming obligatory cartels and quasi monopolies, particularly in agriculture), from loans, and from a substantial rise in government orders. Any definitive improvement in foreign trade indices was halted, however, by quantitative restrictions and, of course, a chronic foreign currency shortage.[27]

Additional incentives were of course significant in the rise in production at the time that the countries of the region were breaking out of the crisis. I mean here export prospects that preferential trade agreements of a distinct political undercurrent opened before certain countries (the Italian-Hungarian-Austrian Danubian Agreement signed in Rome in 1934, and the agreements between Danubian and Balkan countries and Germany).[28] So was specialization in agriculture, the relatively high quality of the produce offered by the Baltic countries, Hungary, and Bulgaria, and last but not least, the demand, rising after 1935, for strategic raw materials (nonferrous metals from Yugoslavia, crude oil from Romania, and to a lesser extent, bauxite from Hungary and coal from Poland).[29]

As I mentioned earlier, East and Central Europe, like other regions, cast aside the liberal theories based on the theory of comparative advantage and referring to the existing international division of labor. Instead, these countries looked for a justification of a policy that would enable them to survive the crisis at a relatively small cost. Protectionism in East and Central Europe thus acquired—as it had shortly after World War I—a predominantly defensive and restrictive character. Those traits were particularly distinct in foreign trade policy, which unexceptionally (with maybe Poland least engaged in such dealings) consisted of the beggar-my-neighbor tactics and of dumping.

In the summer and autumn of 1931, many countries, especially in East-Central Europe, imposed import quotas and foreign currency restrictions with the aim of extending control over all the balance-of-payments items. Behind their decisions lay the fall in agricultural prices (which was more serious than in the case of prices for manufactures and which became even sharper with the onset of the Great Depression), a decisive halt to the inflow of capital and its sudden withdrawal aggravated by the outflow of local capital, and the depreciation of the British pound and the U.S. dollar.[30]

Import quotas make a useful instrument of foreign trade policy; they allow the fluctuation of domestic prices to be separated from world prices for the equivalents subjected to restrictions, and thus to protect domestic production. Exchange control, for its part, makes it possible to reduce the costs of adjusting the national economy to the relative fall in prices abroad.[31] Theoreticians were not of one mind on the usefulness of those instruments. If they usually agreed that duties could be advantageously replaced with exchange control, they doubted the nationwide economic benefit of quotas.[32] But their opinions sounded logical only within the framework of liberal economics.[33]

However, more important than theoretical arguments was the practical line of economic policy in the 1930s, which gave emphasis to quotas and exchange control. I do not think it necessary to present in detail the issue of imposing quotas as a tool for controlling imports. Suffice it to say that most generally quotas were broken up into general and specific ones.[34] The countries of the region had to resort to them, and some of them (such as Poland, Romania, and Lithuania) sooner than others (e.g., Latvia). Initially they tended to employ general quotas (although Greece and Turkey did it the other way around). Import (and sometimes export) licenses made an additional instrument enabling a strong interference with foreign trade, which at the same time strengthened the tendency to impose import and—automatically!—export quotas. In time, all the countries of the region that imposed import quotas began to apply both general as well as specific quotas.[35] Particularly in the period of 1931–1935/36, in their foreign trade policies they were employing both licenses and quotas. The publication of increasingly long and detailed lists of goods subject to import control was the clearest expression of the widening of import restrictions. Its most glaring example was provided by Czechoslovakia, where, from the first half of 1932 until March 1934, it was easier to make a list of goods unsubjected than subjected to these regulations.[36] Meanwhile, Latvia and Estonia were the only countries in the region that temporarily scrapped the system of import quotas.[37] Additionally, quotas were meant to retaliate for similar regulations introduced by other countries and to strengthen one's own bargaining position. Exchange control, along with its basic task of balancing the demand for and the supply of foreign exchange, was also aimed at protecting particular branches and industries. Therefore it is not easy to discern the motives behind the use of both of those instruments or the aims and results the relevant countries wished thus to achieve. One can say that if import quotas were usually imposed to protect domestic manufacturers, then exchange control was also implemented to help stabilize currency.[38] The scope of particular functions performed by these instruments eventually widened and to some extent overlapped.

The growth in compensatory trade, treated as an attempt to overcome the barrier of the hard-currency shortage, was the inevitable effect of exchange control. The development of various forms of compensation, especially the private one (particularly popular in Greece and Bulgaria),[39] allowed the economy to escape the import-and-foreign-exchange restrictions and to raise the volume of exports above the fixed quota. Also, the countries of the region largely used the previously unknown clearing system (to the extent permitted by mutual liabilities, however). Although the systems of import quotas and clearing coincided with each other, they did not have a common origin.[40] Agreements between the clearing-system countries and between them and the countries that imposed exchange control were meant to promote bilateral trade—and indeed they achieved that goal.[41] Yet, in the crisis-ridden 1930s, restrictions worked with redoubled strength, thus creating increasing difficulties in international trade.[42]

I have already mentioned that the assessment of the motives behind the use of such instruments and of the results they produced is not unequivocal (even in theory). One must realize that it was not protectionism that was the prime motive for quotas. Latvia comprised a unique case. In that country, despite official assurances, import quotas were introduced precisely to protect local products. The Latvian authorities saw the quotas as the condition that would ensure the home market to the products so far exported. The expanding lists of goods subject to import restrictions, published from October 1931, included meat products and fats in particular, in keeping with the general orientation of the country's economic policy. (It is a different issue that from mid-1934 the same effect was achieved by a system that was a combination of import quotas, licenses, and duties.[43])

In general, however, when choosing the relevant instruments the governments of the debtor countries (Latvia among them) were guided not so much by protectionist motives as by the intention of keeping their currencies stable. They usually resorted to exchange control, although such countries as Greece, Estonia, and Poland first tried to attain their aim through import quotas, and only when these proved to be insufficiently effective did they resort to the exchange policy—for example, to devaluation, which Greece did in April 1932, and Estonia in June 1933.[44] Still, in the same Greece, by exempting a large volume of food products and raw materials from import duties and other restrictions, and by severely reducing imports of luxury goods, consciously or unconsciously the government provoked a protectionist effect. This policy strongly stimulated the development of industry, and of light industry in particular.[45] It subsequently led Greece to a marked widening of the system of bilateral compensation in 1935.[46]

Estonia included import quotas in the system of exchange control (November 1931), primarily with the aim of keeping its currency, the kroon, stable. In 1932 import quotas were imposed on nearly all imports of manufactures and, needless to say, farm produce. As the government was aware of the protectionist consequences of those restrictions, it was simultaneously trying (in keeping with the priority of the foreign exchange policy then in force) to apply measures that would prevent a growth in the production that made such protectionist effects possible. For example, when restrictions on imports of textiles caused a rise in their prices in the domestic market and, as a result, a greater demand on textile machinery, the government refused to license its imports[47] (which presumably had a negative effect on employment).

In Poland (and in Latvia[48]) the authorities did not resort to a devaluation or depreciation of the zloty or, until 1936, to exchange control. Unlike in Greece and, to a lesser degree, Estonia,[49] it was a very stern policy of deflation combined with the customary import bans and restrictions that allowed Poland and Latvia to keep their currencies stable.[50] The spread of those practices was relatively moderate. Contemporaries maintained all the same that economic nationalism permeated Polish policy.[51] Their opinion resulted, I believe, from an utterly wrong interpretation. Poland did undertake retaliatory measures or imposed restrictions upon particular countries, guided by economic motives—as in the case of Czechoslovakia—or political motives—as during the customs war and toward the close of the 1930s in the case of Germany.[52] Yet, until the establishment of exchange control, import restrictions were actually the basic method of protection of Poland's balance of trade. As for the government's strong leanings toward economic nationalism, probably of greater importance in this respect was the early (1930) strict imposition by Poland of compensatory trade or, in fact, barter (at the beginning, with some of the Balkan and Danubian countries, including Austria and Germany).[53]

Romania, for its part, in order to obtain an export surplus necessary to keep its currency—the leu—stable, imposed exchange control in May 1932 and, in November of the same year, import quotas as well. In August 1933 Romania unilaterally suspended its debt payment, and in July 1935 it in fact depreciated the leu.

Bulgarians originally assumed that import restrictions would be an element of a modest exchange rationing, which had started in October 1931, but already by April the following year they curtailed their debt servicing and actually depreciated the lev.

Hungarians imposed exchange control in July 1931. A year later they blocked foreign debt servicing with the intention of keeping the pengő's rate of exchange steady. They achieved their aim, but at a great cost to the economy.

Yugoslavia introduced new restrictive exchange regulations in October 1931, and in April the following year it curtailed its foreign debt payment. All the same, in October the dinar was actually devalued.[54]

Czechoslovakia, although the only creditor country in the region, relatively quickly took the path of import restrictions. In October 1931 it established exchange control as well. The aim of those moves was twofold: to defend the stability of the koruna and, in the longer term, to protect domestic manufacturers. Twice, however, in February 1934 and in September 1936, Czechoslovakia gave priority to the second aim by devaluing the koruna,[55] which, thanks to that country's relatively favorable foreign exchange position, it could better afford than the debtor countries.

In sum, Greece, Estonia, Romania, and to some extent Poland and Lithuania—in order not to devalue their currencies and to improve their balance of payments—tried to make use of quotas, sometimes along with exchange control. Austria, Czechoslovakia, Yugoslavia, Bulgaria, and Hungary strove to keep their balance of payments in equilibrium by means of exchange regulations (including default or suspension of foreign debt payment). Latvia was closer to the first than to the second group of countries. It was a standard rule in the region that the chief reason for import quotas and exchange control was the protection of currency and the desire to equilibrate the balance of payments (usually by import restrictions). Protection of domestic production seldom was the primary motive; it usually was a by-product of the decision of the first kind. On the whole, the governments of the region underestimated the latent potentialities inherent in the use of those instruments in the interest of the protectionist policy.

The steps that some countries (e.g., Estonia) took to halt industrial growth do not seem to be an adequate response to the threats posed by crisis—all the more so because already by 1930/31 the terms of trade of all the countries of the region, save Austria and Czechoslovakia, were unfavorable. The weight of the problem is indicated by very general (and none-too-precise) data concerning the terms of trade of particular countries. In the years 1929 and 1931 they were as follows (1928 = 100): Austria 128 and 143 respectively, Czechoslovakia 101 and 115, Poland 98.5 and 104, Latvia 91 and 79, Hungary 92 and 85, Estonia 100 and 86, Yugoslavia 105 and 88, Bulgaria 147 and 57, and Romania (1929 = 100) 56. These data show very clearly the extent of the shock the sudden change in the terms of trade gave the agricultural economies in the first years of the crisis.[56] As time went by, those countries' terms of trade deteriorated—for example, in Hungary they were at their lowest in 1933 (80), in Yugoslavia in 1932 (86)—but in the industrialized Czechoslovakia they improved continuously (in 1934, 132).[57] It was only on the eve of World War II that the terms of trade of the agricultural countries improved, although they were still below the pre-crisis level.[58]

Such evolution of the terms of trade had a painful impact on the balance of trade and the balance of payments. To remedy that situation would require an impetus to industrial growth, and this was at the initial stage of the Great Depression. However, either such an argument was not raised or, if it was, it did not carry enough weight against the advocates of the economic policy oriented primarily toward keeping the currency stable, and thus toward a policy that was in fact deflationary. The exchange problem played too critical a role in the policy of the majority of the region's countries in the 1930s, and until 1935/36 in particular.

Seen in the context of the policy of deflation, the exchange difficulties disclosed one more crucial problem: The premises of the deflation policy were incompatible with subsidizing and encouraging exports. The countries that wanted to favor more actively or even aggressively their exports should have, in order to score greater success, suspended free foreign exchange (which, in fact, all of them except Czechoslovakia did), and as a result, abandoned deflation. In practice, they acted depending on circumstances. If it was possible in Poland, for example, to stimulate exports without resorting to foreign exchange restrictions (but, due to this, to a smaller extent and at a greater effort), then to break with deflation was in fact necessary to give the country some maneuvering space and its economic policy an export orientation. Therefore we should not be surprised that the countries of the region—for various reasons compelled to export their products in any amount and at any price—imposed foreign exchange restrictions (e.g., by suspending the transfer of their outstanding liabilities) or manipulated the exchange rates and, sooner or later, actually abandoned the policy of deflation. Bulgaria, Romania, Greece, Hungary, Yugoslavia, Latvia, Estonia, and Czechoslovakia did so in 1933/34, Lithuania in 1935, and Poland as late as the spring of 1936. The latter, unlike other countries of the region, did not depreciate its currency—not even when in September 1936 such economically and financially much stronger countries of the Golden Bloc as France, the Netherlands, and Switzerland took that step.[59] Thus Poland found itself in a situation that was even worse. It is no coincidence that in those debtor countries that stuck to a free currency exchange, that is, Poland and Lithuania, economic recovery was visibly slower in coming than elsewhere in the region.

Let us now consider the possibilities of estimating and measuring (even most roughly) the extent and effectiveness of the protective measures applied. Attempts at assessing the level of protection were made already before the war. Those attempts were inaccurate, however (because of the unreliability of the source material), and methodologically questionable—for example, they took into account only one element (and index), that of the customs tariffs.[60] The data produced particularly by H. Liepmann lead to judgments too categorical, I believe, in the evaluation of the policies of the countries of East and Central Europe. When studying these data one should bear in mind their merely subsidiary character. However, in view of the scantiness of the statistical material, it is doubtful whether the currently constructed indices (interesting even though complicated)[61] are of any use to the examination of the degree of protection of the region's economies in the years 1918–1939. It is doubtful, moreover, whether one can clearly distinguish nontariff measures that affect both domestic production and market. It might be assumed that the purpose leading the whole or only a fragment of the economic policy should be recognized as the basic distinguishing criterion. Still, this does not solve the problem entirely. For example, how to determine relations between the two forms of intervention in those numerous cases in which the short-term government intervention intertwined closely with an intervention of a purely protectionist nature?

When this question is viewed from yet another angle, it seems particularly difficult to separate the measures that go beyond the so-called simple means of intervention (earlier described as tactical and operational protectionisms). In the second half of the 1930s, they acted as a powerful engine of growth. I mean here the policy of inflationary growth promotion. Tariff protection and other instruments of trade and exchange policies admittedly are necessary measures, but they are only subsidiary to the new methods of stimulating domestic production, combating unemployment, and boosting demand. It would be too much to say that the growth promotion policy including particular elements of this policy were always devised as tools of protectionism, but they did add to its effectiveness. In the 1930s the countries of East and Central Europe employed those instruments of protectionism in variable proportions. Indirect methods of trade policy seemed to be the most popular. Along with the already mentioned tariff impediments and rate-of-exchange manipulations, there were the policies of transport charges, export bonuses, lump tax, tax reliefs, and so on. Those were measures that actually did not go beyond the moderate variety of protectionism. Austria and Czechoslovakia seemed to use the whole assortment, and Poland many of them.[62]

Yet, even though such countries as Romania and Bulgaria (and to a lesser extent, Hungary) were trying to give coherence to their protectionist policies, other reasons (e.g., the needs of the budget) compelled them to abandon that goal. The tasks set before the tariff policy conflicted most seriously, I believe, with fiscal interests, because the import-discouraging aim of the former obstructed the drawing of a regular revenue from customs duties (a major part of the budget revenue). In the low-income countries, the revenues drawn from customs played a very important role. In the years preceding the Great Depression, the share of customs duties in the country's tax revenues amounted to 45 percent in Romania (in 1925), somewhat over 32 percent in Albania and Bulgaria (in 1925/26), 25 percent in Yugoslavia (1929/30) and Poland (1925/26), 21 percent in Hungary (1925/26), 17 percent in Czechoslovakia, and 23 percent, 33 percent, and 21 percent in Estonia, Latvia, and Lithuania (in 1928/29), respectively. These data are not comparable, however. In any case, as a result of reductions in imports and of tax reforms, in the 1930s those percentages were markedly reduced.[63]

The assessment of the share of the so-called fiscal duties (e.g., on tropical foods) in the budget revenue is another matter. We can agree with a Polish economist that a large share of fiscal duties in the total customs receipts indicates a less restrictive character in the tariff (e.g., in Great Britain the percentage was 40), whereas a smaller share (e.g., in Poland, where it was a mere 22 percent at the beginning of the 1930s),[64] indicates the tariff's more protectionist tinge.

This notwithstanding, one should be cautious of hazarding an assessment based on such an assumption, considering that rich countries import many more tropical foods than poor countries do.[65] Hence the share of the so-called fiscal duties in the total of the customs receipts in the former is larger than in the latter. This does not mean, however, that the level of protection in the rich countries is any lower than in the poor countries. What is more, Poland as well as other countries were generous with autonomous tariff rebates and conventional duties. Taking these and other factors into account prompts a very prudent acceptance of opinions on the level of protectionism in a given country (e.g., of the prevalent opinion on Poland as extremely protectionist).

The data indicating the average tariff-load of imports, expressed by the ratio between the total custom receipts and the value of all imports, can serve as some gauge of protection. According to S. F. Królikowski, in the year 1934/35 that proportion was 17 percent in Poland, 11 percent in Czechoslovakia, but as much as 29 percent in France, 27 percent in Great Britain, 30 percent in Germany, and 29 percent in Bulgaria.[66] Yet, do these percentages provide anything more accurate than a mere approximation? What is more, these data raise many reservations.

First, from the methodological point of view, it should be noted that the data refer to single instances. To determine a more general trend it is necessary to have longer and more diversified series of statistics. But even then, more general conclusions regarding one country, drawn on the basis of such series, would prove more useful if they were comparable with data and conclusions regarding other countries. This basic requirement, however, is to all intents and purposes unrealizable (due, among other things, to ununiformness of the data).

Second, the inaccuracy of the information thus acquired consists also in that it does not consider the fact that the total of duties collected depends, for example, on the extent of the protection-induced fall in imports.[67]

Third, we do not always know how the percentages were calculated. This is a reservation of minor importance, however. What seems to be more important here is that a more profound analysis would have to include other elements too, as the index of the tariff-load of imports does not comprise a sufficient gauge of protectionism. This is why sometimes another index is used, that of the share of the reimbursed tariffs in the total of customs receipts. In case of Poland, the reimbursements were within the range of several and several dozen million zlotys.[68] Reckoning them in would inevitably reveal the protectionist bias of the Polish economic policy. Yet, with regard to Poland, only very scanty data are available. Still, the comparison of the two indices demonstrates that to refer to the first index alone in order to determine the level of protectionism can give a false picture (it can imply that the level of protection in Poland was lower than in Great Britain). Thus the information concerning the amount of reimbursed tariffs fulfills the role of the first index corrector. In trying to establish the level of actual protection, however, should one not take into consideration other forms of subsidy as well?

My other doubt, a more serious one, I believe, concerns the very recognition of these indices as adequate gauges of the level of actual protection. In the 1930s the tariff policy lost much of its significance as a weapon of protectionism everywhere. Therefore, we could ponder whether data indicating the quantitative changes in import bans would not make a more objective criterion. But here, too, further questions are bound to arise.

First, was it really the interest of the domestic manufacturers that decided on the imposition or annulment of bans on importing certain goods or raw materials? Or were those rather (as in the 1930s) purely foreign-exchange reasons? Second, we must keep in mind that there were frequent changes in the lists of banned imports (licenses to import specific goods or from a specific country were usually valid for a certain time only). Third, aggregate data on the quantitative changes in the lists of banned imports would hardly add to our knowledge of the real significance of particular decisions.[69] Therefore, it seems unlikely that such a comparison of the lists of banned imports (which in itself would be a very difficult job to do) might lead to any more definite comparative conclusions. Finally, even if it were possible to gather reasonably complete series of statistics and indices, we must still beware of overgeneralized conclusions. Such conclusions would still take no account of the effect of other measures to protect the economy, for example, tax reliefs, subsidies, and tax reimbursements. If, finally, even these instruments yield to some approximate quantification, it is still difficult or downright impossible to gauge the effect of indirect instruments such as economic legislation, even though it is otherwise clear that their effect is very significant.

What choice are we then left if we essentially cannot apply Corden's or Balassa's indices *to the economy as a whole*? I think that there are, after all, certain slim possibilities of finding indices of the level of protection. For example, besides what has already been mentioned, we could recognize as an index—albeit a very much *indirect* one—the ratio of agricultural to industrial prices ("scissors effect") or the ratio of domestic to world prices. But even then, the ratios as such do not reflect a full scale of protection. Only when compared to consumption and production indices could these ratios indicate, possibly more reliably but still very vaguely, the effectiveness of the policy of protectionism and the condition of the economy in general. Data concerning import substitution could be used as an additional (again indirect) index of the effectiveness of the protectionist measures employed (yet, to be presented in a descriptive form rather than a quantitative form). Hence the following hypothesis: The smaller the decline in the production involved in import substitution, the more effective was believed to be the protection of domestic manufacturers. In this case, protectionism was carried out through the relevant tariff policy and foreign exchange control. Here too, however, great caution is recommended, especially as it is difficult to distinguish clearly import substitution from other sorts of production.[70]

Notes

1. See, for example, M. John Bell Condliffe, *World Economic Survey: Fifth Year, 1935* (Geneva, 1935), pp. 54, 84; League of Nations, *Commercial Policy in the Interwar Period: International Proposals and National Policies* (Geneva, 1944), pp. 52, 77, 87, 121, 124, 133; Henryk Tennenbaum, *Europa Środkowo-Wschodnia w gospodarce światowej* (London, 1941).

2. League of Nations, *Report on Exchange Control* (Geneva, 1938), p. 5.

3. See, for example, League of Nations, *The World Economic Conference* (Geneva, 1927); L. Pasvolsky, *Economic Nationalism of the Danubian States* (London, 1928); T. E. Gregory, "Economic Nationalism," *Economic Affairs*, vol. X, no. 3, 1931; H. V. Hodson, *Slump and Recovery, 1929–1937* (London, 1938); A. Basch, *The Danube Basin and the German Economic Sphere* (London, 1944). For similar postwar opinions, see F. Hertz, *The Economic Problem of Danubian States: A Study in Economic Nationalism* (London, 1947); J. M. Montias, "Economic Nationalism in Eastern Europe: Forty Years of Continuity and Change," *Journal of International Affairs*, vol. XX, no. 1, 1966; C. A. Macartney and A. W. Palmer, *Independent Eastern Europe: A History* (London, 1962); I. T. Berend and G. Ránki, *Economic Development in East-Central Europe in the 19th and 20th Centuries* (New York and London, 1974); J. Rothschild, *East Central Europe Between Two World Wars* (Seattle and London, 1974).

4. See Pasvolsky, *Economic Nationalism.*

5. W.A.S.H., "Protection," in *Encyclopaedia Britannica*, vol. 18 (London, 1960), p. 604. See also Rothschild, *East Central Europe.*

6. See Z. Landau and J. Tomaszewski, *Gospodarka Polski międzywojennej 1918–1939*, vol. 1, *W dobie inflacji 1918–1923* (Warsaw, 1967), and *Polska w Europie i świecie 1918–1939* (Warsaw, 1984); V. Průcha, ed., *Historia gospodarcza Czecho-*

słowacji XX wieku (Warsaw, 1979); Ż. Z. Natan, V. Khadzhinikolov, and L. Berov, eds., *Ikonomikata na Bŭlgariya*, vol. 1 (Sofia, 1969); M. Mirković, *Ekonomska historija Jugoslavije* (Zagreb, 1968); Royal Institute of International Affairs (RIIA), *The Baltic States: A Survey of the Political and Economic Structure and the Foreign Relations of Estonia, Latvia, and Lithuania* (London, 1938); M. C. Kaser, ed., *The Economic History of Eastern Europe 1919–1975*, vol. 2, *Interwar Policy, the War, and Reconstruction* (Oxford, 1986), chapters 9, 11, 12.

7. N. Spulber, *The State and Economic Development in Eastern Europe* (New York, 1966), chapters 1, 4; Berend and Ránki, *Economic Development in East Central Europe*, chapters 5, 6; Berend and Ránki, *The Development of Manufacturing Industry in Hungary, 1900–1944* (Budapest, 1960); *The Tariff and Its History* (Washington, D.C., 1934); RIIA, *The Balkan States. I. Economic* (London, 1936); RIIA, *The Baltic States*; RIIA, *South Eastern Europe: The Political and Economic Survey* (London, 1939); V. N. Bandera, *Foreign Capital as an Instrument of National Economic Policy: A Study Based on the Experience of East European Countries Between the World Wars* (The Hague, 1964); R. Olšovský et al., *Přehled hospodářského vývoje Československá v letech 1918–1945* (Prague 1961); Natan, Khadzhinikolov, and Berov, eds., *Ikonomikata na Bŭlgariya*; Mirković, *Ekonomska historija*; Landau and Tomaszewski, *Gospodarka Polski międzywojennej,I* vol. 1, and *Gospodarka Polski międzywojennej*, vol. 2, *Od Grabskiego do Piłsudskiego: Okres kryzysu poinflacyjnego i ożywienie koniunktury 1924–1929* (Warsaw, 1971). See also contributions by Drabek, Ránki and Tomaszewski, Iancu Spigler, and R. Nötel in Kaser, ed., *Economic History*, vol. 2.

8. G. Ránki and J. Tomaszewski, "The Role of the State in Industry, Banking, and Trade," in Kaser, ed., *Economic History*, vol. 2, p. 12; Landau and Tomaszewski, *Gospodarka Polski międzywojennej*, vol. 1, p. 326; Průcha, ed., *Historia gospodarcza*, p. 56; Pasvolsky, *Economic Nationalism*, p. 78.

9. See Ránki and Tomaszewski, "The Role of the State," p. 15.

10. Ibid., pp. 14–21; Olšovský et. al, *Přehled hospodářského*, pp. 67–69.

11. Austria and Czechoslovakia in 1922, Bulgaria in 1924, Hungary and Yugoslavia in 1925, Poland in 1924 and 1926; Romania in 1927, Greece in 1929, Lithuania and Latvia in 1922, and Estonia in 1923 and 1927. These dates concern the stabilization de facto. Formal stabilization took place usually after stabilization credit was provided on the initiative or with the support of the League of Nations. See R. Nötel, "International Credit and Finance," in Kaser, ed., *Economic History*, vol. 2, pp. 181–213; Berend and Ránki, *Economic Development in East-Central Europe*, pp. 214–221; RIIA, *The Baltic States*, p. 131; Bandera, *Foreign Capital*, p. 26; Heinrich Heuser, *Control of International Trade* (London, 1939), p. 33; RIIA, *The Balkan States*; League of Nations, *Reconstruction Schemes in the Inter-War Period* (Geneva, 1944), pp. 164–187.

12. This optimism was reflected during the proceedings of the international economic conferences in Brussels (1920), Portosa (1921), Genoa (1922), and the Geneva World Economic Conference (1927). See League of Nations, *Commercial Policy*, pp. 17–32, 102ff.

13. See K. Polanyi, *The Great Transformation* (Boston, 1957), chapter 2; Keynes, in Pollard, ed., *The Gold Standard and Employment Policies Between the Wars* (London, 1970), pp. 27–33 (reprint of the article from 1925); L. Robbins, *The Great Depression* (London, 1934), pp. 97ff.

14. League of Nations, *Commercial Policy*, chapter 1, para. 3, and chapter 5, para. 2.

15. Ibid., pp. 35ff.; Landau and Tomaszewski, *Gospodarka Polski międzywojennej*, vol. 3, *Wielki kryzys 1930–1935*, chapter 13.

16. League of Nations, *Commercial Policy*, p. 37; Pasvolsky, *Economic Nationalism*, pp. 83–86; Z. Sládek and J. Tomaszewski, "Próby integracji gospodarczej Europy Środkowej i Południowo-Wschodniej w latach dwudziestych XX w.," *Roczniki Dziejów Społecznych i Gospodarczych*, vol. XL, 1979, pp. 5ff.

17. Pasvolsky, *Economic Nationalism*, pp. 81ff.; Ránki and Tomaszewski, "The Role of the State," p. 16.

18. Which can lead ultimately to the abolishment of capitalism. See W. Röpke, *International Economic Disintegration* (London, 1942), pp. 56ff.

19. See Berend and Ránki, *Economic Development in East-Central Europe*, pp. 243, 255–257; I. T. Berend, "Agriculture," in M. C. Kaser, ed., *The Economic History of Eastern Europe, 1919–1975*, vol. 1; Józef Orczyk, *Produkcja rolna Polski w latach wielkiego kryzysu gospodarczego (1929–1935)* (Poznań, 1971); V. Lacina, *Velká hospodářská krize v Československu 1929–1934* (Prague, 1984), p. 153, and *Krize československého zemědělství 1928–1934* (Prague, 1974), chapter 7; RIIA, *The Baltic States*, pp. 145–148.

20. Berend and Ránki, *Economic Development in East-Central Europe*, p. 244, table 10.1.

21. O. S. Morgan, ed., *Agricultural Systems of Middle Europe* (New York, 1933); J. Ciepielewski, *Polityka agrarna rządu polskiego w latach 1929–1935* (Warsaw, 1968), chapter 4; Berend, "Agriculture," pp. 176–182; Landau and Tomaszewski, *Gospodarka Polski międzywojennej*, vol. 3, chapter 5; RIIA, *The Baltic States*, pp. 146–148.

22. RIIA, *South Eastern Europe*, p. 117; Georges Servakis and C. Pertounzi, "The Agricultural Policy of Greece," in O. S. Morgan, ed., *Agricultural Systems*, pp. 147, 170; Berend, "Agriculture."

23. Průcha, ed., *Historia gospodarcza*, p. 80; Lacina, *Velká hospodářská krize*, pp. 153, 164, and *Krize československého zemědělství 1928–1934* (Prague, 1974), chapter 4; Berend, "Agriculture," pp. 180–182; Ránki and Tomaszewski, "The Role of the State," p. 22; J. Held, "The Interwar Years and Agrarian Change," in J. Held, ed., *The Modernization of Agriculture: Rural Transformation in Hungary, 1848–1975* (Boulder, 1980), p. 227; Natan, Khadzhinikolov, and Berov, eds., *Ikonomikata na Bŭlgariya*, chapter 4.

24. Landau and Tomaszewski, *Gospodarka Polski międzywojennej*, vol. 3, pp. 140–144; O. von Frangeš, "Fighting the Crisis in the Peasant Countries of the Danube Basin," in *Proceedings of the Third International Conference of Agricultural Economics* (London, 1935), pp. 97ff.

25. RIIA, *The Baltic States*, pp. 145–149; J. Hampden-Jackson, *Estonia* (London, 1948), pp. 187ff., 197.

26. See Z. Drabek, "Foreign Trade Performance and Policy," in M. C. Kaser, ed., *Economic History*, vol. 1, pp. 432–444; R. Nötel, "International Credit and Finance," in M. C. Kaser, ed., *Economic History*, vol. 2, pp. 217ff., 233, 243, 246; RIIA, *The Baltic States*, pp. 151, 155; I. Svennilson, *Growth and Stagnation in the European Economy* (Geneva, 1954), table A.66; Landau and Tomaszewski, *Polska w Europie*, pp. 142–152.

27. See Heuser, *Control*; Drabek, "Foreign Trade."

28. Basch, *The Danube*, chapter 10; Macartney and Palmer, *Independent Eastern Europe*, p. 342; J. B. Hoptner, *Yugoslavia in Crisis, 1934–1941* (London, 1962), pp. 97–105; Dietrich Orlow, *The Nazis in the Balkans: A Case Study of Totalitarian Politics* (Pittsburgh, 1968), pp. 101ff.; Berend and Ránki, *Economic Development in East-Central Europe*, pp. 267–274, 283ff.; A. Teichova, *An Economic Background to Munich: International Business and Czechoslovakia, 1918–1938* (Cambridge, 1974); Lotte Zumpe, *Wirtschaft und Staat in Deutschland 1933 bis 1945* (Berlin, 1980), p. 169.

29. RIIA, *The Baltic States*, p. 166; S. D. Zagoroff, "Agriculture and Food in Bulgaria Before and During World War," in Zagoroff, Jenö Végh, and Alexander D. Blimovitch, *The Agricultural Economy of the Danubian Countries, 1933–45* (Stanford, 1955), p. 376; Berend and Ránki, *Economic Development in East-Central Europe*, pp. 272, 282–284; E. A. Radice, "Raw Materials and Energy," in M. C. Kaser, *Economic History*, vol. 1, pp. 210–218; Józef Krynicki, *Problemy handlu zagranicznego Polski 1918–1939 i 1945–1955* (Warsaw, 1958), pp. 165, 176; M. M. Drozdowski, *Polityka gospodarcza rządu polskiego 1936–1939* (Warsaw, 1963), pp. 161–163.

30. See Heuser, *Control*, p. 3.

31. Ibid., pp. 257ff.

32. Ibid., p. 258.

33. See J. Robinson, "Beggar-my-Neighbour Remedies for Unemployment," in *Essays in the Theory of Employment* (London, 1937).

34. See S. F. Królikowski, *Zarys polskiej polityki handlowej* (Warsaw, 1938); and Heuser, *Control*.

35. Lithuania was an exception. In that country imports were limited by import licenses alone. See Heuser, *Control*, pp. 80, 86ff., 94–97.

36. Ibid., pp. 135–137.

37. Import quotas were substituted by very high tariffs, amounting to 400–600 percent of the value of imported commodities. Ibid., p. 243.

38. Ibid., pp. 3, 5.

39. Ibid., p. 99. See also Zagoroff, "Agriculture and Food in Bulgaria," p. 376; Nikola Momchiloff, *Ten Years of Controlled Trade in South-eastern Europe* (Cambridge, 1944).

40. Different forms and degrees of clearing were analyzed by Howard S. Ellis, *Exchange Control in Central Europe* (Cambridge, Mass., 1941), pp. 1–8. The first clearing agreement was signed in November 1931 between Switzerland and Hungary. See Heuser, *Control*, p. 69.

41. By the end of 1937 Germany had signed fifteen clearing agreements, and before the outbreak of the war, twenty-six. The noneconomic factors played a role in Germany's approval of such agreements. Poland, for its part, signed only seven clearing agreements until 1938. See Heuser, *Control*, p. 71; and Królikowski, *Zarys*, p. 164.

42. See, for example, Momchiloff, *Ten Years*, p. 20, for the analysis of the impact of the quota system on world trade.

43. See Heuser, *Control*, p. 19.

44. *Mały Rocznik Statystyczny 1939*, p. 236; RIIA, *The Baltic States*, p. 171. Both countries joined the Sterling Bloc, thus increasing their export possibilities.

45. See Heuser, *Control*, pp. 34ff. Compared with 1928, industrial production in Greece increased by 27 percent in 1934 and by 83 percent in 1938. Basch, *The Danube*, pp. 148ff.

46. See Heuser, *Control*, p. 37; Basch, *The Danube*, pp. 150ff.

47. Heuser, *Control*, p. 39.

48. RIIA, *The Baltic States*, p. 174.

49. Bandera, *Foreign Capital*, pp. 51, 53; RIIA, *The Baltic States*, p. 172. Latvia continued with the deflation policy until September 1936.

50. Landau and Tomaszewski, *Gospodarka Polski międzywojennej*, vol. 3, p. 364; Drozdowski, *Polityka gospodarcza*, p. 3; Jan Kofman, *Lewiatan a podstawowe zagadnienia ekonomiczno-polityczne Drugiej Rzeczypospolitej. Z dziejów ideologii kół wielkokapitalistycznych w Polsce* (Warsaw, 1986), pp. 135–145.

51. See Heuser, *Control*, p. 86.

52. For more on this topic, see Barbara Ratyńska, *Stosunki polsko-niemieckie w okresie wojny gospodarczej 1919–1930* (Warsaw, 1968); Karol J. Błahut, *Polsko-niemieckie stosunki gospodarcze w latach 1919–1939* (Wrocław, 1975); Czesław Łuczak, *Od Bismarcka do Hitlera: Polsko-niemieckie stosunki gospodarcze* (Poznań, 1988), part III. See also J. Tomaszewski, "Związki gospodarcze państw sukcesyjnych a Polska," in Z. Landau and J. Tomaszewski, *Druga Rzeczpospolita. Gospodarka—społeczeństwo—miejsce w świecie* (Warsaw, 1977), pp. 363–398.

53. Landau and Tomaszewski, *Gospodarka Polski międzywojennej*, vol. 3, p. 366.

54. For Romania, Hungary, Yugoslavia, and Bulgaria, see *Chronology of Political and Economic Events in the Danube Basin, 1918–1938: Hungary* (Paris, 1938), p. 48; Heuser, *Control*, p. 41; Jan Kostanecki, *Naddunajski problem gospodarczy* (Warsaw, 1937), pp. 76–78; Nötel, "International Credit and Finance," pp. 228ff.; Ránki and Tomaszewski, "The Role of the State," p. 27; Natan, Khadzhinikolov, and Berov, eds., *Ikonomikata na Bŭlgariya*, p. 542. In Bulgaria and Hungary, for example, devaluation was effected through surcharges on foreign currency sales.

55. Kostanecki, *Naddunajski problem*, p. 76; Olšovský et al., *Přehled*, p. 395; Nötel, "International Credit and Finance," p. 228.

56. See Heuser, *Control*, p. 56; Drabek, "Foreign Trade," p. 469 (Table 7.45). For Poland, my own calculations based on *Koniunktura gospodarcza Polski w liczbach i wykresach w latach 1928–1938*, Instytut Badania Koniunktur Gospodarczych i Cen, special fascicle no. 12, 1939, p. 34.

57. Nötel, "International Credit and Finance," p. 217, table 12.21.

58. Ibid., pp. 246, 247, tables 12.38, 12.39. For Poland, my own calculations based on *Koniunktura gospodarcza*.

59. A. G. Kenwood and A. L. Lougheed, *The Growth of the International Economy 1820–1960* (London, 1971), p. 109; C. P. Kindleberger, *The World in Depression, 1929–1939* (London, 1973), chapter 14.

60. For the 1920s and the beginning of the 1930s, see Walter T. Layton and Charles Rist, *The Economic Situation of Austria* (Geneva, 1925); Hertz, *The Economic Problem*; H. Liepmann, *Tariff Levels and Economic Unity of Europe* (London, 1938).

61. Proposed, for example, by Corden and Balassa. See chapter 5, notes 29 and 30.

62. See Królikowski, *Zarys*, pp. 176–179.

63. RIIA, *The Baltic States*, p. 139; I. Spigler, "Public Finance," in Kaser, ed., *Economic History*, vol. 2, pp. 153–159; Drabek, "Foreign Trade," p. 413.

64. Królikowski, *Zarys*, pp. 119ff.

65. Ibid.

66. Ibid., p. 126. For Bulgaria, see Ivan Stefanov, "Vynshnata tŭrgoviya na Bŭlgariya sled voynata," in *Trudove ne Statisticheski Institut za Stopanski Prouchvaniya pri Sofiyskiya Dŭrzhaven Universitet*, no. 2-3, 1938, p. 37, table 15.

67. See Zora Pryor and Frederic L. Pryor, "Foreign Trade and Interwar Czechoslovak Economic Development, 1918–1938," in *Vierteljahrschrift für Sozial- und Wirtschaftsgeschichte*, vol. 62, no. 4, 1975, p. 506.

68. *Mały Rocznik Statystyczny 1938*, p. 330, table 21; *Mały Rocznik Statystyczny 1939*, p. 387, table 23.

69. For example, a ban on the export to Germany of a hundred Polish commodities would have been of a lesser significance to the Polish economy and exports than a ban on exporting hard coal to Germany.

70. For example, it is obvious that the decisions to produce aluminum in Hungary and Yugoslavia, taken in 1938 and 1939, were not cases of pure import substitution. Both countries owned rich bauxite deposits and faced no competitors in Europe. The level of production of aluminum in Hungary and Yugoslavia visibly depended on Germany's demand.

7

Protectionism in the Region: The Experience of Poland, Czechoslovakia, and Bulgaria

Poland

Formal criteria based on changes in the customs tariffs[1] permit the distinction of the following stages of protectionism in prewar Poland: (1) until January 1, 1924, (2) from January 1924 to June 1928, (3) from mid-1928 to October 1933, and (4) from October 1933. The indicated stages reflect first and foremost changes in trade policy, and it is in this context that they appear in the literature of the subject.[2] This approach only indirectly tallies with the division of protectionism into stages on the basis of substantive criteria (see Chapter 5). I propose the following presentation of the evolution of interwar protectionism:

The first stage lies in the period between 1919 and the beginning of 1924. It consists of two subperiods: that of the war economy, based (until 1921) almost entirely on administrative control, and that of reconstruction, coinciding with the period of inflation and closed by the introduction of the zloty into circulation. Inasmuch as the protectionist character of Poland's economic policy until 1921 does not require any explanation, the protectionism of the later years, especially in foreign trade, was only an indirect effect of the growing inflation and, as a result, of the conditions facilitating exports and restricting imports.[3] It must be remembered, moreover, that the European environment in which Polish economic policy was formulated definitely drove policymakers to measures that smacked of both rationing and protectionism.

The years after 1924 consist of two successive—although of different lengths—stages of protectionism. The tariffs from January 1924 and October 1933 were particularly eloquent examples of protectionist industrial policy. As they were imposed in different external economic circumstances (the year 1924 preceded or ushered in the world boom, whereas 1933 was a consecutive year of the world crisis), they served different purposes, and they carried different weights. The first tariff, levied during the time of economic prosperity, was to all intents and purposes subordinated to an essential task of raising both domestic production and demand. The other was meant to defend the Polish economy, particularly as by 1936 Poland's primary political goal was to cope with deflation. It should be emphasized that in the 1930s the significance of the tariff policy as the method of protecting local manufacturers turned out to be incomparably smaller than in the period of 1924–1930. In the situation outlined here, the tariff laws comprised landmarks in the interwar history of protectionism.

The protectionist trend of the post-1924 economic policy was characterized and at the same time encouraged by other events as well. Of prime importance among them were the outbreak of the Polish-German tariff war and its aftermath, and also the import and export bans, compensation, quota, and clearing systems that were universal from 1930/31. It must be kept in mind, however, that according to the deflation dogma of the time, any reference to protectionist methods led to a contradiction in terms, thus shaking its doctrine-required consistency. Foreign exchange restrictions and suspension of currency transfers and other payments, imposed in April and May 1936, were only a partial solution to this contradiction. At the same time, they were a turning point in the further development of protectionism. In effect, exports and imports were brought under the near-complete control of the state. Those moves coincided with the formation of the Central Industrial Basin (COP)and with the attempts to include in the country's economic policy elements of self-sufficiency in raw materials.

This cursory glance at the issue is enough to provide detailed characteristics of the successive stages of protectionism in the years 1918–1939.

In the first period, until 1924, government control over the economy was more often than not an ad hoc reaction to outside stimuli and to the economy's domestic problems, and monetary and foreign currency difficulties in particular.

The imposition of a new customs tariff in 1924 officially inaugurated the second period, which lasted until 1931. More consequential, however, was the outbreak of the tariff war between Germany and Poland.

The relapse into import bans in 1932 and a new customs tariff in 1933 began the third period. These notwithstanding, the already mentioned decisions taken in the spring of 1936 were a turning point initiating a separate subperiod.

The first period, at least until 1921/22, was characterized by the state's domination over foreign trade. Government control was exercised primarily through quotas. The provisional customs tariff from 1919 was another standard method applied. The quota system was concerned, among other things, with the reduction in imports of luxury goods and in exports of food products and fuel (essentially coal). The developed quota system was managed by government institutions, first in each of the territories formerly under partition, and later on the entire territory of the Polish state. The Central Office of Exports and Imports banned trade in particular commodities.[4] The Central Office's other task was to provide the war-ravaged country with food. That meant the opening of the domestic market to foreign food products, particularly from the United States. A relatively small part of those imports were obtained as grants.[5]

In that early period, protection of industry was expressed primarily in wide government assistance to private manufacturers, in low duties on raw materials, and the like.[6] Local farming did not need any special protection, as nearly every agricultural product had a ready market at home. (It was rather the transitional speculation in agricultural products that was a problem.)

In mid-1921 the rules of free trade were restored, and in the years 1922–1924 the remaining restrictions were lifted. Bans were confined primarily to exports of certain food products; once quotas were abolished, preferential duties were imposed on imports of necessities.[7] In both cases, liberalization served social needs, particularly the need for food.

The second period (1924–1931) does not yield to an easy definition with respect to protectionist measures. The imposition of a new customs tariff was no doubt crucial. Although contemporaries found it exceptionally protectionist on imported manufactures,[8] I think that was an exaggerated opinion. Until 1928 the theoretically prohibitive tariff had been attenuated by all sorts of preferential duties (especially on imports).[9] The further development of the tariff instruments consisted of the imposition of specific duties and, on a large scale, of the so-called offensive (maximum) tariff aimed (although not charged before 1932) essentially against Germans.[10] There is no doubt, however, that the tariff indexation in February 1928, caused by the change in the Polish zloty parity, and import bans (from September 1925 they applied to eighty-nine items of the customs tariff) escalated protectionism.[11] The relevant decisions were taken, among other things, to strengthen Poland's bargaining position. It is difficult to formulate a single opinion on them. One can say nevertheless that all those duties as well as other measures motivated by the tariff war were favorable to industry: By closing the market to specific German commodities, they spurred the development of new industries, led to a substantial geographical reorientation of Polish foreign trade, and last but not least, reduced the country's economic dependence on Germany.[12] The authorities also resorted to other tools to protect local manufactures: the already mentioned bans on imports as well as—though less regularly—bans on exports (of grain in particular); tariff reimbursements (from 1925); export subsidies; and the intervention procurement of grain, feed, and so on—that is, for instruments having a decisive effect on domestic prices.[13]

The situation regarding protection of agriculture was equivocal. On the one hand, since the improvement in the food market in 1924, the list of agricultural products banned from exports had been gradually cut down until all the bans had been lifted. This way the agricultural incomes might grow. On the other hand, some of those bans were reintroduced temporarily when supplies were inadequate, for example, in the autumn of 1925 charges on grain and on flour exports were raised. At the same time, import duties on these were either suspended or put at a low rate.[14] From the point of view of the so-called policy of protecting the consumer, political and social reasons were more important than the economic criterion. Consumer protection demanded that the government counteract high prices.[15] It was only in the boom years of 1926–1929 that this notion was abandoned for the sake of a more active protection of agriculture. Thus, for instance, at the end of 1929 import duties were levied on rye and wheat to curb the as yet faint dwindling trend of agricultural prices.[16]

Another method to step up food production was to standardize the process and to organize exports. For example, in 1928, the state gave the syndicate of cattle exporters the right to divide the export quota among its members and also introduced standardization regulations with regard to some agricultural products (e.g., eggs).[17] In the third decade, the tendency (distinct not only in Poland) grew markedly stronger.

The so-called grain reserve was yet another means of protection. The institution of grain reserve was set up in mid-1927. The way it worked indicated the wavering of agricultural policy. Generally, it was more absorbed with food supplies and the current market situation than with protection, that is, the strengthening (and possibly the restructuring) of the farming industry.[18] To illustrate the wavering of the policy it is enough to mention the typical divergence of opinion among Polish economists at the end of 1929—at the eve of the Great Depression—on the purposes the grain reserve was to serve. Minister of Industry and Trade Eugeniusz Kwiatkowski saw in it first and foremost a spur to the market and a hindrance to a drastic rise in grain prices, and, indirectly, a boost to the demand for manufactures. However, Minister of Agriculture Kazimierz Niezabytowski and Labor and Welfare Minister Stanisław Jurkiewicz, each for different reasons, treated the reserve as a contrivance to swiftly supply the population with provisions in an emergency.[19]

Yet none of the disparate opinions related grain reserve to measures on behalf of the greater profitability of agriculture. The ministers' proposals simply reflected the liberal economic concepts then prevailing among economists who did not even consider a possibility of using the reserve for any other purpose than to improve the current economic situation or to supply the population with provisions. This short analysis of the mere suggestion of the grain reserve seems to be a good example of how economic policy makers (in Poland and elsewhere) were confused by the contradictions of the time.[20]

The customs tariff from 1933 (and other related measures) showed the rise in protectionist tendencies.[21] Formally strongly protectionist, the tariff was predominantly used as a bargaining chip. But in view of the wide use of preferential and conventional duties, the actual tariff burden was lighter than it might seem judging from fixed rates alone.[22] Thus producers relied more on other methods more appropriate for the situation than on customs protection. Local manufacturing was protected indirectly through the support for industrial and agricultural exports. This was the aim of the system deployed in the years 1930–1935 of duty reimbursements, of subsidies, and of preferential tariffs for exports of coal, steel, and agricultural products in particular. Duty reimbursements played a special role here. Introduced in Poland in 1925, with time they embraced rolled metal sheets, bacon, ham, and grain in particular. Duty reimbursements were of greater significance in supporting agricultural than industrial exports. Also, the reimbursement paid to farmers was higher, but even then it was merely to cushion the severe impact of the agricultural crisis. In the fiscal years 1929/30–1934/35, the reimbursement paid to farmers amounted to 234 million zlotys, or 69 percent of the total sum of duty reimbursements, and in the fiscal years 1929/30–1938/39 it amounted to 396 million zlotys, or 72 percent of the total.[23]

As I have noted, support for agricultural and industrial exports was indirect protection of a sort. Although no trifle—compared, for instance, to the increasingly widespread quota system—its significance was relatively puny (even though, e.g., dumping in the years 1929–1936 required subsidies to the tune of 500 million zlotys a year,[24] to this one should add tax reliefs for exporters or below-cost railway charges).[25]

In agriculture the situation was grim as produce prices plummeted. The state did not support farming to an extent comparable to that in the majority of East-Central European countries,[26] even though it had procured a definite quantity of grain and other products, allowing for the possibility of exporting some of it. This no doubt costly operation was meant to produce a twofold effect: to thwart the fall in agricultural prices and to tilt the balance of payments.[27] In fiscal year 1933/34 the State Granaries acquired 176,000 tons of grain, and in 1933/34 as much as 801,000 tons at a cost of 46 million zlotys (super-bounties included), and nearly 700,000 tons in 1934/35. Despite this operation, the direct cost of which in the years 1930–1935 was estimated at 206 million zlotys,[28] grain prices failed to reach the required level, which was none too extravagant anyway. Although, thanks to a considerable financial effort, Poland (like the other countries to have persisted in the policy of intervention in agriculture) managed to make domestic prices for food products surpass the world level, it did not yet mean that agricultural production became profitable. World prices were very low as almost all exporting countries dumped their goods. Some feeble efforts in the 1930s to resist the tendency to substantially increase plant production proved unsuccessful as well.[29]

Moreover, the authorities took steps indirectly to boost livestock prices by subsidizing animal exports. Starting at the end of the 1920s, this issue was frequently raised at government meetings. Previously, subsidies to exports of livestock were relatively rare and mainly confined to the refunds of export duties on a few products. The policy of steadfast protection of one's own livestock products adopted by countries that until recently had imported such products, and the alarm raised by the farming lobby,[30] forced the Polish authorities to intervene more actively in this area. The aim of the government intervention was to adjust domestic production to competition in foreign markets.[31] Concurrently, in the second half of 1933, the government reversed its policy of livestock exports. Promoting production for the local market, the government levied practically prohibitive export duties on livestock products. In rare cases only, when the government found specific exports lucrative, it assisted them with special, prudently distributed bounties.[32] This was an original measure, adopted by no other country in the region. Yet, from the point of view of protectionism, the assessment of this move is equivocal. From the macroeconomic perspective, state subsidies to unprofitable exports, if granted on a large scale, would be costly primarily because of the current zloty exchange rate. At first glance, the only legitimate reason behind this policy was the protection of national assets against sellout. It was hoped, moreover, that strong export incentives could, at least in the short run (considering the drastically diminishing home demand on animal products), play a positive role.

The preceding discussion can lead to the conclusion that the Polish protectionism of the years 1930–1935—an intricate composition of quota systems, bans, compensation and clearing accounts, subsidies, reimbursement of customs duties and services—was to an extent greater than elsewhere (excepting the protection of certain manufactures) something forced upon it, imposed by military and defense needs. Protectionism in Poland was in great measure a mere reaction to the steps taken by other countries, not a result of the adoption in an economic policy of the clear and fully formed ideological tenets of protectionism. I would even say that the policy—by disregarding the critical opinions of representatives of the farming and industrial interest groups,[33] by supporting deflation, and by accepting almost to the end Poland's presence in the Golden Bloc—was genuinely ill-disposed toward any protectionist provisions. Yet, irrespective of their theoretical leanings, it was obvious to the majority of the economic policy makers that, for instance, the assent by Poland, with no preliminary conditions, to conventions aimed against quotas, discussed at the end of the 1920s, would threaten the interests of the local producers.[34] Compared to the previous statement, this one seems inconsistent—and it should be recognized as such if we were to analyze the matter from the extreme liberal point of view. Yet, from the perspective of the development interests of the country and in the context of the open tariff war with Germany, Poland's negative attitude toward those projects was understandable. It must once again be emphasized that the practice of the Polish economic policy reflected the authorities' ambivalent attitude toward protectionism.

During the boom of 1936–1939, Poland made economic restructuring, industrialization, its aim. In the situation of the increased role of the state (and state industry), economic policy should have almost automatically adopted a more distinctly protectionist line. Still, the matter was not all that obvious. It turned out that the economic growth led to radical cuts in the export subsidies through reimbursement of duties, which was a treadmill procedure in the years 1930–1935. The resources for export subsidies were very severely limited,[35] and so was the number of export products to which duty reimbursement applied (e.g., from March 1937 until August the following year no duties on grain were reimbursed, and starting from the second half of 1935 no superbonus was offered to those who had purchased grain in order to export it).[36] With time, some of the import bans, imposed in May 1936, were selectively suspended.[37] In the Government Economic Committee's principles of the customs policy laid down in September 1937, it suggested the use of other instruments to stimulate exports.[38]

Conditions of growth of national production (including the range of protection against foreign competition) depended directly on export and import control and on quotas. In May 1936 a Commodity Commission was appointed to control exports and the prerogatives of the already mentioned Central Commission for Imports were broadened, and in November of that year the Polish Institute for Settlements to control foreign trade was established.[39] Some of these changes were inevitable in view, for example, of the foreign exchange control and of the suspension of the onerous transfer of the majority of liabilities (this way it was no longer imperative to obtain foreign currency at any price in order to save the balance of payments). The instruments listed here did not differ much, if at all, from those applied in other countries of the region that either set up similar institutions or broadened the prerogatives of the already existing institutions (e.g., central banks).[40]

The changes were not equally acceptable to particular interest groups, especially to exporters. In the literature of the subject it is usually argued that currency restrictions imposed earlier would have lessened the burden to the treasury and the consumers who were together bearing the weight of dumping.[41]

There is some merit in this argument. Yet the reduction in dumping meant at least a partial resignation from the direct influencing of the rise in domestic prices.[42] If the domestic market was narrow and small, as in Poland, cuts in various export subsidies could seriously threaten the existence of even strong industries. In this situation, they tried to carry out the cartel and other monopoly agreements signed earlier in order to raise their prices to the level guaranteeing larger profits.[43] The extensive commodity rationing, enabling control of the majority of imports (e.g., in 1936, as much as 90 percent[44]) served the producers' purpose. Although the commodity rationing protected them against foreign competition, it had an adverse effect, at least in the short run, on the competitiveness of their own product on the foreign market. Then again, resignation from subsidies meant an automatic withdrawal from competition on the third market.

So much for the theory. In practice the economic recovery in the years 1936–1939, reflecting the world recovery and the state's intentional influencing the demand (the COP, the overhauling of military equipment, etc.), and even the uncertain effect of the above-mentioned instruments of foreign exchange, customs and trade policies neutralized the negative consequences of the drastic cuts in rewarding exports (although one can ponder whether customs and exchange policies could not have been better synchronized).

Scarce tax reliefs and cheap loans were still other indirect tools of protectionism. For example, the government began on a large scale to apportion important—from the point of view of protectionism—special-purpose investment grants, territorially limited to the COP, only in 1938. Because of those grants' selectivity, spokespeople for large industry found them substantially inadequate.[45]

No doubt the fact that economic policy hardly resorted to boosting demand through inflation had an effect on narrowing the range of indirect protectionism. Inflation bonus could have encouraged growth in exports.

Measures to provide greater encouragement to exports than before 1936 (treated as an instrument of indirect protection) with regard to the tax, customs, loan, or organizational (export syndicates) area, were not significant enough to make up for the reduction in duty reimbursements.

A novelty in the economic policy was an attempt to devise a separate policy to ensure the country's greater self-reliance in raw materials.[46] Widening the extent and scale of protectionism would be one of this policy's consequences. Yet it was first and foremost the tense international situation, and only then economic reasons and theoretical options, that compelled policymakers on the adoption of definite proposals. Autarky-oriented policy did not reach the practical stage. Contrary to the intentions of its firm advocates (primarily from military circles), it was confined to discussions. The few positive steps taken included the setting up, starting in mid-1936, of state-run agencies and offices for raw materials. They were to ensure continuous supplies to the key industries and this way to guarantee the feasibility of investment plans. In July 1938 defense arguments led to the establishment of the Ministry of Industry and Trade's Department for Raw Materials to monitor the supplies of the raw materials the army needed.[47] Nonetheless, the efficacy of these institutions was questioned. Meanwhile, the policy of transport tariffs changed (the basic modifications from January 1939 were thought to be of particular consequence).[48] But this time, too, other considerations were more important,[49] only a few of which could be recognized as pertaining to a broadly understood protectionism.[50]

Polish interwar economic policy was characterized by inconsistency between the recurrent protectionist tendency and the basic rules governing this policy. It turned out that support for local production and commerce understood as a form of protectionism was hardly concurrent with the general economic line. This divergence had its impact on measures intended as growth incentives. It was particularly clear at the time of deflation and also later, during the cautious inflationary growth promotion.

In Poland's economic circumstances, agricultural protectionism could play a distinct role, especially in the 1930s. Abided by only erratically (it is worth remembering here that a more clearly defined policy of protectionism was pursued only with respect to grain export bounties), it could not prevent a big fall in prices, which was disastrous to the profitability of agriculture, at least in the short run. To make things worse, the falling trend in prices was being strengthened by the pitiful supply of agricultural products from small and even medium-sized holdings.[51] To increase farming profitability would require aiding the traditional stringent means of protection with the whole gamut of other methods, such as a radical and swift lowering of agricultural taxes, followed by a much more decided (compared with the decisions to this end in the years 1933–1935 and in October 1937) reduction of liabilities,[52] at least to the extent that it was done in the rest of the region.[53] It would mean therefore resorting to measures that, along with short-term effects, would also take into consideration such structural changes as agricultural growth and crop restructuring.

This does not mean, though, that the economic policy was characterized by industrial protectionism. For the greater part of the period discussed here, the economic policy was intended to further the interests of agriculture rather than of industry. In practice, however, foreign-exchange and financial considerations in general were the most consequential.[54]

Besides divergences from the economic policy or its ideological principles, protectionism itself was not coordinated and coherent enough. Unlike in some other countries of the region, it was defective and defensive. This form of protectionism in Poland resulted, among other things, from the already mentioned excessive attachment of economists and policymakers to the traditional liberal notion that protectionism was simply a necessary evil resorted to only in emergency. This is why Kwiatkowski, deputy premier for the economy in the years 1935–1939, who opposed protectionist experiments, hoped for a positive impact on the economy from the global recovery; it was only at the end of the 1930s that he stressed the significance of internal incentives.[55]

Was it at all possible, in Poland or anywhere else for that matter, to confine oneself to traditionally understood protectionism, that is, to what I described as operational protectionism? To be more precise, was it possible, in an industrial-agricultural country such as Poland, in the situation resulting from World War I and the Great Depression, to give up customs protection, import-export bans, compensation systems, intervention procurement, and promotion of industrial and agricultural exports by any possible means? These questions are rather rhetorical. Irrespective of the preferences of the economic authorities and their distinct desire to adhere to the classical rules, the balance of payments was the necessary and at the same time sufficient condition to justify the use of the above-mentioned tools of intervention. The example of the Balkan countries, to say nothing of Czechoslovakia, Latvia, or Estonia, shows that it was possible (and perhaps even necessary in hard times) to reach for the plentiful tools of protection and, above all, to use them on a much larger scale. However, the indispensable preliminary condition of this policy was to revise the entire philosophy of the economic policy, useless particularly in the 1930s. It required, as I have said, the rejection of at least the concept of deflation and of the principle of unconstrained foreign-exchange transactions. This was not the case in Poland, although at the end of the 1930s numerous signs indicating such a revision began to appear.

We may therefore pose a thesis that almost in the entire twenty-year interwar period Poland did not carry a coordinated and coherent policy of protectionism, especially with regard to agriculture. No doubt this was due to the fact that the people at the helm of the state's economy did not see development ideology in protectionism and therefore did not treat it as a possible driving force behind development and restructuring. In effect, they at best carried out (not always consistently) a policy that I have defined as tactical protectionism.

Czechoslovakia

As in the Polish case, the evolution of Czechoslovak protectionism followed certain distinct stages. But in Czechoslovakia, perhaps more than elsewhere, the decisive impact of the Great Depression on protectionism as such, and thus on its division into particular stages as well, was evident. It was all the more evident that in the 1920s, after the authorities relatively swiftly removed the postwar restrictions on foreign exchange, import and export, and domestic trade (in 1921, the most painful ones, and then in 1923 and 1924 the rest),[56] protectionism in Czechoslovakia took a relatively moderate form, compared to the situation elsewhere in the region.[57]

Postwar Czechoslovak historiography usually questions this view of the scale and attributes of protectionism. Among Czechoslovak historians there prevails an opinion that the country took, almost from the day of its founding, a firm protectionist line, first in manufacturing and then, from 1925, in agriculture as well.[58]

A separate opinion has it that insufficient protection—virtually in the entire interwar period—gave industry over to fierce competition. Save for the industries or products absolutely indispensable (e.g., the automobile or aircraft industry, superphosphate, synthetic silk), the government was unwilling to boost industry to the degree that would allow the authentic breaking down of foreign customs barriers. Subsidies, reliefs and duty exemptions (notably with regard to the import of textile raw materials), tax reliefs, and the like were too small and the policy of government intervention uncoordinated.[59] Also unfavorable to industry was the insufficient customs protection against aggressive foreign competition for the local market, which in times of slump caused serious adaptation problems.

The two opposing interpretations referred to here contain, however, an unexpected, tacitly allowed for, ethnic undercurrent. In considerations of protectionism, one cannot avoid this factor or treat it as of minor importance. It was a critical element in the international policy of Czechoslovakia, in the 1930s in particular. The position of the majority of Czechoslovak scholars (even if they do not quite realize this) is to defend their country against the charge, brought especially often by the Sudeten Germans, that by relinquishing or misdirecting its protection, the government permitted or even led to the collapse of Sudeten industries. (The anti-Czech propaganda was inclined to emphasize the latter.)[60]

The charge of ethnic bias somehow coincides with the reasoning typical of the business circles, particularly those related to the textile, leather, and ceramic industries. They were usually located in the Sudeten and worked primarily for export.[61]

When looking at those German charges from the point of view of the national question in the Republic, one can perceive a relationship between their varying strength and the current business situation and the assessment of the customs system and of the economic policy in general. The boom of the 1920s largely neutralized the adverse effect of tariffs on the imports of raw materials, and this way lessened the edge of the German charges. In the following decade, especially at the time of the 1930–1934 policy of deflation, this negative correlation was more obvious, thus giving substance to the arguments of the political and economic organizations of the Sudeten Germans.[62]

Leaving aside extreme opinions—which on the one hand went too far in downplaying the extent and degree of protectionism in the 1920s and underestimated its importance in the next decade,[63] and on the other, stressed the omnipresence of the customs and other forms of protection ("Czechoslovakia has become one of the countries with the world's most impenetrable customs barriers . . . ")[64]—it seems that those who believed that the tendency to protect manufactures was particularly strong in Czechoslovakia in the 1930s were right. All the reservations notwithstanding, that tendency was relatively moderate (with the exception of explicit and strong efforts with regard to agriculture); it was undoubtedly weaker than elsewhere in the region.[65]

At the start of its independent existence, Czechoslovakia applied the undoubtedly protectionist Austro-Hungarian tariff from 1906. The postwar supply difficulties led to a certain modification of the tariff by the suspension of import taxes on agricultural products, thus enabling the rise of imports of staple foods.[66] During the short period of quite moderate inflation of the years 1919–1921 duties were being continuously increased, but in such a way as to ensure that the rise in rates was faster than the rise in wholesale prices.[67] (Such old and new industries as engineering, aircraft, and selected parts of the chemical industry enjoyed special protection.[68]) Perhaps from the point of view of protection, more important was a developed and centralized system of import and export licenses, sometimes described as a fragment of the command economy.[69] Such moves enabled a further improvement in protectionism's effectiveness. The so indisputably protectionist practice could be explained by the requirement of taking care of the economic and social needs of the transitional period. But the preservation of tariff multipliers after the koruna ultimately became stable in 1923, after the abandonment of the principles of the "command economy," and in the situation of a typically sharp fall in prices (except, e.g., the prices for imported textile raw materials) meant an actual strengthening of tariff protection.[70]

In the prosperous years of 1926–1930 the advances of protectionism were checked, particularly with regard to the import tax: Through customs agreements the rates on more than a half of the 2,000-odd tariff items (usually manufactures) were reduced.[71] In a good business situation worldwide, this move could not harm local industry.

It is interesting that it was then that agricultural protectionism was born, and in the following decade, it became very expansive. Until 1925 the government had carried out the so-called consumer-oriented policy and therefore had not restricted food imports. In June of that year it imposed percentage duties on certain produce, making the tariff rates dependent on the increase in average domestic prices. This did not satisfy farming circles, however. A year later the Agrarians caused the abolition of percentage duties. Instead, high minimum rates on grain, flour, vegetable oil, eggs, fruit, vegetables, and animals were fixed. Some (usually industrial) raw materials were either duty-free or required low duties.[72] Generally however, as I have noted, the edge of the customs protection was not very sharp. Other forms of protection did not yet play the role they played later, although even at the beginning, agriculture benefited from protection more than industry.[73]

In the years 1930 and 1931, Czechoslovakia returned to protectionism. The country began to extend and enhance the existing customs protection. The already mentioned customs decisions from 1930 constituted a new element; the astounding revision of tariffs even provoked a tariff war with Hungary and made trade with the agricultural countries of the region difficult.[74] Import duties on grain and flour were increased 70–90 percent, and those on animal products were increased markedly as well. Imports of farm produce were made additionally difficult by the restrictive policy that permitted no more than 25 percent of ground wheat and 5 percent of ground rye to be imported.[75]

Customs protection was clearly acquiring prohibitive traits. Reasons were diverse—sheer protectionism as well as the desire to limit foreign-exchange spending and to raise customs revenues in a situation in which other sources of income were drying up. Thus, for instance, at the end of 1932 Czechoslovakia markedly increased the duties on coffee and tea (the respective coefficients went from 10 to 13 and 15); in mid-July 1933 the duty on linoleum, woolen products, and felt was raised 268 percent (from 225 to 600 koruny per 100 kilograms); in January 1934 the duty on salted and unsalted butter grew 100 percent (from 210 to 240 koruny per

100 kilograms), and two months later by another 50 percent[76] (and that was not the final rise). Needless to say, tariffs fluctuated in keeping with the actual or anticipated changes in local and export prices.[77] In Czechoslovakia this was possible because of the special powers pertaining to the economy that the government obtained in 1933, although they became binding only in June 1937, and because of yet other special powers granted to the government through the 1936 law on the country's defenses, which was in force until September 1938.[78]

Prior to the 1933 International Economic Conference that was to discuss the prospects of the as yet barren idea of a customs truce, business circles in Czechoslovakia and other countries, uncertain whether the Conference's decision would be favorable to them, insisted on successive tariff changes. The Agrarians, as usual, demanded a general increase in import levies on agricultural products. Ultimately, in June 1933, on the eve of the conference, the General Assembly granted the Agrarians' demand: From the tariff including 657 items, duty was raised on 165; only a few of these concerned manufactures. The lion's share of the raises fell to farm rates; in addition, abundant minimum duties on food products were restored.[79] New rates did not apply, though, to imports from the countries with which Czechoslovakia had signed relevant conventions.[80]

So what was the real extent of protectionism in Czechoslovakia? As I have already said, the statistical data quoted in the literature are, for various reasons, hardly comparable. Yet, despite all these reservations, protection in Czechoslovakia undeniably increased.

In Czechoslovakia in the 1920s, the customs duty amounted to 21.5–31 percent of the imported products' value, according to the estimates by Layton and Rist; 19 percent (but 27 percent on manufactures), according to the League of Nations' economic service; and 36 percent (46 percent on machinery, and 36 percent on farm produce), according to the Austrian Committee of the International Chamber of Commerce. In 1931 the general level of the so-called potential duties was 50 percent (84 percent on farm products), according to conservative estimates.[81] However, the extent of the so-called effective protection, reckoned according to the Balassa-Corden method, was smaller, standing in 1929 at 24 percent.[82] Since as yet no attempt has been made to assess this coefficient for other years or for other countries of the region in the interwar period, it is difficult to say whether Czechoslovakia's rate of protectionism was in fact moderate. There are basically no reliable data concerning the years that followed. Still, in the light of the economic policy carried out at the time, it is obvious that tariff protection in Czechoslovakia distinctly intensified.[83]

It soon turned out that, as everywhere, tariff policy did not constitute an impenetrable barrier to foreign goods, especially the dumped ones. Therefore it was necessary to resort to other instruments of protection, pertaining to all possible areas of economic life. Expansion of the protection of farm prices was particularly impressive. The tariff decisions of 1930 were indicative of that expansion's range. Farming protection arrived at a new stage of extending interventionism to the areas of production, purchases, and distribution. The trend was clearly gaining in significance. The list of protection instruments comprised minimum prices for farm produce and measures taken to fix the so-called rewarding prices. For example, in 1931 Czechoslovakia passed laws to protect agriculture directly by, among other things, allowing for the stabilization of wheat prices. The years 1932–1936 brought new solutions such as the grain syndicate (1932) and then monopoly (1934) on an unprecedented scale in the region; very far-reaching intervention in the milling industry; deciding on the acreage under particular plants; banning the extension of the growing and producing of certain agricultural products, and the imposition of their mandatory consumption; diversification of production in order to make the country more self-sufficient in farm produce (to this end, Czechoslovakia banned imports of some more agricultural products); and, finally, support for agricultural exports.[84] A transitory upswing at the end of the 1930s did not stem this wave of protectionism. For instance, in 1936, the Agrarians demanded that higher tariffs be imposed on porkers, fats, and butter. They also planned to protect the local production of feed and natural fertilizers and to syndicate the breeding of and trade in animal products.[85] To their old reasons, which in prosperous years did not seem very convincing, the authorities added the need for self-reliance in case the country's defenses were attacked[86] (which in those years sounded very reasonable).

To protect domestic production, Czechoslovakia tried also to subsidize both production and exports, to grant tax reliefs, import-export licenses, to demand veterinary and import certificates (the former being one of the most effective methods of curbing the inflow of foreign food products),[87] to control foreign exchange, to impose quotas, and to manipulate the foreign-exchange rate.

I have already mentioned the defensive aspect of some of those instruments (e.g., the policy of foreign-exchange rates). Tax reliefs for domestic producers and middlemen undoubtedly had a positive impact on domestic production. At least one interesting attempt has been made in recent years to demonstrate the thesis that the Czechoslovak tax policy played a positive role in fighting the effects of the Great Depression.[88] Thus we may conclude that it had a positive protective impact as well.

As regards the foreign-exchange control imposed in Czechoslovakia in October 1931, its protective quality was fully exploited in agriculture. In the hands of the Agrarians, it became the "basic tool of struggle against agricultural imports," as the Polish commercial counselor in Prague put it.[89] Import quotas and prohibitions played no less a protectionist role. At the beginning of 1932 a special commission was established at the finance ministry. The commission started its operations with limiting the number of import licenses, with regard to food products in particular, which had been the Agrarians' (partly satisfied) ambition all the time. By August the list of prohibitions had become so long that temporarily it was easier to publish the list of unprohibited imports.[90] These new restrictions permitted a further intensification of the protection of local agricultural and industrial production.[91] Thus, for instance, in 1933 according to Industry and Trade Minister Josef Matoušek, import restrictions affected 37 percent of the customs tariff, which, for its part, applied to 48 percent of the total value of imports.[92]

Despite attempts to avoid the protectionist bias,[93] it nevertheless remained very distinct, especially in agriculture. Of this line of Czechoslovak economic policy there were no doubts, at least not among keen foreign observers or individual native business circles. Representatives of the government, business circles, consumer associations, and economists, although often starting from different assumptions, willingly emphasized the pros and cons of the protectionist option. In the 1930s its advocates openly began to prefer local interests to the theoretical principles of liberalism, until then formally prevailing in economics and in business life. For instance, the memorandum that the Prague School of Political Science prepared for an international conference on the role of the state in the economy stated blankly that Czechoslovakia should woo the sales market, home as well as foreign, for its advanced industry. At the same time, however, it had to protect local agriculture, which "is as important as our industry," even though, they admitted, this position made trade negotiations, especially with agricultural countries, difficult.[94]

That memorandum was in no way an expression of an extreme attitude; on the contrary, against other declarations of the proponents of protectionism, it was very moderate. It went without saying that such views enforced in practice the affected export possibilities of industry. All the interested parties were aware of the memorandum's inconsistency: Concern for the foreign market had to take for granted a freer access to the home market for imported food products. Yet the alignment of political forces was increasingly becoming a factor eliciting a proagrarian protectionist option. The agrarian circles, seeing a cure-all in protectionism, included it in their program. More often than not in their demands they did not even attempt to conceal their openly selfish motives. For example, in the second half of 1932 the agriculture ministry demanded from the finance ministry's foreign-exchange commission that, under compensation agreements, imports of indispensable industrial raw materials be balanced by exports of not industrial but agricultural commodities.[95] The same demand, although in a modified form, was repeated at the Republican Party congress in January 1936. It was recognized then that compensatory industrial exports to agricultural countries should be linked with exports of farm produce to the allied countries of Romania and Yugoslavia—in exchange for the imports of feed and, needless to say, a limited amount, at an increased duty, of natural fats.[96] This proposition (which ultimately did not become the underlying principle of compensation agreements) should be seen in the context of the intricate political game that participants in the government coalition played with changing luck (usually in the Agrarians' favor).

All in all, those demands, repeated in various forms and years,[97] showed that even among the Agrarian elite particularistic interests took precedence over more general reasons. The rigid agricultural protectionism provoked defensive reactions (protests and retaliations) in Czechoslovakia's agricultural partners.[98] As the American historian Joseph Rothschild correctly observed, this blindness to the needs of the other party actually indicated Czechoslovakia's disinclination to help the Danubian countries out of their agricultural surplus.[99] Let me add here that this stance had a grave effect on Czechoslovakia's foreign policy and international position, particularly in the decade of 1930s.[100] Czechoslovak politicians accepted Premier Milan Hodža's famous 1936 plan as evidence of their openness to the agrarian problems of the region. That program presumed unrealistically, however, that West European countries would import the region's surplus food on preferential terms.[101] But to make this plan come into effect required that Czechoslovakia essentially abandon its extreme agricultural protectionism, at least toward its allies, which, of course, did not take place.[102]

The proagrarian bias of the policy had some adverse influence on political and economic processes in Czechoslovakia, especially if examined in the context of the complicated vocational and residential structures. It contributed to the increase in the tensions in various areas: between industry and agriculture, workers and peasants, town and village, particular parts of the country and, in consequence, between the Sudeten Germans and the Czechs.

This last variance, in a sense, closed the chain of causes and effects. This allows us to look at protectionism in the same way we did at the beginning of this section, that is, from the perspective of the national question. Among the many consequences of agricultural protectionism, which reflected the Agrarians' prevailing upon other members of the government coalition and the parties supporting it (German parties among them), the cumulative psychological effect was eminent. I mean here the majority of Czechoslovak Germans' growing impression or even belief that the economic policy's proagrarian line had led to the collapse of German-owned industry and to the extreme poverty of the German working and lower-middle classes. This was certainly an exaggerated belief. Yet to some extent (presumably small, because other powers interfered there[103]) this impression or belief had some substantiation. The German feelings were only one aspect, and not the principal one, of that multifarious issue.

My last question is, How does the Czechoslovak version of protectionism fit into the tripartite division of protectionism proposed earlier? Assuming that as in Poland and elsewhere, in Czechoslovakia, too, the outbreak of the Great Depression made protectionism undergo a qualitative change, we can propound the following hypothesis: Inasmuch as in its general outline the economic policy quickly passed from the traditionally understood to a moderate protectionism, then as regards agricultural protectionism, it was fast becoming an integral development ideology. As a matter of fact, this is what it was believed to be by some of the Agrarian politicians and ideologues, such as M. Hodža, J. Zadina, E. Reich, and L. K. Feierabend, who applied protectionism to planning, thus trying to build a solid ideological-and-economic structure.[104]

Bulgaria

The policy of protectionism had a long tradition in Bulgaria, dating back to the 1880s and 1890s and the time of Ivan Geshov, minister of finance in the years 1894–1897 and prime minister from 1911 to 1913.[105] By and large, the policy was characterized by the desire to extend strong protection over domestic industry; the significance of agricultural protection became apparent only in the 1930s.[106] Unlike in Poland, in Bulgaria the particular stages (whether distinguished according to formal or substantive criteria) of the evolution of interwar protectionism overlap. Except for the years described everywhere in the region as the period of the postwar consolidation (which in Bulgaria lasted until 1921),[107] in the evolution of Bulgarian protectionism one can distinguish two crucial subperiods: until 1930/31, and the subsequent subperiod, which in 1936 brought about substantial changes.[108]

The first subperiod represented more or less the continuation of the policy of promoting industry, which went back to the pre–Balkan Wars time. In the years 1885, 1905, and 1909 that policy enacted the laws on the promotion of local industry, and the law from 1928 referred to the earlier legislation. According to Bulgarian economists, the first three laws provided the legal foundation necessary to the building of the substructure for national industry.[109] While underwriting this view, one must empha-size, however, that the law of 1928, combined with the high import bar-rier, served first and foremost the purpose of ascertaining and consolidat-ing the position that producers and wholesalers were already occupying in the local market, and of blocking any greater foreign competition. To the foreign observers of Bulgaria's economic life the motives behind the law were obvious.[110] Indeed, even before the passing of the 1928 law, Bul-garians had taken certain legal steps that produced similar results.

Because of the Treaty of Neuilly, in the years of postwar administrative control (1919–1921), Bulgaria could not change the customs tariff. Pro-tecting itself against foreign competition, Bulgaria introduced a conver-sion coefficient to the rates of import duty, which grew more than seven times. The first postwar tariff from 1922 (to which 600 items were added) started with raising the rates on imported manufactures by 100–300 per-cent. In 1923 and 1924 the rates rose again. The customs law enacted in 1926 lifted export and import bans still in force but increased all customs rates.[111] Meanwhile, Bulgaria continued to use other instruments to boost local production. For instance, state institutions and communes were in-structed to purchase locally manufactured goods even though they were 10–15 percent more expensive than comparable imported merchandise (customs duty included). Then, by the 1928 law on the promotion of do-mestic industry, the government could decide on customs rates at its own discretion. Ostensibly it was to lead to the lowering of the customs barri-ers. But the law was accompanied by the raising of the customs conver-sion coefficient from 15 to 20, which increased the duty on the bulk of im-ports, especially imported manufactures, by as much as 100–200 percent of their respective price. Bulgarian industrialists themselves admitted that in keeping with the new tariff and after the further raising of the co-efficient to 27, the customs duty on nearly half of imported goods was simply prohibitive.[112]

In other words, the actual customs burden on imports is today esti-mated at 35–36 percent of its value in the years 1928–1930, and at 51 per-cent in 1931/32 against the average of 21 percent in 1912/13.[113] However, adhering to the concept of potential customs duties, the actual burden was substantially greater, amounting to an average of 67.5 percent of the price in 1927 and to 96.5 percent in 1931. The duty on semifinished prod-ucts totaled 65 percent, and on industrial products 75 percent and 90 per-cent, respectively. It was the highest rate of protectionism in Europe.[114]

Still, in order to stimulate the development of local industry, customs reliefs were given. They were given, to the extent of total duty exemption, to imports of raw materials, machines, and spare parts necessary to start and carry on production.[115] Customs exemptions made the main con-stituent (as much as 45.2 percent in 1931/32) of the total reliefs allocated to industry (1,401 million leva).[116] One must not forget the bargaining significance of the rates fixed as well. This implies the need to be cautious about conclusions as to the real magnitude of industrial protectionism.

As in other countries, in Bulgaria, too, customs tariffs gave way to other instruments of protection. Thus, for instance, industry was offered a tax rebate through government contracts. The share of this rebate in the total of the reliefs awarded to industry grew to 42 percent.[117] One must also take into consideration the protectionist impact of the fifteen-year tax holiday and reliefs granted to local industry, particularly to large industry, in 1925, and other preferences given, for example, to export products, in 1933.[118]

The foregoing information deserves a brief comment. The high proportion of noncustoms reliefs in 1932 (one of the most difficult years of the Great Depression),[119] presumably resulted from a more rapid decline in the value of industrial imports rather than the decline in the total sum of the government contracts. This is what is indicated by the comparison of the total sum of noncustoms reliefs with the value of production, or industrial profits, or of import reliefs with the value of industrial imports. It appears that in 1932 the first kind of relief amounted to 20.6 percent of the value of industrial production and to as much as 48 percent of industry's gross profit; the share of import duty relief exceeded 118 percent of the imports' value.[120]

But the share of industrial raw materials in total imports can be most appealing to the imagination as an indirect indicator of the significance of all sorts of duty reliefs and refunds, reduced railway fares, government orders, and so on. For example, in 1930 and 1937 imports accounted for 87 percent and 82.5 percent, respectively, of raw materials in the government-promoted metallurgical industry, 80 percent and 56 percent in the textile industry, 76 percent and 75 percent in the leather industry, and 64 percent and 79 percent in the paper industry. If, moreover, we regard the considerable dependence of the metal, milling, and textile industries on imported fuel,[121] we can fully appreciate the reliefs' fundamental significance to the growth of industry. Without those privileges industry would not have had enough resources to import the necessary volume of raw materials, semifinished products, and machinery—with all the adverse consequences on the other areas of the economy.

Bulgarian protectionism traditionally lavished care on nascent industries. In the interwar period such attention was devoted to food and canning, chemical, some branches of metallurgical, textile, and rubber industries. Encouragement to the latter found its expression, for example, in the swift and tremendous rise of certain customs rates by as much as several thousand percent.[122] The Bulgarian case leaves no doubt that the high customs barrier had created conditions very advantageous to industry at least until 1936, that is, until the enactment of the new industrial law. Such cozy conditions were offered also, although to a lesser extent, to industrial establishments that did not enjoy special protection (of, for example, the law on the promotion of domestic industry) and that could even be small and backward.[123] To allow any fiercer competition would either have prevented the starting of many businesses, particularly small ones, or would have doomed them to a prompt winding-up. The entrepreneurs involved were aware of this potential risk and therefore demanded that statutory protections, similar to those extended to large industry, be offered to smaller-sized businesses as well.[124]

The 1930s, when the overall economic situation got worse, ushered in a new stage in the development of Bulgarian protectionism. It involved a return, in October 1931, to foreign-exchange control (which had been, to all intents and purposes, suspended in 1928) and to the extension of the system of import licenses[125] as an answer to the budget deficit and serious difficulties (from 1931) in meeting foreign obligations.[126] In 1931 and 1932 Bulgaria's foreign debt and its servicing amounted to 3 percent of the gross national product (GNP) and to 20–30 percent of export revenues (hence, compared to Hungary or Romania, Bulgaria's condition was not so bad).[127]

Desperately seeking new sources of revenue, the government found it necessary by the end of 1931 once again to raise the ad valorem tax from 3 percent to 8–25 percent of a commodity's price (although raw and intermediate materials indispensable to production remained duty-free), and in May 1933 to 20–60 percent of the price. Moreover, duty was imposed on imported machinery and spare parts, which until then the promoted industries had been importing duty-free. Not even half of the old list of 1,300 duty-free items remained.[128] The striving after budget equilibrium impelled higher and new taxes. The withdrawal of tax rebates to industry was the most striking change.[129]

At this point, one might ask about the consistency between the 1930s policy of taxation, foreign-exchange, and customs restrictions on the one hand, and the provisions of the policy of protecting industry on the other. It seems that in everyday economic practice, such consistency could often be observed. The tax burden to the population was relatively heavy (one should bear in mind that half of Bulgaria's yield was subsistence crops and that this kind of agriculture produced 50–56 percent of GNP at the time[130]), especially compared to developed countries. Nevertheless, with 82 percent of the taxation as indirect taxes, it affected the consumer rather than industry.[131]

The same can be said about inhibitory exchange restrictions. The authorities tried to offset the impact of the restrictions or even to use them for protectionist purposes. Thus the government limited or squarely refused access to foreign exchange to the importers of those manufactures that either competed or might compete in the future with similar domestic products.[132]

The Bulgarians attempted also to link the customs policy with their supreme aim, namely, industrialization, which was even more difficult to achieve. In any event, the new customs policy, combined with a more consistent enactment of the law on the promotion of local industry, was more rational than the former practice of giving industry unlimited access to imported raw and intermediate materials.[133] Additionally, the restructuring of the customs tariff was to reduce the waste of resources and to oblige industry, at least in theory, to adhere to profitability criteria when choosing external and internal raw-material suppliers.

Keeping all these in mind, we should once again emphasize that instruments other than customs tariff were typical of the policy of protecting one's own manufactures and domestic market at the time. More important were, for example, foreign trade quotas and the system of clearing accounts (which nearly from the start applied to 70–75 percent of foreign trade).[134] By insulating the economy from the effects of foreign prices, the tightened exchange control that went together with the deepening of the crisis was in fact conducive, among other things, to the creation of Bulgaria's own raw-materials basis for industry and gave an autarkic tint to the country's economic development.[135] That protectionist reorientation toward the development of Bulgaria's own raw-materials resources had only a slight impact on buyers' preferences, which was related to the general backwardness of local agriculture.[136]

The already mentioned industrial law of 1936 represented a turning point in the second stage of protectionism.[137] Having learned a lesson from the transgressions of the earlier regulations, and being still eager to protect the local industry, the authorities gave more attention to the so-called rationalization of industry.[138] The law formally changed the status of enterprises included among the promoted industries and made inclusion criteria stricter. Some industries lost their previously privileged status, which involved, among other things, customs protection.[139] Opinions about this law were not in agreement, ranging from moderately favorable to critical. Spokespeople for large industries, while approving of it, pointed to the concealed possibilities of using it against cartels. Actually, they had opposed any similar projects since 1933. For the same reasons, advocates of unassociated enterprises found the law to be generally discriminatory to free enterprise and favorable to some businesses (the big ones or those carrying out government orders) at the expense of the others (the small ones).[140] Agricultural circles, for their part, saw no substantial change in their own position in the new law. Several years later, proponents of state enterprises lamented over the wasted possibilities of stimulating the development of new industries that the law had offered to the state. Those wasted possibilities included a wider use of tariff exemptions regarding imported raw and intermediate materials recognized as crucial to the fulfillment of government orders.[141]

All in all, although the law allowed for a very far-reaching state intervention in not just industrial relations alone,[142] and despite some criticism on the part of industrial organizations, they nevertheless approved it (just as they had approved the law of 1928).[143] It is interesting to note that the provisions for limiting protection found favor with the British, who had been very critical of the rules governing Bulgaria's economic policy.[144]

The positions outlined here should be seen in the broad context of Bulgarian disputes about the limits of protection, and of industrial protection in particular. Advocates of stimulating development through protectionism clashed with those championing free enterprise as a proven regulator of growth and a guarantor of a smooth, although slower, entry into the international division of labor and into industrialization.[145] After all, approval of protectionism was not unequivocal. Those who saw in it a merely temporary means were in the minority. They urged a cautious use of high duties or bounties and other privileges on the domestic market, and therefore they opposed those who "construct new theories and take pains to justify the realization of 'secular' protectionism."[146] This view can be seen as a veiled disapproval of Manoilescu's concept. Proponents of a decided but rational protectionist policy prevailed. Among the latter was K. Bobchev, a well-known economist and politician, director of the industry department of the ministry of trade, industry, and labor, and the author, among other things, of the 1936 industrial law. At the beginning of the decade Bobchev said, for example, that industrial protectionism was simply a must. He regretted that it was not used on a large enough scale. Protection tariffs, he argued, were sometimes (in crisis) favorable not only to the producers but to the entire economy. He came down in favor of Manoilescu's theory.[147] Several years later, after the experience of the Great Depression, Bobchev observed that the classical theory of foreign trade was "unrealistic" and that "economists were always intuitively aware of the cases where protectionism could be economically justified."[148] It goes without saying that he included Bulgaria among such cases. Still, he was careful when assessing the positive results of industrial protection. Others, Konstantin Klaev, for instance, took a very favorable opinion of protectionism. He charged (indirectly, though quite unjustly) the 1928 law on the promotion of industry with actually restricting protection to tariff policy alone, instead of extending it also to other areas.[149]

In the picture of Bulgarian industrial protectionism, the already-mentioned rule that the state promotes selected industries and specializations is prominent. According to this rule in its formalized version (unmet in any other country of the region), to place a given enterprise in the promoted category quantitative criteria were taken into consideration, such as the enterprise's size and workforce, along with less precise criteria, such as the enterprise's significance to national output. Businesses having government support enjoyed tax-reliefs, including on import taxes, as well as subsidies. In theory, reliefs allowed the government to influence the sphere of industrial production.[150] (In practice, it was not that obvious.) The importance of reliefs to total industrial output was growing. The following approximate data seem to prove the trend: In 1921, of the 1,544 enterprises nationwide, 454 had the government's backing; they secured 47 percent of large-industry output and 40 percent of total industrial output. In 1929, when conditions were good, the number of promoted enterprises swelled to 1,158. By 1937 it had dropped to 907, but these provided as much as 65 percent of total industrial output.[151]

The decline in the number of promoted industries was partly a result of the industrial law and partly of interesting changes brought about in 1930 in the government's policy vis-à-vis the industries promoted. By broadening the interpretation of the law on the promotion of industry, the ministry of trade, industry, and labor, on the recommendation of the Union of Bulgarian Industrialists, issued a circular letter authorizing an Industrial Council to recognize particular industries as "saturated." This was equivalent to recognizing a given industry as sufficiently developed (compared with the needs of the domestic market and export possibilities). It involved the refusal to issue licenses to set up new enterprises in the same industries or to increase production (and production capacities) in the businesses already existing. In 1931 as many as thirty industries were found to be "saturated."[152] To be sure, such practice had a stabilizing effect on the market and the position of the leading producers, yet it was conducive to the ossification of the organizational structures, to the actual monopolization of production, and to the lowering of the competitiveness of Bulgarian products on the foreign market.

In the years 1931–1933, the advocates of the view (particularly the Agrarians) that to win the struggle against economic depression it was necessary to liberalize the economy to some degree, to cut budgetary spending, and to narrow the excessive industrial protectionism carried the abandonment of the policy of promoting large businesses. This also involved the abandonment of the new "saturation" principle as formally inadmissible and economically unjustified.[153] By that time, however, the industrial lobby had grown so strong that several years later, in October 1935, it coerced the authorities into decreeing a return to the old policy. The decree received an additional sanction from the industrial law of 1936, which offered greater possibilities of recognizing various industries as "saturated."[154] Thus in 1936, in virtue of the decree, at the request of the trade ministry's Industrial Council, it was formally recognized that the production in fifteen specialties important to the economy was "saturated." That "saturation" concerned primarily the agricultural-and-food industry (commercial mills, production of sugar, spirits, beer, vinegar and oil, rice mills), light industry (leather products, cotton and woolen cloths), and the metal and glass industries. In some parts of the country every milling activity was recognized as "saturated."[155] Altogether, two-thirds of industrial production in the years 1935 and 1936 was estimated to be "saturated."[156]

The principle of "saturation" of industry was "unjustified by the present stage of development and harmful to economic development," as one Bulgarian economist put it. He saw rather the rationalization described above as the remedy. After all, as I see it, the 1936 law stipulated the establishment of competitive relations on the monopolistic market. It would lead to a drop in prices for manufactures and a rise in sales. Together with some auxiliary measures concerning loans (the lowering of the bank rate), it would allow the reduction of the possibility of "saturation" of certain industries[157] and would help the restructuring of Bulgarian industry in general.[158]

As I have mentioned, industrial protectionism had its opponents, especially among agricultural economists and spokesmen for the peasant movement. In industrial protectionism they saw the cause of rural poverty. It should be kept in mind that at that time the rural population amounted to three-quarters of Bulgaria's total. Their opposition had continued from at least the time of Stamboliyski's rule, which was in fact antiurban and anti-industrial. That charismatic peasant leader condemned the exploitation of the rural by the urban population and subscribed to a tax system adverse to the development of town and industry.[159] That is why the Agrarians, advocating the necessity of basing economic growth predominantly on agriculture, insisted that the state should develop the instruments of agricultural protection.[160] The Popular Bloc cabinets tried to conquer the mutual distrust of industry and agriculture, of town and village. From the protectionist point of view, although the Bloc tried in its economic policy to maintain balance between its subjects, the policy still gave more attention to agriculture (more about which later) than to industry; what is more, the policy went against the "sacred" "saturation" principle, thus eliciting the displeasure of a part of the promoted industries.[161]

Yet outside observers, too, disapproved of the policy of industrial protectionism. They usually believed that industrial protection had seriously poisoned the relations between town and village.[162] Economists and financiers from industrialized countries shared that view, and Bulgaria had to reckon with their opinion, inasmuch as it was they who routinely sat on the Finance Committee and other League of Nations institutions and belonged to groups with a decisive say on the international finance policy. In 1929, still before crisis, Otto Niemeyer voiced the opinion, shared by Sir Friderick Leith-Ross, the Foreign Office's chief financial expert, that Bulgaria's future lay in agriculture and that the customs policy geared to the promotion of industry had not a ghost of a chance of success.[163] This was not an isolated assessment; experts of the League of Nations, and others as well, agreed with it. The same experts monitored how the National Bank of Bulgaria realized the recommendations of the Finance Committee and how Bulgaria met its obligations subsequent to the stabilization loan it had taken on.[164]

Certain assessments made by British diplomats are indicative of the position of some of the Western politicians. In 1930 the British legate to Sofia emphasized the decisively negative effects of the 1928 law on the promotion of industry. Another diplomat did not hesitate in September 1933 to write about Bulgarian protectionism that it was one of the reasons for that country's ruin and that since the imposition of restrictionist tariffs in March 1926 industrialization had become the obsession and principal aim of Bulgaria's economic life.[165] The main victims of the policy naturally were peasants and consumers.[166] Needless to say, as the Great Depression set in, diplomats' opinions became even more critical. They did not change even when business was booming.[167]

In the 1930s Bulgarian protectionism embraced also other areas of economic life. It encompassed foreign trade to further the interests of agriculture. I shall not go here into details of the conditions of agricultural development (the problems related to the patterns of ownership and employment, rural overpopulation, the financing system, the supplies of machinery and other farm equipment, the culture of farming, the yield per hectare, etc.).[168] We should only keep the following in mind: Except for the economically peculiar peasants' rule of the years 1919–1923, which generally coincided with the postwar administrative control of the economy,[169] it was only the Popular Bloc that pledged itself to any policy of protection of agriculture, originally launched by the Andrei Liapchev government.[170]

A serious fall in agricultural prices and, until 1933, the increasingly wide opening of the price scissors,[171] the drastically diminishing peasant incomes and their growing debt,[172] and the decline in the value of agricultural exports, which comprised the lion's share of Bulgaria's foreign sales (and amounted in 1933 to barely 41 percent of their 1929 level)[173] were, as in the agricultural countries elsewhere in the region, the most obvious symptoms of the Great Depression. In this situation the demands of the country's balance of payments and the growing foreign-exchange deficit were enough to decide the extending of protection first to grain, and then to livestock and other kinds of farming as well.[174]

The establishment of a Khranoiznos Board was an expression of those large-scale plans with regard to protection.[175] Initially the board was to make intervention procurements of and to trade in grain; thus it was conceived as a temporary institution. Yet agriculture's increasing difficulties compelled the permanence of the board and its functions. In January 1934 it practically assured itself of the monopoly of procurement of and trade in (including exports of) wheat and rye.[176] This way Khranoiznos was transformed from a temporary institution into an instrument of structural intervention.

It should be pointed out that substantial changes in internal policy furthered such evolution: First, the Popular Bloc came to power in June 1931; then, the new government that was installed as a result of the coup d'état of May 19, 1934, adopting the pattern of Italy, Germany, and the Soviet Union, programmatically resorted to state interventionism in all areas, including the economy.[177]

From autumn 1934 the monopoly-holding Khranoiznos procured agricultural products other than grain, such as cotton, hemp, sunflower seeds, and from 1936, flax. Meanwhile the Bulgarian Agrarian Bank controlled the prices for rose flower and oil and the production of unhulled rice and tobacco.[178] Moreover, the state used the Board to regulate the volume, standard, and kind of grain and industrial-crops cultivation.[179] No doubt the systematic attempts by the Popular Bloc coalition, and then by the cabinets of Kimon Georgiev and Andrei Toshev, to solve the problem of rural debt were a form of protection extended to Bulgarian agriculture.[180] The National Bank's foreign exchange policy also played an important role. Related to increased private compensations, the bank's policy favored clearing foreign trade transactions and the reorientation of the Bulgarian economy toward the satisfaction of demand in the Third Reich's, for raw materials in particular, first under the Schacht plan, and then under the four-year plan.[181]

It should also be noted that, as in Czechoslovakia, Bulgaria, too, tried to make plans regarding the development of agriculture in general and of its specific areas in particular. The Bulgarians, however, talked about the need for a plan rather than actually planning anything, probably because at the end of 1930s this idea was more cherished by individual agrarian economists and advocates of etatism than by government politicians.[182] It was only the harsh requirements of the war that made the decisions pertaining to agriculture resemble planning.[183]

The assessment of the results of Bulgarian protectionism, especially with regard to industry, remains a controversial question. Bulgaria's relatively swift getting over the intense crisis (both agriculture and industry markedly increased their output) indirectly proves the thesis that, ultimately, beneficial elements prevailed.

Agricultural protectionism definitively did not take on the proportions of industrial protectionism. All the same—irrespective of the initially critical view of such Bulgarian historians as Tsonev, Berov, and Natan—in my opinion, the positive results of Bulgarian agricultural protectionism clearly outnumber the negative ones.[184] It also seems to me that the economic policy of the second half of 1930s was characterized by efforts at a more equal treatment of protectionism's main subjects. This does not mean that this tendency prevailed. The proindustrial orientation was undoubtedly more vigorous.

The controversial, elaborate mechanism for promoting Bulgarian industry worked at the expense of the Bulgarian consumer, primarily of the largest social stratum, that is, the peasants. It operated either directly, through the price and tax systems, or indirectly, through subsidies and government orders for industry.

Still, it remains an open question whether any other form of development was possible at all in Bulgaria and in other similarly backward agricultural countries, particularly in 1930s. Needless to say, theoretically, it would be best if Bulgaria and the other countries could develop through agricultural exports. But to achieve this they would need a large market for their agricultural products. The absence of such a market caused Bulgarian agricultural protectionism to become, as suggested by Alexander Gerschenkron, a vacillating policy, lacking the vigor to give an impetus to the country's industrial development and consequently to overcome Bulgaria's underdevelopment.[185] In the entire interwar period, not just in Stamboliyski's time, economic policy too often yielded to pressure from the advocates of agrarianism. Successive governments could not afford an economic policy that, in the name of industrialization, would increase the peasants' burden.[186] Inasmuch as one can agree with Gerschenkron as regards Bulgarian industrial protection policy, his interpretation of the political context gives rise to reservations.

We should also give some attention to Bulgarian protectionism's place in the tripartite classification that I propose. Inasmuch as in the cases of Poland and Czechoslovakia one could wonder whether their respective protectionism was something more than merely tactical, the case of Bulgaria does not raise such doubts, especially as far as industrial protectionism is concerned. Ideologically, Bulgarian protectionism was surely conspicuous for its holistic ambitions. It showed traits of the development ideology (and this already in the 1920s) that held protectionism to be the best remedy for nearly all the ailments of backwardness. Practice, however, did not have much in common with this ideological message.

In any case, it seems justified to conclude that thanks to certain specific institutions (laws on the promotion of industry, the concept of "saturation," etc.) Bulgarian protectionism, often identified with industrialism, was something unique in the region.

Nonetheless, doubts persist as to how much Bulgaria's marked economic growth owed to consistent protectionism and how much to the effect of other factors. It is a fact that the protectionist industrial policy in Hungary, Romania, and even Greece, and the comparable protectionism in Estonia and Latvia (and Bulgaria in the second half of the 1930s) brought about a marked economic improvement in those countries. I shall try to give a more complete answer to this question, going beyond the Bulgarian case, in the final part of my inquiry.

Notes

1. These changes were: administrative control, customs tariff from 1924, maximum tariffs from 1928, and a new customs tariff in 1933.

2. S. F. Królikowski, *Zarys polskiej polityki handlowej* (Warsaw, 1938), p. 22. Compare Z. Landau and J. Tomaszewski, *Gospodarka Polski międzywojennej 1918–1939*, vols. 1–3 (Warsaw, 1967–1982). For a different view, see J. Jankowiak, "Polityka celna jako wyraz interwencji gospodarczej państwa polskiego w latach 1929–1939," *Rocznik Dziejów Społecznych i Gospodarczych*, vol. XXXV, 1974.

3. During the hyperinflation of 1923, however, these incentives to the growth of domestic production practically disappeared.

4. Landau and Tomaszewski, *Gospodarka Polski międzywojennej 1918–1939*, vol. 1, *W dobie inflacji 1918–1923* (Warsaw, 1967), chapter 14.

5. Ibid., pp. 317–320.

6. Inflation turned that assistance practically into grants. See J. Krynicki, *Problemy handlu zagranicznego Polski 1918–1939 i 1945–1955* (Warsaw, 1958), pp. 92–96. This assistance was estimated at US$76–91 million, or 12 percent of the private sector's total profit. See Landau and Tomaszewski, *W dobie inflacji*, pp. 91–93, 289ff.

7. Landau and Tomaszewski, *W dobie inflacji*, chapter 14; Landau and Tomaszewski, *Gospodarka Polski międzywojennej 1918–1939*, vol. 2, *Od Grabskiego do Piłsudskiego: Okres kryzysu poinflacyjnego i ożywienia koniunktury 1924–1929* (Warsaw, 1971), chapter 12.

8. F. Hertz, *The Economic Problem of Danubian States: A Study in Economic Nationalism* (London, 1947), p. 71; H. Liepmann, *Tariff Levels and Economic Unity of Europe* (London, 1938).

9. Landau and Tomaszewski, *Od Grabskiego*, chapter 12.

10. Królikowski, *Zarys*, pp. 108ff.

11. Landau and Tomaszewski, *Od Grabskiego*, p. 285.

12. Ibid., chapter 12. See also B. Ratyńska, *Stosunki polsko-niemieckie w okresie wojny gospodarczej 1919–1930* (Warsaw, 1968), chapter 5, and K. J. Błahut, *Polsko-niemieckie stosunki gospodarcze w latach 1919–1939* (Wrocław, 1975).

13. J. Ciepielewski, *Polityka agrarna rządu polskiego w latach 1926–1939* (Warsaw, 1968), chapter 1; Landau and Tomaszewski, *Od Grabskiego*, chapter 12.

14. Landau and Tomaszewski, *Od Grabskiego*, p. 273. Ciepielewski, *Polityka agrarna*, p. 33. Determined as they were by short-term forecasts, the levels of duties were changed as often as several times a year.

15. Landau and Tomaszewski, *Od Grabskiego*, pp. 118, 272; Ciepielewski, *Polityka agrarna*, pp. 32, 40.

16. Landau and Tomaszewski, *Od Grabskiego*, p. 297.

17. Ibid., p. 298.

18. Ibid., pp. 123ff. For the performance of the grain reserve in the years 1927–1928, see Ciepielewski, *Polityka agrarna*, pp. 33–42.

19. In theory, the reserve was meant to be an instrument to respond to the fluctuations in the prices for grain, and for rye in particular (Poland was a major rye exporter). However, when in the spring of 1928 rye prices kept increasing, irrespective of the sale of the grain reserve, the government decided to import 30,000 tons of rye. See Landau and Tomaszewski, *Od Grabskiego*, pp. 120ff.; and Ciepielewski, *Polityka agrarna*, pp. 148ff. This kind of state intervention had nothing to do with the protection of local production.

20. For a critical analysis of the concept of grain reserve, see Landau and Tomaszewski, *Gospodarka Polski międzywojennej 1918–1939*, vol. 3, *Wielki kryzys 1930–1935* (Warsaw, 1982), p. 159.

21. This concerned primarily the offensive (maximum) duties Germans and Poles imposed on each other's products. In the agreement of 1934, Germany and Poland renounced them. See Królikowski, *Zarys*, pp. 242ff., and Błahut, *Polsko-niemieckie stosunki*, p. 223.

22. Królikowski, *Zarys*, p. 126. For a different opinion, see Landau and Tomaszewski, *Wielki kryzys*, p. 373.

23. Królikowski, *Zarys*, pp. 141–143; Ciepielewski, *Polityka agrarna*, pp. 202–204. Data provided in *Mały Rocznik Statystyczny 1937*, p. 362, table 18, and *Mały Rocznik Statystyczny 1939*, p. 387, table 23.

24. Kazimierz Sokołowski, *Dumping* (Warsaw, 1932), p. 133; R. Battaglia, *Zagadnienia kartelizacji w Polsce: Ceny a kartele* (Warsaw, 1933), p. 145, quoted the sum of 300 million zlotys.

25. For example, in 1930 tax reliefs amounted to 50 million zlotys, transport subsidies to 180 million zlotys, and duty reliefs to 121 million zlotys (the latter in 1935). See R. Nötel, "International Credit and Finance," in M. C. Kaser, ed., *The Economic History of Eastern Europe, 1919–1975*, vol. 2, *Interwar Policy, the War, and Reconstruction* (Oxford, 1986), p. 232, table 12.31; R. Gradowski, *Polska 1918–1939: Niektóre zagadnienia kapitalizmu monopolistycznego* (Warsaw, 1959), p. 204.

26. The governments in Estonia, Latvia, Bulgaria, Czechoslovakia, and even Hungary were more successful in coping with their various problems.

27. For the situation in Polish agriculture, see J. Orczyk, *Studia nad opłacalnością gospodarstw rolnych w Polsce w latach 1929–1938* (Warsaw, 1981), and *Produkcja rolna Polski w latach wielkiego kryzysu gospodarczego (1929–1935)* (Poznań 1971). Compare Wojciech Roszkowski, *Gospodarcza rola większej prywatnej własności ziemskiej w Polsce 1918–1939* (Warsaw, 1986).

28. See Ciepielewski, *Polityka agrarna*, p. 202.

29. Landau and Tomaszewski, *Wielki kryzys*, pp. 165ff., 196; Ciepielewski, *Polityka agrarna*, p. 202, table 42. This failure was due to the very low productivity of Polish agriculture.

30. Ciepielewski, *Polityka agrarna*, pp. 164–167; Roszkowski, *Gospodarcza rola*, p. 330.

31. Ciepielewski, *Polityka agrarna*, pp. 167ff.

32. Ibid., pp. 165–169.

33. M. M. Drozdowski, *Polityka gospodarcza rządu polskiego 1936–1939* (Warsaw, 1963), p. 3; Z. Knakiewicz, *Deflacja polska 1930–1935* (Warsaw, 1967); Landau and Tomaszewski, *Wielki kryzys*, chapters 1 and 7; Jan Kofman, *Lewiatan a podstawowe zagadnienia ekonomiczno-polityczne Drugiej Rzeczypospolitej. Z dziejów ideologii kół wielkokapitalistycznych w Polsce* (Warsaw, 1986), chapter 7.

34. Z. Drabek, "Foreign Trade Performance and Policy," in M. C. Kaser, ed., *The Economic History of Eastern Europe, 1919–1975*, vol. 1, *Economic Structure and Performance Between the Two Wars* (Oxford, 1985), p. 410.

35. For a different view, see Błahut, *Polsko-niemieckie stosunki gospodarcze*, p. 274.

36. *Mały Rocznik Statystyczny 1939*, p. 371; Drozdowski, *Polityka gospodarcza*, chapters 2 and 4.

37. Drozdowski, *Polityka gospodarcza*, p. 176; Królikowski, *Zarys*, p. 156.

38. Drozdowski, *Polityka gospodarcza*, p. 176; Błahut, *Polsko-niemieckie stosunki*, p. 273.

39. Królikowski, *Zarys*, p. 156.

40. See H. Heuser, *Control of International Trade* (London, 1939) and N. Momchiloff, *Ten Years of Controlled Trade in South-eastern Europe* (Cambridge, 1944).

41. See Z. Landau, *Plan stabilizacyjny 1927–1930: Geneza, założenia, wyniki* (Warsaw, 1964), p. 275; Z. Landau and J. Tomaszewski, *Zarys historii gospodarczej Polski 1918–1939* (Warsaw, 1981), p. 204; Drozdowski, *Polityka gospodarcza*, p. 53.

42. Drozdowski, *Polityka gospodarcza*, p. 176.

43. Kofman, *Lewiatan*.

44. Drozdowski, *Polityka gospodarcza*, p. 176.

45. Kofman, *Lewiatan*, chapters 8 and 9; J. Gołębiowski, *Sektor państwowy w gospodarce Polski międzywojennej* (Warsaw, 1985), pp. 229ff.

46. Drozdowski, *Polityka gospodarcza*, pp. 81, 174ff.; "Wytyczne państwowej polityki surowcowej (1938)," *Archiwum Akt Nowych, Komitet Ekonomiczny Ministrów*, Collection 27460, pp. 1–25.

47. Drozdowski, *Polityka gospodarcza*, pp. 81, 94.

48. See Adam Rudzki, *Zarys polskiej polityki komunikacyjnej* (London, 1945), p. 20; Landau and Tomaszewski, *Wielki kryzys*, pp. 303–306.

49. On Polish maritime policies after 1925, see Bogdan Dopierała, *Wokół polityki morskiej Drugiej Rzeczypospolitej* (Poznań, 1978), pp. 262–266, 336–341, 351.

50. See Drozdowski, *Polityka gospodarcza*, p. 180, on the promotion of exports to Czechoslovakia.

51. Ciepielewski, *Polityka agrarna*, chapters 2 and 4; Landau and Tomaszewski, *Wielki kryzys*, chapter 5.

52. During the Great Depression the real tax burden actually increased. See Mieczysław Mieszczankowski, "Zadłużenie rolnictwa Polski międzywojennej," *Najnowsze Dzieje Polski*, vol. 6, 1963, pp. 126, 132; Ciepielewski, *Polityka agrarna*,

chapter 5; Ciepielewski, ed., *Wieś polska w latach wielkiego kryzysu 1929–1935: Materiały i dokumenty* (Warsaw, 1965); Landau and Tomaszewski, *Wielki kryzys*, chapter 5.

53. O. von Frangeš, "Fighting the Crisis in the Peasant Countries of Danube Basin," in *Proceedings of the Third International Conference of Agricultural Economics* (London, 1935), pp. 97–100; Edward Patka, "Experience of Debt Adjustment in Czechoslovakia," in *Proceedings of the Fourth International Conference of Agricultural Economics* (London, 1937), pp. 159–162; Drozdowski, *Polityka gospodarcza*, p. 229; Ciepielewski, *Polityka agrarna*, chapter 5. On the situation in the Baltic states, Romania, Yugoslavia, and Hungary, see Louis Tardy, *Report on Systems of Agricultural Credit and Insurance* (Geneva, 1938), pp. 30ff., 61ff.

54. Kofman, *Lewiatan*, chapter 7; Landau and Tomaszewski, *Wielki kryzys*, chapter 2.

55. See Drozdowski, *Polityka gospodarcza*; Hanna Jędruszczak and Tadeusz Jędruszczak, *Ostatnie lata Drugiej Rzeczypospolitej (1935–1939)* (Warsaw, 1970), pp. 170–215; Gołębiowski, *Sektor państwowy*, chapters 6 and 9; Kofman, *Lewiatan*, chapter 9; Landau, "Polityka walutowa rządu polskiego w latach 1936–1939," *Przegląd Historyczny*, vol. 2, 1986, pp. 274–280.

56. L. Pasvolsky, *Economic Nationalism of the Danubian States* (London, 1928), pp. 78, 213ff., 276; R. Olšovský et al., *Přehled hospodářského vývoje Československá v letech 1918–1945* (Prague, 1961), pp. 69, 154ff.; Jozef Faltus, *Povojnová hospodárska kriza v rokoch 1921–1923 v Československu* (Bratislava, 1966), p. 33; *Dejiny štátu a práva na území Československa v obdobi kapitalizmu*, vol. 2, *1918–1945* (Bratislava, 1972), p. 208.

57. On the policies in 1920s, see Z. Pryor and F. L. Pryor, "Foreign Trade and Interwar Czechoslovak Economic Development 1918–1938," *Vierteljahrschrift für Sozial- und Wirtschaftsgeschichte*, vol. 62, no. 4, 1975, p. 505; Pasvolsky, *Economic Nationalism*, pp. 276–279; L. E. Textor, "Agriculture and Agrarian Reform," in R. J. Kerner, ed., *Czechoslovakia* (Berkeley, 1945), pp. 233, 236; E. A. Radice, "General Characteristics of the Region Between the Wars," in Kaser, ed., *Economic History*, vol. 1, p.36; V. Průcha, "Polemika vstoupila do hospodářské historiografie," in *Československy Časopis Historický*, no. 6, 1969, p. 907; Drabek, "Foreign Trade," pp. 400–412, 476 (Tables 7.62 and 7.63).

58. For the discussions in the 1960s and the early 1970s, see three articles by Anatol Dobrý, "Zakladni směry vývoje československého průmyslu v letech 1913–1938, a něktré otázký socialně politícke," in *Československy Časopis Historický*, no. 5, 1965, "O pravdivý obraz hospodářského profilu předmnichovské republiky," in *Československy Časopis Historický*, no. 2, 1969, and "O spornych problémach dosavadniho výzkumu hospodářských dejín Československa," in *Sbornik Historický*, no. 22, 1975; V. Průcha, "Hospodářský profil předmnichovské republiky," in *Nova Mysl*, no. 3, 1968, and "Polemika"; J. Faltus, "Za pravdivý obraz hospodářského profilu predmnichovskiej republiky," in *Československy Časopis Historický*, no. 5/6, 1970; V. Lacina, "Problémy odvětvove struktury československého průmyslu v letech 1918–1930," in *Československy Časopis Historický*, no. 6, 1976. See also Z. Pryor, "Czechoslovak Economic Development in the Interwar Period," in Victor S. Mamatey and Radomir Luža, eds., *A History of the Czechoslovak Republic, 1918–1948* (Princeton, 1973), p. 200. For a political context of these discussions, see J. M. Montias, "Economic Nationalism in Eastern Europe: Forty Years of Continuity and Change," *Journal of International Affairs,*

vol. XX, no. 1, 1966; I. T. Berend, "The Problem of Eastern European Economic Integration in a Historical Perspective," in Imre Vajda and Mihaly Simai, eds., *Foreign Trade in Planned Economy* (Cambridge, 1971).

59. Dobrý, "O pravdivý," pp. 188ff., and "O spornych," pp. 182–184.

60. "The German Minority in Czechoslovakia (by German Bohemian Deputy)" *Slavonic and East European Review*, vol. XIV, no. 41, 1936, pp. 296–299; Jaromir Nečas, "Economic and Social Problems in German Bohemia," *Slavonic and East European Review*, vol. XV, no. 45, 1937, pp. 601–609; *Czechoslovak Cabinet Ministers on the Complaints of the Sudeten German Party in the Czechoslovak Parliament* (Prague, 1937), pp. 42–56; Robert Polzer, "Die Sudetendeutsche Wirtschaft in der Tschechoslowakei," in *Der Göttinger Arbeitskreis Schriftenreihe*, vol. 26 (n.d.); J. César and B. Černý, *Politika německých buržoaznich stran v Československu v letech 1918–1938*, vol. 2, *1930–1938* (Prague, 1962), and "The Policy of German Activist Parties in Czechoslovakia, 1918, 1938," *Historica*, vol. VI, 1962; E. Wiskemann, *Czechs and Germans* (London, 1967); J. W. Bruegel, *Czechoslovakia Before Munich: The German Minority Problem and British Appeasement Policy* (Cambridge, 1973).

61. Wiskemann, *Czechs and Germans*; R. Olšovský, *Světový obchod a Československo 1918–1938* (Prague, 1981), pp. 123–132.

62. See Wiskemann, *Czechs and Germans*; J. César and B. Černy, "The Nazi Fifth Column in Czechoslovakia," *Historica*, vol. IV, 1962, and *Politika*; Bruegel, *Czechoslovakia*. Compare "Memorandum Respecting the General Economic Situation in Czechoslovakia (1931)," *PRO FO 371/16658*, p. 124; "Annual Report, 1933," *PRO FO 371/18383*, p. 6; "Addison to Hoare, 7 August 1935, report 160E," *PRO FO 371/19494*, p. 195; "Newton to Eden, 15 March 1937," *PRO FO 371/21128*, p. 92. The characteristics of the German minority in Czechoslovakia is provided in "Poselstwo RP w Pradze, 25 April 1936," *Archiwum Akt Nowych, Ministerstwo Spraw Zagranicznych*, Collection 5473, pp. 64–67, 97–108; "Chodacki do Kobylańskiego, 30 June 1936," *Archiwum Akt Nowych, Ministerstwo Spraw Zagranicznych*, Collection 5474, p. 24; "Mniejszość niemiecka w Czechosłowacji, Konsulat RP w Morawskiej Ostrawie, June 1936," *Archiwum Akt Nowych, Ministerstwo Spraw Zagranicznych*, Collection 5474, pp. 201–207.

63. Textor, "Agriculture," and Dobrý, "O pravdivý."

64. Faltus, "Za pravdivý," p. 604.

65. For the 1920s, see Liepmann, *Tariff Levels*, pp. 395–399, 413. Compare Pryor and Pryor, "Foreign Trade," pp. 505–511 (data on effective protection in 1929).

66. It continued until 1925. See Pasvolsky, *Economic Nationalism*, pp. 276–278; V. Průcha, ed., *Historia gospodarcza Czechosłowacji XX wieku* (Warsaw, 1979), p. 56; Olšovský et al., *Přehled*, p. 69.

67. Pasvolsky, *Economic Nationalism*, p. 277; Průcha, ed., *Historia gospodarcza*, pp. 56ff.

68. See data quoted by Průcha, "Polemika," p. 907.

69. Olšovský et al., *Přehled*, pp. 137, 152; Faltus, *Povojnová hospodárska kriza*, pp. 33–35.

70. Pasvolsky, *Economic Nationalism*, p. 278; Průcha, "Polemika," p. 907.

71. This concerned custom agreements first of all with France, Italy, Austria, Poland, and Hungary. See Pasvolsky, *Economic Nationalism*, p. 279; Hertz, *The Economic Problem*, p. 71; Průcha, ed., *Historia gospodarcza*, p. 58.

72. Zdeněk Fafl, "Československá obchodní politíka," *Sbirka ČSN*, no. XVII, 1935/36, pp. 3–8; Olšovský, *Světový*, pp. 156–158; Průcha, "Polemika," pp. 907ff.

73. Drabek, "Foreign Trade," p. 412.

74. Fafl, "Československá," pp. 9, 11; V. Průcha, ed., *Hospodářské dejíny Československá v 19 a 20 století* (Prague, 1974), p. 145; Olšovský, *Světovy*, p. 162. Drabek, "Foreign Trade," p. 441. In 1931 Hungarian exports to Czechoslovakia declined by 85 percent and Czechoslovak to Hungary by 71 percent.

75. I. T. Berend and G. Ránki, *Economic Development in East-Central Europe in the 19th and 20th Centuries* (New York, 1974), p. 207; Josef Anthropius, "Obilni monopol v zemědělska krise," *Sbirka ČSN*, no. VI, 1931/32, pp. 7–9.

76. My own estimates and "Münnich do Ministerstwa Przemysłu i Handlu, 10 January and 10 March 1934," *Archiwum Akt Nowych, Ministerstwo Spraw Zagranicznych*, Collection 9425, pp. 15, 77.

77. Between July and October 1933 alone, various tariffs were revised seven times. See the relevant issues of *Sbirka zakonů a nařizeni státu československého*.

78. Leonard Bianchi, *Právne formy monopolizácie za buržoáznej ČSR* (Bratislava, 1965), pp. 102ff.; *Dejiny státu*, pp. 320, 378; Alena Gajanová and Bohumil Lehár, "K charakteru buržoazně demokratického zřizeni v Československu," *Československy Časopis Historický*, no. 3, 1968, p. 391.

79. Fafl, "Československá" p. 9; Królikowski, *Zarys*, p. 107; "Münnich do Ministerstwa Przemysłu i Handlu, 23 March 1933," *Archiwum Akt Nowych, Ministerstwo Spraw Zagranicznych*, Collection 9423, pp. 132, 145. See also "Annual Report, 1933," p. 12.

80. See Fafl, "Československá," p. 9, and Królikowski, *Zarys*, pp. 107ff.

81. Hertz, *The Economic Problem*, pp. ff70.; Liepmann, *Tariff Levels*, pp. 413, 415.

82. Pryor and Pryor, "Foreign Trade," p. 507.

83. As illustrated, for example, by successive increases in the rates of the 1933 customs tariff.

84. See "Observations on the Relations Between the State and Economic Life from the Point of the Czechoslovak Republic," in *The State and Economic Life: First Study Conference (Milan, May 1932)* (Paris, 1932), p. 125; Anthropius, "Obilni monopol," pp. 1–38; J. Kratochvíl, "O zásahu státní moci do soukromého hospodářstvi," *Sbirka ČSN*, no. III, 1934/35, pp. 11–14; A. Basch, "Československé hospodářstvi v krisi," in *Sbirka ČSN*, no. XV, 1936/37, p. 19; Textor, "Agriculture," pp. 234–238; B. Černý, "Některé hospodářskopolitické důsledky obilniho monopolu," *Československy Časopis Historický*, no. 4, 1959; Lacina, *Krize*; J. Faltus, "Štátne zásahy do československého národného hospodářstva v 30 rokoch," *Hospodářské dějiny*, vol. 13, 1985, pp. 139–141.

85. They scored some temporary success in 1933 and at the end of 1930s. See Textor, "Agriculture," pp. 236–238; Lacina, *Krize*, pp. 145–149; Václav Škoda, "Plánovani v zěmědelstvi," *Sbirka ČSN*, no. XVIII, 1934/35, pp. 16–20; Faltus, "Štátne zásahy," p. 142; "Münnich do Ministerstwa Spraw Zagranicznych Wydział P. III, 3 February 1936," *Archiwum Akt Nowych, Ministerstwo Spraw Zagranicznych*, Collection 831, p. 229; "Münnich do MSZ Wydział P. III, 20 January 1937," *Archiwum Akt Nowych, Ministerstwo Spraw Zagranicznych*, Collection 831, pp. 333, 339; "Münnich do MSZ Wydział p. 80, III, 30 February 1937," *Archiwum Akt Nowych, Ministerstwo Spraw Zagranicznych*, Collection 831, p. 540.

86. See A. Basch, *The Danube Basin and the German Economic Sphere* (London, 1944), p. 80, and *Československé hospodářstvi*, p. 23; František Radouš, "Hospodářské otázký vnitřni kolonisace a obrony země," *Sbirka ČSN*, 1935/36. Compare also Agriculture Minister Zadina's addresses to the parliament (November 1937) and to the State Agricultural Council (December 1937) concerning planned economy. See "Papée do Ministerstwa Spraw Zagranicznych Wydział P. III and Münnich do Ministerstwa Spraw Zagranicznych Wydział P. III, 29 November and 2 December 1937," *Archiwum Akt Nowych, Prezydium Rady Ministrów*, Collection 831, pp. 439–444. Compare L. K. Feierabend, "Agriculture in the First Republic of Czechoslovakia," in M. Rechcigl, Jr., ed., *Czechoslovakia Past and Present*, vol. 1, *Political, International, Social, and Economic Aspects* (The Hague, 1968), p. 178.

87. See "Münnich do Ministerstwa Spraw Zagranicznych Wydział P. IV, 1 December 1930," *Archiwum Akt Nowych, Ministerstwa: Spraw Zagranicznych*, Collection 5534, p. 433.

88. Z. Pryor, "Czechoslovak Fiscal Policies in the Great Depression," *Economic History Review*, vol. 22, 1979, pp. 228ff.

89. See "Münnich do Ministerstwa Spraw Zagranicznych Wydział P. III, 28 November 1932," *Archiwum Akt Nowych, Prezydium Rady Ministrów*, Collection 831, p. 35.

90. Heuser, *Control*, pp. 7, 132–137; Basch, *The Danube Basin*, p. 79.

91. See Basch, *The Danube Basin*, pp. 48, 80.

92. Compare "Addison to Simon, 28 November 1933," *PRO FO 371/16658*, p. 178 (Kershaw's memorandum).

93. For example, in 1936 Czechoslovakia lifted 30 percent of its quantity restrictions on imports. See Heuser, *Control*, p. 250; Jaroslav Skorovský, "Československá obchodní politika," *Sbirka ČSN*, no. II, 1937/38, p. 5; Basch, *The Danube Basin*, p. 120.

94. "Observations on the Relations," p. 125.

95. See "Münnich do Ministerstwa Spraw Zagranicznych Wydział P. III, 28 November 1932," *Archiwum Akt Nowych, Prezydium Rady Ministrów*, Collection 831, p. 35.

96. "Münnich do Ministerstwa Spraw Zagranicznych Wydział P. III, 3 February 1936," ibid., p. 230.

97. Compare certain publications representing the point of view of the Agrarians published in the years 1928/29–1938/39 by the Czech Economic Society (ČSN), for example, Bohdan Živanský, *Aktuálni otázký československého průmyslu mlynářského* (Prague, 1929); Vladimir Brdlík, *Zemědělská krise v souvislosti s národním hospodářstvim* (Prague, 1933); Štefan Čačko, "O polnohospodářskych pomerach Slovenska," in K. Stodola et al., *Hospodářské problémy Slovenska* (Prague, 1934); Alfred M. Mayer, *Pět let krise na našem venkově* (Prague, 1935); Škoda, "Plánovani"; Edvard Reich, *Problem zemědělstvi v celkovém plánu hospodářske politiky* (Prague, 1936); B. Živanský, "Úprava obilního hospodářství a kontingentace mlynů," *Sbirka ČSN*, 1936/37, no. XVI (Prague, 1937).

98. Basch, *The Danube Basin*, p. 48 and chapter 9.

99. J. Rothschild, *East Central Europe Between Two World Wars* (Seattle and London, 1974), pp. 123ff.

100. See Basch, *The Danube Basin*, p. 38 and chapter 9. Compare statistical data quoted by Drabek, "Foreign Trade."

101. Robert Kvaček, *Nad Evropu zataženo: Československo a Europa 1933–1937* (Prague, 1966). On planned regional solutions, see Z. Sládek and J. Tomaszewski, "Próby integracji ekonomicznej Europy Środkowej i Południowo-Wschodniej w latach trzydziestych XX w.", *Sobótka*, no. 3, 1979, pp. 377–400.

102. Z. Sládek, "Wyniki gospodarcze działalności Małej Ententy oraz polityczne następstwa jej niepowodzenia," *Studia z Dziejów ZSRR i Europy Środkowej*, vol. XX, 1984, pp. 138, 142, 154.

103. See, for instance, H. Batowski, *Rok 1938 — dwie agresje hitlerowskie* (Poznań, 1985); Rothschild, *East Central Europe*; F. G. Campbell, *Confrontation in Central Europe: Weimar Republic and Czechoslovakia* (Chicago, 1975).

104. The activities and publications of the Agricultural College (Československá Akademie Zemědělska), set up in 1924, were of consequence here. Hodža was the College's first rector.

105. That policy was propagated, particularly at the end of 1880s, by journalists and economists from the circle around the *Promishlenost* paper. See Z. Natan, V. Khadzhinikolov, and L. Berov, eds., *Ikonomikata na Bŭlgariya*, pp. 376–379, 396, 443; A. Gerschenkron, "Some Aspects of Industrialization in Bulgaria, 1879–1939, in A. Gerschenkron, *Economic Backwardness in Historical Perspective* (London and Cambridge, Mass., 1976), p. 218.

106. D. Toshev, *Industrialnata politika na Bŭlgariya sled Pŭrvata svetovna voyna* (Varna, 1943), p. 44; Z. Natan, "Stopanska istoriya na Bŭlgariya," in *Izbrani trudove v dva toma*, vol. I (Sofia, 1977), p. 404; L. Berow, "Państwowo-monopolistyczne regulowanie gospodarki w burżuazyjnej Bułgarii do 1944 r.," *Studia z Dziejów ZSRR i Europy Środkowej*, vol. XIII, 1977, pp. 6–8, and L. Berov, "Direktsiya 'Khranoiznos,' 1930–1944 g.," *Trudove na Visshiya ikonomicheski institut Karl Marks*, no. 1, 1960.

107. Berow, "Państwowo-monopolistyczne regulowanie," p. 12; Ránki and Tomaszewski, "The Role of the State," in Kaser, ed., *The Economic History*, vol. 2, p. 14.

108. According to Toshev, *Industrialnata politika*, p. 44, the turning point occurred in 1929. I myself believe that it was rather the end of 1930. In 1931 the Democratic Alliance lost the elections. For a similar opinion, see K. Bobchev, "Vyrshnata tŭrgovska politika na Bŭlgariya sled voynata," in *Trudove ne Statisticheski institut za stopanski prouchvaniya pri Sofijskiya dŭrzhaven universitet*, no. 4, 1938, pp. 1, 14, 18. As far as the 1936 turning point is concerned, it means also an ultimate consolidation of the authoritarian rule. See Ilczo Dimitrow, "Ewolucja dyktatury faszystowskiej w Bułgarii (1934–1939)," *Studia z Dziejów ZSRR i Europy Środkowej*, vol. X, 1974, pp. 75–92; Vladimir Migev, *Utvŭrzhdavane na monarkho-fashistkata diktatura v Bŭlgariya, 1934–1936* (Sofia, 1977), chapter 1; Natan et al., *Ikonomikata*, p. 533. Compare also Berow, "Państwowo-monopolistyczne regulowanie," pp. 16, 19, and Stefan Tsonev, *Dŭrzhavno-monopolistichniyat kapitalizm v Bŭlgariya* (Varna, 1968), pp. 62–72).

109. Konstantin Klaev, "Bŭlgarskata industriya prez poslednite deset godini," *Ekonomist*, no. 1, 1939, p. 45; Luben Savadiiev, *Les caractères et les effets de la politique du Nationalisme Economique en Bulgarie* (Lyon, 1939), pp. 48–51; Toshev, *Industrialnata politika*, p. 165; Natan et al., *Ikonomikata*, pp. 378, 518.

110. This is mildly suggested in "Annual Report, 1930," *PRO FO 371/14326/ 13789*, p. 173; "Annual Report, 1930," *PRO FO371/15176/C. 1534/1531/7*, p. 111; "Annual Report, 1931," *PRO FO 371/15897/C. 912/912/7*, p. 165; "Balfour to Simon, 30 September 1933," *PRO FO 371/16653, p. 88–92.*

111. Natan et al., *Ikonomikata*, pp. 491, 518; Ránki and Tomaszewski, "The Role of the State," p. 15.

112. Bobchev, "Reglamentirane na vŭnshnata tŭrgoviya i organizirane na vŭnshnata tyrgovska politika," *Bŭlgarsko stopanstvo*, no. 9, 1940, pp. 131–133; Toshev, *Industrialnata politika*, p. 45; Atanas Atanasov, "Za industrialnata politika na dŭrzhavata," *Industrialen pregled*, no. 61, 1933 (quoted in Toshev).

113. L. Berov, *The Economic Development of Bulgaria Between the Two Wars, 1918–1944* (Oxford, 1972), p. 7; A. Teichova, "Industry," in Kaser, ed., *The Economic History*, vol. 1, p. 254.

114. Liepmann, *Tariff Levels*, pp. 170–173, 417.

115. George Clenton Logio, *Bulgaria Past and Present* (Manchester, 1936), p. 132.

116. The author's estimates, based on the data quoted in Toshev, *Industrialnata politika*, p. 44.

117. Ibid.

118. Ránki and Tomaszewski, "The Role of the State," p. 19; Toshev, *Industrialnata politika*, pp. 110ff.; Tsonev, *Dŭrzhavno-monopolistichniyat kapitalizm*, p. 108.

119. Industrial production stood at 74 percent, foreign trade at 46.6 percent, and the level of industrial and agricultural prices at 70 and 53.5 percent, respectively. See Natan et al., *Ikonomikata*, pp. 536, 539, 541.

120. The author's estimates, based on the data quoted in Toshev, *Industrialnata politika*, p. 44, and Asen Chakalov, *Natsyonalniyat dokhod i rozkhod na Bŭlgariya 1924–1945 g.* (Sofia, 1946), p. 114.

121. Gerschenkron, *Economic Backwardness*, p. 214. See also Tsonev, *Dŭrzhavno-monopolistichniyat kapitalizm*, p. 57.

122. Toshev, *Industrialnata politika*, pp. 60, 63.

123. Ibid., p. 59.

124. Ibid., p. 136.

125. Natan et al., *Ikonomikata*, p. 542; Berow, "Państwowo-monopolistyczne regulowanie," pp. 14, 19.

126. I. Spigler, "Public Finance," in Kaser, ed., *The Economic History*, vol. 2, p. 158; Natan et al., *Ikonomikata*, p. 547. In April 1932 Bulgaria temporarily suspended, and then limited, its debt payment. See Berow, "Państwowo-monopolistyczne regulowanie," p. 19; Nötel, "International Credit and Finance," p. 229.

127. See Nötel, "International Credit and Finance," p. 224.

128. Natan et al., *Ikonomikata*, p. 538.

129. Spigler, "Public Finance," p. 158. Taxes were the main source of state revenues. See Chakalov, *Natsyonalniyat dokhod*, p. 141; Tsonev, *Dŭrzhavno-monopolistichniyat kapitalizm*, pp. 120ff.

130. Chakalov, *Natsyonalniyat dokhod*, p. 116.

131. Stancho Cholakov, *Danŭchno naprezheniye na edin narod v mirno i voenno vreme (Teoretichna skitsa)* (Varna, 1940), pp. 70–72, 78; Natan at al., *Ikonomikata*, p. 599.

132. Berow, "Państwowo-monopolistyczne regulowanie," p. 20.

166 Protectionism in Poland, Czechoslovakia, and Bulgaria

133. For example, 120 enterprises that did not meet the relevant conditions were deprived of the privileges. See Tsonev, *Dŭrzhavno-monopolistichniyat kapitalizm*, p. 75; Natan et al., *Ikonomikata*, p. 538.

134. Drabek, "Foreign Trade," p. 451. See also Berow, "Państwowo-monopolistyczne regulowanie," pp. 20–23; Royal Institute of International Affairs, *South Eastern Europe: The Political and Economic Survey* (London, 1939), pp. 111–113; Momchiloff, *Ten Years*.

135. Gerschenkron, *Economic Backwardness*, pp. 213–215; J. R. Lampe, *The Bulgarian Economy in the Twentieth Century* (London, 1986).

136. Gerschenkron, *Economic Backwardness*, pp. 213–215.

137. See Atanasov, "Industrialnata politika na Bŭlgariya prez poslednite godini," in *Spisaniye na Bŭlgarskoto Ikonomichesko Druzhestvo*, no. 5, 1942.

138. Toshev, *Industrialnata politika*, p. 45; G. Svrakov, *Belezhki vŭrkhu noviya rezhim na industriya na presitenostta* (Varna, 1938), p. 4.

139. Toshev, *Industrialnata politika*, pp. 55, 57.

140. Ibid., pp. 46ff.; Svrakov, *Belezhki vŭrkhu*, pp. 37ff.

141. See "Nasokity na industrialnata ni politika," in *Bŭlgarsko stopanstvo*, no. 6, 1939, p. 86; Toshev, *Industrialnata politika*; Svrakov, *Belezhki vŭrkhu*.

142. Toshev, *Industrialnata politika*, pp. 77–79; Svrakov, *Belezhki vŭrkhu*; "Nasokite."

143. Svrakov, *Belezhki vŭrkhu*; Toshev, *Industrialnata politika*.

144. See "Bulgaria: Annual Report, Economic A, 1936," *PRO FO 371/21122/R 2917/40/7*, p. 96.

145. Svrakov, *Belezhki vŭrkhu*, p. 37.

146. Toshev, *Industrialnata politika*, p. 166.

147. K. Bobchev, "Otnosheniye na dŭrzhavata kŭm narodnoto stopanstvo v Bŭlgariya," *Spisaniye na Bŭlgarskoto Ikonomichesko Druzhestvo*, no. 4, 1930, pp. 216ff., "Stopanskata politika v Bŭlgariya prez 1931 g.," *Spisaniye na Bŭlgarskoto Ikonomichesko Druzhestvo*, no. 1, 1931, and "Protektsionisticheskata teoriya na profesor M. Manoilescu," *Spisaniye na Bŭlgarskoto Ikonomichesko Druzhestvo*, no. 8, 1933.

148. K. Bobchev, "Protektsionism i stopanska nauka," *Spisaniye na Bŭlgarskoto Ikonomichesko Druzhestvo*, no. 8/9, 1935, p. 473.

149. Klaev, "Byłgarskata industriia."

150. Toshev, *Industrialnata politika*, pp. 168ff.; Tsonev, *Dŭrzhavno-monopolistichniyat kapitalizm*, p. 69.

151. Natan et al., *Ikonomikata*, pp. 486, 519 (data for 1921); Teichova, "Industry," pp. 287, 309 (data for 1937).

152. Toshev, *Industrialnata politika*, p. 138; Tsonev, *Dŭrzhavno-monopolitichniyat kapitalizm*, p. 71; Berow, "Państwowo-monopolistyczne regulowanie," p. 31.

153. Svrakov, *Belezhki vŭrkhu*, p. 20; Berow, "Państwowo-monopolistyczne regulowanie," p. 31; Tsonev, *Dŭrzhavno-monopolitichniyat kapitalizm*, p. 71.

154. Svrakov, *Belezhki vŭrkhu*, p. 20; Tsonev, *Dŭrzhavno-monopolitichniyat kapitalizm*, pp. 71, 78ff.

155. Svrakov, *Belezhki vŭrkhu*, p. 21.

156. Berov, *The Economic Development*, pp. 9ff.

157. Svrakov, *Belezhki vŭrkhu*, p. 37. Compare Natan et al., *Ikonomikata*, pp. 586ff.

158. According to Berow, "Państwowo-monopolistyczne regulowanie," p. 31, this goal was not achieved.

159. See Chapter 3.

160. Logio, *Bulgaria*, pp. 133ff.

161. N. Oren, *Revolution Administered: Agrarianism and Communism in Bulgaria* (Baltimore, 1973), pp. 13–17; Georgi Naumov, "Antikrizisna zakonodatelna deynost na Narodniya blok (1931–1934 g.)," *Istoricheski pregled*, no. 6, 1973; Berow, "Państwowo-monopolistyczne regulowanie," and Berov, "Direktsiya."

162. Logio, *Bulgaria*, p. 138.

163. "Leith-Ross to Sargent, 7 December 1929," *PRO FO 371/14313/C/12/7*, p. 5.

164. "Sargent's Memorandum, 30 December 1929," *PRO FO 371/14313/C/13/12/7*, pp. 9ff.; "Waterlow to Simon, 3 February 1933," *PRO FO 371/16652/C/1259/74/7*, pp. 29–33; *Twenty-sixth Report of the Commissioner of League of Nations in Bulgaria (Quarter from Nov. 15th, 1932 to Feb. 15th, 1933).*

165. "Bulgaria: Annual Report, 1929," *PRO FO 371/14326/Confidentional/13787*, p. 173; "Bulgarian Industrial Policy, 30 September 1933," *PRO FO 371/16653/C 8781/74/7*, p. 81.

166. For example, "Leith-Ross to Sargent, 7 December 1929."

167. "Bulgaria: Annual Report, 1929," p. 161. See also "Bulgaria: Annual Report, 1930," *PRO FO 371/15176/C 1534/1531/7*, p. 111; "Bulgaria: Annual Report, 1932," *PRO FO 371/16656/C 1766/C*, p. 86; "Bulgaria: Annual Report, Economic A, 1936."

168. See Natan et al., *Ikonomikata*; L. Berov et al., *100 godini ne bŭlgarska ekonomika* (Sofia, 1978); S. D. Zagoroff, "Agriculture and Food in Bulgaria Before and During World War," in Zagoroff et al., *The Agricultural Economy of the Danubian Countries, 1933–45* (Stanford, 1955); Berend and Ránki, *Economic Development in East-Central Europe*; Berend, "Agriculture," in Kaser, ed., *The Economic History*, vol. 1.

169. See Berow, "Państwowo-monopolistyczne regulowanie," pp. 12–15.

170. Ibid., p. 15.

171. Natan et al., *Ikonomikata*, p. 536. See also J. Tomaszewski, "Faktori na ikonomiczeskiya rastezh v Bŭlgariya prez perioda 1930–1939 g.," in Dimitŭr Kinev, ed., *Sŭvremenna Bŭlgariya*, vol. 1 (Sofia, 1984), p. 224; Oscar N. Anderson, "On the Scissors of Prices in Bulgaria," *Trudove ne Statisticheski Institut za Stopanski Prouchvaniya pri Sofiyskiya dŭrzhaven universitet*, no. 1, 1935 (hereafter quoted as *TSISP*), and "Again on the Problem of the Scissors of Prices in Bulgaria," in *TSISP*, no. 3, 1935. Compare N. K., "The Influence of Prices on Some Aspects of Economic Development in Bulgaria, 1926–1937," in *TSISP*, no. 1, 1938.

172. Within four years, until 1934, agricultural debt increased from 10 percent to 45 percent. Berend, "Agriculture," p. 173.

173. Ibid., p. 172; Natan et al., *Ikonomikata*, chapters 2 and 5.

174. Milka Deyanova, "Agrarnata kriza v Bŭlgariya i dŭrzhavnite merki za neynoto preodoliavane," *Arkhiv za Stopanska i Socialna Politika*, no. 4, 1938. See also Natan et al., *Ikonomikata*, chapters 2 and 5.

175. See Berov, "Direktsiia."

176. Ibid., pp. 277–281.

177. Ibid., p. 279. See also "Kharakter na 19-to mayskiya prevrat prez 1934 g.," *Izvestiya na Instituta po istoriya na BKP*, vol. 21, 1969; Migev, *Utvyrozhdavane na*

monarkhofashistkata diktatura v Bŭlgariya; J. Tomaszewski, "Bułgaria 1934: zamach majowy," in Garlicki, ed., *Przewroty i zamachy stanu: Europa 1918–1930* (Warsaw, 1981), pp. 195–209. For an apologetic picture of the Zveno group see, Logio, *Bulgaria*.

178. Berov, "Direktsiya," pp. 280, 296–326; Berow, "Państwowo-monopolistyczne regulowanie," p. 30; also Tsonev, *Dŭrzhavno-monopolistichniyat kapitalizm v Bŭlgariya*, pp. 77, 83–87, 96.

179. Berow, "Państwowo-monopolistyczne regulowanie," pp. 27–29; Tsonev, *Dŭrzhavno-monopolistichniyat kapitalizm v Bŭlgariya*, pp. 83–87.

180. I mean here the five most significant laws: those of April 1932, January and March 1934, March 1935, and several others. See Berow, "Państwowo-monopolistyczne regulowanie," p. 34; Tsonev, *Dŭrzhavno-monopolistichniyat kapitalizm v Bŭlgariya*, pp. 73ff.; Frangeš, "Fighting the Crisis," pp. 101–103; Deyanova, *Agrarnata kriza*, pp. 289–291; Ciepielewski, *Polityka agrarna*, p. 223.

181. See, for example, L. Zhivkova, "Kŭm vŭprosa za ikonomicheskata ekspanziya na Germaniya v Bŭlgariya (1933–1939)" and Berov, "Vŭnshnata tŭrgoviya mezhdu Bŭlgariya i Germaniya mezhdu dvete svetovni voyni (1919–1939 g.)," in *Bŭlgarsko-germanski otnosheniya i vrŭzki: Izsledovaniya i materiali* (Sofia, 1972 and 1979); Berov et al., *100 godini*, pp. 192–195; Wirginia Grabska, *Ekonomiczna ekspansja Niemiec na Wschód w latach 1870–1939* (Wrocław, 1964), chapters 3 and 5.

182. For example, Deyanova, *Agrarnata kriza*, p. 307; Dimitr Kinev, "Dŭrzhavna interventsiya v tiutiunoproizvodstvo," *Stopanski problemi*, no. 1, 1938, pp. 1, 19–25; T. Radomirov, "Neobkhodimiyat stopanski plan," *Stopanski problemi*, no. 9, 1938, pp. 358–362.

183. Berow, "Państwowo-monopolistyczne regulowanie," pp. 30ff.

184. Tomaszewski, "Faktori," p. 225.

185. Gerschenkron, *Economic Backwardness*, pp. 213, 216.

186. Ibid., p. 226.

8

Recapitulation
and Conclusions

The protectionist character of interwar East-Central Europe's economic policy proved to be the outcome of all sorts of elements: of decisions whose effects were included in the reckoning and of measures unintended or even contrary to their initiators' original intentions. I have concerned myself predominantly with the decisions of the first kind.

It goes without saying that when a government adopted a solution, either directly, through its own institutions, or indirectly, for example, through the central bank, each government had various preferences in view, be it general economic considerations, social policy (e.g., combating unemployment)[1] or export policy. In order to understand protectionism it is necessary to examine in greater detail the problem that has emerged in this text: In what measure was the policy of the central financial institutions with regard to protectionism in harmony with the intentions of government institutions?

It is worthwhile to consider the opinion of Heinrich Heuser that the central banks were giving preference to the stable currency at the expense of agricultural or industrial interests (and thus at the expense of the level of production and business upswing), and that they were referring to the obscure rule of economic necessity on the occasion. That was the case, according to Heuser, in Austria, in Estonia, and in Bulgaria in particular. In Hungary and Czechoslovakia specific industrial or sectoral interests exerted a more obvious influence on the currency and import policies as a whole.[2] All the same, not all the cited examples corroborate this opinion. For Heuser Bulgaria and Hungary are cases of different policies of the central banks. From the technical-financial point of view, he is correct on the details, and the policies of the two banks were indeed different. With a closer look, however, one inevitably comes to the conclusion that in both countries the central banks followed a similar economic policy line conscientiously obeying the spirit of industrial protectionism.

Also, there arises the question of whether a clearing system (an important element of the foreign exchange and trade policy in the 1930s) was, as I tacitly assumed, the result of deliberate or of spontaneous protectionism, thrust by circumstances. It was most likely the result of both.

The primary reason behind the clearing system at the time of economic depression was the desire to reduce to a minimum the outflow of foreign exchange and to maintain in the country the foreign-currency reserves indispensable to the functioning of the economy. Nonetheless, it soon turned out that the foreign currency reserves were too meager to sustain even the current trade. As a consequence, the clearing system became a lasting element of not so much foreign exchange as of economic policy and, through its effect on the structure of imports, a handy means of controlling national production. In this sense, it proved to have been a protectionist measure. There is little wonder, then, that in Hungary and in the Balkan countries (but also in Germany) the clearing and compensation systems rose to a peculiar economic philosophy.[3] With the seriously upset balance of payments, sooner or later (sometimes too late) the countries of the region adopted and followed this form of foreign trade until the outbreak of World War II. Thus, for instance, in 1937 in Hungary, Bulgaria, Romania, and Yugoslavia the clearing system comprised 75–86 percent of their total foreign trade, in the Baltic countries about 40–50 percent, and in Poland and Czechoslovakia 20 percent and 30 percent, respectively (which resulted from the policy of reducing their dependence on Germany).[4]

This does not mean, of course, that the governments did not try to prioritize and coordinate their respective policies in order to achieve at least one of the nonprotectionist goals of import restrictions and foreign-exchange control, that is, of stabilization of currency, protection of foreign-exchange reserves, invitation to tenders, and determination of the directions of foreign trade. The regional governments' economic policy had to serve other objectives as well. It is not easy to establish which protectionist and nonprotectionist purposes played the key role in the policy of each of the countries studied.

We may assume, however, that in Yugoslavia and Greece in the 1930s the protectionist factor blended with the foreign-exchange and bargaining concerns. The foreign-exchange control imposed by these two countries at the end of 1931 manifested their desire to further determine the direction of foreign trade.

In Romania protection must have been their prime concern, although from time to time it had to give way to the measures offsetting the effects of the rapidly deteriorating balance-of-payments position. Still, Romania (like other countries of the region) wanted a devaluation of the leu (which it brought about too late, only in November 1936) precisely in order to increase its exports and at the same time to protect its own industry.

Poland's principal aim, particularly in the years 1930–1935, was to keep the zloty stable. Her other priorities remain vague. In Hungary the situation resembled that of Poland, at least at the time of Great Depression. Bulgaria seems to have wanted both to stabilize its currency and to protect its production, predominantly industrial production. Yet the latter aim was rendered difficult by the authorities' disinclination to devalue the lev.

Czechoslovakia was the only country in the region not to have any serious foreign-exchange troubles. When it imposed restrictions it was, despite government declarations, first and foremost to protect its production. The Baltic countries resorted to restrictive measures chiefly to stabilize and to protect their respective currencies either at the old or the new, lowered, rate of exchange. At the same time, the export restrictions and foreign-exchange control imposed by Estonia and Latvia in 1931 and Lithuania in 1935 served agricultural production primarily.[5]

It is also difficult in each case to decide definitively whether it was for the sake of foreign exchange or protectionism that the Central European countries tended to restrict imports. One can only say that for the most part they did not mean protection as such. The measures they actually took were rather a result of the "self-propelling" of the system of foreign-exchange control and of its internal logic, distinguished by its tendency to bar competitive imports and to counter their consequences.[6]

A more general conclusion concerning the resort to quantity restrictions and foreign-exchange control in the region can seem astonishing. In my opinion, economic policy makers either did not see or did not want to see the advantage (not merely economic) such control gave them in stimulating the volume and structure of production. More often than not, if any structural or transitory changes took place as a result, they were—at least initially—unintended. However, no country of the region failed to see the serviceability of such control in trade policy: as a threat of retaliation, as a bargaining chip, or, ultimately, as the retaliatory measure actually taken.

One may say, moreover, that the countries of the region did not follow in the footsteps of France, Great Britain, the Netherlands, and Switzerland, which *consciously* carried on with the restrictive foreign-trade policy in order to protect domestic industry and/or agriculture, although officially they justified this policy by the need to protect their respective currencies.[7] All the same, I wish to stress once again, the import quotas and foreign-exchange restrictions, one and all, strengthened the protectionist tendencies, no matter what their original intention was.

What, then, were the extent and scale of protectionism and its practical results? In each of the countries examined, protectionism as a system of ideas differed from its practical implementation. On the one hand, economic publicists, theoreticians, and economic policy makers could, particularly at the end of the 1930s, more or less convincingly justify the need for extreme protectionism or even autarky. On the other hand, however, when they took into account a particular country's resource endowment, for practical reasons, the realization of undertakings consistent with the original assumptions proved utopian. A protectionism-based growth was inevitably costly and wasteful. It is so even in countries rich in skilled labor, capital, and developed domestic and foreign trade. As a matter of fact, the striving for the most ambitious protectionist goals did not go beyond verbal declarations. To be sure, as I have noted, nonextremist protectionist aspirations were realized, for example, with regard to agriculture in Bulgaria and Czechoslovakia or to certain light industries in agricultural countries.

I shall briefly consider here, in the comparative perspective, the case of Czechoslovakia, which I have amply discussed in Chapter 7. The difference between the effects, for example, of Czechoslovak agricultural protectionism and Bulgarian and Romanian protection of their textile industries can be briefly expressed as follows: Had these countries opened their markets to each other, owing to the generally higher level of Czechoslovakia's economic development, Czech agriculture, especially grain and animal production, would have probably better adjusted itself to the new situation than, for instance, Bulgarian industry.

Yet, if we consider the effects of Czechoslovakia's protectionist policy on the interests of the other countries of the region, the assessment of this policy proves more difficult. Czechoslovak agricultural protectionism struck a blow to foreign competition—to Hungarian, Romanian, and Yugoslav grain[8] and Polish animal production.[9] The Czechoslovaks cut out that competition not so much by lowering their own prices (on the contrary, in Czechoslovakia's domestic market prices for local produce were higher) as by adopting an appropriate tariff policy, and specifically a system of quotas. All in all, however, the costs of agricultural self-sufficiency (pushed by the Agrarians), justified by the need to improve the lot of peasants, were borne by other social strata, primarily by the urban population. In the 1920s, and especially between 1924 and 1929, as a result of a boom in the world trade, Czechoslovak industry, working at full capacity,[10] was able to retain its position in the Danubian market in spite of the emerging and developing local industries and the expansion of the West European, including German, industries. In the following decade the situation changed. Markedly higher duties to protect native industries in Yugoslavia, Romania, Bulgaria, Hungary, and Poland (in which countries they were levied as a retaliation for the policy of the Agrarians), these countries' foreign-exchange restrictions, the diminishing demand for exports, and increasingly intense German competition, particularly from 1934/35—all these had an adverse effect on the sales of Czech industrial products on the markets that used to be theirs.[11] It is therefore clear that objectively strong agricultural protectionism aimed against the industrial interests, even if contrary to the intentions of some of its proponents (though if one bears in mind the Agrarians' diatribes against industry, the sincerity of their declarations seems rather doubtful). Paradoxically, however, such policy indirectly launched, among other things, the restructuring of industry and the redirecting of exports to overseas markets.[12]

The situation of Czechoslovak industry may hence be seen as an inevitable effect of the overall evolution and economic development of the countries of the region, including Czechoslovakia itself. After all, one can argue with some foundation in facts that there was much to be said on the side of the Agrarians, who in any event represented the interests of more than half of the country's population and who were so earnestly and successfully implementing their economic ideas. In the crisis-ridden 1930s it was absolutely impossible to definitively decide the question of which growth path would be best from the point of view of the general economic interests of the country. Theoretically, it was possible to imagine a reciprocal opening of the Danubian markets to Czech (and even Austrian) manufactures and of the Czechoslovak market to agricultural products of the succession states and the Balkan countries. Such a resolution was frequently recommended by the West, which pointed out the hindrance the strong agricultural protectionism was to the Czechoslovak economy. The British researcher Doreen Warriner stressed the need for Czechoslovakia at least to maintain relations with the countries of the region such as they were before 1930. That, she hoped, would restrain the manifestations of radical industrial protectionism in East-Central Europe.[13]

That was possible only in theory, however, as the actual and potential volumes of the Danubian countries' agricultural exports were beyond the import-absorption capacities of Czechoslovakia and Austria. The demolition or very significant lowering of the customs barriers could, moreover, be a menace to the existence and to the already achieved autonomy of the industries in the succession states. It could also cause a transient ruin of Czechoslovak (Slovak rather than Czech) agriculture[14] and add to the influx of rural, particularly Slovak, population to towns and to industries that were unable to absorb the surplus labor.[15] Such arguments leave aside the important ideological reasons behind the position of the Agrarians, who saw in peasants the salt of the earth (and the nation).

Let us now consider the case of Hungary, which, like Czechoslovakia (although of a fundamentally different status), had previously been a part of the Habsburg monarchy. The opinion that within its post-Trianon borders Hungary stood no chance of an autonomous economic development seems theoretically attractive. Such an opinion presupposes that Hungary's development and prosperity hung on its swiftly joining the new, postwar world economy, and extreme protectionism did not comply with this requirement. Theoretically, such point of view was all the more obvious in light of the drastic change that the Hungarian economy underwent compared to the period prior to 1918. For example, as a result of border modifications, Budapest, Hungary's only large industrial center, was cut off from its old (hitherto domestic) markets and at the same time from its raw-material supplies. As for Hungarian agriculture—which until 1918 had been able to sell all of its surplus production—increasingly often, specifically at the beginning of the 1930s, it had to adjust itself to the radically declining internal market. As a result of the fierce competition from grain and animal growers in South America and the old British dominions, the overseas markets were virtually closed to the products of Hungarian agriculture.[16] There were also other restrictive factors, such as the agricultural protectionism of industrialized countries (including Czechoslovakia, which until 1930 had been a ready market for Hungarian agricultural produce[17]), the previously mentioned preferential tariffs within the old colonial empires, and Central Europeans' total inability to adopt a comprehensive regional resolution (a customs union, the Tardieu plan and its variations, and other concepts, for example, the somewhat later Hodža plan, did not go beyond the stage of initial projects).[18] Even the Italian-Hungarian-Austrian Danubian Agreement, on the strength of which Hungary was by the year 1937 (and then, 1938) to supply each of these countries with 100,000 tons of grain, or German orders for Hungarian crops from the years 1933–1935, did not solve the problem of Hungarian agricultural surpluses.[19]

In spite of the generally unfavorable circumstances, Hungarians decided that industrialization, which they had launched at the turn of the century when the situation had been altogether different, was the only way to develop the country. Hungarians treated industrialization as a demographic imperative, as one close observer put it.[20] The need to become more autonomous vis-à-vis other countries gave further encouragement to industrialization. The industrialization option inevitably resorted to protectionist measures. The new customs tariff from May 1925[21] and its successive frequent modifications were to exert pressure on trade partners, and together with the selective foreign-exchange restrictions from July 1931[22] were to protect industry.

Protectionism-shielded industrialization was thus the route Hungary chose to follow. It proceeded chiefly at the expense of the rural population, which comprised 70 percent of Hungary's total. It must be emphasized that, specifically in the 1930s, industrial policy increased the economic distance between particular areas of the old monarchy.

It remains to be answered whether Hungary could have chosen any other route. One must observe that Hungary's room for maneuver was known in advance and even more restricted than in other countries, perhaps with the exception of Bulgaria. This was the result primarily of such political reasons as Hungarian revisionism and the resulting Little Entente's apprehensions as well as a certain adherence, stricter than in the neighboring countries, to the rules of economic nationalism. Hungary's position was in a way doubly disadvantageous: The route theoretically best, that is, economic growth based on the development of new as well as traditional export lines in exchange for imports of manufactures and semifinished products, turned out to be completely impracticable in the given economic (and political) circumstances, especially in the 1930s. Hungarian industry was too weak to compete (without government support) with the Czech, German, and in some branches, Austrian and Polish industries on the Romanian, Yugoslav, Bulgarian markets, let alone that of Poland. Government support was indispensable to ensure even domestic sales. This means that in this particular case, too, arguments for protectionist growth, giving emphasis to industrialization and arduous expansion of the domestic market for indigenous manufactures, holds up quite well.

Let us now consider the question of the degree to which the oft-mentioned policy of import substitution[23] was actually a protectionist or even an autarkic maneuver. By import substitution, one usually understands starting and increasing production of goods hitherto not manufactured in the country and therefore imported (or not imported at all, in which case we are dealing with substitution in a wider meaning). When speaking of substitution, we usually mean manufactures, although there is no reason why the term should not extend to every other product. The slogan of import substitution, particularly popular in backward countries, was and is a distinct element of the development ideology. The first to put forward theoretical assumptions of this strategy, during World War II, were P. N. Rosenstein-Rodan, T. Balogh, and K. Mandelbaum, who were mentioned earlier here.[24] Later, in the 1950s, economists and economic policy makers in Latin America, especially those associated with R. Prebisch, referred to it as well.[25] Import substitution was of course something practiced before but as a spontaneous occurrence.

Import substitution is only another aspect of protectionism, however. Introduced on a wider scale in various countries or in a group of countries, it impaired the existing international division of labor, in which their respective countries occupied a definite place.

Although it is difficult to associate development based on protectionism and autarky with the standard understanding (in economics) of rationality, it is nonetheless possible to gauge the degree of such development's "rationality," which is dependent on the extent and relative costs of substitution. The type of substitution, for its part, affects the degree of autarky and allows an assessment of the economic policy pursued, whether it involves production based on imported or also on local raw materials, and whether it involves a withdrawal from importing a given commodity and its replacement with a domestic product.

The economic policy of Bulgaria provided an example of the first two solutions. In 1930, 80 percent of the Bulgarian textile industry depended on imported raw materials, and in 1937, 56 percent. In 1939 the quantity of raw materials imported by this industry was six times what it was in the years 1925–1930. In order to become at least in part independent from those imports, the Bulgarians began to grow cotton themselves (the sensibleness of this decision is another matter), which in autumn 1934 the Khranoiznos Board began to procure from the growers.[26] The replacement of imported silk and cotton fabrics by the inferior-quality indigenous linen was an example of the third solution.

The policy of import substitution can be credited with the raising of employment in the national economy. This helped to reduce unemployment and the rural surplus of labor and to upgrade workers' skills. Besides their supreme social significance, such results facilitated the extension of the domestic market. The assessment of the rationality of this policy should, moreover, give heed to the period during which the substitution process was taking place.

The 1920s were good for the region because of, for example, the inflow of foreign capital, the generally favorable terms of trade, and the economic boom from 1924 to 1930. In that decade growth based on import substitution was theoretically less advantageous than growth based on traditional exports even though the latter preserved the "peripheral" character of the Central European economies. But in the 1930s all these favorable circumstances were gone. The fall in the share of foreign trade in the economic growth of the region, which, excepting Czechoslovakia and Austria, had been very modest anyway, was serious. Compared to 1928, foreign trade in 1938 had declined in all of the region's countries except Turkey, Bulgaria, and Lithuania.[27] To be sure, this stifled the affected countries' ability to permanently base their growth on nontraditional exports; however, it did not pay to stick with traditional exports except in special circumstances such as *Grossraumwirtschaft*. Nevertheless, one could observe elements of the policy of diversification of exports in various countries of the region, for example, in the Baltic states (processed food products), Poland (besides higher-quality agricultural exports, also more complex chemical and pharmaceutical products), or Hungary (aluminum, pharmaceutical, and metal products). Yet, with the exception of the Baltic states, the volume of those qualitatively new exports was usually very meager.[28]

As a result, *an active* economic policy quite naturally implied the need to resort to import substitution. Albania was the only country of the region that did not resort to it sooner or later, spontaneously or deliberately (and was thus several decades ahead of Prebisch's recommendations). Yet it is difficult to estimate this substitution's real extent. At any rate, the correlation between import substitution and protectionism is beyond any doubt. All the same, it was right to assume that, seen in a short perspective and analyzed in the context of the international division of labor at the time, this option represented a burden to the national economy, and on the macro scale could be treated as wasteful. In a longer perspective, though, this option, being a significant element of the development ideology, seems to have been inevitable in pre–World War II conditions, and of the 1930s in particular.[29]

Another aspect of this complex problem was the region's (excluding Czechoslovakia and Austria) incapacity to strongly stimulate their growth by a foreign trade multiplier. This of course led to the expansion of protectionism, import substitution included. Paradoxically, with regard to economic growth, protectionism was in a way a substitute for foreign trade.

I will address other aspects of the relationship between protectionism and growth based on the substitution of both imports and exports in Chapter 9.

The examples of Poland and Bulgaria indicate that the differentiation of degrees of protectionism was not a rare occurrence in the region. Unlike Poland's economic policy, the excessively protectionist nature of Bulgaria's industrial course was plain. It was manifest in Bulgarian laws and institutions, which extended protection of home industry beyond any comparison.

Irrespective of the declarations of the Romanian authorities, their economic policy was not liberal. Thus, for instance, the 1930s discussion on the paths of development (transmitted or command industrialization) concentrated on the question of whether and to what extent Romania shed the attributes of the mercantilistic, that is, protectionist, economy and whether it would not be better if it followed that path.[30] It was, of course, the latter option that finally triumphed.

At this point it is worthwhile once again to bring up the question of relations among particular elements of economic nationalism. It should be remembered that depending on the country, either the motif of industrialism or that of agrarianism is emphasized. The subsequent economic consequences of one or the other choice were not slow in coming. These consequences materialized in the form of, among other things, alliances between parties otherwise opposed to each other. For example, in Lithuania, Latvia, and Czechoslovakia the message of agrarianism united agricultural circles and state business leadership in defense of agrarian interests against foreign countries and internal pressure.[31] Elsewhere in the region the binding element was the common belief that industrialization was the way that would make extrication from economic backwardness possible.

In keeping with the second opinion, to persist in developing agriculture would be tantamount to perpetuating traditional dependence. Spokesmen for Lewiatan,[32] an organization of Poland's large-scale industry, no doubt could subscribe to the opinion of Romanian economist Stefan Zeletin that an agricultural country, even if formally independent, was in fact a mere liege man of the capitalist metropolis that supplied it with capital and goods,[33] or to similar views advocated by such people as Mihail Manoilescu. During the years of World War II the well-known Polish economist Henryk Tennenbaum spoke in the same strain. As the Germans saw it, he argued, every large economic region consisted of complimentary parts. The East-Central European region played, in their view, the role of raw-materials and food supplier.[34]

However, to define conditions indispensable to industrialization remained an ideological, political, and practical problem. In less developed "open" economies, the process of integrating new industries into the national economy can be disturbed and reduced to enclaves, as was the case more or less until the middle of this century; it can also acquire the features peculiar to the so-called modernization of dependence.[35] Those modern advocates of protectionism (and also certain Marxists and neo-Marxists) who perceive it to be a development ideology deem the "closedness" of the economy to be a prerequisite for industrialization. State support was proposed by such people as Ion I.C. Brătianu, Zeletin, Manoilescu, and Serban Voinea in Romania, etatists and spokesmen for Lewiatan in Poland, ideologues of the Union of Industrialists in Czechoslovakia, and an organization of industrialists in Bulgaria.[36]

The other questions that disturbed economic policy makers in those underdeveloped countries were the importance of the foreboding phenomena provoked by protectionism and the flimsiness of industry, which stood no chance (or hardly any) of exports to the third markets; the worsening balance of payments; and graft in a considerable part of the local bourgeoisie. It is indeed difficult to envision Bulgarian, Romanian, Greek, or Yugoslav commodities (with the exception of a very few textile and similar products) successfully competing in foreign markets. But this was not what the idea of protectionism consisted of. The pivotal point in the Central European region (perhaps with the exception of Austria and

Czechoslovakia) was to build the foundations of industry and to absorb the surplus rural population in the urban market economy. The question was that of what could be the extent of the desired transformation if it was not backed by adequate foreign investments. Even assuming welcome changes in agricultural land ownership, the prospects for achieving this strategic aim were thin if the country concerned were to relinquish primary accumulation. Attempts to use the savings accumulated in the agricultural sector to start industrialization were not a major success.[37] Paradoxically, one of the reasons for failure were the effects of agrarian reforms. This was the case, for example, in Romania, where 40 percent of the arable land was distributed among peasants. As a result, domestic consumption increased, but grain exports, until then Romania's main foreign cash earner, dwindled.[38] The same happened in Poland and presumably also in Yugoslavia, though on a smaller scale. In Latvia and Estonia the situation was somewhat different. Their land reforms had a clearly beneficial influence on agricultural productivity,[39] and more important, the accumulated savings were returning to this sector and to the food-processing industry.

Historians have been arguing whether and in what measure state intervention can substitute for capital (or other factors of production) in industrial development. It is obvious to most that in all Central European countries, even in the industrialized Czechoslovakia, the state tried to stimulate industrialization (more about which in Chapter 9), sometimes trying (especially in Poland) the methods of planning.

As for protectionist aims, it is doubtful whether antimonopolistic measures—in the form of antitrust campaigns in relatively developed countries (such as Poland) or the abandonment of the "saturation" principle in underdeveloped countries (such as Bulgaria)—could dispose of the relative surplus goods. To this effect several other conditions to bring about the extension of the domestic market would have had to be met. Therefore, the antimonopolistic measures seem to have been, at least in the short run, fairly inconsistent with the aims of protectionism.

As regards an assessment of the international consequences of the protectionist policy (or economic nationalism) in the region, I agree with Bertil Ohlin, to whom I refer in Part One as arguing that the scale of the negative consequences of the protectionist policy could not stand comparison with the (transitory) negative consequences of the neoprotectionism of the turn of the century.[40]

To sum up the conclusions with respect to Central European protectionism:

First, governments that pursued protectionism on a large scale (in industry, agriculture, or both), and which in their struggle against the Great

Depression relatively early took appropriate steps in their foreign-exchange policy and foreign trade (even if inconsistent with the hitherto binding principles of economic policy), were more successful than the governments that had been slow or not firm enough in the introduction of remedial measures. Bulgaria, Greece, Romania, maybe also Hungary, Latvia, and Estonia may be included among the first group of countries, and Poland, Albania, and, after all, Czechoslovakia—all its achievements notwithstanding—in the second.

Second, this conclusion needs nevertheless to be qualified. Obviously economic policy, protectionism included, was not the source of the region's every success in the 1930s. We can to some extent agree with the opinion ventured by spokespeople for neoclassical conceptions that economic improvement in Central Europe was primarily a result of external circumstances. It is necessary, however, to examine these circumstances thoroughly. I mean here that had it not been for the barter trade and clearing agreements with Germany, which offered a vast and lucrative market to those countries, for the majority of them it would have been incomparably more difficult, and perhaps even impossible, to get out of stagnation.[41] I believe this hypothesis to be plausible, particularly with regard to Bulgaria, but also Yugoslavia, Romania, Hungary, in some measure Greece and, with some reservations, Latvia and Estonia. With regard to the latter two countries, it should be emphasized that their economic structure was better than elsewhere in the region and that their dependence on foreign capital was less accentuated, and hence their foreign-exchange position was less critical. These two Baltic countries tried to balance their economic relations with Germany by earnestly upholding their ties with the British market.[42] The countries that did not enter into any closer clearing agreements with Germany (e.g., Poland) clearly faced graver economic problems.

Yet the countries that willingly or unwillingly based their economic policy on close economic ties with the Third Reich entangled themselves with the policy of *Grossraumwirtschaft*. It imparted a dynamic character to their protectionism, one that took advantage of economies of scale. The assessment of the economic and especially political consequences of these countries' operating within the *Grossraumwirtschaft* is another matter.[43]

Third, and most important, only the complex economic, political, and social situation in which the countries of the region found themselves in the 1930s could make protectionism leave such a strong mark on their policies. This was the case because protectionism turned out to be a phenomenon whose scale and characteristics actually differed from those in the preceding decade. Only in those new circumstances could the advantages of protectionism come to light. Protectionism was therefore an element of the state interventionism peculiar to that period.

Finally, the preceding conclusion does not oppose this book's recurrent opinion about the universal role protectionism plays in the underdeveloped countries.

I wish to give more thought than in Chapter 7 to the extent of protectionism advanced in the region. As I showed in my analyses, in the interwar period the economic policy of all the countries of the region swiftly passed from traditional to tactical protectionism. In the 1930s it reached its crescendo—at least in words, though not necessarily in practice—adopting the form of a development ideology. This approach is discernible in development programs and in attempts at their implementation. I am inclined to name the protectionist policy of the time "total," as—theoretically—it applied to the whole of economic life. This was particularly so in Romania and Bulgaria; in other countries, "total" protectionism confined itself to selected economic sectors. In Czechoslovakia, for example, it found expression in the aspiration to self-sufficiency in food; the same could be said of the agrarian policies of Estonia and Latvia. In Hungary (and also in Turkey, sometimes mentioned here) this "totality" was reserved for industrial protectionism. In Poland (and seemingly in Yugoslavia too) protectionism never reached the stage of "totality." At the end of the 1930s the role of development ideology was undertaken in Poland by the slogan of industrialization (in the etatist circles additionally strengthened by the demand for planning).

At this point, however, it is necessary to explain that it would be wrong to suppose that, for example, in the countries that emphasized the need for "total" ("holistic," as Henryk Szlajfer aptly puts it[44]) protectionism, other development ideologies remained marginal. This was not so. Both Bulgaria and Romania treated industrialization on a par with protectionism, as a magic key to open the door leading to the modernization of their countries. But these two countries attached much greater weight than the others in the region to protectionism as the comprehensive idea. The extent to which protectionism was carried out in practice justifies the opinion about this idea's exceptional significance in those two Balkan states.

In connection with these conclusions it is apt once again to observe that the doctrine and practice of economic liberalism could not solve the problems facing the countries of the region, particularly in the 1930s. The apparent world trend away from economic liberalism only strengthened the protectionist (etatist or quasi-liberal) tendency in the East-Central European region, which often went hand in hand with demonstrations of nationalism. The latter prompted foreign researchers and watchers to make generalizations that went far beyond the actual conditions. The situation that arose at the time of the Great Depression naturally drove the regional governments to protectionist measures. It was only at that time that such measures became a firm element of economic policy. Supported by various social forces, and expressing all sorts of interests, increasingly often protectionism was a consciously pursued policy. Depending on the point of view, protectionism was a fragment, an expression or an element to imbue the public with nationalism or, as I call it, *economic patriotism.* Adherents of protectionism sometimes (as in Romania) used arguments with some theoretical ambitions, defending particular sectoral interests. Sometimes they flirted with holistic notions that perceived in protectionism and autarky a method to reach the country's development potentials.

Also, it is apt to point to the socially integrating effect of protectionism (which is usually overlooked by researchers).[45] More often than not this effect was noxious, leading, in extreme cases, to xenophobia. It is difficult to say whether the state leaders were always aware of that. In case of Romania, though, their complicity is beyond any doubt; there it had been deliberately used as an instrument of social integration since the turn of the century.[46] In the 1930s protectionism occurred in all the countries of the region, usually as a side effect of a nationalist ideology.

Finally, while seeking an answer to the question of why it was only in the interwar period that a qualitative change in protectionism occurred, one could point to possible relations between protectionism and medium- and long-term business cycles.[47] On this question, hardly examined by researchers, we can propound only hypotheses. I believe that it is easier to associate the rise in protectionist tendencies with the crisis in Juglar's eight-year cycle (because then, e.g., foreign-exchange problems, as a reflection of the crisis stage of the cycle, enforce stricter protection of domestic production) than with the contraction in Kondratieff's long wave model (as Röpke does).[48] However, if we assume that a contraction in Kondratieff's wave fell exactly in the interwar period,[49] then the relevant protectionist concepts and specific measures would take place in a more manifest and organized form, conformably to the depth of contraction. Still, it is one thing to recognize the policy of protectionism as a tool for softening the impact of contraction, that is, as an acceptable means of anticyclical intervention in the Juglar cycle or the three-year, four-year Kuznets cycle, but quite another to recognize protectionism as an ingredient of the development ideology. A myriad of economists and economic policy makers in the region opted for the latter approach, though they of course used a different terminology.

Notes

1. For Hungary and Latvia, see H. Heuser, *Control of International Trade* (London, 1939), pp. 125ff.

2. Ibid., pp. 126–133.

3. Larry Neal, "Economic and Finance of Bilateral Clearing Agreements: Germany, 1934–38," *Economic History Review*, vol. 22, 1979.

4. Clearing and compensation systems embraced 85 percent of Germany's foreign trade. See I. T. Berend and G. Ránki, *Economic Development in East-Central Europe in the 19th and 20th Centuries* (New York, 1974), p. 264; Z. Drabek, "Foreign Trade Performance and Policy" in M. C. Kaser, ed., *The Economic History of Eastern Europe, 1919–1975*, vol. 1, *Economic Structure and Performance Between the Two Wars* (Oxford, 1985), pp. 440, 451ff.; R. Nötel, "International Credit and Finance," in Kaser, ed., *The Economic History*, vol. 2, *Interwar Policy, the War, and Reconstruction* (Oxford, 1986), pp. 248ff. The estimates for the Baltic countries are the author's, based on the less-than-precise data in Royal Institute of International Affairs, *The Baltic States: A Survey of the Political and Economic Structure and the Foreign Relations of Estonia, Latvia, and Lithuania* (London, 1938), pp. 165–167, and Z. Natan, V. Khadzhinikolov, and L. Berov, eds., *Ikonomikata na Bŭlgariya*, vol. 1 (Sofia, 1969), p. 590.

5. See League of Nations, *Enquiry into Clearing Agreements* (Geneva, 1935), pp. 60–64. For Hungary and Bulgaria, see G. Ránki and J. Tomaszewski, "The Role of the State in Industry, Banking, and Trade," in Kaser, ed., *The Economic History*, vol. 2, p. 33; Nötel, "International Credit and Finance," p. 244. For Yugoslavia, see Heuser, *Control*, p. 250; Nötel, "International Credit and Finance," pp. 210, 228. For Greece, see Ránki and Tomaszewski, "The Role of the State," pp. 33–35; Nötel, "International Credit and Finance," pp. 244ff. For the Baltic countries, see *The Baltic States*, pp. 170–176; Heuser, *Control*, pp. 54, 57. For Poland, see Z. Knakiewicz, *Deflacja polska 1930–1935* (Warsaw, 1967), pp. 244–250; M. M. Drozdowski, *Polityka gospodarcza rządu polskiego 1936–1939* (Warsaw, 1963), pp. 30–38, 239–242.

6. See Heuser, *Control*, pp. 139ff.

7. In autumn 1931 none of those currencies was in danger. See Heuser, *Control*, pp. 8, 33. The situation in East-Central Europe was different. Foreign currency reserves in 1931 in Albania were at 91 percent of their 1929 level, in Austria 21 percent, in Czechoslovakia 47 percent, in Greece 42 percent, in Yugoslavia 348 percent, in Poland 16 percent, in Romania 4 percent, in Hungary 30 percent, in Estonia 79 percent, in Latvia 59 percent, and in Lithuania 73 percent. The estimates are the author's, based on K. Romanow-Bobińska, "Wielki kryzys a Europa Wschodnia," *Studia z Dziejów ZSRR i Europy Środkowej*, vol. XVII, 1981, table 6, p. 111; V. N. Bandera, *Foreign Capital as an Instrument of National Economic Policy: A Study Based on the Experience of East European Countries Between the World Wars* (The Hague, 1964), p. 37.

8. Drabek, "Foreign Trade," p. 441; Z. Sládek, "Wyniki gospodarcze działalności Małej Ententy oraz polityczne następstwa jej niepowodzenia," *Studia z dziejów ZSRR i Europy Środkowej*, vol. XX, 1984, pp. 142–148.

9. Z. Landau and J. Tomaszewski, *Gospodarka Polski międzywojennej 1918–1939*, vol. 3, *Wielki kryzys 1930–1935* (Warsaw, 1982), pp. 380–382.

10. Except some branches of the food-processing and textile industries. See A. Dobrý, "O sporných problémach dosavadního výzkumu hospodářských dějín Československá," *Sborník historický*, no. 22, 1975, pp. 178–184; V. Průcha, ed., *Historia gospodarcza Czechosłowacji XX wieku* (Warsaw, 1979), pp. 68, 72ff.

11. Czech exports to Austria, Poland, Hungary, Romania, and Yugoslavia diminished from 40 percent in 1924 to 21 percent in 1937. For 1924, see Průcha, ed., *Historia gospodarcza*, p. 97; for 1937, see J. Tomaszewski, "Związki gospodarcze państw sukcesyjnych a Polska" in Z. Landau and J. Tomaszewski, *Druga Rzecz-pospolita: Gospodarka—społeczeństwo—miejsce w świecie* (Warsaw, 1977), p. 368.

12. Inasmuch as in 1924 exports to the new markets made up 8.1 percent of the total, in 1937, 25.2 percent. See Průcha, ed., *Historia gospodarcza*, p. 97.

13. Doreen Warriner, "Czechoslovakia and Central European Tariffs," *Slavonic and East European Review*, vol. IX, no. 33, 1933, p. 555.

14. See J. Faltus and V. Průcha, *Prehl'ad hospodárskego vyvoja na Slovensku v rokoch 1918–1945* (Bratislava, 1969), pp. 184, 212.

15. J. Tomaszewski, "Gospodarka krajów Europy Środkowej i Południowo-Wschodniej," in J. Żarnowski, ed., *Dyktatury w Europie Środkowo-Wschodniej 1918–1939* (Wrocław, 1973), pp. 69–71.

16. L. Pasvolsky, *Economic Nationalism of the Danubian States* (London, 1928), pp. 336, 338; I. T. Berend and G. Ránki, *Underdevelopment and Economic Growth: Studies in Hungarian Economic and Social History* (Budapest, 1979), pp. 114–177.

17. Already by the end of 1920s about 50 percent of Czechoslovakia's flour imports came from overseas countries, not from the neighboring agricultural nations. See Berend and Ránki, *Underdevelopment*, p. 116.

18. See J. Hanč, *Tornado Across Eastern Europe: The Path of Nazi Destruction from Poland to Greece* (New York, 1942); Z. Sládek and J. Tomaszewski, "Próby integracji gospodarczej Europy Środkowej i Południowo-Wschodniej w latach dwudziestych XX w.," *Roczniki Dziejów Społecznych i Gospodarczych*, vol. XI, 1979, and "Próby integracji ekonomicznej Europy Środkowej i Południowo-Wschodniej w latach trzydziestych XX w.," *Sobótka*, 1979, no. 3.

19. See Berend and Ránki, *Economic Development in East-Central Europe*, pp. 269–273; A. Basch, *The Danube Basin and the German Economic Sphere* (London, 1944), chapter 10; D. E. Kaiser, *Economic Diplomacy and the Origins of the Second World War: Germany, Britain, France, and Eastern Europe, 1930–1939* (Princeton, 1980), pp. 62ff.; Neal, "Economics and Finance of Bilateral Clearing Agreements."

20. Pasvolsky, *Economic Nationalism*, p. 366.

21. Ibid., p. 371; Ránki and Tomaszewski, "The Role of the State," pp. 15–18.

22. See quarterly reports to the League of Nations by Royall Tyler, *Financial Position of Hungary in the . . .* (Geneva, 1932–38); Berend and Ránki, *Economic Development in East-Central Europe*, pp. 258–260.

23. Compare W. A. Lewis, *Growth and Fluctuations, 1870–1913* (London, 1978), chapter 7.

24. P. N. Rosenstein-Rodan, "Industrialization of Eastern Europe," *Economic Journal*, vol. LIII, 1943, pp. 210–211; Kurt Mandelbaum, *The Industrialization of Backward Areas*, 4th ed. (Oxford, 1961); T. Balogh, *Unequal Partners*, vol. 1, *The Theoretical Framework* (Oxford, 1963).

25. Prebisch, *The Economic Development of Latin America and Its Principal Problems*, ECLA (Lake Success, N.Y., 1950). Among the Polish authors, see, for example, H. Szlajfer, *Modernizacja zależności: Kapitalizm i rozwój w Ameryce Łacińskiej* (Wrocław, 1985).

26. A. Gerschenkron, *Economic Backwardness in Historical Perspective* (London, 1976), p. 214; Natan et al., eds., *Ikonomikata*, pp. 578, 589.

27. League of Nations, *Europe's Trade* (Geneva, 1941), tables 17 and 18.

28. For example, in 1938 Poland's exports of machinery, tools, and equipment amounted to 2 percent of total exports, whereas exports of processed food amounted to 14.8 percent. Estonia's 1936 agricultural exports amounted to 42.4 percent, and of manufactures to 22.5 percent of the total. In the years 1928–1930 Hungary's exports of machinery and vehicles amounted to 6.3 percent, and in 1938 reached 9.6 percent of the total. See *Mały Rocznik Statystyczny 1939*, p. 173; *The Baltic States*, p. 161; Drabek, "Foreign Trade," p. 472 (Table 7.52).

29. Compare the development of Japan in the late 1930s. See, for example, Keiichiro Nakagawa, "The Structure and Motives of Investment by Private Enterprises in Japan Before the Second World War," in Herman Daems and Herman van der Wee, eds., *The Rise of Managerial Capitalism* (The Hague, 1974).

30. See D. Chirot, "Neoliberal and Social Democratic Theories of Development: The Zeletin–Voinea Debate Concerning Romania's Prospects in the 1920s and Its Contemporary Importance," and K. Jowitt, "The Sociocultural Bases of National Dependency in Peasant Countries," both in K. Jowitt, ed., *Social Change in Romania, 1860–1940: A Debate on Development in a European Nation* (Berkeley, 1978), pp. 17, 63. See also H. L. Roberts, *Rumania: Political Problems of an Agrarian State* (New Haven, 1951), pp. 164–166.

31. See G. von Rauch, *The Baltic States: Estonia, Latvia, and Lithuania: The Years of Independence, 1917–1940* (Berkeley and Los Angeles, 1974); P. Łossowski, *Kraje bałtyckie na drodze od demokracji parlamentarnej do dyktatury (1918–1934)* (Wrocław, 1972); Toivo U. Raun, *Estonia and the Estonians* (Stanford, 1987), chapter 18.

32. Jan Kofman, *Lewiatan a podstawowe zagadnienia ekonomiczno-polityczne Drugiej Rzeczypospolitej. Z dziejów ideologii kół wielkokapitalistycznych w Polsce* (Warsaw, 1986), chapter 7.

33. Stefan Zeletin, *Burghezia romana* (Bucharest, 1925), p. 120. Quoted in Jowitt, "The Sociocultural Bases," p. 17.

34. H. Tennenbaum, *Europa Środkowo-Wschodnia w gospodarce światowej* (London, 1941), pp. 126–130.

35. Szlajfer, *Modernizacja*. See also A. C. Janos, "The Rise and Fall of Civil Society: The Politics of Backwardness on the European Peripheries, 1870–1945" (paper for the conference "Models of Development and Theories of Modernization in Eastern Europe Between the World Wars," Rackeve, September 10–15, 1988).

36. M. Manoilescu, *The Theory of Protection and International Trade* (London, 1931); "Hospodářská politika čs. průmyslu v letach 1918–1938," *USČP*, v roce 1937, Prague; Landau and Tomaszewski, *Gospodarka Polski*, vol. 2, *Od Grabskiego*, chapter 2, and *Wielki kryzys*, chapter 2; J. Gołębiowski, *Sektor państwowy w gospodarce Polski międzywojennej* (Warsaw, 1985); Kofman, *Lewiatan*; Natan et al., eds., *Ikonomikata*; Gerschenkron, *Economic Backwardness*; Ránki and Tomaszewski, "The Role of the State," pp. 9ff.; D. Seers, "The Stages of Economic Growth of a Primary Producer of the Twentieth Century," in Robert I. Rhodes, ed., *Imperialism and Underdevelopment* (New York, 1970); Chirot, "Neoliberal"; Zigu Ornea, "Interwar Romania in Search of Development Model," in *Models of Development*.

37. A. Teichova, "Industry," in Kaser, ed., *The Economic History*, vol. 1, pp. 282–285.

38. According to the none-too-precise data, in 1925 exports per capita declined by more than 50 percent from 1913, down to US$8.25. See Janos, "Modernization," p. 107.

39. See Lindes Truska, "Burżuazyjna reforma agrarna 1922 r. na Litwie," *Roczniki Dziejów Społecznych i Gospodarczych*, vol. XXXIX, 1978; A. Svikis, "Stosunki agrarne na Łotwie w okresie międzywojennym," and Auls Ruusmann, "Zmiany w strukturze agrarnej Estonii w latach 1919–1939," both in *Roczniki Dziejów Społecznych i Gospodarczych*, vol. XL, 1979; *The Baltic States*, pp. 144–150; J. Orczyk, "Przesłanki i rozmiary zmian w strukturze agrarnej Polski międzywojennej na tle porównawczym," in *Badania nad historią społeczno-gospodarczą w Polsce: Problemy i metody* (Warsaw, 1978), pp. 226–236.

40. See B. Ohlin, "Introductory Report on the Problem of International Economic Reconstruction," in *International Economic Reconstruction* (Paris, 1936), pp. 59, 63. In the longer run, however, it turned out that, for example, the American neoprotectionism gave a great boost to the U.S. economy.

41. See the literature quoted in Part One of this book.

42. See *The Baltic States*; A. O. Hirschman, *National Power and the Structure of Foreign Trade*, expanded ed. (Berkeley and Los Angeles, 1980), pp. 113ff.; Bandera, *Foreign Capital*, p. 53.

43. See E. Wagemann, *Der neue Balkan: Altes Land—junge Wirtschaft* (Hamburg, 1939); Basch, *The Danube Basin*, chapter 10; Hirschman, *National Power*; Berend and Ránki, *Economic Development in East-Central Europe*, chapters 10 and 11; J. Chodorowski, *Niemiecka doktryna gospodarki wielkiego obszaru (Grossraumwirtschaft) 1800–1945* (Wrocław, 1972), chapters 3 and 4; A. S. Milward, *The New Order and the French Economy* (Oxford, 1970); Hans-Jürgen Schröder, "Yugoistochna Evropa kao 'Nezvanichna imperiia' ('Informal Empire') Natsionalsocijalistichke Nemachke—primer Yugoslaviia 1933–1939," *Istorijski glasnik*, no. 1-2, 1976, pp. 48–80; K. Romanow-Bobińska, "Związki gospodarcze Europy Południowo-Wschodniej okresu międzywojennego," in A. Czubiński, ed., *Państwa bałkańskie w polityce imperializmu niemieckiego w latach 1871–1945* (Poznań, 1982), pp. 167–172.

44. H. Szlajfer, "Economic Nationalism of the Peripheries as a Research Problem," in Szlajfer, ed., *Essays on Economic Nationalism in East-Central Europe and South America, 1918–1939*, Centre of International Economic History, University of Geneva (Geneva, 1990).

45. See B. C. Shafer, *Faces of Nationalism* (New York, 1972), p. 189 (footnote).

46. For example, see J. Grunzel, *Economic Protectionism* (Oxford, 1916), pp. 192–198, and N. Spulber, *The State and Economic Development in Eastern Europe* (New York, 1966), pp. 98–106.

47. See the contributions by Walt W. Rostow, Simon S. Kuznets, William Arthur Lewis, Ernest Mandel, Bernard Rosier, and Pierre Dockès.

48. W. Röpke, *International Economic Disintegration* (London, 1942), p. 18.

49. See E. Mandel, *Long Waves in Capitalist Development: The Marxist Interpretation* (Paris, 1980), pp. 3–5, 22; Rosier and Dockès, *Rythmes économiques: Crises et changement social, une perspective historique* (Paris, 1983), chapter 5. For Poland, see Z. Landau and J. Tomaszewski, *Polska w Europie i świecie 1918–1939*, 2d ed. (Warsaw, 1984), pp. 145–148.

9

Epilogue: Questions for Discussion, Hypotheses, and Summary

Since the industrial revolution economic growth has become a systemic quality of the world economy. Depending on the interpretation of this process, economic nationalism can be viewed in two ways. According to the neoclassical and liberal version, anything that hampers the deepening of the international division of labor and the joining of the world economy by particular countries curbs this natural process. This point of view implies automatically a negative attitude toward economic nationalism.

Opponents of the liberal interpretation maintain, however, that the so-perceived growth only petrifies the old structure of the world economy and leads to its segmentation and, by amplifying the system's internal contradictions, to the widening of the rift between the worlds of the rich and the poor. It is another matter that the advocates of this view differ among themselves about the major characteristics of the phenomenon and about the ways of solving the dilemmas of global growth. They can argue, for example, about whether it was and still is possible to modernize underdeveloped economies in such a measure that they could shorten the distance between themselves and the industrialized countries (it is a truism, e.g., that Japan has been more successful in this regard than the Soviet Union), or whether this was only a make-believe shortening of the distance—make-believe because at present this modernization nearly always means modernization of dependence, argue some students of the development tendencies in Latin America in the past decades.[1]

But according to the other interpretation of economic nationalism, its occurrence (and even autarky as one of its manifestations) in a backward country may be seen as a stage, unavoidable in the twentieth century, that leads to modernization of the economy. Economic nationalism allows the incorporation of the national economy into the world economy. In this case, analysis of economic nationalism requires that we discount radical opinions—for example, that economic nationalism was (is) always bad or good.

It is striking that students of the problem seem to fail to notice that in the 1930s the practice and ideology of economic nationalism, like nationalism in general, underwent a major transformation, reaching a successive, modern stage. Such important historical events as the economic crisis of 1919–1921, the need for the new states to provide infrastructure, and the need to rebuild the foundations of the already established states that had increased their territory (like Serbia or Romania) were conducive to the transformation. The circumstances helped to strengthen the role of the government in prompting, coordinating, and carrying on with the endeavors in various areas of public and economic life necessary to the normal functioning of the state. Those most interested in the widening of state intervention and promoting the interest of the state were members of the bureaucracy, recruited predominantly from the middle class: civil servants, the intelligentsia, a segment of the bourgeoisie. Their interests concurred with the interests of a specific group of the national bourgeoisie (needless to say, the strength of the group and the degree to which their interests concurred differed greatly in the various countries of the region).

Yet, contrary to the liberal-minded politicians and economists (and also certain researchers), this strong etatist trend should not be unduly associated with those states' proclivity to separate themselves from the others—particularly plain in the first postwar years, which allegedly was the result of their economic nationalism.[2] To be sure, the policy of pressing for one's own industrial or agricultural production or for one's transport policy had some effect on the process. But it seems that the respective "separatist" policies resulted first and foremost from the authorities' desire to insure their country against the added impact of untoward events that might magnify internal crises, such as the transfer of inflation from outside, a flight of capital, or the inflow of foreign industrial and agricultural goods at extremely low prices, which was ruinous to the local industries and led to mounting unemployment.[3] This isolationist tendency initially was a result of external circumstances rather than of any conscious plan[4] on how to run the integral national economy according to the principles of economic nationalism.

When discussing the economic aspect of the phenomenon, we should agree with the opinion that one of the results of the establishment of independent economic systems in the region was the tendency to support the production of goods in short supply in the domestic market and to export the surplus commodities outside the old common tariff zone.[5]

Inasmuch as with regard to the Danubian countries a search for completely new markets could be recognized as, to some extent, an objection—rejoicing at their new independence, they took for granted the possibility (not necessarily a real one) of renewing mutual relations for granted[6]—no such doubt arises with regard to the Baltic states. In their case, any creation anew of economic ties with the former Russian empire was out of the question. Also, we should bear in mind that those states operated similar economic structures (this holds true particularly of Estonia and Latvia)[7] and therefore even in several dozen years their economies could not become complementary. The case of Poland was even more complicated.

The cause of the isolation of national economies traced here points to only one aspect of the problem. Yet it does not reveal the mechanism behind such tendencies. For example, in the face of agricultural competition from Hungary, Romania, Yugoslavia, and Poland in the Slovak domestic market, nothing remained for the Slovak Agrarians but to defend their crops with tariff barriers. Or could the other countries of the region put up with the unlimited expansion of Czech, Hungarian, or Polish industry? It is also worth remembering here that every newly emergent country sought a certain degree of autonomy in arms production (which Bulgaria, Romania, Yugoslavia, and the Baltic countries did not actually achieve). Thus, as a result of this and other postwar adjustment difficulties, the new states' inclination to separate their economy (until recently forming a whole within vast economic areas) received a fresh impulse. The Great Depression, with its traumatic experience and effects, of which many of the contemporaries were well aware, produced one more reason for separation. National and ethnic animosities and grudges provided an additional incentive for the isolation of autonomous economic organisms.

A comparison between conclusions concerning inward-oriented economic nationalism with certain of Albert Breton's provisions should permit a new evaluation of his concept. For one thing, it is easier to assert whether and to what extent a definite economic policy is nationalistic if it is inward-oriented rather than outward-oriented. In the latter case, it is difficult to determine anything, as a clear picture of the situation can seldom be obtained, except in such circumstances as tariff war and restrictions.

Protectionist policy as such, even if very restrictive, does not prove discrimination when it is equally hostile to all foreign countries. It is only from the point of view of economic liberalism that it can be recognized as discriminatory. In case of inward-oriented nationalism, the picture is clearer. Various kinds of economic aggressiveness can be directed toward minorities, and with variable intensity. With regard to the countries of East-Central Europe, the general conclusion is obvious. In the 1930s the degree of economic discrimination against minorities varied between rather low (in Czechoslovakia, Bulgaria, Greece, and the Baltic countries), to somewhat higher (in Poland) or quite high (in Hungary and Romania).

This is additionally related to the economic and political status of the territories occupied by a national minority or by people believing themselves to be one. Breton approached this problem in analyzing the position of Quebec. Other researchers tackled this problem, for example, in the context of the position of Slovakia and Transcarpathian Ruthenia in Czechoslovakia. It is difficult to agree with the view heard in the 1950s that Slovakia played the role of a colony or semicolony in the state,[8] yet this was not an unusual view among social scientists. Thus, for instance, certain Ukrainian scholars implied that the predicament of Western Ukraine under Polish rule, as in fact of Poland's internal colony, was even worse.[9]

Whatever one might say about ethnic relations in Poland and Czechoslovakia, the "colonial" argument did not play any significant role in the domestic economic policy. The situation in those two countries resembled rather that in Italy at the turn of the century and later. I mean here the polarization of their basic economic and social structures: the emergence of the developed and the backward parts of the country (the north and the south in the case of Italy), which resulted from spontaneous economic, demographic, and political processes. It is only in this context that one may ponder whether, for example, between the Czech Lands on the one hand and Slovakia and Transcarpathian Ruthenia on the other, or between western and central Poland and its eastern borderland there did not come to be a quasi–center-periphery arrangement (I am consciously referring to the terminology of Andre Gunder Frank and Immanuel Wallerstein).

Secondly, even though Breton's conception jibes with the opinions of those historians of social and political movements who see in the middle class (particularly in the lower middle class) the main representative of the idea of nationalism, things were not that simple in the region and beyond. Large sections of the national bourgeoisie and sometimes even the gentry subscribed to that ideology. The specific character of the region lay, moreover, in the conflict within the middle class overlapping an ethnic conflict—hence the serious difficulty in the direct application of the model, which uses a simplified dichotomous social and national structure (the middle and the working classes, francophones and Anglo-Saxons) to the societies of the region. We must keep in mind that in the post-1918 circumstances the ethnic status of a part of the old middle class and capitalists was markedly reduced under the new socioeconomic and political system. They lost their position derived from their membership in the ruling nation to become a psychologically, politically, and socially inferior national minority. (This is what happened to Germans in Poland,

Czechoslovakia, and the Baltic countries and to Hungarians in Slovakia, Romania, and Yugoslavia.) It was upon these classes, who until recently had been representing the nationalism of the rulers, that the presently ruling and until recently oppressed (or believing themselves to be oppressed) classes retaliated.

Thirdly, it is difficult to approve unreservedly of the way Breton analyzes the behavior of the working class. He attributes the impact of nationalism on workers to their peculiar intoxication with this ideology. All the same, this impact can be ascribed also to other influences. In East-Central Europe workers were financially interested in the materialization of the slogans of economic nationalism. German workers in Upper Silesia and in Lodz, for instance, particularly at the time of the Great Depression, competed for jobs with Poles. In Czechoslovakia, too, the competition between the Czech and the German labor force became a principal problem, causing serious repercussions at home and abroad. The nationalism of the Poles and the Czechs was aimed, although with different intensity, against various sections of the German community: against the ethnically alien bourgeoisie, the middle class (including the lower middle class), and also the workers. In the region, especially in the 1930s, there were consolidating fronts, ethnically differentiated and clearly opposed, based primarily on national solidarism but also, though only to a small degree, on class solidarism. The specific character of East-Central Europe, additionally affected by the singularly painful impact of the Great Depression, contributed to a public support for the policy of economic nationalism that was not restricted to the middle class, as suggested by Breton.

Inasmuch as one cannot be expected to be anything but critical of an inward-oriented economic nationalism that manifested itself in xenophobia or downright racism, the opinion on the role it played in economic reconstruction, economic intervention, and industrialization must take many factors into account. All in all, this opinion must be, as I have tried to show, more favorable.

One should agree with Ingvar Svennilson that the prewar economic nationalism had its roots in the social trends of the time.[10] Returning to our initial discussion of various kinds of nationalism, we cannot recognize, for example, the region's industrialization drive as a clear indication of political nationalism. This drive was first and foremost a result of the people's understanding that unless they industrialized, they would prolong their backwardness.

One may hypothesize that in the interwar period economic nationalism was peculiar primarily to eastern and southern European authoritarian regimes, and only then to totalitarian systems. The difference was crucial. In the former, economic nationalism was an essential element, justified by state interest and used to support the social groups interested in the preservation of the current form of government. Therefore, objectively, in the 1930s it acted as a neutralizing agent in the face of danger from radical movements, chiefly fascism but also communism. (Students of authoritarian regimes do not notice this role of economic nationalism at all.) The extent and importance of economic nationalism to a given system of power were decided by the social forces most eager to refer to it. Under totalitarian regimes (Italy, Germany, the Soviet Union) it was merely an additional, although consequential, element of the ruling ideology. In the democratic countries of Europe its significance was relatively small: ideologically puny, somewhat wider in the economic and political realities of the 1930s. Although of rather minor importance, it played a certain role, for instance, in France, which sought self-sufficiency in food. Czechoslovakia, where agricultural nationalism proved to be indeed a very important element of economic policy and practice, was the only exception here.

It seems that we should at long last try to answer the fundamental question, Can every program and the practical measures aimed at either fuller economic independence or the restructuring of the economy by yet another "big push," particularly through industrialization, be described as economic nationalism? First we should ask, What alternatives are there in the so posed a problem? Explicitly the second part of the question (the restructuring of the economy through industrialization) is logically identical to its first part (fuller economic independence). Clearly this is so; the problem so posed only apparently lacks sense. Even the proponent of neoclassical concepts must give an affirmative answer to the question posed in the first part of this quasi alternative. It is exactly according to the liberal doctrine that the right to independence is an inalienable right of individuals and nations. All the same, to the second part of the question the neoclassicist will usually give a negative answer even though it is nothing else but the concretizing of the abstract notion of independence.

This brief exposition partially reveals the actual foundation of the opinion that determined as nationalistic the region's policy to lay down an economic basis for their independence. This opinion is a result of the influence that neoclassical concepts exert on researchers' way of thinking. For my part, I believe that those attempts at economic takeoff should be understood as simply Eastern and Central Europe's aspiration to cut the distance between themselves and the industrialized Western Europe. These were not unequivocally nationalistic aspirations (precisely in the light of the liberal doctrine). One could of course meet among the politicians and economists of the countries involved advocates of the view that nationalism combined with autarky and with anachronistic conceptions of internal economic order (based either on agrarianism of the collectivist version proposed by local parafascist or fascist movements) was an instrument for attaining political, military, and economic power.[11] It is only in this meaning that economic nationalism took on total proportions. These people, however, misread the development trends in the world economy and the actual condition and potential of their own national economies. The authors of social and economic programs connected with radical nationalist movements were particularly inclined to develop such conceptions.[12]

From this it follows that at least with reference to the interwar history of the region it would be more appropriate to speak not of economic nationalism but of economic patriotism or of economic quasi nationalism if, in its outward orientation, it was defensive in nature or, using miscellaneous protectionist measures, tried to build foundations for economic independence. "Economic patriotism"[13] transformed into nationalism, however, when it became aggressive and served purposes that were more or less imperialistic. After all, the economic nationalism of the industrialized countries or one oriented primarily toward political and military purposes, as in Nazi Germany or Fascist Italy, was not identical with the economic nationalism of, say, the Balkan countries (where in 1937/38, annual national income per capita equaled US$70–80).[14] I do not think that we may agree with the narrow opinion on such occurrences, prevalent in the literature. We must see the differences between these two nationalisms and judge them accordingly. The terminological differentiation I propose is tantamount to cutting ourselves off from the approach to the issue discussed here, which is derived from neoclassical theories.

I am aware that the differentiation I propose can give rise to several methodological doubts. The most serious would concern the absence of a clear-cut criterion allowing a line to be drawn between economic patriotism and economic nationalism. Nevertheless, even this differentiation as it is allows us to carry out a more penetrating and precise analysis of the economic history of the region. Besides, I contest seeing in economic nationalism or, to put it more precisely, in economic patriotism adverse effects only. This ideology was the product of objective state-building processes, and with respect to the economy, of the tendency to question the former division of labor (in the 1930s made additionally strong by the aftermath of the Great Depression).

What social forces were interested in those processes, and to what degree? What methods did those forces employ, and how did these methods affect the political system? Did they really contribute to economic

growth? Did they really make it possible to get over the dysfunction resulting from the disintegration of the previous large political entities?
How does this intricacy appear in the light of some famous development
ideas?

To give even the vaguest answer to these questions one should consider (1) the development options theoretically and practically open to
the countries of East-Central Europe, and (2) the pros and cons of the
methods proposed.

Earlier I raised the question of economic development based on import
substitution, on diversification of exports, or on both (Chapter 8). It is not
easy to assess the usefulness of each of these solutions. In any case, we
should show the unique relationship between the diversification of exports and the substitution of imports—the former is usually the result of
the latter, as was the case in Hungary and Czechoslovakia. Experts in underdeveloped economies argue that because of lower social and economic costs, escape from backwardness is swifter if the emphasis is laid
on the diversification of exports.

Industrial countries were in a better position than agricultural ones to
carry out successfully the policies of diversification of exports and substitution of imports. Due to their exports' greater susceptibility to falls in
world prices and demand, agrarian economies found diversification of
their exports much more difficult. When it came to import substitution,
especially with regard to agricultural imports, the odds were even more
positively in favor of the industrialized countries, as their generally
higher level of economic development made it easier for them to deal
with the troubles they encountered in agricultural production. Sometimes those countries argued that their seeking independence from imports was a result of their greater susceptibility to crisis, caused by the insufficient complementariness of their economy.[15] However, in light of the
liberal theories that economists and spokespeople for business circles in
the developed countries upheld, the argument seems to have been blocking their policy of substitution of food imports.[16] To put it briefly, in underdeveloped countries export-oriented growth—as opposed to import-
oriented growth—is by definition antiautarkic, irrespective of the
structure of exports. It suffices to observe the situation in the 1920s, when
protectionism did not cause any basic reorientation or transformation of
the economic development of the countries of East-Central Europe. But
even in the 1930s, which brought about a major reorientation—either enforced or voluntary—toward import substitution, the significance of this
policy as an element of autarky proved to be fairly small. Along with
subjective reasons (e.g., some ideological motives), it was first and foremost the very serious balance of payments deficit that forced strict aus-

terity measures, reduced imports, and induced policies to alleviate urban unemployment and rural overpopulation. These and other reasons spoke for import substitution and for the previously mentioned beggar-my-neighbor policies. The drastically reduced foreign trade of each of the countries was thus a mere external symptom of the policy of import substitution.

A larger-scale diversification of exports took place in the region also only in the 1930s. It was a spontaneous reaction above all to the shrinking revenues from traditional exports and the need to earn foreign currency in free markets.[17] Traditional exports dwindled markedly: In the relatively more developed Czechoslovakia they fell by 73 percent and in Poland by 53 percent, whereas in Yugoslavia by 27 percent and in Bulgaria by a mere 6 percent.[18]

Deviations from the established export (and import) patterns offered a vague proof that diversification of the economy was taking place. For instance, in Hungary industrialization's rising share in the national income was accompanied by the rising shares of industrial goods in exports and of raw materials in imports. Likewise, changes in agriculture went hand-in-hand with the relative increase in the exports of innovative, processed food products from Poland, Latvia, and Estonia.[19] Yet those changes did not mean any qualitative turning point, with Czechoslovakia being perhaps the only exception. Food products, timber, coal, bauxite, and non-ferrous ores continued to be the main export items.[20]

Taken together, the positive effects of diversified exports in the interwar period were limited in advance, because diversification concerned primarily those products for which international demand was shrinking as the result of the industrialized countries' drive for self-sufficiency in food. However, an increase in the exports of industrial goods required competitiveness, an ability East-Central European countries did not quite have. Hence the inability to further diversify their exports threatened the underdeveloped countries of the region with the continuation of their old pattern of production.

The share of foreign trade in national income and the patterns of exports and imports are useful indicators in the assessment of the economic level achieved and in showing the ultimate limits the economy can reach. The first points to the economy's ties with the international market; the other (considering the specific circumstances of the interwar period) helps in the assessment of the actual possibilities of economic growth as implied by the foreign trade pattern.

In the prosperous 1920s the share of foreign trade in the national product of Czechoslovakia was estimated at 20–25 percent, of Hungary at 14 percent, and of Bulgaria, Romania, and Yugoslavia at 10 percent. In Poland the share must have been larger than Hungary's but smaller than

Czechoslovakia's. In Latvia and Estonia it was, I suppose, closer to the Czechoslovak index.

As regards the pattern of foreign trade, at the end of the 1930s Czecho-slovakia, whose industrial exports comprised three-quarters of its total foreign sales, was the only country of the region where agriculture was not the main foreign-cash earner. All the other countries' imports did not change much, although toward the end of that period East-Central Europe markedly increased its imports of machinery and equipment.[21] No doubt this was due to their increasing industrialization. Industrialization was those countries' answer to the serious decline in world food prices. Combined with the growing popularity of economic nationalism, the situation inevitably favored a reformulation of the economic policy line that would stress the need for a growth based on import substitution. That could lead to an increase in domestic demand through inflation and protectionism (going together or separately). As for protectionism, some economists maintain that it really could advance economic development, although in the longer run it could curb an increase in domestic demand, understood as the engine of growth.[22] In this sense, either a spontaneous or a deliberate protectionist policy in the region was a sensible alternative to purely liberal solutions. This, however, inevitably led to greater autarkic or quasi-autarkic tendencies in economic ideology and practice.

Pressing the idea of self-sufficiency was the natural reaction of a segment of the political elites to the only recently shed subordination to foreign imperial powers, or to their country's economic and cultural underdevelopment, or to both. Suffice it to say here that the autarkic policy tools do not actually differ from those of the protectionist policy, although in the case of the former the ranges of interests and of the measures applied are significantly wider. Consistently advanced autarky can bring a qualitative change; by and large, it means a much more frequent government intervention in the economy at the expense of private enterprise. It was not by chance that it was usually the state bureaucracy, routinely abetted by the military, that spread the idea of self-sufficiency in the region.

In practice, however, it turned out that pure autarky—that is, the building, preferably on one's own, of a productive base that would encompass all stages and areas of production—was simply unattainable. And indeed, after all, the majority of economic policy makers did not advance self-sufficiency thus understood.[23]

Still, it is difficult to classify as a manifestation of nationalism and autarky the aspiration to lay the foundations of infrastructure and industry.[24] What is more, the extent of the protectionist-autarkic instruments resorted to hardly ever depended on the will of the government alone. This extent depended first and foremost on the coincidence of a myriad of internal and external factors. It is significant that all those instruments were directed against the countries at a similar level of development, not against the more industrialized nations capable of retaliation. At any rate, were it not this sometimes radical protectionism, the countries of East-Central Europe would have been flooded with German, British, French, and Italian merchandise. At the same time, though, all the various instruments used to abet local production had, as I have mentioned, only a small effect on the foreign trade pattern. In this situation, the countries of the region—with the exception of Czechoslovak industry and particular sectors of Austrian, Hungarian, Polish, Estonian, and Latvian industries—could not compete seriously with the industrialized countries. At best (which of course was of considerable significance to their balance of trade), the intensive import substitution (and much more infrequently, diversification of exports) boosted the home demand and this way alleviated to some extent the region's dependence on foreign supplies and changed the character of foreign trade. In the case of the industrialized Czechoslovakia, it also meant a strict protective policy toward its own agriculture and the country's drive for self-sufficiency. Agricultural countries, in contrast, which suffered from a chronic shortage of foreign currency, were ready to export their agricultural surpluses at any price. Looking at the situation from those countries' point of view and considering their usually unfavorable terms of trade (they exported food products and raw materials), one could not expect of economic policy makers that in the name of faithfulness to theoretical principles they should abandon the policy of protectionism, nor could one recognize the protection of the region's industry as excessive in each case. What is more, we should not forget that the drive for self-sufficiency in the 1930s was forced on those countries (precisely by the impact of the Great Depression) with much greater intensity than in the previous decade.

The social groups that supported the program for industrialization in the region were relatively small, for several reasons: (1) the anachronistic occupational and residential patterns of the population (in all of these countries peasants made up a vast majority); (2) a relatively poor social infrastructure (differing from country to country but usually including a poor literacy level, a shortage of adequate vocational schooling, very unsatisfactory health care, welfare, and similar systems); (3) an anachronistic status system; and (4) the low appeal of the slogan of industrialization to a part of the middle and the lower classes because it offered only slim prospects for social promotion.

As regards the first two reasons, the relevant indices increased at the close of the 1930s, in some countries even remarkably.[25] Regarding the fourth reason, the fifteen-year plan for the development of the Polish economy conceived by Deputy Premier Kwiatkowski was the only attempt to hold out such a prospect. In other countries promotion was striven for either through the redistribution of the income already produced or of the assets accumulated by selected groups. Economic nationalism and the prospect for the elimination of internal "foreign" competition attracted not only the lower and middle urban strata fighting for a limited number of jobs in industry, trade, and the professions, and the rural population eager to get rid of the annoying creditors and sometimes of the landowners, but the local upper classes as well. The gentry in Poland, Hungary, and even Czechoslovakia wanted to divert dispossessed and smallholders' attention from their own estates, and the native bourgeoisie wanted to add to their own possessions at the expense of the Jewish, German, or Hungarian bourgeoisie. If we take no account of the nostrification and nationalization processes of the early 1920s, only in Hungary and Romania did redistribution of income involve the change of the Jewish minority's status through dispossessing them of their property and of certain civic rights. That was a plain, negative nationalistic message meant to please selected circles of the middle class. It is worth adding here that the underdevelopment of the middle class was that factor which, particularly in the 1930s, contributed to the abandonment of economic liberalism in domestic policy.

The removal of the anachronistic status system, the third reason for the low level of support for industrialization, was linked closely with the changes in the second and fourth factors, poor social infrastructure and prospects for social mobility.

The programs for economic reconstruction announced from time to time, and those for the development of local industry formulated in the 1930s, took various points of departure. Particularly often they resulted from a fairly superficial observation of the development path the industrialized countries had once followed. Discussions of the issue were usually reduced to the questions of which industries to develop; of whether to invest primarily in traditional or in new industries, whether in the light and food industries, as insisted by the economic elites of the developed countries,[26] or in the selected heavy and raw-materials industries, which seemed expedient in view of the country's natural resources, economic independence, national defense, and ambitions of the elite; of whether the economic reconstruction should be accomplished in the traditional way, that is, by private enterprises, or rather through the development of the etatist economy. The list could go on. Depending on the importance of particular vested interests (private or public) and on the international political and business situation, the disposition of options could differ. In the political and economic press, champions of state-in-

duced industrialization seemed to outnumber advocates of private enterprise. The former favored the development of the raw-materials and
heavy industries as well as (and perhaps this is merely my own supposi-
tion, which cannot be borne out without a thorough study[27]) traditional
technologies, as they were more labor-intensive (structural unemployment and agrarian overpopulation was endemic in the overwhelming
part of the region).

There is no one answer, except the most evasive "yes," to the question
of whether the middle class, and especially the local bourgeoisie, supported the vast industrialization program. Only the question about the
more precise understanding of this program gives us some acumen as to
the preferences of the bourgeoisie who seldom were at one.

The groups whose direct interests linked them with international cartels
or with groups of foreign capital, that is, usually the spokespeople for raw-
materials industries, were inclined to declare themselves in favor of the
preservation of the old economic structure. For example, in Poland such
conservatives were the Górnośląski Związek Przemysłowców Górniczo-
Hutniczych [Upper Silesian Union of Mining and Metallurgical Industrial-
ists] and, to a lesser degree, Lewiatan; in Romania, the oilmen associated
with British capital; in Czechoslovakia, capital groups involved in the coal
and metallurgical industries (e.g., those with close relations with the
Schneider-Creusot concern); in Yugoslavia and Hungary, groups strictly
subordinated to foreign and local companies interested specifically in the
extraction of nonferrous ores (Yugoslavia) and bauxite (Hungary).

The groups of bourgeoisie interested primarily in production for the domestic market (many of them representing the middle, unpooled (members of no cartel), and also agrarian bourgeoisie) favored a more intensive
development of processing industries, from the metal and machine to the
textile and food industries.[28] This distinction of course remains a mere approximation, a trend that is by no means explicit. Industrialization preferences of particular groups of the bourgeoisie and of other social circles,
their desire to preserve or to change the economic structure were decided
each time by a definite coincidence of reasons. However, research into this
area has not gone beyond preliminary findings.

All the same, one may observe that between large- or small-scale plans
for industrialization and their actual implementation there was a gap,
sometimes a yawning one. The economic policy of the East-Central European countries was again and again faced with barriers (especially as regards infrastructure, skilled labor, and capital) that turned their ambitions to industrialize into, if not a bubble, then at least a very distant
project. Willy-nilly, they were developing those industries that preserved
the archaic economic structure. In Bulgaria, for instance, a greater part of
investments went to the food industry and agriculture. Hungary and

Greece were more inclined to put their money in light rather than heavy industry, and in traditional rather than new industries. In the Baltic countries, industrialization was clearly subordinated to the interests of peasants and the agricultural sector.

However, we must not forget an interesting change. In Poland it appeared as a four-year economic plan and a six-year plan for the development of the defense industry; in Hungary, as the Győr Program and in a greater emphasis on the development of the aluminum and certain other metalworking industries; in Czechoslovakia, as the takeoff of the restructuring of industry and the achieving of self-sufficiency in food; in Estonia, as a marked rise in the output of oil and its by-products obtained from bitumen. Moreover, Hungary, Romania, Bulgaria, Yugoslavia, and Greece attempted to modernize agriculture.[29] The change was a result of various factors, including these countries' need to protect themselves against the effects of the Great Depression, the increasingly firm conviction—and not on the part of the elites alone—that the country required economic restructuring, the ambition to secure a minimum defense potential, and in the case of the Danubian (Hungary and Romania) and the Balkan countries, their coming within the Third Reich's sphere of influence. The Reich was quite effective in enlisting those countries (and also the Baltic countries, but with less success) for the development of definite types of agricultural products to serve the needs of the German economy or for the development of the local industries that exported their manufacture to Germany. This tendency was, on the one hand, a distinct expression of the idea of *Grossraumwirtschaft,* and on the other, a major incentive to a transformation of the economy. All the same, the evaluation of the *direction* and *effects* of those transformations was and has remained debatable.[30]

The problem of protectionism links up with the dualism of the country's economy, of its agricultural (backward) *and* industrial (modern) character, penetratingly analyzed against the example of interwar Poland by Zbigniew Landau.[31] Politicians who considered how to remedy their country's backwardness had to go into the question of how to get over this dualism. Should it take place through an intense industrialization that would lead to the reduction of the backward agriculture's share in the national income?[32] Or through the stepping-up of the economic demand of the region's most populous social stratum, the peasants?

The latter solution, founding development on an increase in the rural market, assumed that local manufactures, especially necessities, would be cheap. This required a moderate industrial protectionism, because only under such protection was it possible to fight monopoly prices that reduced rural demand. It seemed logical that this policy could go hand-in-hand with agricultural protectionism. The former solution, for its part, gave emphasis to the development of industry at the expense of the agricultural population. The concept stemmed from a paltry accumulation of capital and thus insufficient resources at the disposal of industry (and town) and the state. In the situation like this, a decidedly proindustrial, protectionist policy seemed to be the only answer. Theoretically, each of these solutions could overcome this dualism. The dilemma reared its head in the region particularly in the 1930s, when the dualistic character (i.e., the autonomous operations of industrial and agricultural sectors, of town and village) of the economy was even more apparent (though perhaps not in Latvia, Estonia, Czechoslovakia, and Austria), during the period of a serious fall in agricultural prices and decline in the rural market. Demand even for necessities, which would seem relatively inelastic, diminished at the time.[33]

Admittedly in those days it was impossible to apply the latter solution (the "pro-agrarian" option). Nevertheless many theoreticians believe that it might perhaps be more rational in small countries with a prosperous peasant stratum, placed along trade routes toward vast markets, with a generally educated and enterprising population. Inasmuch as it may be assumed that Latvia and Estonia met those conditions, the Danubian and the Balkan countries, for example, certainly did not. The import-substitution solution, however, aroused the resistance of both peasants and Agrarians as well as criticism from the industrialized countries. The two solutions had one trait in common, however. They both referred to government intervention, including an unequivocally protective policy.

When assessing those solutions' chances of succeeding, we should remember that in the interwar period it was quite improbable that the allocation of a lion's share of any country's resources to agriculture and the extension of its rural market could enable that country to extricate itself relatively quickly from backwardness (the stage of Gerschenkron's "spurts"). A different concept, namely, an industrialization policy supported by protectionism and emphasizing the stepping-up of urban demand and public orders, would offer, at least in theory, greater possibilities to the countries with the so-called minimum industrial complex (Hungary, Poland, and perhaps Romania). I rather subscribe to Gerschenkron's opinion that to hope that in the truly backward country industry can grow from agriculture is not very well founded. The view that agriculture will be modernized as a result of the continuing process of industrialization seems more accurate. This latter view implies a rapid liberation of industry from its dependence on an agricultural environment,[34] and it thus seems to agree with the notion of the total separateness of industry and agriculture in the greater part of the region.

The case of the Danubian countries, remaining in the sphere of German influence, goes to prove indirectly that the burden of the proindustrial solution did not necessarily lie on the agricultural population alone. Assuming, as I do, that at the end of the 1930s those countries' trade with Germany was profitable to the agricultural population and that it was primarily the town people who paid for the rise in import duties on manufactures,[35] one can believe that, contrary to prevalent opinion, the cost for conceivable industrialization could be more evenly distributed among particular social strata. One can ponder whether economic policy was able to lead the economies of these countries to the stage of the first or successive takeoff. In the 1930s only Latvia, Estonia, and, surprisingly, Poland were either at the threshold of or had already embarked upon the takeoff stage.

Although it goes beyond the main thrust of the present work, it is worth noting here that economists sensitive to the problems of backwardness opted for the solution that emphasizes the need to develop first and foremost industry. Manoilescu, Zeletin, Tennenbaum, Rosenstein-Rodan, Balogh, Mandelbaum, and later, for instance, W. W. Rostow, let alone the whole spectrum of advocates of dependency theory, including the proponents of the world-system approach (Wallerstein and others), approved of this variant either directly or indirectly. They often regarded protectionism as part and parcel of that solution. In the 1960s and 1970s economic historians gave particular attention to the concept, mentioned earlier, of leaps in economic development, embraced and built up by Gerschenkron.[36] Gerschenkron, too, considered protectionism to be an instrument of development policy.

Researchers often ask about the relationship between the form of regime and the country's economic development. They ponder whether and to what extent the form of regime decides this development and vice versa— whether the type of economic development affects the formation of the regime. Does this involve a causal or a more complex relationship? It is popularly believed that in underdeveloped market economies a strong impact of the political regime on economic development is less likely than in countries with a centralized, import-substituting economy and collective ownership. This is what, for instance, Guillermo O'Donnell says in reference to Latin America,[37] and, to some extent, Nicos P. Mouzelis in his work on political transformations in the Balkan countries and in South America in conditions of delayed industrialization (before 1939).[38]

As for the reverse relationship, certain conclusions follow from the analysis by Eliezer Ayal. The cases of nationalist ideology's practical effect on the economic development of Japan, Atatürk's Turkey, and Israel, he found, did not support the argument that dictatorship was necessary to latecomers' development.[39] It turned out that Turkey, ruled by the strictest dictatorial regime, was the one that scored the least success.

Ayal's generalization may be intuitively recognized as legitimate, yet the proof of it is so weak that it cannot be accepted as anything more than a mere hypothesis.

Even if authoritarian rule was inevitable in the region, there is much to indicate that such rule was a consequence of causes other than economic (see Part One). The question of whether the authoritarian regime was favorable to the region's development should become a subject of a separate study.

To evaluate the region's policies of industrialization and protectionism, it is important that we answer the question of whether the efforts of the East-Central European countries to abolish the prejudicial international division of labor were effective. The outcome of World War I and of the crisis-ridden years of 1929–1935 do not allow definite conclusions. But the relatively swift adjustment of particular countries, especially the new ones, to new circumstances helps us to understand the problem. Both Hungary (which had lost more than half of its former territory) and Poland (which had regenerated on the territories of three partitioning sectors[40]) seemed unable to depend on themselves. Yet these two as well as the Baltic countries (having practically no industry of their own, and cut off from the former Russian Empire) proved to be able to lay foundations of their own, actually new, economies. To some degree they managed to rectify the hitherto international division of labor.

Some authors argue that the rate of growth in the provinces that were formerly parts of Austria-Hungary, in the Russian Empire, and in the German Reich was at the turn of the century higher than in the interwar period.[41] This argument seems pointless. Methodologically it is open to doubt even for the reason that the economic role of those provinces within the former large-territory economies was different from what it was after 1918. What is more, the economic growth in other countries of Europe was also more rapid before 1914 than in the interwar years, especially in the 1920s. From this it does not result, of course, that the economic problems of the region would have been any less painful had, for instance, the succession and Baltic countries not imposed tariffs higher than those charged in the three former empires.[42] Maybe they would have been less painful, but it is not at all certain. In short, the disintegration of Austria-Hungary and, it should be added, the political consequences of the defeat of the Reich and Russia did not mean an economic disaster to the region. It was not the customs tariffs that were the most important here. Tariffs, the policy of industrialization, the striving after self-sufficiency in food, the establishment of separate and different monetary, communications, transport, foreign-trade, and other systems, all of this was naturally breaking down the large territories that had until recently been all of a piece economically. It was also breaking down the recent division of labor among the lands that had made up those large economic territories. Their having been of a piece, however, only petrified the organization of the large economic territory, its intrinsic contradictions included. Even if we put aside the fundamental significance of national and political ambitions that acted as dynamite exploding the already anachronistic political and territorial formations, from the point of view of counterfactual analysis we can say that it is not at all sure that the further development of the territories that had made up, for example, Austria-Hungary (assuming that the monarchy would have survived) would have been any more rapid than the one actually reached by the new succession states. On the contrary, considering that in the interwar period economic growth ceased in the entire world economy, which was related, as I have noted, with the long cycle's stagnation phase, the Austro-Hungarian economy would have not escaped that slowdown, either.

I return now to fundamental questions. In the light of certain development concepts celebrated in recent decades, how to describe the economic development of the region? Do modernization theories (otherwise often criticized)[43] allow one to define the economic development of the majority of the region's countries as the modernization stage or, on the contrary, as a stagnation or the modernization of their dependence on the advanced countries? The latter definition, let me remind the reader, fits in with the broadly interpreted concepts of dependent development. It implies that the countries of the region (with the exception of Czechoslovakia and Austria), even if they made some economic progress, were still placed in the periphery. The more optimistic researchers willingly observe that in certain countries economic growth and development recast them for new roles in the world economy, that they no longer had to act as the supplier of agricultural and raw materials for the industrialized countries. Therefore it would perhaps be pertinent to include, for instance, Poland, Latvia, and Estonia among the countries that were treading the path toward the status of a strong and relatively lasting semiperiphery.[44] Changes in the occupational structure or the enclaves of modern industry in those countries brought evidence of such trend. Yet the fact that the changes in the occupational structure did not reach a break-even point calls this evidence into question. As for the region as a whole, its economic structure did not change substantially. Even though certain countries initiated the modernization of agriculture, backward agriculture definitely prevailed over industry in the region. The failure of the majority of the East-Central European countries to develop the rudiments of their own machinery production is yet another factor that serves to question this evidence. Thus returning to the questions formulated in the preceding paragraph and following a counterfactual approach to the region's development prospects, I support the opinion that certain countries, such as Latvia, Estonia, and Poland, did indeed see the chance to extricate themselves quickly from economic underdevelopment, from the position described as the periphery (or even semiperiphery).[45]

Summary

1. The spread of the ideology and practice of economic nationalism in East-Central Europe in the interwar period was an effect of manifold factors, in particular:

- the determination of social elites to achieve the economic and administrative unity of their new states;
- those elites' conviction that political sovereignty was incomplete without economic independence, the latter being infeasible without industrialization;
- the impact of strictly political factors, especially the fear that their respective country's territorial integrity could be questioned (e.g., by their bordering neighbors) and the rise in nationalistic feelings;
- the aspirations of the people who wished to extricate themselves from their backwardness;
- the rise in the authoritarianism of the East-Central European regimes;
- the rapid rise in the 1930s of the state's share in the economy;

and

- the impact on the region of the political, economic, and social changes in totalitarian Germany, Italy, and the Soviet Union.

Economic nationalism was oriented outward, against the interests of other countries, and inward, against national minorities. In the economic and political conditions of the time, the outward-oriented nationalism was mostly defensive in character, particularly when it concerned more advanced industrialized countries. But when it was inward-oriented, more often than not it antagonized the public and brought about obnoxious effects. It meant a redistribution of the national wealth and income, not their growth.

The middle class, and especially the state bureaucracy, was a vehicle of economic nationalism. Finding its actual beneficiaries is more difficult. The ideology and practice of economic nationalism narrowly understood furthered vital particularistic interests of the national bourgeoisie (its minority segments included), much more infrequently peasants, and last but not least, some specific group, such as the army. In the first instance, industrialism becomes the main attribute of nationalism; in the second, agrarianism; and in the last, external security interests of the state. In the long-term perspective, if it was able to look after more than mere particularist interests, economic nationalism did serve, for better or for worse, the achievement of common national interests.

2. The growth of protectionism, an important ingredient of both the ideology and practice of economic nationalism in the region, was not merely a result of the ruling elites' conviction that protectionism was indispensable to the achievement of the adopted economic and political goals. No doubt protectionism was bolstered by the economic and social consequences of the Great Depression, the decline of 1938, and the impact of the international situation on the position of the countries of the region. The downswing phase of the Kondratieff waves, which fell in the interwar period, also fostered the development of protectionism.

The main task of the policy of protectionism, which in practice was the effect of different factors and interests, was to protect and support local manufactures. In the complex situation of the time, it was necessary to develop an arsenal of protectionist instruments (quantitative and foreign-exchange restrictions, increase in dumping, introduction of complicated systems of tax reliefs and subsidies, etc.). In the 1930s changes acquired such proportions that one may speak of a qualitative leap in the evolution of protectionism. Having gone through the traditional (operational) stage, in the 1920s it reached the tactical stage, and in the following decade it became a holistic, self-contained ideology of development in such countries as Romania and Bulgaria. The most ardent advocates of protectionism wanted it to proceed in an organized rather than a spontaneous (or transmitted) fashion.

3. Vying with other ideologies, economic nationalism no doubt did stamp economic life durably, and as an ideology of development it played a greater role in the region than anywhere else in the world. The endeavors the East-Central European countries made, particularly in the 1930s, to free themselves from the vicious circle of backwardness might be most generally described as an attempt, under new circumstances and in a modified way, to follow the path the industrialized world had trodden. The instruments of the "new" protectionism, built into the also new economic nationalism (or, as I emphasize throughout the book, economic patriotism rather) were to serve this ultimate goal. The concrete measures adopted by the region's countries were relatively homogeneous; they were taken in response to similar challenges and because of a similar (excepting Austria and Czechoslovakia) social and economic structure.

Although the rationality of economic patriotism or protectionism can be questioned from the microeconomic point of view, it must nevertheless be admitted that in the broader perspective these ideologies played a positive role. This hypothesis differs from the opinions that blame those ideologies for the region's economic and political failures. The same ideologies became a lever to induce beneficial, albeit modest, changes in the international division of labor, for the benefit of the underdeveloped countries of East-Central Europe.

Notes

1. H. Szlajfer, *Modernizacja zależności: Kapitalizm i rozwój w Ameryce Łacińskiej* (Wrocław, 1985). See also R. Stemplowski, "Modernizacja—teoria czy doktryna?" *Kwartalnik Historyczny*, no. 3, 1979, pp. 742–754.

2. See I. T. Berend and G. Ránki, *Economic Development in East-Central Europe in the 19th and 20th Centuries* (London, 1974), pp. 201, 209.

3. For a more nuanced opinion, see A. Basch, *The Danube Basin and the German Economic Sphere* (London, 1944), p. 28, and Z. Landau and J. Tomaszewski, *Gospodarka Polski międzywojennej 1918–1939*, vol. 1, *W dobie inflacji 1918–1923* (Warsaw, 1967); Z. Natan, V. Khadzhinikolov, and L. Berov, *Ikonomikata na Bŭlgariya*, vol. 1 (Sofia, 1969); J. Faltus, *Povojnová hospodárska kriza v rokoch 1921–1923 v Československu* (Bratislava, 1966); I. T. Berend and G. Ránki, *The Hungarian Economy in the Twentieth Century* (London, 1985).

4. L. Pasvolsky, *Economic Nationalism of the Danubian States* (London, 1928), p. 74, and F. Hertz, *The Economic Problem of Danubian States: A Study in Economic Nationalism* (London, 1947).

5. E. A. Radice, "General Characteristics of the Region Between the Wars," in M. C. Kaser, ed., *The Economic History of Eastern Europe, 1919–1975*, vol. 1, *Economic Structure and Performance Between the Two Wars* (Oxford, 1985), p. 36.

6. For example, immediately before World War I, the industry of the future Czechoslovakia exported a mere 20 percent of its output outside the monarchy borders. See Faltus, *Povojnová*, p. 20.

7. Royal Institute of International Affairs, *The Baltic States: A Survey of the Political and Economic Structure and the Foreign Relations of Estonia, Latvia, and Lithuania* (London, 1938); Aleksander A. Drizul, ed., *Istoriia Latviiskoi SSR* (Riga, 1971); P. Łossowski, *Kraje bałtyckie na drodze od demokracji parlamentarnej do dyktatury (1918–1934)* (Wrocław, 1972); *Soviet Estonia* (Tallin, 1980); M. Meshkanskiene, *Promyshlennost' Litvy v period monopolisticheskogo kapitalizma* (Vilnius, 1981).

8. See Richard Wagner, *Panství kapitalistických monopolů v ČSR* (Prague, 1958), p. 169; Pawel Rapoš, *Priemysel Slovenska za kapitalizmu* (Bratislava, 1957). For criticism of this approach, see J. Faltus and V. Průcha, *Prehl'ad hospodárskego vyvoja na Slovensku v rokoch 1918–1945* (Bratislava, 1969), pp. 301–305.

9. See V. N. Bandera, *Foreign Capital as an Instrument of National Economic Policy: A Study Based on the Experience of East European Countries Between the World Wars* (The Hague, 1964), p. 73.

10. I. Svennilson, *Growth and Stagnation in the European Economy* (Geneva, 1954), p. 36, and "The Concept of the Nation and Its Relevance to Economic Analysis," in Edward Austin G. Robinson, ed., *Economic Consequences of the Size of Nations* (London, 1963), pp. 4, 334.

11. On the Romanian case, see papers by K. Hitchins, "Rumanian Peasantism: The Third Way," and Z. Ornea, "Interwar Romania in Search of a Development Model," both in *Models of Development*.

12. For Poland, see the ONR program, *Zasady programu narodowo-radykalnego* (Warsaw, 1937); Szymon Rudnicki, *Obóz Narodowo-Radykalny: Geneza i działalność* (Warsaw, 1985); J. Majchrowski, *Silni—zwarci—gotowi: Myśl polityczna Obozu Zjednoczenia Narodowego* (Warsaw, 1985). For other countries, see C. A. Macartney, *October Fifteenth: History of Modern Hungary, 1929–1945*, vol. 1, 2d ed. (Edinburg, 1961); H. Rogger and E. Weber, eds., *The European Right: A Historical Profile* (London, 1965); P. Sugar and I. J. Lederer, eds., *Nationalism in Eastern Europe* (Seattle, 1973); N. M. Nagy-Talavera, *The Green Shirts and Others: A History of Fascism in Hungary and Rumania* (Stanford, 1970); Łossowski, *Kraje bałtyckie*.

13. The Czech bourgeoisie used this term, although in a different sense, in their struggle against German superiority. See J. Chlebowczyk, *Procesy narodowotwórcze we wschodniej Europie Środkowej w dobie kapitalizmu (od schyłku XVIII do początków XX w.)* (Warsaw and Kraków, 1975), pp. 265ff.

14. E. Lethbridge, "National Income and Product," in Kaser, ed., *The Economic History*, vol. 1, p. 532.

15. See League of Nations, *Commercial Policy in the Interwar Period: International Proposals and National Policies* (Geneva, 1942), p. 125.

16. Compare W. Röpke, *International Economic Disintegration* (London, 1942), pp. 137, 165ff.

17. See Z. Drabek, "Foreign Trade Performance and Policy," in Kaser, ed., *The Economic History*, vol. 1, p. 457.

18. Ibid., p. 458.

19. *The Baltic States*, pp. 122ff., 148, 161. See also Chapter 8 of this book, note 28.

20. Drabek, "Foreign Trade," p. 458.

21. Ibid., pp. 430ff. Data concerning foreign trade per capita in the Baltic countries provide some orientation in foreign trade's importance. In 1929 foreign trade per capita in Latvia was 3.26 times that of Yugoslavia or Romania, in Estonia almost 3 times, and in Lithuania one-third larger. In the years 1926–1929 average annual exports of manufactured goods were smaller than imports, in the case of Romania by 50 times, Lithuania more than 7 times, Poland 3 times, Latvia almost 2 times, and Hungary 3.5 times. See Drabek, "Foreign Trade," pp. 470–474 (Tables 7.46–7.58); *The Baltic States*, p. 163; F. Hilgerdt, *Industrialization and Foreign Trade* (Geneva, 1945), p. 84. See also Chapter 8 of this book, note 28.

22. See G. M. Meier, *The Problem of Limited Economy* (New York, 1974).

23. For an analysis of some theoretical aspects of this question, see P. J. Burnell, *Economic Nationalism in the Third World* (Brighton, 1986), chapter 1. For the interwar approaches, especially the German and Italian, see, for example, Kurt Baumann, "Autarkia a gospodarka planowa [1933]," in Jerzy Łoziński, ed., *Szkoła frankfurcka* (Warsaw, 1985), pp. 231–249; F. Lantini et al., *L'Autarchia: Economica della nazione* (Rome, 1939); *The State and Economic Life: First Study Conference (Milan, May 1932)*

(Paris, 1932); *The State and Economic Life: A Record of a Second Study Conference (London 29 V — 2 VI 1933)* (Paris, 1934); J. Chodorowski, *Niemiecka doktryna gospodarki wielkiego obszaru (Grossraumwirtschaft) 1800–1945* (Wrocław, 1972); and E. Teichert, *Autarkie und Grossraumwirtschaft in Deutschland 1930–1939* (Munich, 1984). For the Soviet approach, see Alec Nove, *An Economic History of the USSR* (Harmondsworth, 1975), and Roger Munting, *The Economic Development of the USSR* (New York, 1982).

24. See J. Kleer, *Gospodarka światowa: Prawidłowości rozwoju* (Warsaw, 1975), pp. 45ff.

25. See Éva Ehrlich, "Infrastructure," in Kaser, ed., *The Economic History*, vol. 1, pp. 323–378; G. von Rauch, *The Baltic States: Estonia, Latvia, and Lithuania: The Years of Independence, 1917–1940* (Berkeley and Los Angeles, 1974), chapter 3; T. U. Raun, *Estonia and the Estonians* (Stanford, 1987), pp. 129–137; A. L. Miskes, "Statistical Evidence and the Concept of Tertiary Industry," *Economic Development and Cultural Change*, vol. III, no. 4, 1955, pp. 366–372.

26. See, for example, "Manifest finansistów," in *Przemysł i Handel*, 1926, p. 47; E. Wagemann, *Der neue Balkan: Altes Land—junge Wirtschaft* (Hamburg, 1939), and Chodorowski, *Niemiecka doktryna.*

27. See, however, J. Gołębiowski, *Spór o etatyzm wewnątrz obozu sanacyjnego w latach 1926–1939* (Kraków, 1978), and Jan Kofman, *Lewiatan a podstawowe zagadnienia ekonomiczno-polityczne Drugiej Rzeczypospolitej: Z dziejów ideologii kół wielkokapitalistycznych w Polsce* (Warsaw, 1986).

28. See the previously cited contributions by Biały, Drozdowski, Popkiewicz, Ryszka, Kofman, Landau, Tomaszewski, Berov, Tsonev, Natan, Černy, Teichova, and Radice.

29. See Kaser, ed., *The Economic History*, vol. 1, chapters 1, 3, and 5; vol. 2, chapters 9 and 10; Berend and Ránki, *Economic Development in East-Central Europe*, chapters 10 and 11; M. M. Drozdowski, *Polityka gospodarcza rządu polskiego 1936–1939* (Warsaw, 1963), chapters 2 and 3; A. F. Freris, *The Greek Economy in the Twentieth Century* (London, 1980); Z. Landau and J. Tomaszewski, *Zarys historii gospodarczej Polski 1918–1939*, 4th ed. (Warsaw, 1981), chapters 6 and 7; V. Průcha, ed., *Historia gospodarcza Czechosłowacji XX wieku* (Warsaw, 1979), chapters 3 and 4; A. Teichova, *The Czechoslovak Economy, 1918–1980* (London, 1988), chapter 3; Natan et al., eds., *Ikonomikata*, chapters 5 and 6; H. L. Roberts, *Rumania: Political Problems of an Agrarian State* (New Haven, 1951); RIIA, *The Baltic States*, part two, chapter 1.

30. Apart from the authors mentioned earlier, see, for example, Andrej Mitrović, "Erganzungswirtschaft: The Theory of an Integrated Economic Area of the Third Reich and Southeast Europe (1933–1941)," and Leposava Cvijetić, "The Ambitions and Plans of the Third Reich with Regard to the Integration of Yugoslavia into Its So-called Grosswirtschaftsraum," both in Pero Morača, ed., *The Third Reich and Yugoslavia, 1933–1945* (Belgrade, 1977), pp. 7–45, 184–196; Czesław Madajczyk, *Faszyzm i okupacje 1938–1945: Wykonywanie okupacji przez państwa Osi w Europie*, vol. 2 (Poznań, 1984), pp. 537–555.

31. Z. Landau, "Hamulce rozwoju gospodarczego związane z dwusektorową strukturą gospodarki," in Z. Landau and J. Tomaszewski, *Druga Rzeczpospolit. Gospodarka—społeczeństwo—miejsce w świecie* (Warsaw, 1977), pp. 70–92.

32. In 1938 agriculture's share in the net national product (in current prices) was 32 percent in Czechoslovakia, 36–39 percent in Hungary, Greece, and Poland,

and 52–63 percent in Yugoslavia, Romania, and Bulgaria. See I. T. Berend, "Agriculture," in Kaser, ed., *The Economic History*, vol. 1, p. 207.

33. Inasmuch as in the much smaller, western, part of the region, trade between town and village, industry and agriculture, helped to develop the market also for the products of new industries, in the remaining areas no more than 30 percent of the agricultural output went to the market. It is estimated too that, for example, in Romania, Bulgaria, and Yugoslavia barely 20 percent of total industrial output reached the countryside. The situation in Hungary, Greece, and Poland was only slightly better. See *Economic Development in S.E. Europe: Political and Economic Planning* (London, 1945). According to very rough estimates, in the year 1931/1932 an average peasant spent 37 zlotys (US$4.1) on necessities (salt, sugar, kerosene, footwear, clothing, medicines). In 1934 an average Pole used 10.4 boxes of matches (against 24 in 1929). See J. Ciepielewski, ed., *Wieś polska w latach wielkiego kryzysu 1929–1935: Materiały i dokumenty* (Warsaw, 1965), pp. 36ff.

34. A. Gerschenkron, *Economic Backwardness in Historical Perspective* (London, 1976), p. 216.

35. Compare Röpke, *International Economic Disintegration*, p. 40, footnote 8, apparently the only renowned economist of the time to have emphasized this point.

36. Apart from *Economic Backwardness*, see "The Typology of Industrial Development as a Tool Analysis" in his *Continuity in History and Other Essays* (Cambridge, Mass., 1968), *Europe in the Russian Mirror: Four Lectures in the Economic History* (Cambridge, 1970), and *An Economic Spurt that Failed: Four Lectures in Austrian History* (Princeton, 1977). For criticism of his hypotheses, see, for example, Andrew Shonfield, *Modern Capitalism: The Changing Balance of Public and Private Power* (London, 1969), chapter 3; Simon S. Kuznets, *Economic Growth of Nations: Total Output and Production Structure* (Cambridge, Mass., 1976), chapter 1; Rondo Cameron, "Explanations of International Inequalities in Economic Development: History and Theory," and A. S. Milward, "Comments on Some Theories of Historical Changes," both in Jürgen Kocka and G. Ránki, eds., *Economic Theory and History* (Budapest, 1985). See also M. Kula, "Aleksandra Gerschenkrona uwagi o zacofaniu gospodarczym," *Prace i Materiały*, no. 1, 1966; Jerzy Kleer, *Drogi wyjścia z zacofania* (Warsaw, 1974).

37. Guillermo A. O'Donnell, *Modernization and Bureaucratic Authoritarianism* (Berkeley, 1973), pp. 13–15, 113.

38. N. P. Mouzelis, *Politics in Semi-Periphery: Early Parliamentarism and Late Industrialization in the Balkans and Latin America* (London, 1988), pp. 72, 220.

39. E. B. Ayal, "Nationalist Ideology and Economic Development," *Human Organization*, vol. 25, no. 3, 1966, p. 238.

40. For example, in 1910, 67 percent of the exports of the Kingdom of Poland were directed eastward, primarily to Russia; the industrialized Upper Silesia and the modern Great-Poland agriculture were economically integrated into the German empire. See Andrzej Jezierski, *Handel zagraniczny Królestwa Polskiego 1815–1914* (Warsaw, 1967), p. 192.

41. Hertz, *The Economic Problem*. See also I. T. Berend and G. Ránki, *Underdevelopment and Economic Growth: Studies in Hungarian Economic and Social History* (Budapest, 1979), pp. 110–119.

42. See J. M. Montias, "Economic Nationalism in Eastern Europe: Forty Years of Continuity and Change," *Journal of International Affairs*, vol. XX, no. 1, 1966, p. 46.

43. See, for example, Kocka and Ránki, eds., *Economic Theory and History*, and Gerschenkron, *An Economic Spurt*, pp. 142–146.

44. On the concept of the semiperiphery, see I. Wallerstein, *The Capitalist World-Economy* (Cambridge, 1979), pp. 95–118. For a penetrating criticism of this concept, see D. Chirot and Thomas D. Hall, "World-System Theory," *Annual Review of Sociology*, vol. 8, 1982.

45. So described not just by adherents of the dependence theory alone. See, for example, D. Chirot, "Successes or Failures? Evaluating Progress and Models of Development in Eastern Europe Between the Two World Wars," in *Models of Development* conference.

Bibliography

List of Abbreviations

AAN	*Archiwum Akt Nowych* (Archives of New Files)
ASSP	*Archiw za stopanska i socialna politika*
BS	*Bŭlgarsko stopanstvo*
BU	*Biuletyn Urzędniczy*
CS	*Current Sociology*
ČČH	*Československý Časopis Historický*
EDCC	*Economic Development and Cultural Change*
EEQ	*East European Quarterly*
EHR	*Economic History Review*
EJ	*Economic Journal*
FA	*Foreign Affairs*
FO	Foreign Office
HO	*Human Organization*
HQ	*Hungarian Quarterly*
IA	*International Affairs*
IBK GiC	Instytut Badania Koniunktur Gospodarczych i Cen (Institute of Research on Economic Situation and Prices)
IG	*Istorijski glasnik*
IP	*Istoricheski pregled*
JIA	*Journal of International Affairs*
JMH	*Journal of Modern History*
JPE	*Journal of Political Economy*
JSS	*Jewish Social Studies*
KEM	*Komitet Ekonomiczny Ministrów* (Economic Committee of Ministers)
KH	*Kwartalnik Historyczny*
Conference on Models of Development	Conference on *Models of Development and Theories of Moderniztion in Eastern Europe Between the World Wars* (Rackeve, 10–15 September 1988), duplicated manuscripts
MRSt	*Mały Rocznik Statystyczny* (Small Statistical Annual)
MSZ	Ministerstwo Spraw Zagranicznych (Ministry of Foreign Affairs)
NDP	*Najnowsze Dzieje Polski: Materiały i studia z okresu 1914–1939 (The Newest History of Poland: Materials and studies from 1914 to 1939)*
ONR	Obóz Narodowo-Radykalny (National and Radical Front)

OZN	Obóz Zjednoczenia Narodowego (United National Front)
PEEE	Paper in East European Economics
PH	*Przegląd Historyczny*
PP	*Przegląd Powszechny*
PRM	*Prezydium Rady Ministrów* (Presidium of the Council of Ministers)
PRO	*Public Record Office*
PSQ	*Political Science Quarterly*
RDSiG	*Rocznik Dziejów Społecznych i Gospodarczych*
RIIA	Royal Institute of International Affairs
RP	Rzeczpospolita Polska (Republic of Poland)
SBID	*Spisaniye na Bŭlgarskoto Ikonomichesko Drŭzhestvo*
Sbirka ČSN	*Sbirka přednašek pořadaných Českou společností národohospodá řskou v obdobi*
SDEŚ	*Studia z dziejów ZSRR i Europy Środkowej*
SEER	*Slavonic and East European Review*
SH	*Sbornik historycký*
Sobótka	*Śląski Kwartalnik Historyczny "Sobótka"*
SP	*Stopanski problemi*
TSISP	*Trudowe na Statisticzeski institut za stopanski prouchvaniya pri Sofiyskiya dŭrzhaven universitet*
TWII	*Trudove na Visshiya ikonomicheski institut Karl Marks*
USČP	*Ústředni svaz československých prŭmyslniku v roce . . .* (annals from 1921 to 1938)
VSWG	*Vierteljahrschrift für Sozial- und Wirtschaftsgeschichte*
WA	*Weltwirtschaftliches Archiv.*
Weekly Report	*Weekly Report of the German Institute for Business Research*
WEP	Wielka encyklopedia powszechna PWN (The Great Universal Encyclopedia PWN)

I. Archives

Archiwum Akt Nowych (Archives of New Files) — teams:
Komitet Ekonomiczny Ministrów (Economic Committee of Ministers)
Konsulat RP w Morawskiej Ostrawie (Polish Consulate in Ostrava)
Ministerstwo Przemysłu i Handlu (Ministry of Industry and Commerce)
Ministerstwo Spraw Zagranicznych (Ministry of Foreign Affairs)
Poselstwo RP w Budapeszcie (Polish Mission in Budapest)
Poselstwo RP w Pradze (Polish Mission in Prague)
Prezydium Rady Ministrów (Presidium of the Council of Ministers)
Public Record Office — team:
Foreign Office

II. Journals

(Annals included in the work)

Annual Review of Sociology 1982
Archiv za stopanska i sotsialna politika 1938
Banker 1936
Biuletyn Urzędniczy 1931, 1935, 1939
Bŭlgarsko stopanstvo 1939, 1940
Československý Časopis Historický 1956, 1959, 1965, 1968, 1970, 1976, 1978
Current Sociology 1973
East European Quarterly 1971
Economic Development and Cultural Change 1955
Economic History Review 1978, 1979
Economic Journal 1938, 1943
Economist 1939
Ekonomista 1932
Foreign Affairs 1932, 1933, 1937
Godishnik na Sofiyskiya universitet Filosofsko-istoricheskiya fakultet 1970
Historica 1962
Hospodářské dejíny 1985
Human Organization 1966
Hungarian Quarterly 1941
Industrialen pregled 1933
International Affairs 1930–1932, 1934
Internationale Agrarrundschau 1940
Istoricheski pregled 1973
Istorijski glasnik 1976
Izvestiya na Instituta po istoriya na BKP 1969
Jewish Social Studies 1946, 1966
Journal of International Affairs 1966
Journal of Modern History 1972
Journal of Political Economy 1932, 1964, 1965
Kwartalnik Historyczny 1972, 1979
Najnowsze Dzieje Polski, Materiały i studia z okresu, 1914–1939, 1963
New Statesman and Nation 1933
Nova Mysl 1968
Political Science Quarterly 1965
Prace i Materiały (Międzyuczelniany Zakład Problemowy Krajów Słabo Rozwiniętych) 1966
Przegląd Historyczny 1986
Przegląd Powszechny 1985
Przemysł i Handel 1926
Review Fernand Braudel Center for Study of Economies, Historical Systems, and Civilization 1988
Roczniki Dziejów Społecznych i Gospodarczych 1974, 1978, 1979
Sbornik Historický 1975
Slovenské historické studie 1968
Slavonic and East European Review 1933, 1936, 1939
Spisaniye na Bŭlgarskoto Ikonomichesko Druzhestvo 1930, 1933, 1935, 1942
Stopanski problemi 1938

Studia z dziejów ZSSR i Europy Środkowej 1974, 1977, 1981, 1984, 1985
Śląski Kwartalnik Historyczny "Sobótka" 1979
Trudove na Statisticheski institut za stopanski prouchvaniya pri Sofiyskiya dŭrzhaven universitet 1935, 1938
Trudove na Visshiya ikonomicheski institut Karl Marks 1960
Vierteljahrschrift für Sozial- und Wirtschaftsgeschichte 1975
Weekly Report of the German Institute for Business Research 1938
Weltwirtschaftliches Archiv 1931, 1940

III. State and Statistical Publications

M. J. B. Condliffe. *World Economic Survey: Fifth Year, 1935.* Geneva 1935.
Czechoslovak Cabinet of Ministers on the Complaints of the Sudete German Party in the Czechoslovak Parliament, Prague 1937.
Europe's Trade, League of Nations, Geneva 1941.
International Economic Conference (Geneva, May 1927), *Principal Features and Problems of the World Economic Position from the Point of View of the Different Countries*, 3d and 4th ser., League of Nations, Geneva 1927.
Koniunktura gospodarcza Polski w liczbach i wykresach w latach 1929–1938, special edition IBKGiC 1938, No. 12, Warsaw 1939.
Mały Rocznik Statystyczny, 1937–1939.
Sejm Rzeczypospolitej Polskiej. IV kadencja. Stenography reports.
The Tariff and Its History, 2d ed., Washington, D.C., 1934.
Twenty-sixth Report of the Commissioner of League of Nations in Bulgaria (Quarter from November 15, 1932, to February 15, 1933).
R. Tyler. *Financial Position of Hungary in the . . .* , Geneva 1932–1938.
The World Book Encyclopedia, Field Enterprises Educational Corporation, Vol. 15.
The World Economic Conference: Final Report, League of Nations. Geneva 1927.

IV. Publications of Organizations (National and International), Informational Publications (Encyclopedias, Dictionaries, Abstracts, Etc.), Collection of Documents and Law Regulations, Speeches

The Balkan States. I. Economic, RIIA, London 1936.
The Baltic States: A Survey of the Political and Economic Structure and the Foreign Relations of Estonia, Latvia, and Lithuania, RIIA, London, New York, and Toronto 1938.
Chronology of Political and Economic Events in the Danube Basin, 1918–1936: Hungary, Paris 1938.
J. Ciepielewski (elaboration and introduction). *Wieś polska w latach wielkiego kryzysu 1929–1935: Materiały i dokumenty*, Warsaw 1965.
H. Delpar (ed.). *Encyklopedia of Latin America*, New York 1974.
K. W. Deutsch. *Interdisciplinary Bibliography of Nationalism, 1933–1953*, Cambridge 1954.
Dizionario Enciclopedico Italiana, Vol. 8, Rome 1958.

Doctionar Enciclopedic Roman, Vol. 3, Bucharest 1965.

Enciclopedia Italiana, Vol. 22, Rome 1934.

The Encyclopedia Americana, Vol. 19, New York, Chicago, and Washington, D.C. 1958.

Encyclopaedia Britannica, Vol. 18, Chicago, London, and Toronto 1960.

Encyklopedia nauk politycznych, Vol. 2, Warsaw 1937.

J. Gould, W. L. Kolb (eds.). *A Dictionary of the Social Sciences*, Glencoe, Ill., 1969.

A. S. Hornby with A. P. Cowie (eds.). *Oxford Advanced Learner's Dictionary of Current English*, 7th impression, Oxford 1980, reprinted Warsaw 1981.

"Hospodářská politika čs. průmyslu v letech 1918–1938,"in *USČP* v roce 1937, Prague.

International Encyclopedia of the Social Sciences, Vols. 8, 11, Chicago 1968.

Konstytucja Królestwa Rumunii z dnia 27 lutego 1938 r., 2d emended edition, Warsaw 1938.

Mała encyklopedia ekonomiczna, Warsaw 1958.

Nowe konstytucje, Warsaw 1925.

K. S. Pinson. *Bibliographical Introduction to Nationalism*, New York 1935.

South Eastern Europe: The Political and Economic Survey, RIIA, London 1939.

A. Stamboliyski. *Izbrani proizvedeniye*, Sofia 1979.

J. B. Sykes (ed.). *The Concise Oxford Dictionary of Current English*, 6th ed., Oxford 1978.

J. Tomaszewski. "Kwestia narodowa w Jugosławii i Grecji w raportach polskich poselstw," *SDEŚ*, Vol. 21 (1985).

J. Tomaszewski. "Kwestia narodowa w Rumunii w 1931 r. w raportach polskich konsulatów i poselstwa," *SDEŚ*, Vol. 20 (1984).

USČP, 1921–1938.

V. Elaborations

A. Ajnenkiel. "Ewolucja systemów ustrojowych w Europie Środkowej 1918–1939," in J. Żarnowski (ed.), *Dyktatury w Europie Środkowo-Wschodniej 1918–1939*. Wrocław, Warsaw, Kraków, and Gdańsk 1973.

W. Alter. *Antysemityzm gospodarczy w świetle cyfr*, Warsaw 1937.

Ameryka Łacińska: Dyskusja o rozwoju (selection and introduction R. Stemplowski), Warsaw 1987.

S. Amin, G. Arrighi, A. G. Frank, I. Wallerstein. *Dynamics of Global Crisis*, New York and London 1982.

O. N. Anderson. "Again on the Problem of Scissors of Prices in Bulgaria," *TSISP*, 1935, No. 3.

O. N. Anderson. "On the Scissors of Prices in Bulgaria," *TSISP*, 1935, No. 1.

J. Anthropius. "Obilni monopol v zemědělska krise," *Sbirka ČSN* 1931/32, No. 6, Prague 1932.

H. Arendt. *The Origins of Totalitarianism*, New York 1973.

H. W. Arndt. "Development Economics Before 1945," in J. Bhagwati, R. S. Eckaus (eds.), *Development and Planning: Essays in Honour of Paul Rosenstein-Rodan*, Cambridge, Mass., 1973.

A. Atanasov. "Industrialnata politika na Bŭlgariya prez poslednite godini," *SBID* 1942.

A. Atanasov. "Za industrialnata politika na drzhavata," *Industrialen pregled*, 1933.

E. B. Ayal. "Nationalist Ideology and Economic Development," *HO*, Vol. 25 (1966), No. 3.

S. L. Baily. "Nationalism," in H. Delpar (ed.), *Encyclopedia of Latin America*, New York 1974.

B. Balassa. "The Structure of Incentives in Semi-industrial Economies," in B. Balassa et al., *Development Strategies in Semi-industrial Economies*, Baltimore and London 1984.

W. Balcerak. *Powstanie państw narodowych w Europie Środkowo-Wschodniej*, Warsaw 1974.

T. Balogh. *Unequal Partners*, Vol. 1, *The Theoretical Framework*, Oxford 1963.

T. Balogh. "Some Theoretical Aspects of the Central European Credit and Transfer Crisis," *IA*, Vol. XI (1932), No. 3.

V. N. Bandera. *Foreign Capital as an Instrument of National Economic Policy: A Study Based on the Experience of East European Countries Between the World Wars*, The Hague 1964.

A. Basch. "Československé hospodářství v krisi", *Sbirka ČSN*, 1936/37, No. 15, Prague 1937.

A. Basch. *The Danube Basin and the German Economic Sphere*, London 1944.

A. Basch. *The New Economic Warfare*, New York 1941.

A. Basch. *A Price for Peace: The New Europe and World Markets*, New York 1945.

H. Batowski. *Austria i Sudety 1919–1938*, Poznań 1968.

H. Batowski. *Z polityki międzynarodowej XX wieku*, Kraków 1979.

H. Batowski. *Między dwiema wojnami: Zarys historii dyplomatycznej*, Kraków 1988.

H. Batowski. *Rok 1938 — dwie agresje hitlerowskie* (1st joint ed.), Poznań 1985.

R. Battaglia. *Zagadnienia kartelizacji w Polsce: Ceny a kartele*, Warsaw 1933.

K. Baumann. "Autarkia a gospodarka planowa," in *Szkoła frankfurcka* (introduction and transl. J. Łoziński), Warsaw 1985.

C. Beaud. "The Interests of the Union Européenne in Central Europe," in A. Teichova, P. L. Cottrell (eds.), *International Business and Central Europe, 1918–1939*, New York 1983.

J. D. Bell. *Peasants in Power: Alexander Stambolijski and the Bulgarian Agrarian National Union, 1899–1923*, Princeton 1977.

I. T. Berend. "Agriculture," in M. C. Kaser (gen. ed.), *The Economic History of Eastern Europe, 1919–1975*, Vol. 1, M. C. Kaser, E. A. Radice (eds.), *Economic Structure and Performance Between the Two Wars*, Oxford 1985.

I. T. Berend. "The Problem of Eastern European Economic Integration in a Historical Perspective," in I. Vajda, M. Simai (eds.), *Foreign Trade in Planned Economy*, Cambridge 1971.

I. T. Berend, G. Ránki. *The Development of Manufacturing Industry in Hungary, 1900–1944*, Budapest 1960.

I. T. Berend, G. Ránki. *Economic Development in East-Central Europe in the 19th and 20th Centuries*, New York and London 1974.

I. T. Berend, G. Ránki. *Underdevelopment and Economic Growth: Studies in Hungarian Economic and Social History*, Budapest 1979.

I. T. Berend, G. Ránki. *The Hungarian Economy in the Twentieth Century*, London and Sydney 1985.

I. T. Berend, G. Ránki. *The European Periphery and Industrialization, 1780–1914*, Budapest 1982.

I. Berlin. "Nationalism: Past Neglected and Present Power," in I. Berlin, *Against the Current: Essays in the History of Ideas*, Oxford 1981.

L. Berov. "Appearance of Ideas for a Co-operative ('Intermediate') Road of Socioeconomic Development in Bulgaria During the Period Between Two World Wars, Conference on *Models of Development*.

L. Berov. *The Economic Development of Bulgaria Between the Two Wars, 1918–1944*, PEEE, Oxford 1972.

L. Berov. "Direktsiya 'Khranoizos'" 1930–1940 g.," *TWII* 1960, No. 1.

L. Berow [Berov]. "Państwowo-monopolistyczne regulowanie gospodarki w burżuazyjnej Bułgarii do 1944 r.," *SDEŚ*, 1977, Vol. 13.

L. Berov et al. *100 godini na bŭlgarska ekonomika*, Sofia 1978.

L. Berov. "Vŭnshnata tŭrgoviya mezhdu Bŭlgariya i Germaniya meżdu dvete svetovni voyni (1919–1939 g.)," in *Bŭlgarsko-germanski otnosheniya i vrŭzki: Izsledovaniya i materiali*, Vol. 1, Sofia 1972.

F. Biały. *Górnośląski Związek Przemysłowców Górniczo-Hutniczych 1914–1932*, Wrocław, Warsaw, and Kraków 1967.

L. Bianchi. *Právne formy monopolizácie za buržoáznej ČSR*, Bratislava 1965.

K. J. Błahut. *Polsko-niemieckie stosunki gospodarcze w latach 1919–1939*, Wrocław and Warsaw 1975.

K. Bobchev. "Otnosheniye na dŭrzhavata kŭm narodnoto stopanstvo v Bŭlgariya," *SBID*, 1930, Vol. 1.

K. Bobchev. "Protektsionism i stopanska nauka," *SBID*, 1935, Vols. 8–9.

K. Bobchev. "Protektsionisticheskata teoriya na profesor M. Manoilescu," *SBID*, 1933, Vol. 8.

K. Bobchev. "Reglamentirane na vŭnshnata tŭrgoviya i organizirane na vŭnshnata tŭrgovska politika," *BS* 1940.

K. Bobchev. "Vŭchnata tŭrgovska politika na Bŭlgariya sled voynata," *TSISP*, 1938, Vol. 4.

G. Bombach, H.-J. Ramser, M. Timmermann, W. Wittmann (Hrsg.). *Der Keynesianismus*, Vol. I: *Theorie und Praxis Keynesianischer Wirtschaftspolitik*, Berlin, Heidelberg, and New York 1976.

J. W. Borejsza. *Mussolini był pierwszy . . .* , Warsaw 1979.

V. Brdlík. "Zemědělská krise v suvislosti s národním hospodářstvím," *Sbirka ČSN*, 1932/33, No. 1, Prague 1933.

Y. S. Brenner. *Theories of Economic Development and Growth*, London 1966.

A. Breton. "The Economics of Nationalism," *JPE*, Vol. LXXII (August 1964), No. 4.

A. Brożek. "Polityka imigracyjna w państwach docelowych emigracji polskiej (1850–1939)," in A. Pilch (ed.), *Emigracja z ziem polskich w czasach nowożytnych i najnowszych (XVIII–XX w.)*, Warsaw 1984.

J. W. Bruegel. *Czechoslovakia Before Munich: The German Minority Problem and British Appeasement Policy*, Cambridge 1973.

P. J. Burnell. *Economic Nationalism in the Third World*, Brighton 1986.

E. B. Burns. *Nationalism in Brazil: A Historical Survey*, New York 1968.

E. Busière. "The Interests of the Banque de l'Union Parisienne in Czechoslovakia, Hungary, and the Balkans, 1939–40," in A. Teichova, P. L. Cottrell (eds.), *International Business and Central Europe, 1918–1939,* New York 1983.

M. Byé. "Międzynarodowa polityka handlowa, jej skutki i założenia," in Z. Kamecki, J. Sołdaczuk (selection and ed.), *Teoria i polityka handlu międzynarodowego w kapitalizmie,* Warsaw 1960.

Š. Čačko. "O polnohospodářskych pomerach Slovenska," in K. Stodola, *Hospodářské problemy Slovenska,* Prague 1934.

R. Cameron, "Explanations of International Inequalities in Economic Development: History and Theory," in J. Kocka, G. Ránki (eds.), *Economic Theory and History,* Budapest 1985.

F. G. Campbell. *Confrontation in Central Europe: Weimar Republic and Czechoslovakia,* Chicago 1975.

F. Capie. "The British Tariff and Industrial Protection in the 1930s," *EHR,* 2d ser., Vol. XXXI (August 1978), No. 3.

E. H. Carr (ed.). *Nationalism: A Report by a Study Group of Members of the RIIA,* Oxford 1939.

E. H. Carr. "States and Nationalism: The Nation in European History," in J. Held et al. (eds.), *States and Societies,* Oxford 1985.

B. Černý. "Některé hospodářskopolitické důsledky obilniho monopolu," *ČČH,* 1959, No. 4.

J. César, B. Černý. "The Nazi Fifth Column in Czechoslovakia," *Historica,* Vol. 4, Prague 1962.

J. César, B. Černý. "O ideologii československého agrarizmu," *ČČH,* 1959, No. 2.

J. César, B. Černý. "The Policy of German Activist Parties in Czechoslovakia, 1918–1938," *Historica,* Vol. 6, Prague 1962.

J. César, B. Černý. *Politika nemeckych buržoaznich stran v Československu v letech 1918–1938,* Vol. 2, *1930–1938,* Prague 1962.

Chakalov. See Czakałow.

"Kharakter na 19-to mayskiya prevrat prez 1934 g.," *Izvestiya na Instituta po istoriya na BKP,* Vol. 21, Sofia 1969.

D. Chirot. "Neoliberal and Social Democratic Theories of Development: The Zeletin–Voinea Debate Concerning Romania's Prospects in the 1920s and Its Contemporary Importance," in K. Jowitt (ed.), *Social Change in Romania, 1860–1940: A Debate on Development in a European Nation,* Berkeley 1978.

D. Chirot. "Successes or Failures? Evaluating Progress and Models of Development in Eastern Europe Between the Two World Wars," Conference on *Models of Development.*

D. Chirot, T. D. Hall. "World-Systems Theory," *Annual Review Sociology,* Vol. 8, Palo Alto 1982.

J. Chlebowczyk. *Między dyktatem, realiami a prawem do samostanowienia: Prawo do samookreślania i problem granic we wschodniej Europie Środkowej w pierwszej wojnie światowej oraz po jej zakończeniu,* Warsaw 1988.

J. Chlebowczyk. *Procesy narodowotwórcze we wschodniej Europie Środkowej w dobie kapitalizmu (od schyłku XVIII do początków XX w.),* Warsaw and Kraków 1975.

J. Chodorowski. *Niemiecka doktryna gospodarki wielkiego obszaru (Grossraumwirtschaft) 1800–1945,* Wrocław, Warsaw, Kraków, and Gdańsk 1972.

A. Chojnowski. *Koncepcje polityki narodowościowej rządów polskich w latach 1926–1939*, Wrocław, Warsaw, Kraków, and Gdańsk 1979.

Cholakov. See Czołakow.

J. Ciepielewski, I. Kostrowicka, Z. Landau, J. Tomaszewski. *Dzieje gospodarcze świata do roku 1980*, 4th emended edition, Warsaw 1985.

J. Ciepielewski, *Polityka agrarna rządu polskiego w latach 1926–1939*, Warsaw 1968.

G.D.H. Cole. *Studies in World Economies*, London 1934.

Commercial Policy in the Interwar Period: International Proposals and National Policies, League of Nations, Geneva 1944.

W. M. Corden. "Tariffs and Protectionism," in *International Encyclopedia of the Social Sciences*, Vol. 8, Chicago 1968.

W. M. Corden. *The Theory of Protection*, Oxford 1971.

P. L. Cottrell. "Aspects of Western Equity Investment in the Banking Systems of East Central Europe," in A. Teichova, P. L. Cottrell (eds.), *International Business and Central Europe, 1918–1939*, New York 1983.

M. Coulborne. *Economic Nationalism*, London 1933.

R. J. Crampton. *A Short History of Modern Bulgaria*, Cambridge, London, and New York 1987.

L. Cvijetić. "The Ambitions and Plans of the Third Reich with Regard to the Integration of Yugoslavia into Its So-called Grosswirtschaftsraum," in P. Morača (ed.), *The Third Reich and Yugoslavia, 1933–1945*, Belgrade 1977.

B. Cywiński. *Potęga jest i basta: Z minionych doświadczeń ruchów społecznych na wsi*, Paris 1983.

A. Czakałow [Chakalov]. *Natsionalniyat dokhod i rozkhod na Bŭlgariya 1924–1945 g.*, Sofia 1946.

S. Czołakow [Cholakov]. *Danŭchno naprezheniye na edin narod v mirno i voenno vreme (Teoretichna skitsa)*, Varna 1940.

A. Czubiński, ed., *Rola mniejszości niemieckiej w rozwoju stosunków politycznych w Europie 1918–1945*, Poznań 1984.

A. Czubiński, ed., *Państwa bałkańskie w polityce imperializmu niemieckiego w latach 1871–1945*, Poznań 1982.

M. Dejanowa [Deyanova]. "Agrarnata kriza v Bŭlgariya i dŭrzhavnite merki za neynoto preodolyavane," *ASSP*, 1938, Vol. 4.

Dejiny štátu a práva na území Československa v obdobi kapitalizmu, Vol. 2, *1918–1945*, Bratislava 1975.

J. Demel. *Historia Rumunii*, Wrocław, Warsaw, and Kraków 1970.

R. F. Dernberger. "The Role of Nationalism in the Rise and Development of Communist China," in H. G. Johnson (ed.), *Economic Nationalism in Old and New States*, London 1968.

K. W. Deutsch. *Nationalism and Social Communication: An Inquiry into the Foundations of Nationality*, 2d ed., Cambridge, Mass., 1967.

Deyanova. See Dejanowa.

I. Dimitrov. "Bŭlgarskata demokratichna obshtestvenost fashizmŭt i voynata 1934–1939," *Godishnik na Sofiyskya universitet Filosofsko-istoricheskiya fakultet*, kniga II, *Istoriya*, Vol. LXIV (1970), No. 2.

I. Dimitrow. "Ewolucja dyktatury faszystowskiej w Bułgarii (1934–1939)," *SDEŚ*, Vol. 10 (1974).

A. Dobrý. "O pravdivý obraz hospodářského profilu předmnichovskě republiky," *ČČH*, 1969, No. 2.

A. Dobrý. "O spornych problémach dosavadniho výzkumu hospodářských dejín Československá," *SH*, No. 22. Prague 1975.

A. Dobrý. "Zakladni směry vývoje československého průmyslu v letech 1913–1938, a některé otaźký socialně politícke," *ČČH*, 1965, No. 5.

H. Donath. *Przemiany ustrojowo-prawne na Węgrzech 1939–1949*, Wrocław, Warsaw, Kraków, and Gdańsk 1978.

B. Dopierała. *Wokół polityki morskiej Drugiej Rzeczypospolitej*, Poznań 1978.

Z. Drabek. "Foreign Trade Performance and Policy," in M. C. Kaser (gen. ed.), *The Economic History of Eastern Europe, 1919–1975*, Vol. 1, M. C. Kaser, E. A. Radice (eds.), *Economic Structure and Performance Between the Two Wars*, Oxford 1985.

A. A. Drizul (ed.). *Istoriya Latvijŭskoŭ SSR*, 2d supplemented ed., Riga 1971.

M. M. Drozdowski. *Polityka gospodarcza rządu polskiego 1936–1939*, Warsaw 1963.

K. Dziewanowski. "Kto płaci za rację stanu?" *PP*, 1985, No. 12.

Economic Development in S.E. Europe: Political and Economic Planning, London 1945.

The Economic Development of Latin America and Its Principal Problems, Economic Commission for Latin America, Lake Success, N.Y., 1950.

"The Economic Fate of the Sudeten Germans in the Czechoslovak Republic," *Weekly Report*, 7 X 1938.

É. Ehrlich. "Infrastructure," in M. C. Kaser (gen. ed.), *The Economic History of Eastern Europe, 1919–1975*, Vol. 1, M. C. Kaser, E. A. Radice (eds.), *Economic Structure and Performance Between the Two Wars*, Oxford 1985.

H. S. Ellis. *Exchange Control in Central Europe*, Cambridge, Mass., 1941.

Enquiry into Clearing Agreements, League of Nations, Geneva 1935.

Etatyzm w Polsce (foreword A. Krzyżanowski), Kraków 1932.

Z. Fafl. "Československá obchodní politíka," *Sbirka ČSN*, 1935/36, No. XVII, Prague 1936.

J. Faltus. *Povojnová hospodárska kriza v rokoch 1921–1923 v Československu*, Bratislava 1966.

J. Faltus. "Štátne zásahy do československého národného hospodářstva v 30 rokach," *Hospodářské dějíny*, Vol. 13, Prague 1985.

J. Faltus. "Za pravdivy obraz hospodářského profilu predmnichovskiej republiky," *ČČH*, 1970, No. 5-6.

J. Faltus, V. Průcha. *Prehl'ad hospodárskego vyvoja na Slovensku v rokoch 1918–1945*, Bratislava 1969.

L. K. Feierabend. "Agriculture in the First Republic of Czechoslovakia," in M. Rechcigl (ed.), *Czechoslovakia Past and Present*, Vol. 1, *Political, International, Social, and Economic Aspects*, The Hague 1968.

R. de Felice. *Interpretacje faszyzmu* (transl. M. de Rosset-Borejsza), Warsaw 1976.

V. Fic. "Národní sjednocení v politické strukture buržoazniho Československá v letech 1934–1935," *ČČH*, 1978, No. 1.

S. Fischer-Galati. *Twentieth-Century Rumania*, New York and London 1970.

A.G.B. Fisher. *Self-Sufficiency*, London 1939.

O. von Frangeš. "Fighting the Crisis in the Peasant Countries of the Danube Basin," in *Proceedings of the Third International Conference of Agricultural Economies*, London 1935.

A. F. Freris. *The Greek Economy in the Twentieth Century*, London 1980.

C. J. Friedrich (ed.). *Totalitarianism*, 2d ed., New York 1964.

A. Gajanová. "Přispevek k objasněni příčin roztržasky v táboře česke buržoazie v roce 1934," *ČČH*, 1956, No. 4.

A. Gajanová, B. Lehár. "K charakteru buržoazně demokratického zřizeni v Československu," *ČČH*, 1968, No. 3.

N. M. Gelber. "Jewish Life in Bulgaria," *JJS*, Vol. VIII (April 1946), No. 2.

L. Gembarzewski. "Konstytucje Jugosłáwi, Portugalii, Albanii," *BU* 1931, No. 11-12; 1935, No. 5-6; 1939, No. 3-4.

[German Bohemian Deputy.] "The German Minority in Czechoslovakia," *SEER*, Vol. XIV (1936), No. 41.

A. Gerschenkron. *An Economic Spurt That Failed: Four Lectures in Austrian History*, Princeton 1977.

A. Gerschenkron. *Europe in the Russian Mirror: Four Lectures in the Economic History*, Cambridge 1970.

A. Gerschenkron. *Economic Backwardness in Historical Perspective*, 3d printing, London and Cambridge, Mass., 1976.

A. Gerschenkron. "The Typology of Industrial Development as a Tool Analysis," in A. Gerschenkron, *Continuity in History and Other Essays*, Cambridge, Mass., 1968.

S. Głąbiński. *Ekonomika narodowa: Teoria ekonomiki narodowej*, Lwów 1927.

F. H. Golay, R. Anspach, M. R. Pfanner, E. B. Ayal. *Underdevelopment and Economic Nationalism in Southeast Asia*, Ithaca and London 1969.

J. Gołębiowski. *Sektor państwowy w gospodarce Polski międzywojennej*, Warsaw and Kraków 1985.

J. Gołębiowski. *Spór o etatyzm wewnątrz obozu sanacyjnego w latach 1926–1939*, Kraków 1978.

M. N. Goranowicz. *Krach zielonego internacionała*, Moscow 1967.

J. Górski. "Protekcjonizm," in *Mała encyklopedia ekonomiczna*, Warsaw 1958.

J. Górski, W. Sierpiński. *Historia powszechnej myśli ekonomicznej (1870–1950)*, 3d ed., Warsaw 1979.

W. Grabska. *Ekonomiczna ekspansja Niemiec na Wschód w latach 1870–1939*, Wrocław, Warsaw, and Kraków 1964.

R. Gradowski. *Polska 1918–1939: Niektóre zagadnienia kapitalizmu monopolistycznego*, Warsaw 1959.

T. E. Gregory. "Economic Nationalism," *IA*, Vol. X (1931), No. 3.

K. Grünberg. *Niemcy i ich organizacje polityczne w Polsce międzywojennej*, Warsaw 1970.

R. Grunberger. *A Social History of the Third Reich*, London 1977.

J. Grunzel. *Economic Protectionism*, Oxford 1916.

M. Grzyb. *Narodowościowo-polityczne aspekty przemian stosunków własnościowych i kadrowych w górnośląskim przemyśle w latach 1922–1939*, Katowice 1978.

G. Haberler. *The International Trade*, Edinburgh 1936.

J. Hampden-Jackson. *Estonia*, 2d ed., London 1948.

J. Hanč. *Tornado Across Eastern Europe: The Path of Nazi Destruction from Poland to Greece*, New York 1942.

M. Hauner. "Human Resources," in M. C. Kaser (gen. ed.), *The Economic History of Eastern Europe, 1919–1975*, Vol. 1, M. C. Kaser, E. A. Radice (eds.), *Economic Structure and Performance Between the Two Wars*, Oxford 1985.

R. Havranková, Z. Sládek, J. Valenta. "O močnosti integračniho pojetí. Studia dějin 'vychodni Evropy' ve 20 stoleti," *Slovenské historické studie*, Vol. VII, Prague 1968.

C.J.H. Hayes. *Essays on Nationalism*, New York 1926.

C.J.H. Hayes. *Nationalism: A Religion*, New York 1960.

E. F. Heckscher. *Mercantilism*, London 1955.

M. A. Heilperin. *Studies in Economic Nationalism*, Geneva and Paris 1960.

M. A. Heilperin. *The Trade of Nations*, London, New York, and Toronto 1946.

J. Held. "The Interwar Years and Agrarian Change," in J. Held (ed.), *The Modernization of Agriculture: Rural Transformation in Hungary, 1848–1975*, Boulder 1980.

F. Hertz. *The Economic Problem of Danubian States: A Study in Economic Nationalism*, London 1947.

H. Heuser. *Control of International Trade*, London 1939.

A. Heydel. "Etatyzm," in *Encyklopedia nauk politycznych*, Vol. 2, Warsaw 1937.

F. Hilgerdt. *Industrialization and Foreign Trade*, Geneva 1945.

A. O. Hirschman. *National Power and the Structure of Foreign Trade*, expanded edition, Berkeley, Los Angeles, and London 1980.

K. Hitchins. *Rumanian Peasantism: The Third Way*, Conference on *Models of Development*.

G. G. Hodgson. *Economic Nationalism*, New York 1933.

H. V. Hodson. *Slump and Recovery, 1929–1937*, London 1938.

J. B. Hoptner. *Yugoslavia in Crisis, 1934–1941*, London 1962.

M. Hroch. *Evropská národní hnutí v 19 stoleti: Společenské předpoklady vzniku novodobých národů*, Prague 1986.

G. Ionescu. "Eastern Europe," in G. Ionescu, E. Gellner (eds.), *Populism: Its Meanings and National Characteristics*, London 1969.

M. F. Iovanelli, *Industria Româneasca 1934–1938*, Bucharest 1975.

J. Jankowiak. "Polityka celna jako wyraz interwencji gospodarczej państwa polskiego w latach 1929–1939," *RDSiG*, Vol. XXXV (1974).

A. C. Janos. "Modernization and Decay in Historical Perspective: The Case of Romania," in K. Jowitt (ed.), *Social Change in Romania, 1860–1940: A Debate on Development in European Nations*, Berkeley 1978.

A. C. Janos. "The One-Party State and Social Mobilization: East Europe Between the Wars," in S. P. Huntington, C. H. Moore (eds.), *Authoritarian Politics in Modern Society: The Dynamics of Established One-Party Systems*, New York and London 1970.

A. C. Janos. *The Rise and Fall of Civil Society: The Politics of Backwardness on the European Peripheries, 1870–1945*, Conference on *Models of Development*.

H. Janowska. "Emigracja z Polski w latach 1918–1939," in A. Pilch (ed.), *Emigracja z ziem polskich w czasach nowożytnych i najnowszych (XVIII–XX w.)*, Warsaw 1984.

O. Jászi. "Kossuth and the Treaty of Trianon," *FA*, Vol. 12 (October 1933), No. 1.

The Jews of Czechoslovakia: Historical Studies and Surveys, Vol. 1, Philadelphia 1968.

A. Jezierski. *Handel zagraniczny Królestwa Polskiego 1815–1914*, Warsaw 1967.

H. and T. Jędruszczak. *Ostatnie lata Drugiej Rzeczypospolitej (1935–1939)*, Warsaw 1970.

H. G. Johnson. "An Economic Theory of Protectionism, Tariff Bargaining, and the Formation of Custom Unions," *JPE*, Vol. 73 (June 1965).

H. G. Johnson. "The Ideology of Economic Policy in the New States," in H. G. Johnson (ed.), *Economic Nationalism in Old and New States*, London 1968.

H. G. Johnson. "Notes on Some Theoretical Problems Posed by the Foreign Trade in Centrally Planned Economy," in A. A. Brown, E. Neuberger (eds.), *International Trade and Central Planning: An Analysis of Economic Interactions*, Berkeley and Los Angeles 1968.

H. G. Johnson. "A Theoretical Model of Economic Nationalism in New Developing States," *PSQ*, Vol. LXXX (1965), No. 2.

H. G. Johnson. "Theory" (in "International Trade"), in *International Encyclopedia of the Social Sciences*, Vol. 8, Chicago 1968.

K. Jowitt. "The Sociocultural Basis of National Dependency in Peasant Countries," in K. Jowitt (ed.), *Social Change in Romania 1860–1940: A Debate on Development in a European Nation*, Berkeley 1978.

N. K. "The Influence of Prices on Some Aspects of Economic Development in Bulgaria, 1926–1937," *TSISP*, 1938, No. 1.

E. Kaczyńska, K. Piesowicz. *Wykłady z powszechnej historii gospodarczej (od schyłku średniowiecza do I wojny światowej)*, Warsaw 1977.

D. E. Kaiser. *Economic Diplomacy and the Origins of the Second World War: Germany, Britain, France, and Eastern Europe, 1930–1939*, Princeton 1980.

O. Kána. "Mniejszość niemiecka pod wodzą Konrada Henleina na ziemiach czeskich," in H. Batowski (ed.), *Irredenta niemiecka w Europie Środkowej i Południowo-Wschodniej przed II wojną światową*, Katowice and Kraków 1971.

B. H. Kaplan (ed.). *Social Change in the Capitalist World Economy*, Beverly Hills and London 1978.

J. F. Karcz. "Reflections on the Economics of Nationalism and Communism in Eastern Europe," *EEQ*, Vol. V (June 1971), No. 2.

A. Kemiläinen. *Nationalism: Problem Concerning the World: The Concept and Classification*, Jyväskylä 1964.

A. G. Kenwood, A. L. Lougheed. *The Growth of the International Economy, 1820–1960*, London 1971.

J. M. Keynes. "National Self-Sufficiency," *New Statesman and Nation*, 8 VII 1933.

J. M. Keynes. *The General Theory of Employment, Interest, and Money*, London 1936.

C. P. Kindleberger. *The World in Depression, 1929–1939*, London 1973.

D. Kinev. "Dyrżawna interwencija w tiutonoproizwodstwo," *SP*, 1938, Vol. 1.

R. R. King. *Minority Under Communism: Nationalities as a Source of Tension Among Balkan Communist States*, Cambridge, Mass., 1973.

D. Kirk. *Europe's Population in the Interwar Years*, Princeton 1946.

B. Kisiel-Łowczyc. *Protekcjonizm w handlu zagranicznym w teorii i historii myśli ekonomicznej: Przyczynek do analizy polityki handlowej rozwiniętych krajów kapitalistycznych*, Gdańsk 1974.

D. Kiss. "The Jews of Eastern Europe," *FA*, Vol. 15 (January 1937), No. 2.

A. J. Klawe, A. Makać. *Zarys międzynarodowych stosunków ekonomicznych*, Warsaw 1977.

J. Kleer. *Drogi wyjścia z zacofania*, Warsaw 1974.

J. Kleer. *Gospodarka światowa: Prawidłowość rozwoju*, Warsaw 1975.

B. Klein. "Hungarian Politics and the Jewish Question in the Interwar Period," *JSS*, Vol. XXVIII (April 1966), No. 2.

L. R. Klein. *The Keynesian Revolution*, 2d ed., London 1968.

K. Kłajew [Klaev]. "Bŭlgarskata industriya prez poslednite deset godini," *Ekonomist*, 1939, Vol. 1.

Z. Knakiewicz. *Deflacja polska 1930–1935*, Warsaw 1967.

D. Koen. "Demografsko i sotsialno-ikonomichesko polozheniye na bŭlgarskite evrei (1926–1946)," in *Prouchvaniya za istoriyata na evreyskoto naseleniye v bŭlgarskite zemi XV–XX vek*, Sofia 1980.

J. Kofman. *Lewiatan a podstawowe zagadnienia ekonomiczno-polityczne Drugiej Rzeczypospolitej. Z dziejów ideologii kół wielkokapitalistycznych w Polsce*, Warsaw 1986.

H. Kohn. *The Idea of Nationalism: A Study in Its Origins and Background*, 8th ed., New York 1967.

H. Kohn. "Nationalism," in D. L. Sills (ed.), *International Encyclopedia of the Social Sciences*, Vol. 11, Chicago 1968.

E. Kołodziej. *Wychodźstwo zarobkowe z Polski 1918–1939: Studia nad polityką emigracyjną II Rzeczypospolitej*, Warsaw 1982.

P. Korzec. "Antisemitism in Poland as an Intellectual, Social, and Political Movement," in J. Fishman (ed.), *Studies on Polish Jewry, 1919–1939*, New York 1974.

J. Kostanecki. *Naddunajski problem gospodarczy*, Warsaw 1937.

M. Koźmiński. "Mniejszości narodowościowe w basenie Dunaju a węgierski rewizjonizm terytorialny," in J. Żarnowski, *"Ład wersalski" w Europie Środkowej*, Wrocław, Warsaw, Kraków, and Gdańsk 1971.

J. Kratochvíl. "O zásahu státní moci do soukromého hospodářství," *Sbirka ČSN*, 1934/35, No. III, Prague 1934.

S. F. Królikowski. *Zarys polskiej polityki handlowej*, Warsaw 1938.

J. Krynicki. *Problemy handlu zagranicznego Polski 1918–1939 i 1945–1955*, Warsaw 1958.

M. Kula. "Aleksandra Gerschenkrona uwagi o zacofaniu gospodarczym," *Prace i Materiały* (Międzyuczelnianego Zakładu Problemowego Gospodarki Krajów Słabo Rozwiniętych), 1966, No. 1.

M. Kula. *Historia Brazylii*, Wrocław, Warsaw, Kraków, Gdańsk, and Łódź 1987.

M. Kula. *Polonia brazylijska*, Warsaw 1981.

S. S. Kuznets. *Economic Growth of Nations: Total Output and Production Structure*, Cambridge, Mass., 1976.

R. Kvaček. *Nad Evropu zataženo: Československo a Evropa 1933–1937*, Prague 1966.

V. Lacina. *Krize československého zemědělstvi 1928–1934*, Prague 1974.

V. Lacina. "Problémy odvětvove struktury československého průmyslu v letech 1918–1930," *ČČH*, 1976.

V. Lacina. *Velká hospodářská krize v Československu 1929–1934*, Prague 1984.

J. R. Lampe. *The Bulgarian Economy in the Twentieth Century*, London and Sydney 1986.

J. R. Lampe, M. R. Jackson. *Balkan Economic History, 1550–1950: From Imperial Borderlands to Developing Nations*, Bloomington, Ind., 1982.

Z. Landau. "Hamulce rozwoju gospodarczego związane z dwusektorową strukturą gospodarki," in Z. Landau, J. Tomaszewski, *Druga Rzeczpospolita: Gospodarka—społeczeństwo—miejsce w świecie*, Warsaw 1977.

Z. Landau. "Oligarchia finansowa," in Z. Landau, J. Tomaszewski, *Druga Rzeczpospolita: Gospodarka—społeczeństwo—miejsce w świecie*, Warsaw 1977.

Z. Landau. *Plan stabilizacyjny 1927–1930: Geneza, założenia, wyniki*, Warsaw 1964.

Z. Landau. "Polityka walutowa rządu polskiego w latach 1936–1939," *PH*, 1986, Vol. 2.

Z. Landau, J. Tomaszewski, *Anonimowi władcy. Z dziejów kapitału obcego w Polsce (1918–1939)*, Warsaw 1967.

Z. Landau, J. Tomaszewski. *Gospodarka Polski międzywojennej 1918–1939*, Vol. 1, W dobie inflacji 1918–1923, Warsaw 1967; Vol. 2, *Od Grabskiego do Piłsudskiego: Okres kryzysu poinflacyjnego i ożywienia koniunktury 1924–1929*, Warsaw 1971; Vol. 3, *Wielki kryzys 1930–1935*, Warsaw 1982.

Z. Landau, J. Tomaszewski. *Polska w Europie i świecie 1918–1939*, 2d emended ed., Warsaw 1984.

Z. Landau, J. Tomaszewski. *Sprawa żyrardowska*, Warsaw 1983.

Z. Landau, J. Tomaszewski. *Zarys historii gospodarczej Polski 1918–1939*, 4th emended ed., Warsaw 1981.

O. Lange. "Nacjonalizm gospodarczy," in *Dzieła*, Vol. 1, *Kapitalizm*, Warsaw 1973.

F. Lantini et al. *L'Autarchia: Economica della nazione*, Rome 1939.

W. T. Layton, C. Rist. *The Economic Situation of Austria*, Geneva 1925.

R. Lekachman. *The Age of Keynes*, London 1967.

E. Lethbridge. "National Income and Product," in M. C. Kaser (gen. ed.), *The Economic History of Eastern Europe, 1919–1975*, Vol. 1, M. C. Kaser, E. A. Radice (eds.), *Economic Structure and Performance Between the Two Wars*, Oxford 1985.

W. A. Lewis. *The Theory of Economic Growth*, London 1956.

W. A. Lewis. *Growth and Fluctuations, 1870–1913*, London 1977.

H. Liepmann. *Tariff Levels and Economic Unity of Europe*, London 1938.

J. J. Linz. "From Falange to Movimiento-Organización: The Spanish Single Party and the Franco Regime, 1936–1969, in S. P. Huntington, C. H. Moore (eds.), *Authoritarian Politics in Modern Society: The Dynamics of Established One-Party Systems*, New York and London 1970.

E. Lipiński. *Historia powszechnej myśli ekonomicznej do roku 1870*, Warsaw 1968.

G. C. Logio. *Bulgaria Past and Present*, Manchester 1936.

L. L. Lorwin. "Economic Nationalism and World Co-operation," in L. L. Lorwin, *Time for Planning: Social-economic Theories and Program for Twentieth Century*, New York and London 1945.

J. L. Love. "Modelling Internal Colonialism: History and Prospect," Conference on *Models of Development*.

J. L. Love. "Theorizing Underdevelopment: Latin America and Romania, 1860–1950," *Review: Fernand Braudel Center for Study of Economies, Historical Systems, and Civilizations*, Vol. XI (1988), No. 4.

T. Łepkowski (ed.). *Dzieje Ameryki Łacińskiej od schyłku epoki kolonialnej do czasów współczesnych*, Vol. 3, 1930–1975/80, Warsaw 1983.

T. Łepkowski. "Region karaibski," in T. Łepkowski (ed.), *Dzieje Ameryki Łacińskiej od schyłku epoki kolonialnej do czasów współczesnych*, Warsaw 1983.

P. Łossowski. "Ideologie reżimów autorytarnych (kraje bałtyckie 1926– 1934–1940)," in J. Żarnowski (ed.), *Dyktatury w Europie Środkowo-Wschodniej 1918–1939*, Wrocław, Warsaw, Kraków, and Gdańsk 1973.

P. Łossowski. *Kraje bałtyckie na drodze od demokracji parlamentarnej do dyktatury (1918–1934)*, Wrocław, Warsaw, Kraków, and Gdańsk 1972.

P. Łossowski. *Po tej i tamtej stronie Niemna: Stosunki polsko-litewskie 1883–1939*, Warsaw 1985.

P. Łossowski. "Problem mniejszości narodowych w Europie Środkowo-Wschodniej na przykładzie państw bałtyckich 1919–1940," in J. Żarnowski (ed.), *"Ład wersalski" w Europie Środkowej*, Wrocław, Warsaw, Kraków, and Gdańsk 1971.

P. Łossowski. "Związki Niemców bałtyckich z państwem niemieckim 1919–1940," in A. Czubiński (ed.), *Rola mniejszości niemieckiej w rozwoju stosunków politycznych w Europie 1918–1945*, Poznań 1984.

A. Łuczak. *Społeczeństwo i państwo w myśli polityczenj ruchu ludowego II Rzeczypospolitej*, Warsaw 1982.

C. Łuczak. *Od Bismarcka do Hitlera: Polsko-niemieckie stosunki gospodarcze*, Poznań 1988.

C. A. Macartney. *October Fifteenth: History of Modern Hungary, 1929–1945*, Vol. I, 2d ed., Edinburg 1961.

C. A. Macartney, A. W. Palmer. *Independent Eastern Europe: A History*, London 1962.

G. Macesich. *Economic Nationalism and Stability*, New York and Philadelphia 1985.

F. Machlup. *A History of Thought on Economic Integration* (London, 1977).

C. Madajczyk. *Faszyzm i okupacje 1938–1945: Wykonywanie okupacji przez państwa Osi w Europie*, Vol. II, *Mechanizmy realizowania okupacji*, Poznań 1984.

V. Madgearu. "The New Economic Policy in Rumania," *IA*, Vol. IX (1930), No. 1.

A. Maizels. *Growth and Trade*, Cambridge 1970.

J. Majchrowski. *Silni—zwarci—gotowi: Myśl polityczna Obozu Zjednoczenia Narodowego*, Warsaw 1985.

E. Mandel. *Long Waves in Capitalist Development: The Marxist Interpretation*, Paris 1980.

K. Mandelbaum. *The Industrialization of Backward Areas*, 4th ed., Oxford 1961.

"Manifest finansistów," *Przemysł i Handel*, 1926, Vol. 47.

M. Manoilescu. *Der Einzige Partei*, Berlin 1941.

M. Manoilescu. *Rostul şi destinul burgheziei romanesti*, Bucharest 1942.

M. Manoilescu. *Le siècle du corporatisme*, Paris 1936.

M. Manoilescu. "Die theoretische Problematik des Aussenhandels: Synthese-Beweisführung-Polemik," *WA*, Bd. 51 (1940), HF. 1.

M. Manoilescu. *The Theory of Protection and International Trade*, London 1931.

M. Manoilescu. "Le triangle économique et social des pays agricoles: La ville, le village, l'étranger," *Internationale Agrarrundschau*, June 1940.

H. Martins. "Ideology and Development: 'Development Nationalism' in Brazil," *Sociological Review Monography*, 1967, No. 11.

J. P. Maxton. "Planning Measures for the Protection of British Agriculture," in *Proceedings of the Third International Conference of Agricultural Economics*, London 1935.

A. M. Mayer. "Pět let krise na našem venkově," *Sbirka ČSN*, 1934/35, No. XIII, Prague 1935.

W. O. McCagg, Jr. "Hungary's 'Feudalized' Bourgeoisie," *JMH*, Vol. 44 (1972), No. 1.

D. McCord Wright. *The Keynesian System*, New York 1961.

G. M. Meier. *Leading Issues in Economic Development*, 3d ed., New York 1977.

G. M. Meier. *The Problem of Limited Economy*, New York 1974.

G. M. Meier, R. E. Baldwin. *Economic Development: Theory, History, Policy*, New York and London 1957.

V. Mencl, J. Menclová. "Náčrt podstaty a vývoje vrcholné sféry předmnichovske československe mocensko-politické struktury," *ČČH*, 1968, No. 3.

E. Mendelsohn. *The Jews of East Central Europe Between The World Wars*, Bloomington, Ind., 1983.

M. Meszkanskiene [Meshkanskiene]. *Promyszhlennost' Litvy v period monopolisticheskogo kapitalizma*, Vilnius 1981.

W. Michowicz. "Problem mniejszości narodowych," in J. Tomicki (ed.), *Polska Odrodzona 1918–1939*, Warsaw 1982.

M. Mieszczankowski. "Zadłużenie rolnictwa Polski międzywojennej," *NDP*, Vol. 6, Warsaw 1963.

V. Migev. *Utrvŭrzhdavane na monarkhofashistkata diktatura v Bŭlgariya, 1934–1936*, Sofia 1977.

A. S. Milward. "Comments on Some Theories of Historical Changes," in J. Kocka, G. Ránki (eds.), *Economic Theory and History*, Budapest 1985.

A. S. Milward. "Fascism and the Economy," in W. Laqueur (ed.). *Fascism: A Reader's Guide*, Berkeley and Los Angeles 1978.

A. S. Milward. *The New Order and the French Economy*, Oxford 1970.

A. S. Milward. *War, Economy, and Society, 1939–1945*, Harmondsworth 1977.

S. Miłkowski. *Agraryzm jako forma przebudowy ustroju społecznego*, Warsaw 1934.

M. Mirković. *Ekonomska historija Jugoslavije*, Zagreb 1968.

A. L. Miskes. "Statistical Evidence and the Concept of Tertiary Industry," *EDCC*, Vol. III (1955), No. 4.

D. Mitrany. *Marx Against Peasant: A Study in Social Dogmatism*, London 1951.

A. Mitrović. "Erganzungswirtschaft: The Theory of an Integrated Economic Area of the Third Reich and Southeast Europe (1933–1941)," in P. Morača (ed.), *The Third Reich and Yugoslavia, 1933–1945*, Belgrade 1977.

N. Momchiloff. *Ten Years of Controlled Trade in South-eastern Europe*, Cambridge 1944.

Money Policy and the Depression, RIIA, Oxford 1933.

J. M. Montias. "Economic Nationalism in Eastern Europe: Forty Years of Continuity and Change," *JIA*, Vol. XX (1966), No. 1.

J. M. Montias. "Notes on the Romanian Debate on Sheltered Industrialization: 1860–1906," in K. Jowitt (ed.), *Social Change in Romania, 1860–1940: A Debate on Development in a European Nation*, Berkeley 1978.

N. P. Mouzelis. *Politics in Semi-Periphery: Early Parliamentarism and Late Industrialization in the Balkans and Latin America*, London 1986.

T. Munk. *Le débat sur le libre échange et le protectionnisme à la lumière des structures nationales,* Geneva 1953.

R. Munting. *The Economic Development of the USSR,* New York 1982.

"Nacjonalizm," *WEP,* Vol. VII, Warsaw 1966.

N. M. Nagy-Talavera. *The Green Shirts and Others: A History of Fascism in Hungary and Romania,* Stanford 1970.

K. Nakagawa. "The structure and Motives of Investment by Private Enterprises in Japan Before the Second World War," in H. Daems, H. van der Wee (eds.), *The Rise of Managerial Capitalism,* The Hague 1974.

M. Nash. "Economic Nationalism in Mexico," in H. G. Johnson (ed.), *Economic Nationalism in Old and New States,* London 1968.

"Nasokite na industrialnata ni politika," *BS* 1939, Vol. 6.

Zh. Natan. "Stopanska istoriya na Bŭlgariya," in Zh. Natan, *Izbrani trudove v dva toma,* Vol. 1, Sofia 1977.

Zh. Natan, V. Khadzhinikolov, L. Berov (eds.). "Ikonomikata na Bŭlgariya do sotsialisticheskata revolutsiya," in *Ikonomikata na Bŭlgariya,* Vol. 1, Sofia 1969.

"Nationalism," in J. B. Sykes (ed.), *The Concise Oxford Dictionary of Current English,* 6th ed., Oxford 1978.

"Nationalism," in: A. S. Hornby with A. P. Cowie (eds.), *Oxford Advanced Learner's Dictionary of Current English,* 7th impression, Oxford 1980, reprinted Warsaw 1981.

G. Naumow [Naumov]. "Antikrizisna zakonodatelna deynost na Narodniya blok (1931–1934 g.)," *IP* 1973, No. 6.

"L'nazionalismo economico," in *Dizionario Enciclopedico Italiana,* Vol. VIII, Rome 1958.

L. Neal. "Economics and Finance of Bilateral Clearing Agreements of Germany, 1934–38," *EHR,* Vol. 22 (1979).

J. Nečas. "Economic and Social Problems in German Bohemia," *SEER,* Vol. XV (1937), No. 45.

F. L. Neumann. *Behemoth: The Structure and Practice of National Socialism,* 2d ed., New York 1944.

R. Nötel. "International Capital Movements and Finance in Eastern Europe," *VSWG,* Bd. 61 (1975), Hf. 1.

R. Nötel. "International Credit and Finance," in M. C. Kaser (gen. ed.), *The Economic History of Eastern Europe, 1919–1975,* Vol. 2, M. C. Kaser, E. A. Radice (eds.), *Interwar Policy, the War, and Reconstruction,* Oxford 1986.

A. Nove. *An Economic History of the USSR,* Harmondsworth 1975.

"Nowite zadachi na nashata stopanska politika," *BS* 1939, Vol. 19.

R. Nurske et al. *International Currency Experience: Lessons of the Inter-war Period,* Princeton 1944.

"Nuzhdata ot plan zemedeleto," *BS* 1939, Vol. 1.

"Observations on the Relations Between the State and Economic Life from the Point of the Czechoslovak Republic, in *The State Economic Life: First Study Conference* (*Milan, May 1932*), Paris 1932.

G. A. O'Donnell. *Modernization and Bureaucratic Authoritarianism,* Berkeley 1973.

B. Ohlin. "Introductory Report on the Problem of International Economic Reconstruction," in *International Economic Reconstruction,* Paris 1936.

B. Ohlin. "Protection and Non-competing Groups," *WA*, Bd. 33 (1931), Hf. 1.

R. Olšovský et al. *Přehled hospodářského vývoje Československá v letech 1918–1945*, Prague 1961.

R. Olšovský. *Světový obchod a Československo 1918–1938*, Prague 1981.

J. Orczyk. *Produkcja rolna Polski w latach wielkiego kryzysu gospodarczego (1929–1935)*, Poznań 1971.

J. Orczyk. "Przesłanki i rozmiary zmian w strukturze agrarnej Polski międzywojennej na tle porównawczym," in *Badania nad historią społeczno-gospodarczą w Polsce (problemy i metody)*, Warsaw and Poznań 1978.

J. Orczyk. *Studia nad opłacalnością gospodarstw rolnych w Polsce w latach 1929–1938*, Warsaw 1981.

N. Oren. *Revolution Administrated: Agrarianism and Communism in Bulgaria*, Baltimore and London 1973.

D. Orlow. *The Nazis in the Balkans: A Case Study of Totalitarian Politics*, Pittsburgh 1968.

Z. Ornea. "Interwar Romania in Search of Development Model," Conference on *Models of Development.*

G. Orwell. "Uwagi o nacjonalizmie," in G. Orwell, *Eseje*, London 1985.

S. Ossowski. *O ojczyźnie i narodzie* (introd. J. Szacki), Warsaw 1984.

S. Ossowski. "O osobliwościach nauk społecznych," in *Dzieła*, Vol. IV, Warsaw 1967.

G. C. Paikert. *The Danube Swabians*, The Hague 1967.

L. Pasvolsky. *Bulgaria's Economic Position*, Washington D.C. 1930.

L. Pasvolsky. *Economic Nationalism of the Danubian States*, London 1928.

E. Patka. "Experience of Debt Adjustment in Czechoslovakia," in *Proceedings on the Fourth International Conference of Agricultural Economics (held at St. Andrews, Scotland, 30 VIII–6 IX 1936)*, London 1937.

"Patriotism," in A. S. Hornby with A. P. Cowie (eds.), *Oxford Advanced Learner's Dictionary of Current English*, 7th impression, Oxford 1980, reprinted Warsaw 1981.

"Patriotyzm," in *WEP*, Vol. VIII, Warsaw 1966.

S. G. Payne. *Fascism: Comparison and Definition*, Madison, Wisc., 1983.

J. Petras, R. LaPorte, Jr. "U.S. Response to Economic Nationalism in Chile," in J. Petras (ed.), *Latin America: From Dependence to Revolution*, New York, Washington, Sydney, and Toronto 1973.

K. Polanyi. *The Great Transformation*, 2d ed., Boston 1957.

S. Pollard (ed.). *The Gold Standard and Employment Policies Between the Wars*, London 1970.

S. Pollard. *European Economic Integration, 1815–1970*, London 1974.

S. Pollard. *Peaceful Conquest: The Industrialization of Europe, 1760–1970*, Oxford 1981.

R. Polzer. *Die Sudetendeutsche Wirtschaft in der Tschechoslowakei*, Der Göttinger Arbeitskreis Schriftenreihe, Hf 26, Kitzinger/Main.

J. Popkiewicz, F. Ryszka. *Przemysł ciężki Górnego Śląska w gospodarce Polski międzywojennej (1922–1939)*, Opole 1959.

S. Potocki. *Położenie mniejszości niemieckiej w Polsce 1918–1939*, Gdańsk 1969.

V. Průcha (ed.). *Historia gospodarcza Czechosłowacji XX wieku* (transl. P. Godlewski, H. Szwedo), Warsaw 1979.

V. Průcha (ed.). *Hospodářské dejíny Československá v 19 a 20 století*, Prague 1974.

V. Průcha. "Hospodářský profil předmnichovskě republiky," *Nowa Mysl*, 1968, No. 3.

V. Průcha. "Polemika vstoupila do hospodářské historiografie," *ČČH*, 1969, No. 6.

Z. Pryor. "Czechoslovak Economic Development in the Interwar Period," in V. S. Mamatey, R. Luža (eds.), *A History of the Czechoslovak Republic, 1918–1948*, Princeton 1973.

Z Pryor. "Czechoslovak Fiscal Policies in the Great Depression," *EHR*, Vol. 22 (1979).

Z. Pryor, F. L. Pryor. "Foreign Trade and Interwar Czechoslovak Economic Development, 1918–1938," *VSWG*, Bd. 62 (1975), Hf. 4.

B. Puchert. *Ekspansja gospodarcza niemieckiego imperializmu w Europie Środkowej i Wschodniej 1900–1933*, Warsaw 1975.

S. Raczew [Rachev]. "Borbata na bŭlgarskiya narod za spasyavane ne evreite ot unishtozhvane prez Vtorata svetowna voyna (1939–1944)," in *Prouchvaniya za istoriyata na evreyskoto naseleniye v bŭlgarskite zemi XV–XX vek*, Sofia 1980.

E. A. Radice. "General Characteristics of the Region Between the Wars," in M. C. Kaser (gen. ed.), *The Economic History of Eastern Europe, 1919–1975*, Vol. 1, M. C. Kaser, E. A. Radice (eds.), *Economic Structure and Performance Between the Two Wars*, Oxford 1985.

E. A. Radice. "Raw Materials and Energy," in M. C. Kaser (gen. ed.), *The Economic History of Eastern Europe, 1919–1975*, Vol. 1, M. C. Kaser, E. A. Radice (eds.), *Economic Structure and Performance Between the Two Wars*, Oxford 1985.

T. Radomirov. "Neobkhodimiyat stopanski plan," *SP* 1938, Vol. 9.

F. Radouš. "Hospodářské otázký vnitřni kolonisace a obrony země," *Sbirka ČSN*, 1935/36, Prague 1936.

G. Ránki. "The Hungarian General Credit Bank in the 1920s," in A. Teichova, P. L. Cottrell (eds.), *International Business and Central Europe, 1918–1939*, New York 1983.

G. Ránki, J. Tomaszewski. "The Role of the State in Industry, Banking and Trade," in M. C. Kaser (gen. ed.), *The Economic History of Eastern Europe, 1919–1975*, Vol. 2, M. C. Kaser, E. A. Radice (eds.), *Interwar Policy, the War, and Reconstruction*, Oxford 1986.

P. Rapoš. *Priemysel Slovenska za kapitalizmu*, Bratislava 1957.

W. E. Rappard. "Economic Nationalism," in *Authority and Individual*, Cambridge, Mass., 1937.

W. E. Rappard. *Le nationalisme économique et la Société des Nations*, Recueil des Cours de l'Academie du Droit International de la Haye, 1937, III, Paris 1937.

B. Ratyńska. *Stosunki polsko-niemieckie w okresie wojny gospodarczej 1919–1930*, Warsaw 1968.

G. von Rauch. *The Baltic States: Estonia, Latvia, and Lithuania: The Years of Independence, 1917–1940*, Berkeley and Los Angeles 1974.

T. U. Raun. *Estonia and the Estonians*, Stanford 1987.

Reconstruction Schemes in the Inter-war Period, League of Nations, Geneva 1944.

E. Reich. "Problém zemědělstvi v celkovém plánu hospodářske politiki," *Sbirka ČSN*, 1935/36, No. V, Prague 1936.

Report on Exchange Control, League of Nations, Geneva 1944.

J. Rézler. "The Hungarian Manufacturing Industry," *HQ*, Vol. VI (Summer 1941), No. 1.

L. Robbins. "Economic Nationalism and Monetary Policy," *Banker*, June 1936, No. 125.

L. Robbins. *The Economic Problem in Peace and War*, London 1947.

L. Robbins. *The Great Depression*, London 1934.

H. L. Roberts. *Rumania: Political Problems of an Agrarian State*, New Haven 1951.

J. Robinson. *Economic Heresies: Some Old-fashioned Questions in Economic Theory*, New York 1971.

J. Robinson. "Beggar-my-Neighbour Remedies for Unemployment," in *Essays in the Theory of Employment*, London 1937.

J. Robinson. *Introduction to the Theory of Employment*, Cambridge 1937.

H. Rogger, E. Weber (eds.). *The European Right: A Historical Profile*, London 1965.

D. Roksandić. "Agrarne ideologije i teorije modernizacije u Jugoslaviji od 1918 do 1941 godine," Conference on *Models of Development*.

K. Romanow-Bobińska. "Wielki kryzys a Europa Wschodnia," *SDEŚ*, Vol. XVIII (1981).

K. Romanow-Bobińska. "Związki gospodarcze Europy Południowo-Wschodniej okresu międzywojennego," in A. Czubiński (ed.), *Państwa bałkańskie w polityce imperializmu niemieckiego w latach 1871–1945*, Poznań 1982.

H. Roos. *A History of Modern Poland*, London 1966.

W. Röpke. *International Economic Disintegration* (with App. by A. Rüstow), London, Edinburgh, and Glasgow 1942.

P. N. Rosenstein-Rodan. "Industrialization of Eastern Europe," *EJ*, Vol. LIII (1943), No. 210-211.

B. Rosier, P. Dockès. *Rythmes économiques: Crises et changement social, une perspective historique*, Paris 1983.

W. Roszkowski. *Gospodarcza rola większej prywatnej własności ziemskiej w Polsce 1918–1939*, "Monografie i opracowania" SGPiS, No. 191, Warsaw 1987.

J. Rothschild. *The Communist Party of Bulgaria: Origins and Development, 1883–1936*, New York 1959.

J. Rothschild. *East Central Europe Between Two World Wars*, Seattle and London 1974.

J. S. Roucek. *The Politics of the Balkans*, New York and London 1939.

S. Rudnicki. *Obóz Narodowo-Radykalny: Geneza i działalność*, Warsaw 1985.

A. Rudzki. *Zarys polskiej polityki komunikacyjnej*, London 1945.

A. Ruusmann. "Zmiany w strukturze agrarnej Estonii w latach 1919–1939," *RDSiG*, Vol. XXXIX (1978).

F. Ryszka. "Autorytaryzm i faszyzm: Wprowadzenie semantyczne," *KH* 1972, No. 2.

F. Ryszka. *Państwo stanu wyjątkowego*, 3d emended ed., Wrocław, Warsaw, Kraków, Gdańsk, and Łódź 1985.

A. Salter. The Future of Economic Nationalism," *FA*, Vol. 11 (October 1932), No. 1.

L. Savadiev. *Les caractères et les effets de la politique du Nationalisme Economique en Bulgarie*, Lyon 1939.

L. Schapiro. *Totalitarianism*, London 1972.

C. P. Schleicher. "Nationalism," in J. Gould, W. L. Kolb (eds.), *A Dictionary of the Social Sciences*, Chicago 1969.

P. C. Schmitter. "Reflections on Mihail Manoilescu and the Political Consequences of Delayed-Dependent Development on the Periphery of Western Europe," in K. Jowitt (ed.), *Social Change in Romania, 1860–1940: A Debate on Development in a European Nation*, Berkeley 1978.

C. Schrecker. "The Growth of Economic Nationalism and Its International Consequences," *IA*, Vol. XIII (1934), No. 2.

H. J. Schröder. "Jugoistoczna Ewropa kao 'Nezwaniczna imperija' ('Informal Empire') Nacionalsocijalisticzke Nemaczke—primer Jugoslawija 1933–1939," *IG* 1976, No. 1-2.

D. Seers. "The Stages Economic Growth of a Primary Producer of the Twentieth Century," in R. I. Rhodes (ed.), *Imperialism and Underdevelopment*, New York 1970.

G. Servakis, C. Pertounzi. "The Agricultural Policy of Greece," in O. S. Morgan (ed.), *Agricultural Systems of Middle Europe*, New York 1933.

B. C. Shafer. *Faces of Nationalism*, New York 1972.

B. C. Shafer. *Nationalism*, New Brunswick 1954.

A. Shonfield. *Modern Capitalism: The Changing Balance of Public and Private Power*, London, Oxford, and New York 1969.

S. Sierpowski. "Polityka mniejszościowa Niemiec w Lidze Narodów," in A. Czubiński (ed.), *Rola mniejszości niemieckiej w rozwoju stosunków politycznych w Europie 1918–1945*, Poznań 1984.

R. Skidelsky (ed.), *The End of the Keynesian Era*, London 1977.

V. Škoda. "Plánovani v zemědělstwi," *Sbirka ČSN*, 1934/35, No. XVIII, Prague 1935.

J. Skorovský. "Československá obchodní politika," *Sbirka ČSN*, 1937/38, No. II, Prague 1937.

Z. Sládek. "Wyniki gospodarcze działalności Małej Ententy oraz polityczne następstwa jej niepowodzenia," *SDEŚ*, Vol. XX (1984).

Z. Sládek, J. Tomaszewski. "Próby integracji gospodarczej Europy Środkowej i Południowo-Wschodniej w latach dwudziestych XX w.," *RDSiG*, Vol. XI (1979).

Z. Sládek, J. Tomaszewski. "Próby integracji ekonomicznej Europy Środkowej i Południowo-Wschodniej w latach trzydziestych XX w.," *Sobótka*, 1979, No. 3.

A. D. Smith. "Nationalism: A Trend Report and Bibliography," *CS*, Vol. XXI (1973), No. 3.

A. D. Smith. *Nationalism in the Twentieth Century*, Oxford 1979.

L. L. Snyder. *The Meanings of Nationalism*, New Brunswick 1954.

K. Sokołowski. *Dumping*, Warsaw 1932.

W. Sombart. *Die deutsche Volkswirtschaft im neunzehten Jahrhundert*, Berlin 1903.

Soviet Estonia, Tallin 1980.

I. Spigler. "Public Finance," in M. C. Kaser (gen. ed.), *The Economic History of Eastern Europe, 1919–1975*, Vol. 2, M. C. Kaser, E. A. Radice (eds.), *Interwar Policy, the War, and Reconstruction*, Oxford 1986.

T. Spira. *German-Hungarian Relations and the Swabian Problem: From Károlyi to Gömbös, 1919–1936*, Boulder 1977.

N. Spulber. *The State and Economic Development in Eastern Europe*, New York 1966.

The State and Economic Life: First Study Conference (Milan, May 1932), Paris 1932.

The State and Economic Life: A Record of a Second Study Conference (London 29 V — 2 VI 1933), Paris 1934.

I. Stefanov. *"Vŭnshnata tŭrgoviya na Bŭlgariya sled voynate,"* TSISP, 1938, No. 2-3.

R. Stemplowski. *Zależność i wyzwanie: Argentyna wobec rywalizacji mocarstw anglosaskich i III Rzeszy,* Warsaw 1975.

R. Stemplowski. "Modernizacja: Teoria czy doktryna?" *KH* 1979, No. 3.

A. Stepan (ed.). *Authoritarian Brazil: Origins, Policies, and Future,* New Haven and London 1973.

Studia nad faszyzmem i zbrodniami hitlerowskimi, Vol. III, *Faszyzm—teoria i praktyka w Europie (1922–1945),* Wrocław 1977.

P. F. Sugar. "External and Domestic Roots of Eastern European Nationalism," in P. F. Sugar, I. J. Lederer (eds.), *Nationalism in Eastern Europe,* Seattle and London 1973.

P. F. Sugar, E. Weber (eds.). *Native Fascism in the Successor States, 1918–1945,* Santa Barbara, Calif., 1971.

B. Supple. "States and Industrialization: Britain and Germany in the Nineteenth Century," in J. Held et al. (eds.), *States and Societies,* Oxford 1985.

I. Svennilson. "The Concept of the Nation and Its Relevance to Economic Analysis," in E.A.G. Robinson (ed.), *Economic Consequences of the Size of Nations,* London 1963.

I. Svennilson. *Growth and Stagnation in the European Economy,* Geneva 1954.

A. Svikis. "Stosunki agrarne na Łotwie w okresie międzywojennym," *RDSiG,* Vol. XL (1979).

G. Svrakov. *Belezhki vŭrkhu noviya rezhim na industriya na presitenostta,* Varna 1938.

A. Szefer. *Mniejszość niemiecka w Polsce i Czechosłowacji w latach 1933–1938,* Kraków and Katowice 1967.

A. Szefer. "Niemcy sudeccy jako narzędzie agresji przeciw Czechosłowacji," in A. Czubiński (ed.), *Rola mniejszości niemieckiej w rozwoju stosunków politycznych w Europie 1918–1945,* Poznań 1984.

T. Szentes. *Theories of World Capitalist Economy,* Budapest 1985.

H. Szlajfer. "Economic Nationalism of the Peripheries as a Research Problem," in H. Szlajfer (ed.), *Essays on Economic Nationalism in East-Central Europe and South America, 1918–1939,* Centre of International Economic History, University of Geneva, Geneva 1990.

H. Szlajfer. *Modernizacja zależności: Kapitalizm i rozwój w Ameryce Łacińskiej,* Wrocław, Warsaw, Kraków, Gdańsk, and Łódź 1985.

F. Tachau. "Patriotism," in *The World Book Encyclopedia,* Vol. 15, Field Enterprises Educational Corporation.

L. Tardy. *Report on Systems of Agricultural Credit and Insurance,* Geneva 1938.

E. Teichert. *Autarkie und Grossraumwirtschaft in Deutschland 1930–1939,* Munich 1984.

A. Teichova. *An Economic Background to Munich: International Business and Czechoslovakia, 1918–1938,* Cambridge 1974.

A. Teichova. "Industry," in M. C. Kaser (gen. ed.), *The Economic History of Eastern Europe, 1919–1975,* Vol. 1, M. C. Kaser, E. A. Radice (eds.), *Economic Structure and Performance Between the Two Wars,* Oxford 1985.

A. Teichova. *The Czechoslovak Economy, 1918–1980,* London 1988.

H. Tennenbaum. *Europa Środkowo-Wschodnia w gospodarce światowej*, London 1941.

L. E. Textor. "Agriculture and Agrarian Reform," in R. J. Kerner (ed.), *Czechoslovakia*, Berkeley 1945.

L. Tilkovszky. "Irredenta niemiecka a Węgry," in H. Batowski (ed.), *Irredenta niemiecka w Europie Środkowej i Południowo-Wschodniej przed II wojną światową*, Katowice and Kraków 1971.

J. Tomasevich. *Peasants, Politics, and Economic Change in Jugoslavia*, Stanford and London 1955.

J. Tomaszewski. "Bułgaria 1923: profesor Cankow ratuje monarchię," in *Przewroty i zamachy stanu: Europa 1918–1939* (introd. A. Garlicki), Warsaw 1981.

J. Tomaszewski. "Bułgaria 1934: Zamach majowy," in *Przewroty i zamachy stanu: Europa 1918–1939*, Warsaw 1981.

J. Tomaszewski. "Faktori na ikonomicheskiya rastezh v Bŭlgariya prez perioda 1930–1939 g.," in D. Kinev (ed.), *Sŭvremenna Bŭlgariya*, Vol. 1, Sofia 1984.

J. Tomaszewski. "Gospodarka krajów Europy Środkowej i Południowo-Wschodniej," in J. Żarnowski (ed.), *Dyktatury w Europie Środkowo-Wschodniej 1918–1939*, Wrocław, Warsaw, Kraków, and Gdańsk 1973.

J. Tomaszewski. "Konsekwencje wielonarodowościowej struktury ludności Polski 1918–1939," in H. Zieliński (ed.), *Drogi integracji społeczeństwa w Polsce XIX–XX w.*, Wrocław 1976.

J. Tomaszewski. *Rzeczpospolita wielu narodów*, Warsaw 1985.

J. Tomaszewski. "Związki gospodarcze państw sukcesyjnych a Polska," in Z. Landau, J. Tomaszewski, *Druga Rzeczpospolita: Gospodarka—społeczeństwo—miejsce w świecie*, Warsaw 1977.

D. Toshev. *Industrialnata politika na Bŭlgariya sled Pŭrvata svetovna voyna*, Varna 1943.

L. Truska. "Burżuazyjna reforma agrarna 1922 r. na Litwie," *RDSiG*, Vol. XXXIX (1978).

S. Tsonev. *Dŭrzhavno-monopolistichniyat kapitalizm v Bŭlgariya*, Varna 1968.

Unemployment as International Problem, RIIA, Oxford 1935.

B. Vago. *The Shadow of the Swastika: The Rise of Fascism and Anti-Semitism in the Danube Basin, 1936–1939*, London 1975.

I. Vajda, M. Simai (eds.). *Foreign Trade in Planned Economy*, Cambridge 1971.

J. Viner. Review of M. Manoilescu, *The Theory of Protection and International Trade* (London 1931), *JPE*, Vol. XL (February 1932), No. 1.

J. Viner. *Studies in the Theory of International Trade*, New York 1937.

I. Vinski. *Klasna podjela stanovnistva i nacionalnog dohotka Jugoslavije v 1938*, Zagreb 1970.

W.A.S.H. "Protection," in *Encyclopaedia Britannica*, Vol. 18, Chicago, London, and Toronto 1960.

E. Wagemann. *Der neue Balkan: Altes Land—junge Wirtschaft*, Hamburg 1939.

R. Wagner. *Panství kapitalistických monopolů v ČSR*, Prague 1958.

A. Wakar. "Pojęcie produkcyjności i dochodu społecznego," *Ekonomista*, 1932, Vol. I.

I. Wallerstein. *The Capitalist World-Economy*, Cambridge, London, New York, and Melbourne 1979.

P. S. Wandycz. *France and Her Allies, 1919–1925*, Minneapolis 1962.

B. Ward. *Five Ideas That Changed the World*, New York 1959.

D. Warriner. "Czechoslovakia and Central European Tariffs," *SEER*, Vol. IX (1933), No. 33.

J. B. Whitton. "Nationalism—Internationalism," in *The Encyclopedia Americana*, Vol. XIX, New York, Chicago, and Washington, D.C., 1958.

J. J. Wiatr. *Naród i państwo: Socjologiczne problemy kwestii narodowej*, Warsaw 1969.

P.J.D. Wiles. "Foreign Trade of Eastern Europe: A Summary Appraisal," in A. A. Brown, E. Neuberger (eds.), *International Trade and Central Planning: An Analysis of Economic Interactions*, Berkeley and Los Angeles 1968.

H. A. Winkler (Hrsg.). *Nationalismus*. Verlagsgruppe Athenëum, Main, Scriptor, Hanstein, 1978.

H. A. Winkler. *Statistisches Handbuch der Europöischen Nationalitäten*, Vienna 1931.

J. D. Wirth. *The Politics of Brazilian Development, 1930–1954*, Stanford 1970.

E. Wiskemann. *Czechs and Germans*, 2d ed., London 1967.

E. Wiskemann. *Europe of the Dictators, 1919–1945*, London 1967.

R. L. Wolf. *The Balkans in Our Time*, Cambridge, Mass., 1974.

S. F. Woolf. "Czy istniał faszystowski system ekonomiczny?" in *Faszyzmy europejskie (1922–1945) w oczach współczesnych i historyków* (selection and introd. J. Borejsza), Warsaw 1979.

S. D. Zagoroff. "Agriculture and Food in Bulgaria Before and During World War," in S. D. Zagoroff, J. Végh, A. D. Blimovitch, *The Agricultural Economy of the Danubian Countries, 1933–45*, Stanford 1955.

Zasady programu narodowo-radykalnego, Warsaw 1937.

T. Zavalani. "Albanian Nationalism," in P. Sugar, I. J. Lederer (eds.), *Nationalism in Eastern Europe*, Seattle and London 1973.

H. Zörner. "Agriculture in Germany," in *Proceedings of the Third International Conference of Agricultural Economics*, London 1935.

L. Zumpe. *Wirtschaft und Staat in Deutschland 1933 bis 1945*, Berlin 1980.

F. Zweig. *Zmierzch czy odrodzenie liberalizmu?* Warsaw 1980 (reprint from 1938).

J. Żarnowski. *Społeczeństwo Drugiej Rzeczypospolitej 1918–1939*, Warsaw 1973.

J. Żarnowski. "Reżimy autorytarne w Europie Środkowej i Południowo-Wschodniej w okresie międzywojennym—analogie i różnice," in J. Żarnowski (ed.), *Dyktatury w Europie Środkowo-Wschodniej 1918–1939*, Wrocław, Warsaw, Kraków, and Gdańsk 1973.

B. Živanský. "Aktuálni otázký československého průmyslu mlynářského," *Sbirka ČSN*, 1928/29, No. IV, Prague 1929.

B. Živanský. "Úprava obilního hospodářství a kontingentace mlýnů," *Sbirka ČSN*, 1936/37, No. XVI, Prague 1937.

L. Żiwkowa [Zhivkova]. "Kŭm vŭprosa za ikonomicheskata ekspanziya na Germaniya v Bŭlgariya (1933–1939 g.)," in *Bŭlgarsko-germanski otnosheniya i vrŭzki: Izsledvaniya i materiali*, Vol. I, Sofia 1972.

About the Book and Author

In an era of ever-increasing national consciousness combined, paradoxically, with pressures for regional economic integration, this thought-provoking and exhaustively researched volume will challenge readers' assumptions about optimal paths to national economic development.

Drawing on archival sources as well as published materials in eight languages, Jan Kofman analyzes both the intent and the efficacy of nationalist policies and economic protectionism in Europe's central and eastern regions—traditionally, its weaker and less industrialized states. He concludes that such policies, where implemented, generally succeeded in promoting individual state's economic growth and modernization during the interwar period.

Jan Kofman is professor of history and political science at the University of Warsaw (the Bialystok Branch) and at the Institute of Political Studies of the Polish Academy of Sciences. He is also editor in chief and deputy director of Polish Scientific Publishers PWN, the largest academic publishing house in Poland. He was editor in chief of KRYTYKA (1982–1995), an underground turned official political quarterly established in 1978.

Index